AN MMY MONOGRAPH

Publications of
THE INSTITUTE OF MENTAL MEASUREMENTS
Edited by Oscar Krisen Buros

EDUCATIONAL, PSYCHOLOGICAL, AND PERSONALITY TESTS OF 1933 AND 1934

EDUCATIONAL, PSYCHOLOGICAL, AND PERSONALITY TESTS OF 1933, 1934, AND 1935

EDUCATIONAL, PSYCHOLOGICAL, AND PERSONALITY TESTS OF 1936

THE NINETEEN THIRTY-EIGHT MENTAL MEASUREMENTS YEARBOOK

THE NINETEEN FORTY MENTAL MEASUREMENTS YEARBOOK

THE THIRD MENTAL MEASUREMENTS YEARBOOK

THE FOURTH MENTAL MEASUREMENTS YEARBOOK

THE FIFTH MENTAL MEASUREMENTS YEARBOOK

TESTS IN PRINT

THE SIXTH MENTAL MEASUREMENTS YEARBOOK

READING TESTS AND REVIEWS

PERSONALITY TESTS AND REVIEWS

THE SEVENTH MENTAL MEASUREMENTS YEARBOOK

TESTS IN PRINT II

ENGLISH TESTS AND REVIEWS

FOREIGN LANGUAGE TESTS AND REVIEWS

INTELLIGENCE TESTS AND REVIEWS

MATHEMATICS TESTS AND REVIEWS

PERSONALITY TESTS AND REVIEWS II

READING TESTS AND REVIEWS II

SCIENCE TESTS AND REVIEWS

SOCIAL STUDIES TESTS AND REVIEWS

VOCATIONAL TESTS AND REVIEWS

SOCIAL STUDIES

TESTS AND REVIEWS

SOCIAL STUDIES
TESTS AND REVIEWS

A Monograph
Consisting of the Social Studies Sections of the
SEVEN MENTAL MEASUREMENTS YEARBOOKS (1938–72)
and
TESTS IN PRINT II (1974)

Edited by
OSCAR KRISEN BUROS
Director, The Institute of Mental Measurements

THE GRYPHON PRESS
HIGHLAND PARK · NEW JERSEY
1975

DESIGNED BY LUELLA BUROS

COPYRIGHT 1975 BY OSCAR KRISEN BUROS, PUBLISHED BY THE GRYPHON PRESS,
220 MONTGOMERY STREET, HIGHLAND PARK, NEW JERSEY 08904. No part of this publication may
be reproduced in any form, nor may any of the contents be used in an informational storage,
retrieval, or transmission system without the prior written permission of the publisher.

LC 75-8115, ISBN 910674-22-1

MANUFACTURED BY QUINN & BODEN COMPANY, INC., RAHWAY, NEW JERSEY
PRINTED IN THE UNITED STATES OF AMERICA

To
Eleanor and Herman

TABLE OF CONTENTS

MMY TEST REVIEWERS

Elizabeth C. Adams	4:693, 4:699	Edith M. Huddleston	4:678
Dorothy C. Adkins	3:609	Robert E. Keohane	2:1642
	3:612, 4:684, 4:689	David R. Krathwohl	5:788
Howard R. Anderson	1:950, 1:1146, 2:1616	A. C. Krey	1:1016
	2:1621, 2:1622, 3:590, 3:607, 4:689	Dana G. Kurfman	7:904, 7:906
	5:790, 5:810, 5:841, 6:966, 6:1019, 7:918	Martha E. Layman	4:684
Frederic L. Ayer	4:702	Paul M. Limbert	1:948
Harry D. Berg	3:593, 3:596, 4:664	S. P. McCutchen	1:1016, 2:1628, 2:1634
	5:799, 5:832, 6:974, 6:1000, 7:888, 7:896	Christine H. McGuire	5:812, 5:835
William C. Bingham	6:1020		6:980, 6:1019, 7:901, 7:902
Donald T. Campbell	5:829	Jonathon C. McLendon	6:971, 6:994
Vincent N. Campbell	7:888, 7:928	John Manning	5:820, 5:825
W. H. Cartwright	3:591, 3:610, 3:618		7:913, 7:917, 7:922
Henry Chauncey	6:964, 6:998, 6:1013	I. G. Meddleton	5:830
Clinton C. Conrad	2:1637, 2:1640	Howard D. Mehlinger	7:927, 7:931
Robert A. Davis	3:592	Wilbur F. Murra	1:1015
Alvin C. Eurich	1:951, 1:1150		1:1024, 2:1631, 2:1639
Robert H. Ferrell	5:818	Raymond C. Norris	5:793
James A. Field, Jr.	5:812	Donald W. Oliver	6:971
Warren G. Findley	2:1619	Pedro T. Orata	2:1619
Elaine Forsyth	3:599, 3:600	Jacob S. Orleans	2:1630
Wayne A. Frederick	5:820, 5:834	C. Robert Pace	3:619
Edward J. Furst	7:901	Anna Parsek	2:1626
Kenneth E. Gell	2:1614, 2:1636	Roy A. Price	2:1615, 2:1638, 3:616
J. Raymond Gerberich	2:1641, 3:591	S. A. Rayner	5:792
Grace Graham	2:1632	Edwin H. Reeder	3:598, 3:603, 4:676, 4:678
Hulda Grobman	7:929	Virginia M. Rogers	7:890, 7:895
Richard E. Gross	5:785, 5:792	Giles M. Ruch	2:1619
	6:970, 6:1010, 7:915, 7:916	Douglas E. Scates	1:1154, 5:833
Harold Gulliksen	1:1145A	Robert J. Solomon	6:970
John H. Haefner	5:833, 6:1013a, 6:1020	Frederick H. Stutz	3:608
Lavone A. Hanna	2:1635, 3:591, 3:617		3:611, 5:816, 5:837
David K. Heenan	5:814, 5:836, 6:967	Hilda Taba	1:1154, 2:1618, 4:663

PREFACE

I T IS my considered belief that most standardized tests are poorly constructed, of questionable or unknown validity, pretentious in their claims, and likely to be misused more often than not. This conviction began to form 48 to 50 years ago when I was taking courses in testing at the University of Minnesota. I vividly recall presenting a paper entitled "Common Fallacies in the Use of Standardized Tests" in an advanced educational psychology class taught by Professor W. S. Miller, a paper in which I criticized some of the views of my instructors. Shortly thereafter, I had the good fortune to read a book which was a landmark in the consumer movement—*Your Money's Worth* by Stuart Chase and F. J. Schlink. It was this book which led to the founding of Consumers' Research, Inc., an organization which tests and evaluates commonly used commercial products. This book and the establishment of Consumers' Research stimulated me to begin thinking about a test users' research organization to evaluate tests.

After failing to secure financial support for the initiation of a test users' research organization, I scaled down my objectives to the establishment of a cooperative test reviewing service which would report on and evaluate standardized tests used in education, industry, and psychology. One hundred thirty-three specialists in a wide variety of disciplines cooperated by contributing "frankly critical reviews" for *The 1938 Mental Measurements Yearbook* (also called *The First Yearbook*). Later yearbooks (each volume supplementing earlier volumes) were published in 1941, 1949, 1953, 1959, 1965, and 1972.

The objectives of the *Mental Measurements Yearbooks* (MMY's) have remained essentially the same since they were first presented in detail in *The 1940 Mental Measurements Yearbook* (also called *The Second Yearbook*): (*a*) to provide information about tests published as separates throughout the English-speaking world; (*b*) to present frankly critical test reviews written by testing and subject specialists representing various viewpoints; (*c*) to provide extensive bibliographies of verified references on the construction, use, and validity of specific tests; (*d*) to make readily available the critical portions of test reviews appearing in professional journals; and (*e*) to present fairly exhaustive listings of new and revised books on testing along with evaluative excerpts from representative reviews in professional journals.

As important as the above objectives are, I place even greater importance on these less tangible objectives: (*f*) to impel test authors and publishers to publish better tests and to provide test users with detailed information on the validity and limitations of these tests; (*g*) to inculcate in test users a keener awareness of the values and limitations of standardized tests; (*h*) to stimulate contributing reviewers to think through more carefully their own beliefs and values relevant to testing; (*i*) to suggest to test users better methods of appraising tests in light of their own particular needs; and (*j*) to impress upon test users the need to suspect all tests unaccompanied by detailed data on their construction, validity, uses, and limitations—

even when products of distinguished authors and reputable publishers.

As the number of published tests and, especially, the related literature increased tremendously over the years, the MMY's became increasingly more encyclopedic in scope. Many test users, however, are interested in only one or two areas of testing. To meet their needs, we announced in 1941 plans for publishing monographs in English, foreign languages, intelligence, mathematics, personality, reading, science, social studies, and vocations. Unfortunately, we were too optimistic; it was over a quarter of a century before we were able to finance the publication of the first monograph, *Reading Tests and Reviews* (RTR I), published in 1968.

The next monograph, *Personality Tests and Reviews* (PTR I), was published in 1970. The core of these two monographs, RTR I and PTR I, consists of a reprinting of the reading and personality sections, respectively, of the first six MMY's and a new section listing both in print and out of print tests in the area represented by the monograph.

Despite the use of a large amount of reprinted material, the preparation and publication of these two monographs turned out to be very costly. Since sales later proved insufficient to finance similar monographs in other areas, we temporarily abandoned our plans for additional monographs.

Following the publication of *The Seventh Yearbook* in early 1972, we began devoting all of our time to the completion of *Tests in Print II: An Index to Tests, Test Reviews, and the Literature on Specific Tests* (TIP II). In mid-1974, while TIP II was in press, it suddenly occurred to me that up-to-date monographs could be prepared at a manageable cost by reprinting a given section of TIP II along with the corresponding sections of the seven MMY's. As a consequence, we are now publishing monographs in nine areas: second monographs in personality and reading, and first monographs in English, foreign languages, intelligence, mathematics, science, social studies, and vocations. Hopefully, the publication of these monographs will make our material available to many test users who might otherwise not consult the MMY's and TIP II. Broadening

the readership of our test reviews will bring us closer to achieving our objectives.

This monograph, *Social Studies Tests and Reviews,* reflects the changing state of the art in 50 years of social studies testing. I cannot but wonder why more progress has not been made in developing better instruments to assess social studies achievement. Considering the extensive use of social studies tests—especially as parts of achievement batteries at elementary and secondary school levels—and the effects of testing on the learning process, it is important that we have the best possible tests. To achieve this goal, specialists in social studies education must give more attention to the development, use, and validation of standardized tests which will reflect the wide range of objectives in the social studies. It would be especially helpful if professional journals in social studies education would give more adequate coverage to standardized tests. In addition to more articles on testing, the journals might regularly include reviews of tests, including "closed" tests such as those of the CEEB. If each journal reviewed three to five tests per year, their combined output of reviews would greatly extend the critical coverage now provided by the MMY's. These reviews could then be excerpted in the next MMY.

It has been particularly hectic preparing nine MMY monographs simultaneously. Fortunately, I have been assisted by a dedicated staff. Although other people worked for shorter periods of time, there are seven whom I would like to name for special recognition: Mary Anne Miller Becker, Sandra Boxer Discenza, Doris Greene McCan, Barbara Ruis Martko, Mary T. Mooney, Joan Stein Paszamant, and Natalie J. Rosenthal Turton. I am greatly indebted to my staff colleagues for their assistance in producing these nine derivative monographs.

We plan to publish *The Eighth Mental Measurements Yearbook* in 1977, followed by *Tests in Print III* in 1978. The social studies sections of these volumes will supplement and update the material in this monograph.

OSCAR KRISEN BUROS

Highland Park, New Jersey
February 24, 1975

INTRODUCTION

FOR THE past 40 years we have been providing test users in education, industry, and psychology with a series of publications designed to assist them in the selection and use of tests which best meet their needs. We maintained an annual production schedule for our first four volumes (1935–38); since then, however, the intervals between books have been quite irregular with publication dates 1941, 1949, 1953, 1959, 1961, 1965, 1968, 1970, 1972, and 1974. Our publications through 1974 include three test bibliographies, seven *Mental Measurements Yearbooks,* two monographs, and two *Tests in Print.*[1] Nine derivative mono-

graphs—this volume and eight others—are being published in 1975. A brief description of our first fourteen publications follows.

FIRST THREE PUBLICATIONS

Although the earliest three publications are noncritical bibliographies, the original intent had been to prepare an annual critical review of new tests for journal publication. It soon became apparent, however, that this was far beyond the capacity of a single individual. A more modest goal was substituted, the publication of an annual bibliography of tests, as described in the Introduction to the first one:

To locate the standard tests recently published in specific areas is a laborious task. The usual bibliographic aids for locating periodical, monograph, and book publications are of little value in locating standard tests. New tests are being published so rapidly that the test technicians themselves find it difficult to locate the test titles of the past year without an inordinate amount of searching. For these reasons, the writer has undertaken the task of preparing a bibliography of psychological, achievement, character, and personality tests published in 1933 and 1934. This bibliography will be the first of a series to be published annually by the School of Education, Rutgers University.[2]

This 44-page bibliography lists 257 tests that were new, revised, or supplemented in 1933 and 1934. Many of these tests, usually revised editions, are still in print today.

Similar test bibliographies[3] were published in 1936 and 1937. During this time, attempts were being made to obtain a grant to initiate a

---

[1] The first fourteen publications (1935–1974), edited by Oscar K. Buros and now published by The Gryphon Press, are listed from the most recent to the oldest:
  a) Tests in Print II: An Index to Tests, Test Reviews, and the Literature on Specific Tests, December 1974. Pp. xxxix, 1107. $70.
  b) The Seventh Mental Measurements Yearbook, Vols. I and II, 1972. Pp. xl, 935; vi, 937–1986. $70 per set.
  c) Personality Tests and Reviews: Including an Index to The Mental Measurements Yearbooks, 1970. Pp. xxxi, 1659. $45. For reviews, *see* 7:B120.
  d) Reading Tests and Reviews: Including a Classified Index to The Mental Measurements Yearbooks, 1968. Pp. xxii, 520. $20. For reviews, *see* 7:B121.
  e) The Sixth Mental Measurements Yearbook, 1965. Pp. xxxvii, 1714. $45. (Reprinted 1971) For reviews, *see* 7:B122.
  f) Tests in Print: A Comprehensive Bibliography of Tests for Use in Education, Psychology, and Industry, 1961. Pp. xxix, 479. $15. (Reprinted 1974) For reviews, *see* 6:B105.
  g) The Fifth Mental Measurements Yearbook, 1959. Pp. xxix, 1292. $35. (Reprinted 1961) For reviews, *see* 6:B104.
  h) The Fourth Mental Measurements Yearbook, 1953. Pp. xxv, 1163. $30. (Reprinted 1974) For reviews, *see* 5:B84.
  i) The Third Mental Measurements Yearbook, 1949. Pp. xv, 1047. $25. (Reprinted 1974) For reviews, *see* 4:B71.
  j) The Nineteen Forty Mental Measurements Yearbook, 1941. Pp. xxv, 674. $20. (Reissued 1972) For reviews, *see* 3:788 and 4:B70.
  k) The Nineteen Thirty Eight Mental Measurements Yearbook, 1938. Pp. xv, 415. $17.50. (Reissued 1972) For reviews, *see* 2:B858.
  l) Educational, Psychological, and Personality Tests of 1936: Including a Bibliography and Book Review Digest of Measurement Books and Monographs of 1933–36, 1937. Pp. 141. Out of print. For reviews, *see* 1:B326.
  m) Educational, Psychological, and Personality Tests of 1933, 1934, and 1935, 1936. Pp. 83. Out of print. For reviews, *see* 36:B46.
  n) Educational, Psychological, and Personality Tests of 1933 and 1934, 1935. Pp. 44. Out of print. For a review, *see* 36:B45.

[2] *Educational, Psychological, and Personality Tests of 1933 and 1934,* p. 5.
[3] *Educational, Psychological, and Personality Tests of 1933, 1934, and 1935.*
Educational, Psychological, and Personality Tests of 1936.

research organization which would serve as a bureau of standards for the evaluation of educational and psychological tests. It was only after we despaired of raising such funds that we decided to set up a test reviewing service.

THE SEVEN MMY'S

Since tests, unlike books, were rarely reviewed in professional journals, it was a revolutionary step forward when we published *The 1938 Mental Measurements Yearbook* 37 years ago. In his Foreword, Clarence E. Partch's comments reflect our excitement and mood in those early days:

The publication of *The 1938 Mental Measurements Yearbook of the School of Education, Rutgers University* is likely to prove a landmark of considerable importance in the history of tests and measurements. Heretofore, despite the obvious need of test users for frank evaluations of tests by competent reviewers, few standardized tests have been critically appraised in the professional journals and textbooks for students of education and psychology. Now, for the first time, a large number of frankly evaluative reviews by able test technicians, subject-matter specialists, and psychologists are available to assist test users in making more discriminating selections from among the hundreds of tests on the market.[4]

Except for a few test authors and publishers who objected to unfavorable reviews, *The 1938 Yearbook* (also referred to as *The First Yearbook*) was enthusiastically acclaimed in this country and abroad. It took some time, however, before most of the protesting publishers were able to accept unfavorable test reviews with equanimity.

Before *The 1938 Yearbook* was off the press, we began sending out invitations to review tests for a 1939 yearbook. Unfortunately, because of financing and production problems, we were unable to maintain our annual production schedule. It took us over two years to publish the next volume, *The 1940 Mental Measurements Yearbook*.

Much enlarged and greatly improved over its predecessor, *The 1940 Yearbook* (also referred to as *The Second Yearbook*) has been the prototype for all later yearbooks. In addition to the increased number of tests, reviews, and references, there were many qualitative changes: (*a*) The objectives which have characterized all MMY's were presented in detail for the first time. (*b*) The format was standardized. (*c*) The classification of tests was

4 *The 1938 Mental Measurements Yearbook*, p. xi.

changed from 40 specific categories to 12 broad categories. (*d*) The practice of including very short reviews of 100 words or less was discontinued. (*e*) The review coverage was extended to old tests and to tests previously reviewed as well as new tests. (*f*) The instructions given to reviewers concerning the preparation of their test reviews were presented. (*g*) The reactions of test authors and publishers—most of them objecting strenuously to unfavorable reviews—were reprinted for the first and last time.

In the Preface of *The 1940 Yearbook* we announced that the yearbooks would be published every two years. Because of World War II, however, *The Third Mental Measurements Yearbook* was not published until 1949. Except for its larger size and more thorough preparation, *The Third Yearbook*—like all later yearbooks—is very similar in its coverage, format, indexing, and organization to *The 1940 Yearbook*. There were, however, several improvements: (*a*) The "Classified Index of Tests," an expanded table of contents, was introduced. (*b*) Stars and asterisks were used preceding test titles to indicate, respectively, tests listed in a yearbook for the first time and tests revised or supplemented since last listed. (*c*) Asterisks were used at the end of a reference to indicate that the reference had been examined personally for accuracy and relevance. (*d*) Whenever possible, the abstract in *Psychological Abstracts* was cited for each reference. (*e*) Two improvements were made in the name index. Previously authors of references for specific tests had been indexed merely by citing the test for which the reference appears. After locating the test, one then had to search through the references to find those by that author. The new index eliminated this searching by citing each reference both to the test number and the reference number. Secondly, the index was converted into an "analytic index" in which *"test," "rev," "exc," "bk,"* and *"ref"* were used to indicate whether a citation referred to authorship of a test, review, excerpted review, book, or reference. These five features have been included in all later yearbooks.

In *The Fourth Mental Measurements Yearbook,* published in 1953, our review coverage was extended for the first time to many tests restricted to testing programs administered by organizations such as the College Entrance Examination Board. Six years later, in 1959, *The Fifth Yearbook* was published. Upon the completion of that volume, we were concerned that some cutbacks would be necessary to stem the phenomenal growth of production costs, as well as the ever increasing length of each MMY. As a result, we decided to discontinue specific test bibliographies and almost all reviews of foreign tests. The appreciative reviews *The Fifth Yearbook* received, however, especially those mentioning the value of the specific bibliographies to students of testing, caused us to reconsider. Consequently, despite the expanding literature on specific tests, we decided to continue all features of the earlier volumes. As a result, it took us six years to publish in 1965 *The Sixth Mental Measurements Yearbook,* a 1,751-page volume, approximately one-third larger than the previous yearbook. In addition to its more extensive coverage, *The Sixth Yearbook* presents a comprehensive listing of all tests in print as of mid-1964. The latest yearbook to date, *The Seventh Yearbook,* was published in 1972. This massive two-volume work of 2,032 pages may well be considered the zenith of the MMY's.

Like all other volumes published since 1938, *The Seventh Yearbook* supplements rather than supplants earlier yearbooks. For complete coverage, therefore, a reader must have access to all seven MMY's. A person using only the latest, *The Seventh Yearbook,* will miss a tremendous amount of valuable information in the six earlier volumes. Although the more recent yearbooks—especially the last three—are of greatest value, the third and fourth yearbooks also contain much useful information on many in print tests. Even though the first two yearbooks are mainly of historical interest, they also include some critical information on currently used tests. Our faith in the value of the first four MMY's, published between 1938 and 1953, is attested to by our reissuing of the first and second yearbooks in 1972 and reprinting of the third and fourth in 1974. Consequently, all seven yearbooks are now in print.

EARLIER
MMY MONOGRAPHS

It is with amusement and wonder that we look back at some of the dreams of our youth. *The 1940 Mental Measurements Yearbook* was the first yearbook published by my wife and myself. In those depression days, money was scarce but printing was cheap and penny postcards could be used for advertising. Borrowed capital of $3,500 was sufficient to launch us into book publishing. Even before our first book was off the press we were planning to publish not only a new MMY every two years, but also a series of derivative monographs. Our plans were confidently announced in the Preface of *The 1940 Yearbook* thus:

In order to make the material in the yearbooks more easily accessible to individuals who are interested in only a small part of each volume, a new series of monographs is being planned. If the first two or three monographs prove successful, others will eventually be prepared to cover tests in each of the following fields: business education, English and reading, fine arts, foreign languages, health and physical education, home economics, industrial arts, intelligence, mathematics, sciences, social studies, and vocational aptitudes. The first publication in each field will include: a comprehensive bibliography of all standard tests in print in that area; a reprinting, in part or in full, of all reviews of these tests which have appeared in previous yearbooks or in the journal literature; new reviews written especially for the monograph (to be, in turn, reprinted, in part or in full, in the following yearbook); and an extensive list of references on the construction, validation, use, and limitations of the tests. Separates in each field will be issued every four, six, or eight years depending upon the frequency of test publication. These monographs will range in size from fifty to two hundred pages. This new series will make it possible for an individual to purchase, at a nominal cost, every four, six, or eight years a monograph devoted solely to the tests and reviews of most interest to him.[5]

However, the publishing of the MMY's alone, even at intervals of 4 to 8 years, proved to be so time consuming and difficult that initiating the monograph series had to be continually postponed. But the dreams were never abandoned.

In 1968, 27 years after the monograph series was initially announced, the first monograph, *Reading Tests and Reviews* (RTR I), was published. This 542-page volume consists of a comprehensive bibliography of reading tests as of May 1968 and a reprinting of the reading sections of the first six MMY's. A second monograph, *Personality Tests and Reviews* (PTR I), was published two years later. This 1,695-page volume lists all personality tests as of June 1969 and provides a reprinting of the personality sections of the first six MMY's. The preparation of these two monographs turned out to be too costly and time consuming to justify working on monographs in other areas.

[5] *The 1940 Mental Measurements Yearbook,* p. xx.

TIP I AND TIP II

In 1961, we published the ninth volume in the MMY series: *Tests in Print: A Comprehensive Bibliography of Tests for Use in Education, Psychology, and Industry.* The objectives and nature of *Tests in Print* (hereafter called *Tests in Print I* or TIP I) are described in its Introduction as follows:

The objectives of *Tests in Print* are threefold: first, to present a comprehensive bibliography of tests—achievement, aptitude, intelligence, personality, and certain sensory-motor skills—published as separates and currently available in English-speaking countries; second, to serve as a classified index and supplement to the volumes of the *Mental Measurements Yearbook* series published to date; third, to give a wider distribution to the excellent recommendations for improving test manuals made by committees of the American Psychological Association, the American Educational Research Association, and the National Council on Measurements Used in Education.[6]

TIP I lists 2,967 tests—2,126 in print and 841 out of print as of early 1961, and also serves as a master index to the contents of the first five MMY's. Originally, we had planned to publish a new edition of TIP shortly after the publication of each new MMY, but poor sales of TIP I caused these plans to be abandoned. *The Sixth Yearbook,* in effect, served as a new edition of *Tests in Print* by referring to the tests in TIP I which were still in print as of mid-1964. Surprisingly, however, sales of the 1961 *Tests in Print* began to pick up after publication of *The Sixth Yearbook* in 1965. This unexpected upturn encouraged us to begin devoting all of our time to the preparation of a new edition of TIP immediately after approving the last proofs for *The Seventh Yearbook.*

Tests in Print II: An Index to Tests, Test Reviews, and the Literature on Specific Tests (TIP II) was published in December 1974. Like the 1961 volume, *Tests in Print II* presents: (a) a comprehensive bibliography of all known tests published as separates for use with English-speaking subjects; (b) a classified index to the contents of the test sections of the seven *Mental Measurements Yearbooks* published to date; and (c) a reprinting of the 1974 APA-AERA-NCME *Standards for Educational and Psychological Tests.*

In addition, TIP II introduces the following new features: (d) comprehensive bibliographies through 1971 on the construction, use,

[6] *Tests in Print,* p. xv.

and validity of specific tests; (e) a classified list of tests which have gone out of print since TIP I; (f) a cumulative name index for each test with references; (g) a title index covering in print and out of print tests, as well as inverted, series, and superseded titles in the MMY's and monographs; (h) an analytic name index covering all authors of tests, reviews, excerpts, and references in the MMY's and monographs; (i) a publishers directory with a complete listing of each publisher's test titles; (j) a classified scanning index which describes the population for which each test is intended; (k) identification of foreign tests and journals by presenting the country of origin in brackets immediately after a test entry or journal title; (l) inclusions of factual statements implying criticism such as "1971 tests identical with tests copyrighted 1961 except for format," and "no manual"; (m) listing of test titles at the foot of each page to permit immediate identification of pages consisting only of references or names; and (n) directions on how to use the book and an expanded table of contents printed on the end-pages to greatly facilitate its use.

TIP II contains 2,467 in print test entries, 16.0 percent more than in TIP I. Table 1 presents a breakdown of the number of tests and new references in TIP II by classification. Personality—the area in which we know the least about testing—has, as it did in 1961, the greatest number of tests. Although the percentage of personality tests is 17.9, 44.9 percent of the TIP II references are for personality tests. Three categories—intelligence, personality, and

TABLE 1

TESTS AND NEW REFERENCES
IN TESTS IN PRINT II

Classification	Tests		References	
	Number	Percent	Number	Percent
Achievement Batteries	50	2.0	438	2.6
English	131	5.3	220	1.3
Fine Arts	35	1.4	229	1.4
Foreign Languages	105	4.3	81	.5
Intelligence	274	11.1	4,039	24.4
Mathematics	168	6.8	166	1.0
Miscellaneous	291	11.8	866	5.2
Multi-Aptitude	26	1.1	235	1.4
Personality	441	17.9	7,443	44.9
Reading	248	10.1	837	5.1
Science	97	3.9	72	.4
Sensory-Motor	62	2.5	382	2.3
Social Studies	85	3.4	49	.3
Speech and Hearing	79	3.2	216	1.3
Vocations	375	15.2	1,301	7.8
Total	2,467	100.0	16,574	99.9

vocations—make up 44.2 percent of tests and 77.1 percent of the references in TIP II.

SOCIAL STUDIES TESTS AND REVIEWS

This volume's subtitle, *A Monograph Consisting of the Social Studies Sections of the Seven Mental Measurements Yearbooks (1938–72) and Tests in Print II (1974)*, succinctly describes its contents. In addition to the 10-page reprint from TIP II and the 171-page section of reprints from the seven MMY's, *Social Studies Tests and Reviews* (SSTR) includes a publishers directory, title index, name index, and a social studies scanning index. The TIP II scanning index is reprinted in full also.

TIP II TESTS REPRINT

The section of this volume reprinted from *Tests in Print II,* TIP II Tests, contains a bibliography of in print social studies tests, references for specific tests, cumulative name indexes for specific tests having references, and lists of tests which have gone out of print since appearing in TIP I. (The out of print tests are listed alphabetically following each subsection: General, Contemporary Affairs, Economics, Geography, History, Political Science, and Sociology.) The first three of these categories will be described in more detail.

SOCIAL STUDIES TESTS

The TIP II reprint section lists 85 social studies tests in print as of early 1974—24.8 percent fewer tests than were listed 14 years ago in TIP I (Table 2). In five of the seven categories of tests, the number of available tests has dropped. Economics and sociology are the only areas in which more tests are available now than

TABLE 2
IN PRINT SOCIAL STUDIES TESTS
IN TIP II AND TIP I

Classification	TIP II		TIP I	
	Number	Percent	Number	Percent
General	22	25.9	23	20.4
Contemporary Affairs	5	5.9	7	6.2
Economics	10	11.8	5	4.4
Geography	7	8.2	12	10.6
History	24	28.2	42	37.2
Political Science	13	15.3	21	18.6
Sociology	4	4.7	3	2.7
Total	85	100.0	113	100.1

14 years ago. History tests dropped sharply both in number (from 42 to 24) and in percentage (from 37.2 to 28.2). Of the 85 in print social studies tests, 11.8 percent (10 tests) are new since the 7th MMY; 44.7 percent (38 tests), revised or supplemented. The most significant change in social studies tests has been in the increased number of tests for college accreditation and placement—especially the CLEP examinations.

Unlike the long test entries in the *Mental Measurements Yearbooks,* the TIP II entries in this volume are short entries supplying the following information:

a) TITLE. Test titles are printed in boldface type. Secondary or series titles are set off from main titles by a colon. Titles are always presented exactly as reported in the test materials. Stars precede titles of tests listed for the first time in TIP II; asterisks precede titles of tests which have been revised or supplemented since last listed.

b) TEST POPULATION. The grade, chronological age, or semester range, or the employment category is usually given. Commas are used to indicate separate grade levels. "Grades 1.5–2.5, 2–3, 4–12, 13–17" means that there are four test booklets: a booklet for the middle of the first grade through the middle of the second grade, a booklet for the beginning of the second grade through the end of the third grade, a booklet for grades 4 through 12 inclusive, and a booklet for undergraduate and graduate students in colleges and universities. "First, second semester" means that there are two test booklets: one covering the work of the first semester, the other covering the work of the second semester. "1, 2 semesters" indicates that the second booklet covers the work of the two semesters. "Ages 10-2 to 11-11" means ages 10 years 2 months to 11 years 11 months and "Grades 4-6 to 5-9" means the sixth month in the fourth grade through the ninth month in the fifth grade. "High school and college" denotes a single test booklet for both levels; "High school, college" denotes two test booklets, one for high school and one for college.

c) COPYRIGHT DATE. The range of copyright dates (or publication dates if not copyrighted) includes the various forms, accessories, and editions of a test. When the publication date differs from the copyright date, both dates are given; e.g., "1971, c1965–68" means that the test materials were copyrighted between 1965 and 1968 but were not published until 1971. Publication or copyright dates enclosed in brackets do not appear on the test materials but were obtained from other sources.

d) ACRONYM. An acronym is given for many tests. Following the alphabetical sequence of test titles in the Index of Titles, there is an alphabetical listing of acronyms for tests with 10 or more references.

e) SPECIAL COMMENTS. Some entries contain special notations, such as: "for research use only"; "revision of the *ABC Test*"; "tests administered monthly at centers throughout the United States"; "subtests available as separates"; and "verbal creativity." "For research use only" should be interpreted to mean that the *only* use of the test should be in research designed to assess its usefulness; contrary to what the implications seem to be, "for research use only" does not mean that a test has any use, whatsoever, as a research instrument. Tests used in research studies should have demonstrated validity before being selected as research tools. A statement such as "verbal creativity" is intended to further describe what the test claims to measure.

f) PART SCORES. The number and description of part scores is presented.

g) FACTUAL STATEMENTS IMPLYING CRITICISM. Some of the test entries include factual statements which imply criticism of the test, such as "1970 test identical with test copyrighted 1960" and "no manual."

h) AUTHOR. For most tests, all authors are reported. In the case of tests which appear in a new form each year, only authors of the most recent forms are listed. Names are reported exactly as printed on test materials. Names of editors are generally not reported.

i) PUBLISHER. The name of the publisher or distributor is reported for each test. Foreign publishers are identified by listing the country in brackets immediately following the name of the publisher. The Publishers Directory and Index must be consulted for a publisher's address.

j) FOREIGN ADAPTATIONS. Revisions and adaptations of tests for foreign use are listed in parentheses following the description of the original edition.

k) CLOSING ASTERISK. An asterisk following the publisher's name indicates that the entry was prepared from a first-hand examination of the test materials.

l) SUBLISTINGS. Levels, editions, subtests, or parts of a test which are available in separate booklets are sometimes presented as sublistings with titles set in small capitals. Sub-sublistings are indented with titles set in italic type.

m) CROSS REFERENCES. Except for tests being listed for the first time, a test entry includes a second paragraph with cross references to relevant material which may be found in the MMY reprint sections in this volume, or, in rare instances, the material in other sections of the MMY's. These cross references may be to "additional information" reported in longer entries, or to reviews, excerpts, and references for specific tests.

REFERENCES

The specific test bibliographies in this monograph contain 120 references on the construction, use, and validity of specific tests—78 of these references for tests currently in print. Sixty-eight percent of the references for in print tests are for the last six years reported on, 1966–71. Very little research and writing is being done on standardized tests in social studies—currently about 12 such references per year. Only four of the in print tests have generated bibliographies of 10 or more references: *Test of Economic Understanding,* 29 references; *Sequential Tests of Educational Progress: Social Studies,* 14; *College Board Achievement Test in American History and Social Studies,* 10; and *Test of Understanding in College Economics,* 10.

These specific test bibliographies cover not only the literature of the English-speaking world, but also the literature in English published in non-English-speaking countries. Our goal has been to include all published material —articles, books, chapters, and research monographs—as well as unpublished theses. We do not list as references research reports prepared for internal organizational use, prepublication reports, ERIC material, or abstracts of documents which are reproduced only on receipt of a purchase order (e.g., JSAS manuscripts). Secondary sources (e.g., *Psychological Abstracts*) may provide leads, but if the original publication cannot be located and examined, the reference is not used. We do, however, rely on secondary sources (primarily *Dissertation Abstracts International*) for unpublished theses. Except for doctoral dissertations abstracted in DAI, in recent years all thesis entries have been checked for accuracy by the degree-granting institutions.

References for a given test immediately follow the test entry. They are numbered consecutively for each test as they appear in the first through the seventh MMY and TIP II. References which appeared in earlier volumes are referred to but not repeated; e.g., "7–9. See 5:786." means references 7–9 can be found following test 786 in the section "Fifth MMY Reviews" in this volume.

References are arranged in chronological order by year of publication and alphabetically by authors within years. No references later than 1971 have been included. Supplementary bibliographies will be provided in the forthcoming 8th MMY for those tests which are listed again in that volume; the bibliographies for other tests will be brought up to date in *Tests in Print III,* scheduled for publication after the 8th MMY.

CUMULATIVE NAME INDEXES

A cumulative name index has been provided for every in print test having references to facilitate the search for an author's writings relevant to that test. To simplify indexing, forenames were reduced to initials. Authors not consistent in reporting their names will find their publications listed under two or more citations. On the other hand, a given name may represent two or more persons. In all cases, however, the references present names exactly as they appear in the publication referenced.

TABLE 3

REVIEWS, EXCERPTS, AND REFERENCES
FOR THE 204 SOCIAL STUDIES TESTS
IN THIS VOLUME

Reprint	Tests	Rev's	Exc's	Ref's
TIP II	85			49
7th MMY	53	22	1	15
6th MMY	61	22	1	6
5th MMY	60	30		10
4th MMY	48	15		7
3rd MMY	29	30	2	24
2nd MMY	31	31	1	9
1st MMY	37	16		
Total	204 1	166	5	120

1 The total number of different tests in all publications is 204 —85 in print and 119 out of print.

MMY REVIEWS REPRINT

This chapter is a reprinting of the social studies test sections of the seven *Mental Measurements Yearbooks* presented in their order of publication: 1st MMY (1938, 13 pages), 2nd MMY (1941, 25 pages), 3rd MMY (1949, 23 pages), 4th MMY (1953, 17 pages), 5th MMY (1959, 30 pages), 6th MMY (1965, 33 pages), and 7th MMY (1972, 30 pages). This chapter brings together in a single well-indexed volume a great deal of information on social studies testing covering the past 50 years and more.

This chapter presents 166 original test reviews written by 72 specialists, 5 excerpted test reviews, and 71 references on the construction, use, and validity of specific tests (Table 3). Of the 171 reviews and excerpts, 31.0 percent are for tests currently in print, although not always the most recent editions.

The contributing reviewers represent a wide range of interests and viewpoints. Every effort was made to select reviewers who would be considered highly competent by a sizable group of test users. Our practice of publishing multiple reviews of given tests makes it possible to give representation to differing viewpoints among reviewers. The test reviews in a given yearbook are not limited to new and revised tests; old tests, especially those generating considerable research and writing, are frequently reviewed in successive yearbooks.

In order to make sure that persons invited to review would know what was expected of them, a sheet entitled "Suggestions to MMY Reviewers" was enclosed with each letter of invitation. The suggestions follow:

1. Reviews should be written with the following major objectives in mind:
a) To provide test users with carefully prepared appraisals of tests for their guidance in selecting and using tests.
b) To stimulate progress toward higher professional standards in the construction of tests by commending good work, by censuring poor work, and by suggesting improvements.
c) To impel test authors and publishers to present more detailed information on the construction, validity, reliability, uses, and possible misuses of their tests.
2. Reviews should be concise, the average review running from 600 to 1,200 words in length. The average length of the reviews written by one person generally should not exceed 1,000 words. Except for reviews of achievement batteries, multi-factor batteries, and tests for which a literature review is made, longer reviews should be prepared only with the approval of the Editor.
3. Reviews should be frankly critical, with both strengths and weaknesses pointed out in a judicious manner. Descriptive comments should be kept to the minimum necessary to support the critical portions of the review. Criticism should be as specific as possible; implied criticisms meaningful only to testing specialists should be avoided. Reviews should be written primarily for the rank and file of test users. An indication of the relative importance and value of a test with respect to competing tests should be presented whenever possible. If a reviewer considers a competing test better than the one being reviewed, the competing test should be specifically named.
4. If a test manual gives insufficient, contradictory, or ambiguous information regarding the construction, validity, and use of a test, reviewers are urged to write directly to authors and publishers for further information. Test authors and publishers should, however, be held responsible for presenting adequate data in test manuals—failure to do so should be pointed out. For comments made by reviewers based upon unpublished information received personally from test authors or publishers, the source of the unpublished information should be clearly indicated.
5. Reviewers will be furnished with the test entries which will precede their reviews. Information presented in the entry should not be repeated in reviews unless needed for evaluative purposes.
6. The use of sideheads is optional with reviewers.
7. Each review should conclude with a paragraph presenting a concise summary of the reviewer's overall evaluation of the test. The summary should be as explicit as possible. Is the test the best of its kind? Is it recommended for use? If other tests are better, which of the competing tests is best?
8. A separate review should be prepared for each test. Each review should begin on a new sheet. The test and forms reviewed should be clearly indicated. Your name, title, position, and address should precede each review, e.g.: John Doe, Professor of Education and Psychology, University of Maryland, College Park, Maryland. The review should begin a new paragraph immediately after the address.
9. All reviews should be typed double spaced and in triplicate. Two copies of each review should be submitted to the Editor; one copy should be retained by the reviewer.
10. If for any reason a reviewer thinks he is not in a position to write a frankly critical review in a scholarly and unbiased manner, he should request the Editor to substitute other tests for review.
11. Reviewers may not invite others to collaborate with them in writing reviews unless permission is secured from the Editor.
12. Most tests will be reviewed by two or more persons in order to secure better representation of vari-

ous viewpoints. Noncritical content which excessively overlaps similar materials presented by another reviewer may be deleted. Reviews will be carefully edited, but no important changes will be made without the consent of the reviewer. Galley proofs (unaccompanied by copy) will be submitted to reviewers for checking.

13. The Editor reserves the right to reject any review which does not meet the minimum standards of the MMY series.

14. Each reviewer will receive a complimentary copy of *The Seventh Mental Measurements Yearbook*.

The long test entries in the section Seventh MMY Reviews contain all the information in the short TIP II entries plus the following:

a) INDIVIDUAL OR GROUP TEST. All tests are group tests unless otherwise indicated.

b) FORMS, PARTS, AND LEVELS. All available forms, parts, and levels are listed with copyright dates.

c) PAGES. The number of pages on which print occurs is reported for test booklets, manuals, technical reports, profiles, and other nonapparatus accessories.

d) FACTUAL STATEMENTS IMPLYING CRITICISM. Much more so than short entries, the long entries include factual statements implying criticism of the following type: "no data on reliability," "no data on validity," "no norms," "norms for grade 5 only," "no description of the normative population," "no norms for difference scores," "test copyrighted in 1970 identical with test copyrighted in 1960," and "statistical data based on earlier forms."

e) MACHINE SCORABLE ANSWER SHEETS. All types of machine scorable answer sheets available for use with a specific test are reported: Digitek (OpScan Test Scoring and Document Scanning System), IBM 805 (IBM Test Scoring Machine), IBM 1230 (IBM Optical Mark Reader), MRC (MRC Scoring and Reporting Service), NCS (NCS Scoring and Reporting Service), and NCS Sentry/70, and a few other answer sheets less widely used.

f) COST. Price information is reported for test packages (usually 20 to 35 tests), answer sheets, all other accessories, and specimen sets. The statement "$5.20 per 35 tests" means that all accessories are included unless separate prices are given for accessories. The statement also means 35 tests of one level, one edition, or one part unless stated otherwise. Quantity discounts and special discounts are not reported. Specimen set prices include copies of each level and part—but not all forms—unless otherwise indicated. Since 1970 prices are reported, the latest catalog of a test publisher should be consulted for current prices.

g) SCORING AND REPORTING SERVICES. Scoring and reporting services provided by publishers are reported along with information on costs. Special computerized scoring and interpretation services are sometimes given in separate entries immediately following the test entry.

h) TIME. The number of minutes of actual working time allowed examinees and the approximate length of time needed for administering a test are provided whenever obtainable. The latter figure is always enclosed in parentheses. Thus, "50(60) minutes" indicates that the examinees are allowed 50 minutes of working time and that a total of 60 minutes is needed to administer the test. When the time necessary to administer a test has been obtained through correspondence with the test publisher or author, the time is enclosed in brackets.

RUNNING HEADS AND FEET

To use this volume most efficiently, it is important to take advantage of the information

given at the top and bottom of each page in the test and review sections. Both test entry and page numbers are given in the running heads. However, since all citations in the indexes and cross references are to entry numbers, these numbers, found next to the outside margins on facing pages, can be used as guide numbers in locating a particular test. The entry number on the left-hand page corresponds to the test embodying the first line of type on that page; the entry number on the right-hand page refers to the test containing the last line of type on that page. The test titles corresponding to these guide numbers are given in the running feet at the bottom of the page. Thus, the reader can quickly identify the first and last test discussed on each pair of facing pages.

The first reprint section, from *Tests in Print II,* has guide numbers in the range 1936 to 2020, the second reprint section, from the seven MMY's, has the successive ranges: 1:948 to 1:1154, 2:1614 to 2:1642, 3:590 to 3:619, 4:662 to 4:709, 5:785 to 5:844, 6:963 to 6:1022, and 7:884 to 7:936. The digit preceding the colon in the guide number corresponds to the number of the yearbook being reprinted. The numbers following the colon are the test entry numbers within that yearbook.

TIP II SCANNING INDEX

The complete TIP II Scanning Index, a classified listing of all tests in TIP II, has been reprinted to provide readers with an overview of tests available in areas other than social studies. The 2,467 tests are divided into the categories delineated in Table 1 of this Introduction. Since the social studies section of the TIP II Scanning Index will be of most interest to readers of this monograph, we have reprinted that section (entitled Social Studies Scanning Index) at the end of this volume for convenient reference. This end-of-the-book index is especially useful for locating tests suitable for a given population, since descriptions of these populations are reported immediately following the test titles.

PUBLISHERS DIRECTORY AND INDEX

Instead of giving only the entry numbers of the tests of a given publisher, as in our earlier publications, this Publishers Directory and Index gives both test titles and entry numbers. Stars denote the 11 publishers with test catalogs listing 10 or more tests (not necessarily social studies tests). Tests not originating in the country of publication are identified by listing in brackets the country in which the test was originally prepared and published.

All addresses have been checked by the publishers and are accurate through 1973. However, with such a large number of publishers (including many author-publishers), some address changes must be expected.

The directory lists 19 publishers of social studies tests, 4 of which publish only one social studies test. The five publishers with 8 or more social studies tests are: College Entrance Examination Board, 13 tests; Educational Testing Service, 13; Bureau of Educational Measurements, 9; Cooperative Tests and Services, 8; and Psychometric Affiliates, 8.

INDEX OF TITLES

This cumulative title index includes social studies tests in print as separates as of February 1, 1974, and out of print or status unknown social studies tests.

Citations are to test entry numbers, not to pages. Numbers without colons refer to in print tests listed in the first reprint section (TIP II Tests) in this volume; numbers with colons refer to tests out of print, status unknown, or reclassified since last listed with social studies tests. Unless preceded by the word *"consult,"* all numbers containing colons refer to tests in this volume. To obtain the latest information on a test no longer classified with social studies tests, the reader is directed to consult the last yearbook in which the test appeared. For example, "Cooperative Contemporary Affairs Test for College Students, 1:948; reclassified, *consult* 4:4" indicates that the test was listed as a social studies test in the *First Yearbook* but has been reclassified and for the latest information available, the reader must consult test 4 in the *Fourth Yearbook*. Superseded titles are listed with cross references to the current title. Tests which are part of a series are listed under their individual titles and also their series titles.

INDEX OF NAMES

This cumulative index is an analytical index distinguishing between authorship of a test, test review, excerpted review, or reference dealing with a specific test. Furthermore, the index indicates whether the relevant test is in print or out of print. Numbers with colons refer to out of print or status unknown tests. Unless preceded by the word "consult," all numbers containing colons refer to tests in this volume.

Forenames have been reduced to initials to lower the cost of indexing. Since authors are not always consistent in how they list their names, two or more listings may refer to the same person. On the other hand, the use of initials sometimes results in one name representing two or more persons. Reference to the cited material in the text will resolve these difficulties in almost all cases.

Except for test authors, the use of the Index of Names is a two-step process. For example, if the name index reports *"rev, 1948"* for R. W. Tyler, the reader must look at the cross reference for test 1948 in the TIP II Tests section of this volume to learn where Tyler's review may be found in the yearbook reprints. Similarly, if the name index reports *"ref, 1968"* for E. T. Garman, the reader must look at the Cumulative Name Index for test 1968 to learn where, in this volume, Garman's reference or references on that test may be found. The Cumulative Name Index for test 1968 indicates that Garman is the author of 3 references for this test, each cited by number, so the reader can quickly locate them in the list of references under the test entry.

SOCIAL STUDIES

TESTS AND REVIEWS

SOCIAL STUDIES – TIP II

[1936]

American History—Government—Problems of Democracy: Acorn Achievement Tests. Grades 9–16; 1942–53; 6 scores: growth of a national spirit, growth of democracy, the Constitution, foreign policy, problems of American democracy, total; 1953 test identical with test copyrighted 1942 except for minor changes; Vincent McGarrett; Psychometric Affiliates. *

For additional information and a review by Richard E. Gross, see 5:785; for a review by Howard R. Anderson, see 3:590.

[1937]

American School Achievement Tests: Part 4, Social Studies and Science. Grades 4–6, 7–9; 1941–63; 2 scores: social studies, science; Willis E. Pratt, Robert V. Young (manuals), and Clara E. Cockerille; Bobbs-Merrill Co., Inc. * For the complete battery entry, see 4.

For additional information, see 6:963. For reviews of the complete battery, see 6:2 (2 reviews), 5:1 (2 reviews), 4:1 (1 review), and 3:1 (2 reviews).

[1938]

*CLEP General Examinations: Social Sciences and History. 1–2 years of college or equivalent; 1964–73; for college accreditation of nontraditional study, advanced placement, or assessment of educational attainment; a retired subtest of the *College-Level Examination Program General Examinations* published as a separate for local administration through the *Testing Academic Achievement* program (see 1061); 3 scores: social sciences, history, total; program administered for the College Entrance Examination Board by Educational Testing Service. * For the testing program entry, see 1050.

For additional information concerning earlier forms, see 7:8b. For reviews of the testing program, see 7:664 (3 reviews).

[1939]

*College Board Achievement Test in American History and Social Studies. Candidates for college entrance; 1901–73; test administered on specified dates at centers established by the publisher; inactive forms, entitled *College Placement Test in American History and Social Studies,* are available to colleges for local administration; program administered for the College Entrance Examination Board by Educational Testing Service. * For the testing program entry, see 1048.

For additional information, see 7:884; for a review by Howard R. Anderson of earlier forms, see 6:966; for a review by Ralph W. Tyler, see 5:786 (3 references); for a review by Robert L. Thorndike, see 4:662 (6 references). For reviews of the testing program, see 6:760 (2 reviews).

REFERENCES THROUGH 1971
1–6. See 4:662.
7–9. See 5:786.
10. PUGH, RICHARD C.; MORGAN, JAMES M.; AND LUDLOW, H. GLENN. *Predicting Success for Indiana University Freshmen Using the CEEB Achievement Tests, the CEEB Scholastic Aptitude Test, and High School Rank.* Indiana Studies in Prediction, No. 13. Bloomington, Ind.: Bureau of Educational Studies and Testing, Indiana University, April 1970. Pp. xi, 39. *

CUMULATIVE NAME INDEX

Anderson, H. R.: *rev,* 6:966
Bobbitt, J. M.: 8
Bragdon, H. W.: 7
Chauncey, H.: 4
College Entrance Examination Board: 9
French, J. W.: 8
Ludlow, H. G.: 10
Morgan, J. M.: 10
Newman, S. H.: 8
Pargellis, S.: 2
Pugh, R. C.: 10
Stalnaker, J. M.: 5
Stalnaker, R. C.: 5
Thorndike, R. L.: *rev,* 4:662
Tyler, R. W.: *rev,* 5:786
Warr, C. F.: 1–3
Weber, C. O.: 6

[1940]

*College Board Achievement Test in European History and World Cultures. Candidates for college entrance; 1901–73; test administered on specified dates at centers established by the publisher; inactive forms, entitled *College Placement Test in European History and World Cultures,* are available to colleges for local administration; program administered for the College Entrance Examination Board by Educational Testing Service. * For the testing program entry, see 1048.

For additional information, see 7:885; for a review by David K. Heenan of earlier forms, see 6:967. For reviews of the testing program, see 6:760 (2 reviews).

[1941]

*College Placement Test in American History and Social Studies. Entering college freshmen; 1962–72; reprintings of inactive 1962 and 1964 forms of *College Board Achievement Test in American History and Social Studies;* test available to colleges for local administration; program administered for the College Entrance Examination Board by Educational Testing Service. * For the testing program entry, see 1051.

For additional information, see 7:886. For a review of the testing program, see 7:665. For reference to reviews of the *College Board Achievement Test in American History and Social Studies,* see 1939.

[1942]

*College Placement Test in European History and World Cultures. Entering college freshmen; 1963–72; reprinting of inactive 1963 form of *College Board Achievement Test in European History and World Cultures;* test available to colleges for local administration; program administered for the College Entrance Examination Board by Educational Testing Service. * For the testing program entry, see 1051.

For additional information, see 7:887. For a review of the testing program, see 7:665. For reference to a review of the *College Board Achievement Test in European History and World Cultures,* see 1940.

[1943]

History and Civics Test: Municipal Tests: National Achievement Tests. Grades 3–6, 6–8; 1938–55; subtest of *Municipal Battery;* 3 scores: lessons of history, historical facts, total; 1948–55 tests identical with tests copyrighted 1938–39 except for minor changes; Robert K. Speer and Samuel Smith; Psychometric Affiliates. *

For additional information and a review by Howard R. Anderson, see 5:790; for a review by Harry D. Berg, see 4:664. For reviews of the complete battery, see 5:18 (1 review), 4:20 (1 review), and 2:1191 (2 reviews).

[1944]

*The Iowa Tests of Educational Development: Test 1, Understanding of Basic Social Concepts. Grades 9–12; 1942–67; Forms X-4 and Y-4; more recent Forms X5 and Y5 are not available as separates; prepared under the direction of E. F. Lindquist and Leonard S. Feldt; Science Research Associates, Inc. * For the complete battery entry, see 20.

For additional information and a review by Morey J. Wantman of earlier forms, see 6:969. For reviews of the complete battery, see 6:14 (2 reviews), 5:17 (2 reviews), 4:17 (1 review), and 3:12 (3 reviews).

REFERENCES THROUGH 1971

1. HART, RICHARD LAVERNE. *An Analysis of Factors Related to High and Low Achievement in Understanding Basic Social Concepts.* Doctor's thesis, University of Nebraska (Lincoln, Neb.), 1960. (*DA* 21:2159)

CUMULATIVE NAME INDEX

Hart, R. L.: 1   Wantman, M. J.: *rev,* 6:969

[1945]

*National Teacher Examinations: Social Studies. College seniors and teachers; 1940–73; an inactive form (1966) entitled *Teacher Education Examination Program: Social Studies* is available to colleges for local administration; another inactive form (1968) entitled *Specialty Examinations: Social Studies* is available to school systems for local use as part of the program entitled *School Personnel Research and Evaluation Services;* Educational Testing Service. * For the testing program entry, see 869.

For additional information concerning earlier forms, see 7:889; for a review by Harry D. Berg, see 6:974. For reviews of the testing program, see 7:582 (2 reviews), 6:700 (1 review), 5:538 (3 reviews), and 4:802 (1 review).

[1946]

Primary Social Studies Test. Grades 1–3; 1967; PSST; Ralph C. Preston and Robert V. Duffey; Houghton Mifflin Co. *

For additional information and a review by Virginia M. Rogers, see 7:890.

[1947]

SRA Achievement Series: Social Studies. Grades 4–9; 1963–69; Forms C and D; more recent Forms E and F are not available as separates; Louis P. Thorpe, D. Welty Lefever, and Robert A. Naslund; Science Research Associates, Inc. * For the complete battery entry, see 29.

For additional information, see 7:891. For reviews of the complete battery, see 7:18 (2 reviews), 6:21 (1 review), and 5:21 (2 reviews).

[1948]

*Sequential Tests of Educational Progress: Social Studies. Grades 4–6, 7–9, 10–12, 13–14; 1956–72; 2 editions; Cooperative Tests and Services. * For the complete battery entry, see 35.

a) ORIGINAL SERIES [70 MINUTE TESTS]. 1956–63; Braille and large type editions (grades 4–12) are available from American Printing House for the Blind, Inc.

b) SERIES 2 [45 MINUTE TESTS (GRADES 4–9) AND 60 MINUTE TESTS (GRADES 10–14)]. 1956–72.

For additional information and reviews by Jonathon C. McLendon and Donald W. Oliver of *a,* see 6:971 (1 reference); for reviews by Richard E. Gross, S. A. Rayner, and Ralph W. Tyler, see 5:792. For reviews of the original edition of the complete battery, see 6:25 (2 reviews) and 5:24 (2 reviews, 1 excerpt).

REFERENCES THROUGH 1971

1. See 6:971.
2. McBEE, GEORGE, AND DUKE, RALPH L. "Relationship Between Intelligence, Scholastic Motivation, and Academic Achievement." *Psychol Rep* 6:3–8 F '60. * (*PA* 34:8404)
3. McGUIRE, CARSON. "Sex Role and Community Variability in Test Performances." *J Ed Psychol* 52:61–73 Ap '61. * (*PA* 38:3207)
4. RUSSELL, JAMES WILLIAM. *An Analysis of the Academic Performance of Transfer and Native Students and Their Major Fields in the College of Arts and Sciences at the University of Georgia.* Doctor's thesis, University of Georgia (Athens, Ga.), 1963. (*DA* 25:1668)
5. PEAKE, RONALD EDWARD. *An Examination of the Differences in Problem-Solving Processes of Successful and Nonsuccessful Students Taking Ninth Grade Social Studies.* Doctor's thesis, University of Alabama (University, Ala.), 1964. (*DA* 25:7111)
6. MARTIN, LOUIS. *An Examination of the Test and Item Validity of the Sequential Tests of Educational Progress, Social Studies—Level II, Form B.* Master's thesis, Catholic University of America (Washington, D.C.), 1965.
7. BONEY, J. DON. "Predicting the Academic Achievement of Secondary School Negro Students." *Personnel & Guid J* 44:700–3 Mr '66. * (*PA* 40:8064)
8. CHANDLER, JOSEPH DOUGLAS. *An Analysis of Competence in the Social Sciences by Elementary Education Majors at the University of Tennessee.* Doctor's thesis, University of Tennessee (Knoxville, Tenn.), 1966. (*DA* 27:3246A)
9. MICHAEL, JOAN JOHNSON. *An Experimental Analysis of the Relationship Between the Reliability of a Multiple-Choice Examination and Various Test-Scoring Procedures.* Doctor's thesis, University of Southern California (Los Angeles, Calif.), 1967. (*DA* 28:2561A)
10. MICHAEL, JOAN J. "The Reliability of a Multiple-Choice Examination Under Various Test-Taking Instructions." *J Ed Meas* 5:307–14 w '68. * (*PA* 44:11225)
11. BORNSTEIN, HARRY, AND CHAMBERLAIN, KAREN. "An Investigation of the Effects of 'Verbal Load' in Achievement Tests." *Am Ed Res J* 7(4):597–604 N '70. *
12. PARSLEY, JAMES FRANCIS, JR. *A Comparison of the Ability of Ninth Grade Students to Apply Several Critical Thinking Skills to Problematic Content Presented Through Two Different Media.* Doctor's thesis, Ohio University (Athens, Ohio), 1970. (*DAI* 31:4629A)
13. BORNSTEIN, HARRY. "Some Effects of Verbal Load on Achievement Tests." *Am Ann Deaf* 116(1):44–8 F '71. * (*PA* 47:1603)
14. BORNSTEIN, HARRY, AND KANNAPELL, BARBARA. "More on the Effects of Verbal Load on Achievement Tests." *Am Ann Deaf* 116(6): 575–9 D '71. * (*PA* 48:7769)
For additional references, see the bibliography for the series, 35.

CUMULATIVE NAME INDEX

Boney, J. D.: 7   Chandler, J. D.: 8
Bornstein, H.: 11, 13–4   Duke, R. L.: 2
Chamberlain, K.: 11   Gross, R. E.: *rev,* 5:792

Kannapell, B.: 14
Liggitt, W. A.: 1
McBee, G.: 2
McGuire, C.: 3
McLendon, J. C.: rev, 6:971
Martin, L.: 6
Michael, J. J.: 9–10

Oliver, D. W.: rev, 6:971
Parsley, J. F.: 12
Peake, R. E.: 5
Rayner, S. A.: rev, 5:792
Russell, J. W.: 4
Tyler, R. W.: rev, 5:792

[1949]

*Social Studies: Minnesota High School Achieve-
ment Examinations. Grades 7, 8, 9; 1961–70; a new,
revised, or previously inactive form issued each May;
Midwest High School Achievement Examinations
used as series title through 1962; Form GJ Rev ('70,
with 1973 copyright for grade 8) used in 1970 and
1973 testings; 3 levels; edited by V. L. Lohmann;
American Guidance Service, Inc. *
a) SOCIAL STUDIES GRADE 7. 1961–70.
b) SOCIAL STUDIES GRADE 8. 1962–70.
c) SOCIAL STUDIES GRADE 9. 1962–70.
   For additional information concerning out of print
and inactive forms, see 7:892 and 6:973.

[1950]

Social Studies Test: Acorn National Achieve-
ment Tests. Grades 7–9; 1946–50; 5 scores: human
relations and life situations, products and places, social
ideas and facts, application of knowledge, total; Lester
D. Crow and Everett F. Augspurger; Psychometric
Affiliates. *
   For additional information and a review by Edgar
B. Wesley, see 4:666.

[1951]

Social Studies Test: National Achievement
Tests. Grades 4–6, 7–9; 1937–57; 1945 and 1955–57
tests identical with tests copyrighted 1939 and 1945,
respectively, except for minor changes; 2 levels; Robert K. Speer and Samuel Smith; Psychometric Affiliates. *
a) GRADES 4–6. 6 scores: human relations, life situations, social problems, products and peoples, meaning
of events, total.
b) GRADES 7–9. 7 scores: human relations, life situations, social interpretations, values of products, social
ideas, miscellaneous facts, total.
   For additional information, see 5:798; for a review
by Ray G. Wood, see 3:594.

[1952]

Stanford Achievement Test: High School Social
Studies Test. Grades 9–12; 1965–66; catalog uses
the title Stanford High School Social Studies Test;
subtest of Stanford Achievement Test: High School
Basic Battery; Eric F. Gardner, Jack C. Merwin,
Robert Callis, and Richard Madden; Harcourt Brace
Jovanovich, Inc. * For the complete battery entry,
see 37.
   For additional information, see 7:894. For reviews
of the complete battery, see 7:27 (2 reviews).

REFERENCES THROUGH 1971
1. SMITH, I. LEON. "Validity of Taxonomic Tests." Ed &
Psychol Meas 31(2):475–6 su '71. *

CUMULATIVE NAME INDEX
Smith, I. L.: 1

[1953]

Stanford Achievement Test, 1964 Edition: Social Studies Tests. Grades 5.5–6.9, 7.0–9.9; 1940–68;
catalog uses the title Stanford Social Studies Test;
not available as a separate in the 1973 edition of the
battery; Braille editions are available from American
Printing House for the Blind, Inc.; Truman L. Kelley,
Richard Madden, Eric F. Gardner, and Herbert C.

Rudman; Harcourt Brace Jovanovich, Inc. * For the
complete battery entry, see 36.
   For additional information and a review by Virginia
M. Rogers, see 7:895; for a review by Harry D. Berg
of an earlier edition, see 5:799; for a review by Ray
G. Wood, see 3:595. For reviews of the complete
battery, see 7:25 (1 excerpt), 6:26 (1 review, 1
excerpt), 5:25 (1 review), 4:25 (2 reviews), and
3:18 (2 reviews).

[1954]

*Teacher Education Examination Program: So-
cial Studies. College seniors preparing to teach secondary school; 1957–72; reprinting of inactive 1966
form of National Teacher Examinations: Social Studies; test available to colleges for local administration;
Educational Testing Service. * For the testing program entry, see 898.
   For additional information concerning an earlier
form, see 6:975. For a review of the testing program,
see 5:543. For reference to a review of the National
Teacher Examinations: Social Studies, see 1945.

[1955]

Tests of Academic Progress: Social Studies.
Grades 9–12; 1964–66; Dale P. Scannell and Alvin
H. Schild; Houghton Mifflin Co. * For the complete
battery entry, see 44.
   For additional information and a review by Harry
D. Berg, see 7:896 (1 reference). For a review of
the complete battery, see 7:31.

REFERENCES THROUGH 1971
1. See 7:896.

CUMULATIVE NAME INDEX
Berg, H. D.: rev, 7:896   Goolsby, T. M.: 1

[1956]

*Tests of Basic Experiences: Social Studies.
Prekgn–kgn, kgn–grade 1; 1970–72; Margaret H.
Moss; CTB/McGraw-Hill. * For the complete bat-
tery entry, see 47.
   For additional information, see 7:897. For a review
of the complete battery, see 7:33.

[1957]

Zimmerman-Sanders Social Studies Test. 1, 2
semesters in grades 7–8; 1962–64; first published 1962–
63 in the Every Pupil Scholarship Test series; John
J. Zimmerman and M. W. Sanders; Bureau of Educational Measurements. *
   For additional information, see 7:898.

[Out of Print Since TIP I]

Christian Democracy Test (Civics, Sociology, Eco-
nomics): Affiliation Testing Program for Catholic
Secondary Schools, 6:964 (1 review)
Citizenship: Every Pupil Scholarship Test, 6:965
Cooperative General Achievement Tests: Social Stud-
ies [General Proficiency Series], 6:968 (1 review),
4:668 (3 references)
Cooperative Social Studies Test for Grades 7, 8, and 9,
4:663 (3 reviews)
Graduate Record Examinations Advanced Anthro-
pology Test, 7:546
Greig Social Studies Test, 5:788 (1 review)
Introduction to Social Studies: Achievement Examin-
ations for Secondary Schools, 5:789
Metropolitan Achievement Tests: High School Social
Studies Test, 7:888 (2 reviews)
Shearer Social Studies Test, 5:793 (1 review, 1 refer-
ence)
Social Studies: Every Pupil Scholarship Test, 6:972
T. C. Social Studies Test, 6:978

CONTEMPORARY AFFAIRS

[1958]

*Current News Test. Grades 9–12; 1951–74; formerly called *Newsweek Current News Test;* 2 new tests issued annually: spring term review (covering mid December–mid April) issued each May, fall term review (covering September–mid December) issued each January; available only as part of the Newsweek Educational Program; no manual; Newsweek Educational Division. *

For additional information, see 6:985.

[1959]

*Newsweek NewsQuiz. Grades 9–12; 1951–74; formerly called *Newsweek Monthly Objective Test;* 6 tests (spirit masters for local duplicating) issued annually during school year (October, November, December, February, March, and April); available only as part of the Newsweek Educational Program; no manual; Newsweek Educational Division. *

For additional information, see 6:986.

[1960]

*School Weekly News Quiz. High school; 1947–74; revision of *New York Times Current Affairs Test;* although title implies weekly publication, 8 tests (spirit masters for local duplicating) issued annually during school year (October–May); available only as part of the New York Times Daily School Service Program; no manual; New York Times. *

For additional information concerning the earlier edition, see 6:983.

[1961]

*Time Current Affairs Test. Grades 9–12 and adults; 1935–74; formerly called *Current Affairs Test;* new test issued annually in January; available only as part of the Time Education Program; no manual; Time, Inc. *

[1962]

★The Time Monthly News Quiz. Grades 9–12 and adults; 1969–74; 9 tests (spirit masters for local duplicating) in each of 2 areas, issued annually in August (Summer Review Quiz), September, October, November, December–January, February, March, April, and May; available only as part of the Time Education Program; no manual; Time, Inc. *

a) ENGLISH REVIEW. 1973–74.
b) NEWS QUIZ. 1969–74.

[Out of Print Since TIP I]

Contemporary Affairs: Every Pupil Test, 6:979
Cooperative Test on Foreign Affairs, 6:980 (1 review, 1 excerpt, 1 reference)
Current Affairs: Every Pupil Scholarship Test, 6:981
Nationwide Current Events Examination, 6:982
New York Times Current Affairs Test for Colleges, 6:984

ECONOMICS

[1963]

*CLEP Subject Examination in Introductory Economics. 1 year or equivalent; 1964–73; for college accreditation of nontraditional study, advanced placement, or assessment of educational achievement; tests administered monthly at centers throughout the United States; program administered for the College

Entrance Examination Board by Educational Testing Service. * For the testing program entry, see 1050.

For additional information, see 7:899. For reviews of the testing program, see 7:664 (3 reviews).

[1964]

★[Economics/Objective Tests.] 1 semester high school; 1970; 5 tests; no manual; Perfection Form Co. *

a) CONCEPTS IN ECONOMICS.
b) PRICE, INCOME AND PERSONAL GROWTH.
c) MONEY, BANKING AND INSURANCE.
d) INTERNATIONAL TRADE.
e) FINAL TEST.

[1965]

*The Graduate Record Examinations Advanced Economics Test. Graduate school candidates; 1939–73; Educational Testing Service. * For the testing program entry, see 1053.

For additional information concerning earlier forms, see 7:900; see also 6:987 (1 reference). For reviews of the testing program, see 7:667 (1 review) and 5:601 (1 review).

REFERENCES THROUGH 1971
1. See 6:987.

CUMULATIVE NAME INDEX
Love, J. O.: 1   Riley, R. C.: 1

[1966]

★Modern Economics Test: Content Evaluation Series. Grades 10–12; 1971; Morris G. Sica, Sylvia Lane, and John D. Lafky; Houghton Mifflin Co. *

[1967]

★Primary Test of Economic Understanding. Grades 2–3; 1971; PTEU; Donald G. Davison and John H. Kilgore; Bureau of Business and Economic Research, University of Iowa; distributed by Joint Council on Economic Education. *

REFERENCES THROUGH 1971
1. DAVISON, DONALD G., AND KILGORE, JOHN H. "A Model for Evaluating the Effectiveness of Economic Education in Primary Grades." *J Econ Ed* 3(1):17–25 f '71. *

CUMULATIVE NAME INDEX
Davison, D. G.: 1   Kilgore, J. H.: 1

[1968]

Test of Economic Understanding. High school and college; 1963–64; TEU; test by Committee for Measurement of Economic Understanding, Joint Council on Economic Education; manual by George Leland Bach, Walter R. Jones, and Suzanne R. Meyer; Science Research Associates, Inc. *

For additional information, reviews by Edward J. Furst and Christine H. McGuire, and an excerpted review by Robert L. Ebel, see 7:901 (10 references).

REFERENCES THROUGH 1971
1–10. See 7:901.
11. CAMPBELL, MORRIS W. *Measurement of Economic Understandings of Grade Twelve Students.* Master's thesis, University of Alberta (Edmonton, Alta., Canada), 1964.
12. BACH, G. L., AND SAUNDERS, PHILLIP. "Economic Education: Aspirations and Achievements." *Am Econ R* 55:329–56 Je '65. *
13. BACH, G. L., AND SAUNDERS, PHILLIP. "Lasting Effects of Economics Courses at Different Types of Institutions." *Am Econ R* 56:505–11 Je '66. *
14. MOYER, M. E., AND PADEN, D. W. "On the Efficiency of the High School Economics Course." *Am Econ R* 58:870–7 S '68. *
15. GARMAN, E. THOMAS. *Economic Literacy of Prospective Business Education Teachers.* Doctor's thesis, Texas Tech University (Lubbock, Tex.), 1969. (*DAI* 31:264A)
16. MAHER, JOHN E. "DEEP: Strengthening Economics in the Schools." *Am Econ R* 59(2):230–8 My '69. *

17. VILLARD, HENRY H. "Where We Now Stand." *J Econ Ed* 1(1):60–6 f '69. *
18. WELSH, ARTHUR L., AND FELS, RENDIGS. "Performance on the New Test of Understanding in College Economics." *Am Econ R* 59(2):224–9 My '69. *
19. GARMAN, E. THOMAS. "Economic Literacy of Prospective Business Education Teachers." *Bus Ed Forum* 24(4):35 Ja '70. *
20. GERY, FRANK W. "Mathematics and the Understanding of Economic Concepts." Letter. *J Econ Ed* 2(1):100–4 f '70. *
21. MOYER, M. EUGENE, AND PADEN, DONALD W. "Economics Achievement and Mathematics Training." Letter. *J Econ Ed* 2(1):104–6 f '70. *
22. SAUNDERS, PHILLIP. "Does High School Economics Have a Lasting Impact?" *J Econ Ed* 2(1):39–55 f '70. *
23. GARMAN, E. THOMAS. "College Level Use of the 'Test of Economic Understanding.'" *Ill Sch Res* 7(2):53–5 w '71. *
24. JONES, ROLAND ODELL. *A Study of the Relationship Between Economic Understanding, Business Education Curricula and Certain Personal Factors of Business Education Seniors in Selected Delaware High Schools.* Doctor's thesis, Pennsylvania State University (University Park, Pa.), 1971. (*DAI* 32:4923A)
25. MCKENZIE, RICHARD B. "An Exploratory Study of the Economic Understanding of Elementary School Teachers." *J Econ Ed* 3(1):26–31 f '71. *
26. MORTON, JOHN S., AND REZNY, RONALD R. "Some Teaching Techniques." *J Econ Ed* 3(1):11–6 f '71. *
27. O'TOOLE, DENNIS MARTIN. *An Accountability Evaluation of an In-Service Economic Education Experience.* Doctor's thesis, Ohio University (Athens, Ohio), 1971. (*DAI* 32:2315A)
28. PHILLIPS, JAMES ARTHUR. *The Effects of Instructional Objectives Treatment on Economics Achievement Scores of Students in Selected Community Colleges.* Doctor's thesis, University of Southern California (Los Angeles, Calif.), 1971. (*DAI* 33:992A)
29. WALL, CARLTON DEWEY. *Contributing Factors to the Economic Understanding of High School Seniors.* Doctor's thesis, Ohio State University (Columbus, Ohio), 1971. (*DAI* 32:3581A)

CUMULATIVE NAME INDEX

[1969]

★**Test of Elementary Economics, Revised Experimental Edition.** Grades 4–6; 1971; TEE; developed by Economic Education Enrichment Program, West Springfield Public Schools, West Springfield, Mass.; Joint Council on Economic Education. *

[1970]

Test of Understanding in College Economics. 1, 2 semesters college; 1967–68; TUCE; Committee for a College-Level Test of Economic Understanding, Joint Council on Economic Education; Psychological Corporation; distributed by the Council. *

For additional information and a review by Christine H. McGuire, see 7:902.

REFERENCES THROUGH 1971

1. FELS, RENDIGS. "A New 'Test of Understanding in College Economics.'" *Am Econ R* 57:660–6 My '67. *
2. FELS, RENDIGS. "Hard Research on a Soft Subject: Hypothesis-Testing in Economic Education." *South Econ J* 36(1):1–9 Jl '69. *
3. VILLARD, HENRY H. "Where We Now Stand." *J Econ Ed* 1(1):60–6 f '69. *
4. GERY, FRANK W. "Mathematics and the Understanding of Economic Concepts." Letter. *J Econ Ed* 2(1):100–4 f '70. *
5. HEALEY, RUTH M. "Economic Understandings of Junior College Students." *Bus Ed Forum* 24(7):32–4 Ap '70. *
6. BUCKLES, STEPHEN G., AND MCMAHON, MARSHALL E. "Further Evidence on the Value of Lectures in Elementary Economics." *J Econ Ed* 2(2):138–41 sp '71. *
7. LEWIS, DARRELL R., AND DAHL, TOR. "The Test of Understanding in College Economics and Its Construct Validity." *J Econ Ed* 2(2):155–66 sp '71. *

8. MEINKOTH, MARIAN R. "Teachers of Economic Principles: Effect on Student Achievement and Attitudes." *J Exp Ed* 40(2):66–72 w '71. * (*PA* 47:11806)
9. MEINKOTH, MARIAN R. "Textbooks and the Teaching of Economic Principles." *J Econ Ed* 2(2):127–30 sp '71. *
10. O'TOOLE, DENNIS MARTIN. *An Accountability Evaluation of an In-Service Economic Education Experience.* Doctor's thesis, Ohio University (Athens, Ohio), 1971. (*DAI* 32:2315A)

CUMULATIVE NAME INDEX

[1971]

★**Test of Understanding in Personal Economics.** High school; 1971; TUPE; Joint Council on Economic Education. *

[1972]

*****The Undergraduate Program Field Tests: Economics Test.** College; 1969–73; formerly called *The Undergraduate Record Examinations: Economics Test;* test available to colleges for local administration; Educational Testing Service. * For the testing program entry, see 1062.

For additional information, see 7:903. For reviews of the testing program, see 7:671 (2 reviews).

[Out of Print Since TIP I]

Economics Test: State High School Tests for Indiana, 4:670
High School Economics: Manchester Semester-End Achievement Tests, T:1738
Hills Economics Test, 4:673
Standard Achievement Test in Economic Understanding for Secondary Schools, 6:988
Test of Economic Information, T:1971

GEOGRAPHY

[1973]

Brandywine Achievement Test in Geography for Secondary Schools. Grades 7–12; 1962; no manual; John A. Bonham and Harry R. Martini; [Brandywine Achievement Test]. *

For additional information, see 6:990.

[1974]

*****Economic Geography: Achievement Examinations for Secondary Schools.** High school; 1951–61; a new, revised, or previously inactive form was issued each May from 1951 through 1961; Form 4 ('54) is the only form in print; High School Achievement Examinations and Midwest High School Achievement Examinations have also been used as series titles; Helen Haberman; Bobbs-Merrill Co., Inc. *

For additional information concerning earlier forms, see 5:802.

[1975]

Geography Test: Municipal Tests: National Achievement Tests. Grades 3–6, 6–8; 1938–52; subtest of *Municipal Battery;* 3 scores: geographical ideas and comparisons, miscellaneous facts, total; 1949 and 1952 tests identical with tests copyrighted 1939 and 1938, respectively, except for minor changes; Robert K. Speer and Samuel Smith; Psychometric Affiliates. *

For additional information, see 5:806; for a review by Edwin H. Reeder, see 4:676. For reviews of the complete battery, see 5:18 (1 review), 4:20 (1 review), and 2:1191 (2 reviews).

[1976]

Geography Test: National Achievement Tests.
Grades 6–8; 1938–49; 6 scores: geographical ideas, locating products, uses of products and instruments, economic and human relations, miscellaneous problems, total; Robert K. Speer, Lester D. Crow, and Samuel Smith; Psychometric Affiliates. *

For additional information, see 4:677; for a review by Elaine Forsyth, see 3:600.

[1977]

*The Graduate Record Examinations Advanced Geography Test. Graduate school candidates; 1966–73; 3 scores: human geography, physical geography, total; Educational Testing Service. * For the testing program entry, see 1053.

For additional information concerning earlier forms, see 7:905. For reviews of the testing program, see 7:667 (1 review) and 5:601 (1 review).

[1978]

Hollingsworth-Sanders Geography Test. 1, 2 semesters in grades 5–7; 1962–64; first published 1962–63 in the Every Pupil Scholarship Test series; Leon Hollingsworth and M. W. Sanders; Bureau of Educational Measurements. *

For additional information and a review by Dana G. Kurfman, see 7:906.

[1979]

*The Undergraduate Program Field Tests: Geography Test. College; 1969–73; formerly called *The Undergraduate Record Examinations: Geography Test;* test available to colleges for local administration; Educational Testing Service. * For the testing program entry, see 1062.

For additional information, see 7:907. For reviews of the testing program, see 7:671 (2 reviews).

[Out of Print Since TIP I]

Coordinated Scales of Attainment: Geography, 5:801
Emporia Geography Test, 3:598 (2 reviews)
Geography Achievement Test for Beginning High School Students, 7:904
Geography: Every Pupil Scholarship Test, 6:991
Geography of the Americas: Every Pupil Test, 6:992a1
Geography of the Eastern Hemisphere: Every Pupil Test, 6:992a2
Geography of the World: Every Pupil Test, 6:992b
Physical Geography: Every Pupil Scholarship Test, 6:993
Survey Test in Geography, 6:994 (1 review)
Tate Economic Geography Test, 3:601 (1 review)
World Geography: Every Pupil Scholarship Test, 6:995

HISTORY

[1980]

*Advanced Placement Examination in American History. High school students desiring credit for college level courses or admission to advanced courses; 1956–73; available to secondary schools for annual administration on specified days in May; inactive forms are available to colleges for local administration in the *Testing Academic Achievement* program; program administered for the College Entrance Examina-

tion Board by Educational Testing Service. * For the testing program entry, see 1045.

For additional information concerning earlier forms, see 7:908; for a review by Harry D. Berg, see 6:1000 (1 reference); for reviews by James A. Field, Jr. and Christine McGuire, see 5:812. For reviews of the testing program, see 7:662 (2 reviews).

REFERENCES THROUGH 1971
1. See 6:1000.
2. PARTIN, RONALD L. *The Value of Four Selected Test Scores in Predicting Advanced Placement American History Test Scores.* Master's thesis, Bowling Green State University (Bowling Green, Ohio), 1970.

CUMULATIVE NAME INDEX
Berg, H. D.: *rev,* 6:1000   McGuire, C.: *rev,* 5:812
Field, J. A.: *rev,* 5:812   Partin, R. L.: 2
Graff, H. F.: 1

[1981]

*Advanced Placement Examination in European History. High school students desiring credit for college level courses or admission to advanced courses; 1956–73; available to secondary schools for annual administration on specified days in May; inactive forms are available to colleges for local administration in the *Testing Academic Achievement* program; program administered for the College Entrance Examination Board by Educational Testing Service. * For the testing program entry, see 1045.

For additional information concerning earlier forms, see 7:909; see also 6:1001 (2 references). For reviews of the testing program, see 7:662 (2 reviews).

REFERENCES THROUGH 1971
1–2. See 6:1001.
CUMULATIVE NAME INDEX
Winkler, H. R.: 2

[1982]

★American History: Junior High—Objective. 1, 2 semesters in grades 7–9; 1963–70; revision of *Objective Tests in American History—Jr. H. S.* by John Barrett; 12 tests; no manual; Perfection Form Co. *
a) EXPLORATION AND COLONIZATION.
b) REVOLUTIONARY AMERICA.
c) FOUNDATION OF A STRONG GOVERNMENT.
d) THE DEVELOPMENT OF DEMOCRACY.
e) WESTWARD EXPANSION.
f) FIRST SEMESTER TEST.
g) DIVISION AND REUNION.
h) A MODERN AMERICA.
i) AMERICA BECOMES A WORLD POWER.
j) POST WORLD WAR II.
k) SECOND SEMESTER TEST.
l) FINAL TEST.

[1983]

*American History: Senior High—Objective. 1, 2 semesters high school; 1960–70; revision of *Objective Tests in American History* by Earl Bridgewater; 13 tests; no manual; Perfection Form Co. *
a) THE HERITAGE OF COLONIAL AMERICA.
b) BACKGROUND OF THE REVOLUTIONARY WAR, THE REVOLUTIONARY WAR AND ESTABLISHING A NEW GOVERNMENT (1763–1789).
c) THE UNITED STATES CONSTITUTION.
d) WASHINGTON'S ADMINISTRATION THROUGH THE WAR OF 1812.
e) EXPANSION WESTWARD AND THE JACKSONIAN ERA (1815 THRU 1841).
f) EXPANSION, WAR AND RECONSTRUCTION (1841–1868).
g) FIRST SEMESTER EXAMINATION.
h) THE EMERGENCE OF MODERN AMERICA.

i) THE UNITED STATES BECOMES A WORLD POWER (SPAN-ISH-AMERICAN WAR, WORLD WAR I, AND SETTLEMENT 1896-1921).
j) PROSPERITY AND DEPRESSION (1920 THRU 1940).
k) WORLD LEADERSHIP (1940-PRESENT).
l) SECOND SEMESTER EXAMINATION.
m) FINAL EXAMINATION.
For additional information concerning the earlier tests, see 6:1006.

[1984]
American History Test: National Achievement Tests. Grades 7-8; 1937-56; 5 scores: lessons of history, time concepts, historical associations, miscellaneous problems, total; 1945 and 1956 tests identical with tests copyrighted 1938 and 1939-49, respectively, except for minor changes; Robert K. Speer, Lester D. Crow, and Samuel Smith; Psychometric Affiliates. *
For additional information, see 5:811; for reviews by Jacob S. Orleans and Wallace Taylor, see 2:1630.

[1985]
★CLEP Subject Examination in Afro-American History. 1 semester or equivalent; 1973, c1972-73; for college accreditation of nontraditional study, advanced placement, or assessment of educational achievement; tests administered monthly at centers throughout the United States; program administered for the College Entrance Examination Board by Educational Testing Service. * For the testing program entry, see 1050.
For reviews of the testing program, see 7:664 (3 reviews).

[1986]
*CLEP Subject Examination in American History. 1 year or equivalent; 1970-73; for college accreditation of nontraditional study, advanced placement, or assessment of educational achievement; tests administered monthly at centers throughout the United States; program administered for the College Entrance Examination Board by Educational Testing Service. * For the testing program entry, see 1050.
For additional information, see 7:910. For reviews of the testing program, see 7:664 (3 reviews).

[1987]
*CLEP Subject Examination in Western Civilization. 1 year or equivalent; 1964-73; for college accreditation of nontraditional study, advanced placement, or assessment of educational achievement; tests administered monthly at centers throughout the United States; program administered for the College Entrance Examination Board by Educational Testing Service. * For the testing program entry, see 1050.
For additional information, see 7:911. For reviews of the testing program, see 7:664 (3 reviews).

[1988]
Cooperative Social Studies Tests: American History. Grades 7-8, 10-12; 1964-65; Cooperative Tests and Services. *
For additional information and a review by William J. Webster, see 7:912.

REFERENCES THROUGH 1971
1. DIELMAN, T. E.; BARTON, K.; AND CATTELL, R. B. "The Prediction of Junior High School Achievement From Objective Motivation Tests." *Personality* 2(4):279-87 w '71. * (PA 48:7881)

CUMULATIVE NAME INDEX
Barton, K.: 1   Dielman, T. E.: 1
Cattell, R. B.: 1   Webster, W. J.: *rev*, 7:912

[1989]
Cooperative Social Studies Tests: Modern European History. Grades 10-12; 1964-65; Cooperative Tests and Services. *
For additional information and a review by John Manning, see 7:913.

[1990]
Cooperative Social Studies Tests: World History. Grades 10-12; 1964-65; Cooperative Tests and Services. *
For additional information, see 7:914.

[1991]
Cooperative Topical Tests in American History. High school; 1963-65; CTTAH; 8 tests; Cooperative Tests and Services. *
a) TEST 1, EXPLORATION, COLONIZATION, AND INDEPENDENCE: 1450-1783.
b) TEST 2, FOUNDATIONS OF AMERICAN GOVERNMENT: 1781-1801.
c) TEST 3, GROWTH OF NATIONALISM AND DEMOCRACY: 1801-1840.
d) TEST 4, EXPANSION, CIVIL WAR, AND RECONSTRUCTION: 1840-1877.
e) TEST 5, DEVELOPMENT OF INDUSTRIAL AMERICA: 1865-1898.
f) TEST 6, IMPERIALISM, DOMESTIC REFORM, AND THE FIRST WORLD WAR: 1898-1920.
g) TEST 7, PROSPERITY, DEPRESSION, AND THE NEW DEAL: 1920-1940.
h) TEST 8, THE SECOND WORLD WAR AND AFTER.
For additional information and a review by Richard E. Gross, see 7:915.

[1992]
Crary American History Test, Revised Edition. Grades 10-13; 1950-65; Ryland W. Crary; Harcourt Brace Jovanovich, Inc. *
For additional information and a review by Richard E. Gross, see 7:916; for a review by Frederick H. Stutz of the original edition, see 5:816 (2 references); for a review by Edgar B. Wesley, see 4:688.

REFERENCES THROUGH 1971
1-2. See 5:816.
3. SCOTT, OWEN. "A Comparison of Summer School and Regular Session Achievement in Eleventh Grade American History." *J Ed Res* 59:235-7 Ja '66. * (PA 40:7014)

CUMULATIVE NAME INDEX
Cowne, L.: 2   Stutz, F. H.: *rev*, 5:816
Gross, R. E.: *rev*, 7:916   Townsend, A.: 1
Scott, O.: 3   Wesley, E. B.: *rev*, 4:688

[1993]
Emporia American History Test. 1, 2 semesters high school; 1962-64; first published 1962-63 in the Every Pupil Scholarship Test series; Shirley Meares and M. W. Sanders; Bureau of Educational Measurements. *
For additional information and a review by Howard R. Anderson, see 7:918.

[1994]
*The Graduate Record Examinations Advanced History Test. Graduate school candidates; 1939-73; 3 scores: European history, American history, total; Educational Testing Service. * For the testing program entry, see 1053.
For additional information concerning earlier forms, see 7:919 (1 reference); for a review by Robert H. Ferrell, see 5:818. For reviews of the testing program, see 7:667 (1 review) and 5:601 (1 review).

REFERENCES THROUGH 1971
1. See 7:919.
CUMULATIVE NAME INDEX
Ferrell, R. H.: *rev*, 5:818   Marco, G. L.: 1
Lannholm, G. V.: 1   Schrader, W. B.: 1

[1995]
Hollingsworth-Sanders Intermediate History Test. 1, 2 semesters in grades 5–6; 1962–64; first published 1962–63 in the Every Pupil Scholarship Test series; Leon Hollingsworth and M. W. Sanders; Bureau of Educational Measurements. *
For additional information, see 7:920.

[1996]
Meares-Sanders Junior High School History Test. 1, 2 semesters in grades 7–8; 1962–64; first published 1962–63 in the Every Pupil Scholarship Test series; Shirley Meares and M. W. Sanders; Bureau of Educational Measurements. *
For additional information, see 7:921.

[1997]
Modern World History: Achievement Examinations for Secondary Schools. High school; 1951–54; Form 4 ('54) of a series of tests, currently ('73) entitled *Social Studies Grade 11 (World History): Minnesota High School Achievement Examinations* (see 2000), issued annually for May testing; M. J. Haggerty; Bobbs-Merrill Co., Inc. *
For additional information concerning later and earlier forms, see 2000, 7:924, 6:1009, and 5:821–2.

[1998]
Sanders-Buller World History Test. 1, 2 semesters high school; 1962–64; first published 1962–63 in the Every Pupil Scholarship Test series; M. W. Sanders and Robert Buller; Bureau of Educational Measurements. *
For additional information and a review by John Manning, see 7:922.

[1999]
*Social Studies Grade 10 (American History): Minnesota High School Achievement Examinations. Grade 10; 1951–70; a new, revised, or previously inactive form issued each May; Achievement Examinations for Secondary Schools, High School Achievement Examinations, and Midwest High School Achievement Examinations have also been used as series titles; called *American History* through 1957; Form GJ Rev ('70, some tests have 1973 copyright) used in 1970 and 1973 testings; edited by V. L. Lohmann; American Guidance Service, Inc. *
For additional information concerning out of print and inactive forms, see 7:923, 6:1008, and 5:807; for a review by Howard R. Anderson of Form A (1955) and Form B (1957), see 5:810.

[2000]
*Social Studies Grade 11 (World History): Minnesota High School Achievement Examinations. Grade 11; 1951–70; a new, revised, or previously inactive form issued each May; Achievement Examinations for Secondary Schools, High School Achievement Examinations, and Midwest High School Achievement Examinations have also been used as series titles; various titles have been used such as *Modern World History* and *World History;* Form GJ Rev ('70, some tests have 1973 copyright) used in 1970 and 1973 testings; Form 4 ('54), entitled *Modern World History: Achievement Examinations for Secondary Schools* (see

1997), is available from another publisher; edited by V. L. Lohmann; American Guidance Service, Inc. *
For additional information concerning out of print and inactive forms, see 7:924, 6:1009, and 5:821–2.

[2001]
*The Undergraduate Program Field Tests: History Test. College; 1969–73; formerly called *The Undergraduate Record Examinations: History Test;* test available to colleges for local administration; Educational Testing Service. * For the testing program entry, see 1062.
For additional information, see 7:925. For reviews of the testing program, see 7:671 (2 reviews).

[2002]
*World History/Objective Tests. 1, 2 semesters high school; 1961–70; revision of *Objective Tests in World History* by Earl Bridgewater; 16 tests: 13 unit tests, 2 semester tests, and a final examination; no manual; Perfection Form Co. *
For additional information concerning the earlier tests, see 6:1007.

[2003]
World History Test: Acorn National Achievement Tests. High school and college; 1948–57; 6 scores: social studies terms, world geography, contributions of world peoples to civilization, political history, economic-social-cultural history, total; 1957 direction sheet identical with sheet copyrighted 1948; Vincent McGarrett and Edward H. Merrill; Psychometric Affiliates. *
For additional information and a review by John Manning, see 5:825.

[Out of Print Since TIP I]
American History: Every Pupil Scholarship Test, 6:996
American History: Every Pupil Test, 6:997
American History Test: Affiliation Testing Program for Catholic Secondary Schools, 6:998 (1 review)
American History Test: State High School Tests for Indiana, 4:682
American History: 20th Century Test, 4:683
Ancient History: Every Pupil Scholarship Test, 6:999
Cooperative American History Test, 4:684 (4 reviews, 5 references)
Cooperative Ancient History Test, 4:685 (2 reviews)
Cooperative Modern European History Test, 4:686 (3 reviews)
Cooperative World History Test, 5:814 (3 reviews)
Coordinated Scales of Attainment: History, 5:815
Cummings World History Test, 7:917 (4 reviews, 1 reference)
Emporia History Test, 1:1018
History: Every Pupil Scholarship Test, 6:1004
Kansas American History Test, 3:610 (2 reviews)
Kansas History: Every Pupil Scholarship Test, T:1774
Kansas Modern European History Test, 3:611 (2 reviews)
Kansas United States History Test, 6:1005 (2 reviews)
Ohio History: Every-Pupil Test, T:1779
Survey Test in Introductory American History, 6:1010 (1 review)
Taylor-Schrammel World History Test, 2:1641 (1 review)
Understanding of American History, 4:693 (1 review)
United States History: Manchester Semester-End Achievement Tests, T:1787, 36:724

World History: Every Pupil Scholarship Test, 6:1011
World History: Every Pupil Test, 6:1012
World History Test: Affiliation Testing Program for Catholic Secondary Schools, 6:1013 (1 review)
World History Test: Manchester Semester-End Achievement Tests, T:1791
World History Test: State High School Tests for Indiana, 4:696
World History: 20th Century Test, 4:697

POLITICAL SCIENCE

[2004]

*CLEP Subject Examination in American Government.** 1 semester or equivalent; 1965–73; for college accreditation of nontraditional study, advanced placement, or assessment of educational achievement; tests administered monthly at centers throughout the United States; program administered for the College Entrance Examination Board by Educational Testing Service. * For the testing program entry, see 1050.

For additional information concerning an earlier form, see 7:926. For reviews of the testing program, see 7:664 (3 reviews).

[2005]

Cooperative Social Studies Tests: American Government. Grades 10–12; 1964–65; Cooperative Tests and Services. *

For additional information and a review by Howard D. Mehlinger, see 7:927.

[2006]

Cooperative Social Studies Tests: Civics. Grades 8–9; 1964–65; Cooperative Tests and Services. *

For additional information and a review by Vincent N. Campbell, see 7:928.

[2007]

Cooperative Social Studies Tests: Problems of Democracy. Grades 10–12; 1964–65; Cooperative Tests and Services. *

For additional information and a review by Hulda Grobman, see 7:929 (1 reference).

REFERENCES THROUGH 1971
1. See 7:929.

CUMULATIVE NAME INDEX
Farnen, R. F.: 1   Wills, G. R.: 1
Grobman, H.: *rev,* 7:929

[2008]

★[**Government/Objective Tests.**] 1 semester in grades 11–12; 1970; 6 tests; no manual; Perfection Form Co. *
a) FUNDAMENTALS OF GOVERNMENT.
b) THE EXECUTIVE BRANCH (POLITICAL PARTIES AND ELECTION).
c) THE LEGISLATIVE BRANCH.
d) THE AMERICAN JUDICIARY SYSTEM AND CIVIL LIBERTIES.
e) AMERICAN GOVERNMENT—STATE AND LOCAL GOVERNMENT.
f) FINAL TEST.

[2009]

*The Graduate Record Examinations Advanced Political Science Test.** Graduate school candidates; 1939–73; formerly called *The Graduate Record Exam-*

inations Advanced Tests: Government; Educational Testing Service. * For the testing program entry, see 1053.

For additional information concerning earlier forms, see 7:930; for a review by Christine McGuire, see 5:835. For reviews of the testing program, see 7:667 (1 review) and 5:601 (1 review).

[2010]

★**National Teacher Examinations: Texas Government.** College seniors and teachers; 1972–73; Educational Testing Service. * For the testing program entry, see 869.

For reviews of the testing program, see 7:582 (2 reviews), 6:700 (1 review), 5:538 (3 reviews), and 4:802 (1 review).

[2011]

Patterson Test or Study Exercises on the Constitution of the United States. Grades 9–16 and adults; 1931–53; 1953 test identical with test copyrighted 1937 except for minor changes; Raymond G. Patterson; Bobbs-Merrill Co., Inc. *

For additional information, see 5:838.

[2012]

Principles of Democracy Test. Grades 9–12; 1961, c1960–61; Nathaniel L. Gage, Neil F. Garvey, Charles B. Hagan, and Roland Payette; Science Research Associates, Inc. *

For additional information and reviews by William C. Bingham and John H. Haefner, see 6:1020.

[2013]

Sare-Sanders American Government Test. High school and college; 1962–64; first published 1962–63 in the Every Pupil Scholarship Test series; Harold V. Sare and M. W. Sanders; Bureau of Educational Measurements. *

For additional information and a review by Howard D. Mehlinger, see 7:931.

[2014]

Sare-Sanders Constitution Test. High school and college; 1962–64; first published 1962–63 in the Every Pupil Scholarship Test series; Harold V. Sare and M. W. Sanders; Bureau of Educational Measurements. *

For additional information, see 7:932.

[2015]

*Social Studies Grade 12 (American Problems): Minnesota High School Achievement Examinations.** Grade 12; 1951–70; a new, revised, or previously inactive form issued each May; Achievement Examinations for Secondary Schools, High School Achievement Examinations, and Midwest High School Achievement Examinations have also been used as series titles; *Introduction to Social Science, Introduction to Social Studies,* and *Social Studies* were used as titles through 1962; within past 9 years an alternate subtitle, *Introduction to Social Science,* has been used every third year; Form GJ Rev ('70, some tests have 1973 copyright) used in 1970 and 1973 testings with the subtitle *Introduction to Social Science;* edited by V. L. Lohmann; American Guidance Service, Inc. *

For additional information concerning out of print and inactive forms, see 7:893, 6:976, 5:789, and 5:795.

[2016]

*The Undergraduate Program Field Tests: Political Science Test.** College; 1969–73; formerly called *The Undergraduate Record Examinations: Political Science Test;* test available to colleges for local administration; Educational Testing Service. * For the testing program entry, see 1062.

For additional information concerning an earlier form, see 7:933. For reviews of the testing program, see 7:671 (2 reviews).

[Out of Print Since TIP I]

American Civics and Government Tests for High Schools and Colleges, 6:1013a (1 review)
American Government and Citizenship: Every Pupil Test, 6:1014 (1 review)
American Government: Every Pupil Scholarship Test, 6:1015
Bear Test on United States Constitution, T:1798
Civic Vocabulary Test, 5:830 (1 review, 1 reference)
Civics: 20th Century Test, 4:701
Constitution: Every Pupil Scholarship Test, 6:1016
Cooperative American Government Test, 4:702 (1 review)
Dimond-Pflieger Problems of Democracy Test, 5:833 (2 reviews, 1 reference)
Duke University Political Science Information Test (American Government), 6:1017
Junior High School Civics Test: State High School Tests for Indiana, 4:704
Kansas Constitution Test, 5:836 (1 review)
Mordy-Schrammel American Government Test, T:1807
Patterson Test or Study Exercises on the Declaration of Independence, 5:839
Patterson's Tests on the Federal Constitution, 4:705
Peltier-Durost Civics and Citizenship Test, 6:1019 (2 reviews)
Senior High School Civics Tests: State High School Tests for Indiana, 4:706–7
United States Government Test: Manchester Semester-End Achievement Tests, T:1815, 36:848

SOCIOLOGY

[2017]

*CLEP Subject Examination in Introductory Sociology.** 1 year or equivalent; 1965–73; for college accreditation of nontraditional study, advanced placement, or assessment of educational achievement; tests administered monthly at centers throughout the United States; program administered for the College Entrance Examination Board by Educational Testing Service. * For the testing program entry, see 1050.

For additional information, see 7:934. For reviews of the testing program, see 7:664 (3 reviews).

[2018]

*The Graduate Record Examinations Advanced Sociology Test.** Graduate school candidates; 1939–73; Educational Testing Service. * For the testing program entry, see 1053.

For additional information concerning earlier forms, see 7:935; for a review by J. Richard Wilmeth, see 6:1021. For reviews of the testing program, see 7:667 (1 review) and 5:601 (1 review).

[2019]

Sare-Sanders Sociology Test. High school and college; 1958; Harold Sare and Merritt W. Sanders; Bureau of Educational Measurements. *

For additional information and a review by J. Richard Wilmeth, see 6:1022.

[2020]

*The Undergraduate Program Field Tests: Sociology Test.** College; 1969–73; formerly called *The Undergraduate Record Examinations: Sociology Test;* test available to colleges for local administration; Educational Testing Service. * For the testing program entry, see 1062.

For additional information, see 7:936. For reviews of the testing program, see 7:671 (2 reviews).

[Out of Print Since TIP I]

Sociology: Every Pupil Scholarship Test, 5:844

REPRINTED FROM *The First Mental Measurements Yearbook*

SOCIAL STUDIES — FIRST MMY

REVIEWS BY *Howard R. Anderson, Alvin C. Eurich, Harold Gulliksen, A. C. Krey, Paul L. Limbert, S. P. McCutchen, Wilbur F. Murra, Douglas E. Scates, Hilda Taba, R. M. Tryon, Edgar B. Wesley, and J. Wayne Wrightstone.*

CONTEMPORARY AFFAIRS

[948]
Cooperative Contemporary Affairs Test for College Students: Form 1937. c1937; a new form is scheduled for publication each May 1; 100(110) minutes; 7¢ per test, 10 to 99 copies; 6½¢ per test, 100 or more; 25¢ per specimen set (Form 1937); 10¢ per sample test (Form 1937); A. C. Eurich, E. C. Wilson, and G. A. Hill, with the editorial collaboration of R. D. Casey, A. N. Christensen, R. Faulkner, A. Pepinsky, H. S. Quigley, E. W. Weaver, and E. B. Wesley; Cooperative Test Service.

Paul M. Limbert, Columbia University. This test is designed to measure the extent to which an institution attains one of the objectives of the newer general education, "a functioning interest in the activities and progress of present society." Included in this realm of "contemporary affairs" are not only current events on the economic and political front, nationally and internationally, but developments in literature and drama, music and radio, the movies, and art.

The content of the test was selected on the basis of a survey of articles in twenty-five current magazines and journals that have been found to have the widest appeal on the junior college level. Experts from a number of fields collaborated on the preparation of the items. In its general structure this *Contemporary Affairs Test* maintains the high level of technical craftsmanship for which the Cooperative tests are well known.

In order to make a creditable score on this test a student would have to read the newspapers carefully, to keep abreast of current literary productions, to listen regularly to musical broadcasts, and either to attend the theater frequently or to keep reading reviews of plays and movies. That knowledge of this kind should be part of the repertoire of alert college students is generally accepted in theory but seldom adequately provided for in practice.

Although in most colleges it would be hard to relate the *Contemporary Affairs Test* to any specific course, it would doubtless have definite values (1) in indicating the extent to which students are keeping abreast of current social and cultural developments, both through courses and through incidental learnings, (2) in diagnosing the strong interests and the blind spots of individual students. The range of interests and accuracy of understanding, as revealed by an objective test of this kind, provide probably one of the most reliable indications of the degree to which education is functioning in the daily intellectual life of the student.

At the same time this *Contemporary Affairs Test* has obvious limitations. The basis of selection of items is in many cases frequency of occurrence or popular interest rather than quality. It may reveal what a student knows about current affairs, but gives no adequate clue as to what is worth knowing. Whether H. E. Ekins completed his round-the-world trip in ten, fifteen or eighteen days seems to be of little consequence. One can be pardoned for not knowing—or caring—which soprano sings for the national Ry-Krisp broadcasts or what kind of sculptural ornament adorns Boulder Dam. Although the number of such insignificant items is very small, the fact remains that one should not expect too much of a test of this kind in revealing qualitative standards or critical thinking on the part of the students.

This criticism applies much less to Part I, which deals with current political events. This section assembles 150 items which will give a good clue not only to a student's factual knowledge but to his understanding of underlying factors. One wonders why the section on science is so brief, since scientific developments in relation to social movements are increasingly to the fore.

A new form of the *Contemporary Affairs Test* is to be printed each May 1. College teachers who are interested in testing their students' alertness in relation to their own social and cultural environment may be thankful that such a convenient and comprehensive instrument is readily available.

[950]

Cooperative Current Public Affairs Test for High School Classes: Form 1937. c1937; a new form is scheduled for publication each May 1; 40(45) minutes; printed; 6¢ per test, 10 to 99 copies; 5½¢ per test, 100 or more; 25¢ per specimen set (Form 1937); 10¢ per sample test (Form 1937); A. C. Eurich, E. C. Wilson, and G. A. Hill, with the editorial collaboration of R. D. Casey, A. N. Christensen, H. S. Quigley, E. W. Weaver, and E. B. Wesley; Cooperative Test Service.

Howard R. Anderson, Cornell University. [*Review of Form 1937.*] This examination consists of 100 five-response multiple-choice test items divided almost equally between "national events" and "world events." According to the authors their purpose has been to construct a test measuring the pupil's "interest in the activities and progress of society." The allocation of items was determined after "a survey of thousands of articles in current magazines and journals evaluated in terms of long-time and short-time appeal."

After reading this examination one year following its publication this reviewer is tempted to say that a 1937 current affairs test is about as useful in 1938 as a 1937 calendar. Perhaps this is inevitable and that is why a new form is brought out each spring. Yet it would seem of utmost importance in a current affairs test to include only items bearing on problems of outstanding significance. Fully 10–15 per cent of the items in this particular test must have appeared of ephemeral importance even in the spring of 1937. The following questions are typical of this group: (1) What explosion occurred on March 18? (2) To where did Amelia Earhart launch an unsuccessful flight in March? (10) What is the Townsend Plan? (16) For what did President Roosevelt appeal in his opening message to the 75th Congress? (22) Who was the winner of the Harmon aviation trophy in 1936? (30) The issuance of what 3-cent stamp aroused a storm of protest in the South? (74) How many days did H. R. Ekins require for his round-the-world air trip?

Not only should a current affairs examination include test items bearing on problems of lasting significance but it is equally necessary to

test the pupils' reasoned understanding of the really important aspects of these problems, including background factors, causes, results, etc. The present examination includes a large percentage of "who, what, when, where" type of items. About one-fifth of the total examination concerns the identification of personages ranging from Chiang Kai-shek and Cordell Hull to Sonja Henie, Queen Marie and Beryl Markham.

The form of the test items would be improved if phrased as questions rather than statements. The latter phrasing is often confusing especially when the introductory statement is divided. For example, in item No. 95: "St. Patrick's day riots in a Paris suburb resulted in several deaths and over 300 wounded when a crowd attempted to break up a meeting of the French Social Party (formerly Croix de Feu) a 95(1) communist, 95(2) socialist, 95(3) fascist, 95(4) anarchist, 95(5) monarchist, organization."

Several of the items have the additional weakness, present also in the foregoing item, of including in the introductory statement a series of qualifying remarks which contribute little to an understanding of the element tested. Thus the foregoing item could be greatly shortened and the meaning clarified if the introductory statement were phrased as follows: "What is the nature of the French Social Party (formerly Croix de Feu)?" and followed with the same responses.

J. Wayne Wrightstone, Ohio State University. [*Review of Form 1937.*] This test is designed especially for high school classes and follows generally the same pattern of construction as the *Cooperative Contemporary Affairs Tests,* constructed in the previous years. Items of the test are based, according to the authors, on a survey of thousands of articles in current magazines and journals and evaluated in terms of long-time and short-time appeal of the events. Section A contains 53 items dealing with national events and personages, such as "The new labor weapon used effectively in automobile and other strikes in 1937 was the . . . ," and Section B contains 47 items dealing with world events, such as "The 1936 Nobel peace prize award was bitterly criticized by the German government press because . . ."

Each item is followed by five possible answers of which one is best.

Obviously from the content and structure this test purports to measure recognition and recall of salient facts or concepts selected from a sample of the current national and world events. Honest differences of opinions about the selection of test items may occur. No definitive criteria for selecting items are stated. Although a balance in sampling of items is indicated generally in a handbook, no detailed distribution for such topics as labor, politics, transportation, and so on is supplied. This test provides a valid index of a pupil's acquaintance with public affairs, but it obviously is not intended to measure such teaching objectives as attitudes, interests, and critical thinking about current public affairs.

The test is designed particularly for high school pupils, and the vocabulary and concepts generally are adapted to such pupils. In contrast with the previous contemporary affairs tests in the Cooperative Test Series, which were rather difficult both in vocabulary and concepts, this new test is much better adapted for secondary school classes. The test requires about 40 minutes for its administration.

Judging from past reliabilities of the contemporary affairs test, the reliability of the new edition of the current public affairs test may reasonably be estimated as about .90 for the entire test. Separate scores for sections A and B would be correspondingly lower. Scores of this test or its part scores, nevertheless, might well be used for individual diagnosis of pupil knowledge about current events. In objectivity—that is, consensus among authorities about the best answers—the test meets high standards. The statements of the test items, including answers, are not ambiguous.

Judged upon the criterion of practicability, the test is easy to understand, to administer, to score and to interpret. It certainly should meet a need not now supplied and one urgently felt in most high schools for an index of the pupil's acquaintance with current public affairs happening in the world about him. The so-called norms or frequency distributions of scores on this test are available for a highly selected sampling rather than a random sampling of public school pupils. Although national "norms" have some practical values as points of reference and comparison in interpreting the achievement of groups and individual pupils, local school system "norms" may be used for similar purposes of interpreting achievement. Comparable scores for the various forms of the test are available.

Admitting the useful purpose for which the test is now valid, it may be hoped that its scope will be extended to include tests for such objectives as attitudes, interests, and critical thinking on current public affairs. This suggestion should not be construed in such a way as to detract from the excellent purpose which the test now serves.

[951]

Iowa Every-Pupil Test in Understanding of Contemporary Affairs: Ninth Annual Iowa Every-Pupil High School Testing Program. p1937; a new form is scheduled for publication each May; 4¢ per test; 5¢ per key; 10¢ per summary report of norms; 60(65) minutes; H. R. Anderson and E. F. Lindquist with the collaboration of G. G. Andrews, J. E. Briggs, G. R. Davies, K. E. Leib, E. T. Peterson, H. J. Thornton, and C. W. Hart; edited by [E. F. Lindquist]; distributed by the Bureau of Educational Research and Service.

Alvin C. Eurich, Stanford University. The purpose of this test, according to the authors, is "to find out how widely and thoughtfully" pupils have been reading about current events in newspapers and magazines or have learned about them through the radio or other sources. The test itself consists of 96 single-choice statements with four possible answers for each. Sixty minutes are allowed to complete the test. The form is excellent with the squares preceding the possible answers staggered so that there is little chance of placing the check on the line above or below the answer which the student intends to mark.

The chief defect of the test is that it is *not* a measure of the objective implied by the title: *UNDERSTANDING of Contemporary Affairs.* To the reviewer, at least, "understanding" involves, among other things, interpretation of events, seeing cause and effect relationships, discovering motives which lead to group or individual action, noting relationships between events. Practically none of the items involves these types of responses. On the contrary, 45 of the 96 items call for the identification of countries, states, personalities, or memory of statistics such as: About what per cent of the popular vote favored the reelection of President Roosevelt? (1) 53 per cent, (2) 65 per cent, (3) 78 per cent, (4) 90 per cent. Which country is most friendly toward the Jews? (1) Germany, (2) Rumania, (3) Poland, (4) Russia. Clearly items of this type call for a *"knowledge of"* not an "understanding of" contemporary affairs. To be sure, an occasional item goes beyond the memory for a current event, but such items are few. As a whole, the test might more accurately be labeled a test of the knowledge of facts and events in the contemporary scene. As such, it is a good test. Beyond the measurement of achievement of this objective, however, there is an urgent need for new tests or observational methods that actually provide an index of pupils' "understanding" or interpretation of the events that are taking place in the world about them. Unfortunately, the test under consideration makes no contribution in this direction.

A basis for interpreting the scores in the test in "Understanding of Contemporary Affairs" is provided along with that for other tests in a *Summary Report of Results for the 1937 Iowa Every-Pupil High School Testing Program.* Part 1 on the use and interpretation of test results can be read with profit not only by the users of the Iowa tests but by anyone interested in giving tests and in interpreting results more accurately. Part 2 presents the 1937 norms of achievement. For the *Contemporary Affairs Test,* norms are based upon approximately 4000 pupils in each of the four high school grades: 9, 10, 11, and 12. Tables giving percentile norms make it fairly easy to interpret the relative position in the distribution of scores for each pupil and for each school. A study of these tables reveals a tendency that is apparent in the distribution of scores for most contemporary affairs tests. The medians are low, ranging from about 11 out of a possible score of 96 for Grade 9 to 24 for Grade 12. It appears to be more difficult to adapt current affairs tests to the grade groups for which they are intended than to adapt tests in other fields to specific levels. Two factors probably account for the difference: (1) the field of contemporary affairs is so broad that if a test is to cover it adequately, the sample is certain to include many items which any given pupil does not know and (2) the school curriculum does not include courses which cover contemporary affairs systematically. In general, the data provided by the summary give a basis for interpreting test scores that compares favorably with that available for the best tests and observational techniques.

The mechanical aspects of the test are carefully worked out. The keys for scoring are arranged for maximum accuracy and efficiency.

The test merits consideration from all who have an interest in discovering the relative amounts of knowledge of current events possessed by high school students. The test will not serve, however, as a diagnostic instrument indicating the areas in which the pupil is strong or weak. Nor will it show the degree to which pupils "understand" the events of which they are aware, the title of the test notwithstanding.

ECONOMICS

[952]

Economics Test: State High School Tests for Indiana, 1936–1937 Edition. First, second semesters; p1936–37; 2 levels; a new first-semester form is scheduled for publication each December; a new second-semester form is scheduled for publication each March; mimeographed; 2¢ per test; 15¢ per sample test; 40 (45) minutes; W. F. Mitchell; edited by H. H. Remmers; Division of Educational Reference.

GEOGRAPHY

[989]

Emporia Geography Test. Grades 4–7; p1937; 2 forms; 50¢ per 25 tests, postpaid, 15¢ per specimen set; 30(35) minutes; H. E. Schrammel, E. J. Calkins, H. Bechtoldt, F. Frease, and L. Wharton; Bureau of Educational Measurements.

[990]

Geography Ability Test. Ages 9–11, 12–14; 1 form; 2 levels (ages 9–11: Test No. 1; ages 12–14: Test No. 2); 2s.6d. per 20 tests; 3d. per specimen set; quantity discounts; nontimed (30–35) minutes; Robert Gibson and Sons (Glasgow), Ltd.

[991]

Geography: Every Pupil Test, December 1937 and April 1938. Grades 4–7; p1937–38; a new form is scheduled for publication each December and April; 2¢ per test; 1¢ per key; specimen set free; 40(45) minutes; L. R. Keller; directed by C. H. Roberts; Ohio Scholarship Tests.

[992]

Geography Test: National Achievement Tests. Grades 6–8; c1937; 1 form; $1.50 per 25 tests; 100 or more, 4½¢ per test; 5¢ per specimen set; nontimed (45–60) minutes; R. K. Speer, L. D. Crow, and S. Smith; Acorn Publishing Co.

HISTORY

[1011]

American History: Every Pupil Test, December 1937 and April 1938. Grades 7, 8, 11–12; p1937–38; 2

Iowa Every-Pupil Test in Understanding of Contemporary Affairs

levels; new forms for grade 7 and grades 11–12 are scheduled for publication each December and April; a new form for grade 8 each December; 2¢ per test; 1¢ per key; specimen set free; 40(45) minutes; E. Cottle, G. S. Hug, V. J. Hug, and C. H. Roberts; directed by C. H. Roberts; Ohio Scholarship Tests.

[1012]

American History Test: National Achievement Tests. Grades 7–8; c1937; 1 form; $1.50 per 25 tests; 100 or more, 4½¢ per test; 5¢ per specimen set; non-timed (45–60) minutes; R. K. Speer, L. D. Crow, and S. Smith; Acorn Publishing Co.

[1013]

American History Test: State High School Tests for Indiana, 1936–1937 Edition. First, second semesters; p1936–37; 2 levels; a new first-semester form is scheduled for publication each December; a new second-semester form is scheduled for publication each March; mimeographed; 2¢ per test; 15¢ per sample test; 40 (45) minutes; V. F. Dawald assisted by R. Gilbert and L. Long; edited by H. H. Remmers; Division of Educational Reference.

[1014]

Cooperative American History Test. 1 year: high school; c1937; 40- and 90-minute editions; lithotyped; 25¢ per specimen set (Form 1934 or N); 10¢ per sample test (Form 1937 or N); H. R. Anderson and E. F. Lindquist; Cooperative Test Service.
a) FORM 1937. 4 earlier forms; no further forms scheduled; 90(95) minutes; 6¢ per test, 10 to 99 copies; 5½¢ per test, 100 or more.
b) REVISED SERIES FORM N. A new form is scheduled for publication each May 1; 40(45) minutes; 5¢ per test, 10 to 99 copies; 4½¢ per test, 100 or more; test booklets may be used repeatedly if separate answer sheets are used; 1½¢ per answer sheet, adapted to hand or machine scoring.

Edgar B. Wesley, University of Minnesota. [*Review of Form 1937.*] The work of the Cooperative Test Service has become so extensive and varied as to require at least a three-credit course to attain an understanding of its manifold activities. The details of its program and its procedures are beyond the scope of this review. All that the reviewer undertakes to do is to give some unstatistical comments on the test by Anderson and Lindquist.

This test consists of 185 items divided into three parts, which deal with persons and terms, with dates and events, and with historical judgment. Part I uses the multiple-choice form to test for simple recognition. In so doing, the authors greatly simplify the task of the testee. For example, the person who is asked to recall the name of the Mexican War general who became president (item 22) may be unable to answer. If, however, he is confronted with the names, Van Buren, Polk, Taylor, Scott, and Frémont, he can on a very slender margin of

information check the name of Taylor. The recognition level is far below the recall level and the multiple-choice technique is very space-consuming. In other words, a good score on Part I is not, in the opinion of this reviewer, very good evidence of historical or geographical information.

Part II is devoted to chronology. It presents that confusing device of intervals. It takes a very keen student to understand this within any reasonable time. If the tester could explain and exemplify the procedure it might become less puzzlesome. The interval device, however, is a valid and sound way of measuring one's sense of chronology. The factor of chronology can easily be overemphasized. Pupils and students, and even many grown-ups, have a very fragmentary sense of chronology, sequence, and time intervals, and yet they seem to enjoy their meals and to behave quite normally. The authors have very properly kept this section very short (24 items).

Part III, called historical judgment, involves mostly historical information. What judgment is required to decide, for example (item 152), what plank was inserted repeatedly in the Whig platform. One knows it or he does not. In other words, the difference between Parts I and III is very inconsequential. In Part I the options are names; in Part III they are phrases or clauses, a little more confusing, to be sure, but nevertheless problems of simple recognition.

This is an excellent test. It is long enough to be reliable and its contents indicate its validity. The reputation which its authors have so meritedly won is another evidence of its high quality. The criticisms which appear above could be applied to most objective tests and so apply to this one merely because it belongs to the genre.

[1015]

Cooperative Ancient History Test, Form 1937. 1 year, high school; c1937; 4 earlier forms; no further forms scheduled (this series is being supplemented with a series of 40-minute forms, adapted to hand or machine scoring); 90(95) minutes; lithotyped; 6¢ per test, 10 to 99 copies; 5½¢ per test, 100 or more (future forms will sell at 1¢ less per test); 25¢ per specimen set (Form 1934); 10¢ per sample test (Form 1934); H. R. Anderson and E. F. Lindquist; Cooperative Test Service.

Wilbur F. Murra, Harvard University. This test partakes of all the well-known good features of the Cooperative tests. Thus, it must be rated "excellent" among standardized tests generally. It does, however, deal somewhat less with "functional materials" than do other social studies tests in the Cooperative series and it devotes too much attention to proper names. Its 185 items are distributed as follows: on historical personages, 39; on historical terms, 60; on geographical terms, 16; on dates and events, 24; on historical judgment, 47. The usual scope of ancient history is fully represented, with items touching events from the Old Stone Age to Charlemagne.

[1016]

Cooperative Modern European History Test. 1 year, high school; c1937; 40- and 90-minute editions; lithotyped; 25¢ per specimen set (Form 1934 or N); 10¢ per sample test (Form 1937 or N); H. R. Anderson and E. F. Lindquist; Cooperative Test Service.
a) FORM 1937. 4 earlier forms; no further forms scheduled; 90(95) minutes; 6¢ per test, 10 to 99 copies; 5½¢ per test, 100 or more.
b) REVISED SERIES FORM N. A new form is scheduled for publication each May 1; 40(45) minutes; 5¢ per test, 10 to 99 copies; 4½¢ per test, 100 or more; test booklets may be used repeatedly if separate answer sheets are used; 1½¢ per answer sheet, adapted to hand or machine scoring.

A. C. Krey, University of Minnesota. [*Review of Form 1937.*] This is another of the tests primarily for high school subjects so carefully worked out by Anderson and Lindquist at the University of Iowa. The multiple-choice technique which is used throughout invites the student to make use of the knowledge acquired in the course and minimizes the rewards of purely blind guessing. Very few of the eighty-nine questions, almost none, deal with matters which would not be emphasized in any course in modern history covering the period from the Wars of Religion to the present. It is, therefore, serviceable to schools in all parts of the country.

It is excellent as far as it goes. The criticism which I have to offer applies to all tests of this kind rather more than to this particular test, to the use which may be made of it, rather than to the makers of the test. In its aggregate of leading persons and events, its chronological and geographical relationships, it touches the core of the modern history course. Too many of the questions involve facts heavily underlined by capital letters, italics, or quotation marks and call only for single relationships of the most obvious type. Such material lends itself too readily to last day cramming. Perhaps it is

the fault of the prevailing courses of study and textbooks in modern history that the items in this test are so largely confined to the political. There is very little of the economic and less than that of the social and cultural. In these respects this test is not as good as the one which these same authors have prepared for American history.

However essential a core may be for structure, the most nourishing portion of the fruit usually is found beyond the core. The possession of these core facts does not necessarily indicate that the student has likewise gained all of the nourishment. It does not indicate how much of the history the student knows nor how well he knows it. It does not show how firmly he has mastered the material, what generalizations he has acquired for application to current events or later study, nor how far he has advanced in appreciation of the multiple connections even of the most important events. Success on this test does not prove either that the student is or will be a good student of history. It proves only that he is in possession of some of the materials of history, some of the core facts of modern history. Such material, however, is essential and this test is an excellent means of determining the student's knowledge of it. The larger question of deciding the student's degree of historical knowledge and aptitude remains to be determined through the many additional indices which the teacher's longer association with the student affords. The test is not a comprehensive test and should not be so used. Within its own limits it is excellent. My hope is that the authors will bring its further editions up to the standard they have already reached in American history.

S. P. McCutchen, University of Chicago. [*Review of Form 1937.*] No doubt it is wicked and immoral to criticize an achievement test because it is an achievement test and heir to the evils inherent in that sort of instrument. Some or perhaps most of the criticisms made of this test are protests against the type. By the very nature of the items, it must be given at the end of the course rather than during the year and has diagnostic value for guidance, perhaps, but not for teaching.

Considered independently, apart from other instruments edited by the Cooperative Test Service, this test puts its entire emphasis upon mastery of content. There is no effort made here to ascertain the student's acquisitions of skills in research or abilities in thinking, or to find out whether he will be able to use this information to find solutions for his own problems or the social direction to which he is turning. His attitudes, beliefs and points of view, as they are influenced by this content, are not revealed. All that can be told is the extent of his "reasoned understanding" of the particular content chosen for sampling, which is the objective in terms of which the test measures achievement. And one of the potencies of a testing program is its influence in determining the real, operating objectives of the course. Hence for users of this test, a "reasoned understanding" of the historical past becomes an end-product objective of the social studies, in terms of which achievement is measured. There are those who would prefer to have it only the means to the attainment of other more fundamental purposes. Of course teachers interested in other objectives either would not use this test or could use it in connection with others, such as the *Cooperative Test of Social Studies Abilities.* One wonders, however, whether the two types of tests could not be combined.

The test contains three parts. Part I requires the identification, by selecting from five listed alternatives, of historical personages, historical terms, and geographical terms. Part II deals with dates and events, requiring not a knowledge of exact dates but a knowledge of when events occurred in relation to other events. It seems to this reviewer that more memory than reasoned understanding is required for these first two parts. Many of the items lead one who has lost his pristine enthusiasm for the minutiae and trivia of history to ask, "What of it?" Will it make any real difference in the lives of the citizens of tomorrow whether it was Cavour's or Mazzini's plans for the unification of his country which failed in 1848? or to know that Sully was the chief minister of the first Bourbon king?

Part III, testing historical judgment, goes considerably beyond mere possession of knowledge. Its fundamental idea is well conceived and the items are, in the main, admirably constructed. Perhaps there is some danger, in items dealing with causes or with effects, that students who are required to select one cause for a problem or one effect of a movement

might fall into habits of oversimplifying social issues, but the teaching task thus raised is not a difficult one.

Most teachers of history agree on the value of history in contributing to an understanding of the present. If this is true, the whole test misses a wonderful opportunity when it fails to test the student's ability to see this relationship. There is little or none of the then-now connection brought out.

[1017]

Cooperative World History Test. 1 year of world history: high school; or 2 years of history: grades 10–13; c1937; 3 earlier forms; no further forms scheduled; 90(95) minutes; lithotyped; 6¢ per test, 10 to 99 copies; 5½¢ per test, 100 or more; 25¢ per specimen set (Form 1934); 10¢ per sample test (Form 1934); H. R. Anderson and E. F. Lindquist; Cooperative Test Service.

R. M. Tryon, University of Chicago. This test in world history is one of a large number of the cooperative achievement tests now being sponsored by the American Council on Education. It should be noted at the outset that the achievements the test is expected to measure are limited to the abilities to connect the names of historical personages with one or more of their accomplishments, the ability to identify historical and geographical terms with brief statements of their essential aspects, the ability to arrange events in their correct time relation, and the ability to select for each of a series of incomplete statements the one of four words or phrases that correctly completes it. The selecting involved in this last ability is designated in the test "historical judgment." Such abilities as those of obtaining facts, organizing facts, interpreting facts, and applying generalizations are outside the domain of this test. Neither does it attempt to invade the fields of beliefs and attitudes. On the whole it is traditional in what it aims to test and consequently runs the risk of condemnation by some as being a good instrument for testing the more or less insignificant achievements in world history.

With respect to the administration of the test, ninety minutes are allowed for its completion. Forty of these minutes are assigned to historical personages and historical and geographical terms, fifteen to dates and events, and thirty-five to so-called historical judgments. Such an allotment of time probably has no relation to the relative importance of the various aspects of history suggested by the categories used in naming the various divisions of the test. Further-more, the persons, terms, and dates-events that compose most of the content of the test may be important when viewed from one angle and insignificant when viewed from another angle. It is on such matters as these that the test will probably be rejected by those who are interested in humanizing the traditional course in world history. While an attempt is made to have the content of the test broad in scope; nevertheless, on a careful scrutiny of its contents one finds that the political aspects of the past are much emphasized. Even in the parts of the test in which an effort is made to broaden the content, there is an abundance of terms, names, and dates-events that seem far removed from the needs and interests of present-day society and the youth for whom the test is intended.

In considering the test from the standpoint of certain recognized criteria it seems fair to remark that on validity, reliability, and diag-nostic value it probably ranks low. On ease of administration, objectivity in scoring, cost, and mechanical features it seems to rank high. The aspects on which it ranks high seem less im-portant than those on which it ranks low.

Should the educational world take this and other tests in its class seriously, future cur-riculum advancement would be difficult to achieve. The test would tend to dictate the content of the course in world history. For this reason the content of this course would become static. It could not be forward moving because of the fixed nature of the content of the test. There are those who hope that the test will never pass into general use.

[1018]

Emporia History Test. Grades 5–6, 7–8; p1937; 2 forms; 2 levels; 50¢ per 25 tests, postpaid; 15¢ per specimen set; grades 5–6: 30(35) minutes; grades 7–8: 40(45) minutes; H. E. Schrammel, E. J. Calkins, H. Bechtoldt, F. Frease, and L. Wharton; Bureau of Educational Measurements.

[1019]

Iowa Every-Pupil Test in American Govern-ment: Ninth Annual Iowa Every-Pupil High School Testing Program. p1937; a new form is scheduled for publication each May; 4¢ per test; 5¢ per key; 10¢ per summary report of norms; 60(65) minutes; J. H. Haefner and H. R. Anderson; edited by J. E. Briggs and [E. F. Lindquist]; distributed by the Bureau of Educational Research and Service.

[1020]

Iowa Every-Pupil Test in United States His-tory: Ninth Annual Iowa Every-Pupil High School Testing Program. p1937; a new form is scheduled for

publication each May; 4¢ per test; 5¢ per key; 10¢ per summary report of norms; 60(65) minutes; H. Berg and H. R. Anderson; edited by G. G. Andrews and [E. F. Lindquist]; distributed by the Bureau of Edu-cational Research and Service.

[1021]

Iowa Every-Pupil Test in World History: Ninth Annual Iowa Every-Pupil High School Testing Pro-gram. p1937; a new form is scheduled for publication each May; 4¢ per test; 5¢ per key; 10¢ per summary report of norms; 60(65) minutes; W. Taylor and H. R. Anderson; edited by G. G. Andrews and [E. F. Lindquist]; distributed by the Bureau of Educational Research and Service.

[1022]

Medieval History: Every Pupil Test, April 1938. Grade 9; p1938; a new form is scheduled for publica-tion each April; 2¢ per test; 1¢ per key; specimen set free; 40(45) minutes; N. Wicks; directed by C. H. Roberts; Ohio Scholarship Tests.

[1023]

Modern History: Every Pupil Test, December 1937. Grades 9–10; p1937; a new form is scheduled for pub-lication each December; 2¢ per test; 1¢ per key; speci-men set free; 40(45) minutes; N. Wicks; directed by C. H. Roberts; Ohio Scholarship Tests.

[1024]

Test of Factual Relations in American History. Senior high school; c1936; 1 form; a second form is scheduled for publication; 6 parts, each part covering a given period in American history; a seventh part is scheduled for publication; 45¢ per 25 parts; 25¢ per specimen set of all parts; (15–30) minutes per part; E. S. Farley; Educational Test Bureau, Inc.

Wilbur F. Murra, Harvard University. This is a test of mediocre quality designed to cover conventional topics in American history from 1607 to 1930. It could probably be used on either the junior or senior high school level, although the only norms published are T-scores for twelve-year-old children. Supposedly the test emphasizes relationships and "larger con-cepts," but actually it would seem to reflect to the greatest extent pupils' verbal associations of pat phrases, names, and labels. Some real thinking—in respect to identifying causes and effects—is doubtless demanded, but it would apparently have only a minor influence on the total score.

In form, all items in the test are a modifica-tion of the matching type, so arranged as to make scoring unnecessarily awkward. Technical flaws in test construction are numerous—nota-bly in respect to ambiguities, logical incon-sistency, and lack of homogeneity. The accom-panying manual and norms are both inadequate. Statistical data as to reliability and norms are reported and appear commendable at first glance, but no clue is given as to how the data were derived.

[1025]

Wisconsin American History Test, Form 1937. Grade 12; c1937; a new form is scheduled for publication each spring; less than 100 copies, 5¢ per test; 100 or more, 4¢ per test; 10¢ per specimen test; 50(55) minutes; E. J. Goodrich, in collaboration with the Social Studies Committee of the Wisconsin Education Association, the Department of History, and the Bureau of Records and Guidance, School of Education, University of Wisconsin; E. M. Hale and Co.

[1026]

World History: Every Pupil Test, December 1937 and April 1938. Grade 10; c1937–38; a new form is scheduled for publication each December and April; 2¢ per test; 1¢ per key; specimen set free; 40(45) minutes; M. Davidson; directed by C. H. Roberts; Ohio Scholarship Tests.

[1027]

World History Test: State High School Tests for Indiana, 1936–1937 Edition. First, second semesters; p1936–37; 2 levels; a new first-semester form is scheduled for publication each December; a new second-semester form is scheduled for publication each March; mimeographed; 2¢ per test; 15¢ per sample test; 40 (45) minutes; V. F. Dawald; edited by H. H. Remmers; Division of Educational Reference.

SOCIAL STUDIES, GENERAL

[1144]

Beard-Erbe Social Science Tests: High School Comprehensive. c1937; 1 form; a new form is scheduled for publication every second year; (45) minutes; 5¢ per test; 20¢ per specimen set; M. R. Beard and C. H. Erbe; Holst Printing Co.

Edgar B. Wesley, University of Minnesota. This social studies (erroneously called social science) test is designed as a general measure of the student's achievement in history, government, economics, and sociology. One section in Part I consists of twenty-four items dealing with Millikan, Sandburg, Damrosch, and other persons in cultural fields. The authors must have forgotten their categories when they included such items. Their importance is not in question; it is their relevancy.

This test consists of 148 items. It actually includes materials from government, sociology, American and European history, and a few items relating to economics and contemporary cultural information. It is divided into six parts which involve matching, best answer, multiple-response, chronological sequence, and completion exercises.

A few criticisms of a minor nature may be made. An "act" cannot "inflict" a punishment (item 9); it can merely provide for its infliction. The word "loathe" (item 40) is unhappily chosen. The word "may" (item 54) should be changed to "will" or "is expected to." In feudal days no one except a very naive person would have thought of God as the landlord (item 87). Item 89 contains a downright error. The keyed answer (option 3) is erroneous, and no one of the options is correct. Every item in Part V is, in the opinion of the reviewer, trivial. He would also omit option 2 in Item 140.

In spite of these minor faults, if such they be, this test is a stimulating one. It undoubtedly will differentiate between the capable and the slothful. It therefore deserves wide use.

[1145]

Civics: Every Pupil Test, April 1938. Grades 8–12; p1938; a new form is scheduled for publication each April; 2¢ per test; 1¢ per key; specimen set free; 40 (45) minutes; G. S. Hug; directed by C. H. Roberts; Ohio Scholarship Tests.

[1145A]

Cooperative General Achievement Test: Part I, A Survey Test in the Social Studies. High school and college placement; c1937; a new form is scheduled for publication each May 1; 40(45) minutes; 6¢ per test, 10 to 99 copies; 5½¢ per test, 100 or more; 25¢ per specimen set; 10¢ per sample test; test booklets may be used repeatedly if adapted to hand or machine scoring; 1½¢ per answer sheet; Form N; H. R. Anderson, E. F. Lindquist, and J. E. Partington; Cooperative Test Service.

Harold Gulliksen, University of Chicago. Part I of the *Cooperative General Achievement Test* is intended to give a comprehensive view of the students' performance in social studies. It includes economics, sociology, and civics, as well as ancient, modern European, and American history. There are about 20 four-choice items on each of these six topics making a 120-item test for which 40 minutes is allowed. All except 4 or 5 of the 25 items in the section on civics and American government are simple memory items such as the definition of referendum, veto, customs duty, etc. In all the other sections less than half of the items would be rated as dealing with knowledge of specific facts.

Most items deal with causal relations or broad implications of a given development or specific application of general principles. It is difficult to frame general thought questions without making some relatively easy or obvious and others

dependent on matters of opinion. A few of
the items reflect this difficulty. For example,
according to the key, "An important obstacle
to the development of a united leadership in
Greece was the—*Too pronounced individual-
ism.*" Whether or not historians agree on this
fact the good student would probably get this
answer by elimination since the other alternatives are factually false.

Items seem well distributed within the fields.
In economics, for example, about half of the
items are on economic institutions and half on
economic theory. However, the test attempts
to cover such a wide range in 40 minutes that
one would not be surprised to find that it was
a very fair sample of the courses given in some
institutions and a much less adequate sampling
of the same courses as given in other institutions.

[1146]

Cooperative Test of Social Studies Abilities:
Experimental Form 1936. High school; c1936; 1 form;
no new forms scheduled; 6¢ per test, 10 to 99 copies;
5½¢ per test, 100 or more; 25¢ per specimen set; 10¢
per sample test; 90(95) minutes; J. W. Wrightstone;
Cooperative Test Service.

Howard R. Anderson, Cornell University.
This test consists of four parts, each including
20 to 25 scoring units. Part I, Obtaining Facts,
uses traditional techniques to measure the
pupil's ability to read charts, graphs and maps,
to use an index, etc. Part II, Organizing Facts,
includes a number of different exercises capable
of objective scoring to test the pupil's ability
to recognize the relevancy of materials and to
construct outlines. Part III, Interpreting Facts,
calls for the pupil to mark statements (+)
"true interpretations," (−) "false" or (o)
"not proved" in terms of the content of a given
paragraph. Part IV, Applying Generalizations,
makes use of a complicated technique whereby
the pupil relates generalizations to a description
of an event, and relates reasons to the proper
generalizations. The last section appears rather
difficult for high school pupils.

[1147]

Historical Development and Cultural Change.
Grades 10–18; p1937; 1 form; $2.50 per 25 tests; 15¢
per sample test; 90(95) minutes; mimeographed;
M. Koopman and V. L. Minor; Cooperative Bureau of
Educational Research.

[1148]

Iowa Every-Pupil Test in Economics: Ninth
Annual Iowa Every-Pupil High School Testing Pro-

gram. p1937; a new form is scheduled for publication
each May; 4¢ per test; 5¢ per key; 10¢ per summary
report of norms; 60(65) minutes; H. R. Anderson;
edited by J. E. Partington and [E. F. Lindquist]; distributed by the Bureau of Educational Research and
Service.

[1149]

Junior High School Civics Test: State High
School Tests for Indiana, 1936–1937 Edition. First,
second semesters; p1936–37; 2 levels; a new first-
semester form is scheduled for publication each December; a new second-semester form is scheduled for
publication each March; mimeographed; 2¢ per test;
15¢ per sample test; 40(45) minutes; C. T. Malan;
edited by H. H. Remmers; Division of Educational
Reference.

[1150]

Melbo Social Science Survey Test. Grades 10–16
and adults; c1937; 1 form; 4¢ per test; $3 per 100
tests; 10¢ per handbook; 20¢ per specimen set; nontimed (40–45) minutes; I. R. Melbo; Public School
Publishing Co.

Alvin C. Eurich, Stanford University. This
test is carefully designed to do what the author
claims for it: "to measure one's information
about the existence of the major trends, the
direction of their movement, and the present
status of such important 'currents of events.' "
It grew out of an analysis of 50 selected books
in the social studies, 6132 clippings and references from 29 periodicals and newspapers
issued between July 1, 1932, and February 15,
1936. In addition, items in the test were judged
by competent persons and studied for discriminatory power for different levels of ability
and for successive grades.

Forty-five minutes of testing time are required.

The first 56 items are of the true-false type
most of which refer to a trend as: "The
past decade has witnessed the increasing manu-
facture of luxury and quality goods designed
for low incomes." The remaining 42 items are
of the best-answer type with each statement
involving four possible responses. These items,
likewise, emphasize trends as: "The divorce
rate is tending to (1) increase, (2) decrease
rapidly, (3) decrease slightly, and (4) remain
about the same." The author states that key
responses were determined whenever possible,
by checking with primary and reliable sources
such as government or university research
bureau reports. All evidence indicates that the
test was worked out with extreme care.

Although the author claims that the test may
be used with high school students, college and
university students and adults, norms expressed

in terms of deciles are provided only for "more than 5000" high school seniors.

For different groups of high school seniors reliability coefficients calculated by the "split-half" method range from .810 to .885. In view of the fact that these coefficients are based upon relatively homogeneous groups, they place the test among the most reliable achievement measures. Probably if all the items were of the best-answer type, selected with equal care, the reliability of the instrument would be higher.

The mechanical features of the test are well arranged for efficiency in giving and scoring.

The test is a distinct contribution to the instruments available in the field. It goes beyond a knowledge of events. It provides a measure of knowledge of trends which is of greater significance for thinking about social problems than a knowledge of isolated events.

[1151]

Senior High School Civics: State High School Tests for Indiana, 1936–1937 Edition. First, second semesters; p1936–37; 2 levels; a new first-semester form is scheduled for publication each December; a new second-semester form is scheduled for publication each March; mimeographed; 2¢ per test; 15¢ per sample test; 40(45) minutes; C. T. Malan; edited by H. H. Remmers; Division of Educational Reference.

[1152]

Social Situation Interview. Grades 10–18; p1937; 2 parts (Schedule A: Part I, Social Implications and Part II, Self-Interview on Experience Background; Schedule B: Part I, Personal Implications and Part II, Community Implications); $1.25 per 25 schedules, either form; 15¢ per sample set, both schedules; Schedule A: 55(60) minutes; Schedule B: 45(50) minutes; Cooperative Bureau of Educational Research.

[1153]

Social Studies Test; National Achievement Tests. Grades 3–7, 7–9; c1937; 1 form; 2 levels; $1.75 per 25 tests; 100 or more, 5½¢ per test; 5¢ per specimen set; nontimed (45–60) minutes; R. K. Speer and S. Smith; Acorn Publishing Co.

[1154]

Tests of the Socially Competent Person. Grades 7–12; c1936–37; 1 form; 75(80) minutes; $6.30 per 100 tests; 15¢ per specimen set; P. R. Mort, R. B. Spence, V. C. Arnspiger, and L. K. Eads; Bureau of Publications.

Douglas E. Scates, Cincinnati Public Schools. It is practically impossible to keep teachers vitally concerned about the broad objectives of education when their work is constantly being evaluated in terms of test results which relate only to the formal subject. It is, similarly, difficult for superintendents and boards of

education to convince themselves that it is safe to urge upon their school systems any large attention to the more modern statements of objectives, when their school systems are likely to be surveyed by staffs which employ ordinary standardized tests which are likely to penalize their school systems for having emphasized something other than the formalities.

Fortunately, recent years have seen the production of a number of tests which are designed to cover these newer areas of outcomes of instruction. Some of these newer tests have been in the field of mental hygiene or adjustment. Some have dealt with character knowledge of acceptable practices. Some have dealt with a general scientific attitude, or with its application to practical problems. In this latter field, we may regard the *Orientation Tests* by Lewerenz and Steimetz (1927, 1931, and 1935) as a pioneer, emphasizing the more abstract elements of intellectual caution, suspended judgment, open-mindedness, etc. The Socially Competent Person test is a recent contribution in this general field, emphasizing the applications of factual knowledge to a variety of personal problems.

The test consists of four divisions containing 370 items. The areas covered are health, personal economics, family and community relationships, and social-civic problems. None of the sections is construed in a narrow way, so that the coverage is rather wide. The range is principally the junior high school grades, though the test may be used from the sixth to the twelfth grades.

The test consists of statements suggesting things that might be done in the light of a given set of circumstances. The test thus tends to reflect practical conclusions from studies that have been taken in school, in contrast to purely academic understandings. For example, when a person awakens in the morning with a sore throat, headache, and upset stomach, should he take a strong pain killer? Apply a red flannel to his throat? Plan to spend the day in bed? Have his mother call a doctor? Etc.

It is possible that some teachers will feel that such material is undignified in a school test. The answer may be made that the question used for illustration is one of the easier ones; the material ranges to more difficult and refined application of knowledge. But to the reviewer, the answer lies not in making any apology for

any of the material, but rather in the con‐
viction that such an emphasis as represented
by the test is a very healthy antidote to the ex‐
treme formality and abstractness that education
must constantly be on its guard against. The
improvement of our society is to come about
eventually through raising the level of practices
in regard to the myriad practical problems
which one faces day after day, much more than
through increasing the understanding on the
part of the average person of the more theoreti‐
cal aspects of the various branches of science.
This is not to discourage a comprehensive grasp
of abstract science on the part of a very limited
number; but it is to emphasize that even our
fewer scientists are frequently unable to make
practical application of their knowledge for the
betterment of their own personal conditions,
and the great majority of people are still largely
dependent upon imitation of their companions
and upon advertisements for the guidance of
their personal conduct, notwithstanding what
they have been taught in various science
(physical, biological, or social) courses in
schools.

The content of the test, however, does not
have to be defended by personal opinion, for
it was selected from actual practices at the
present time in a number of schools. Items in
the test are selected from generalizations found
in those courses of study which had been rated
as superior by the Curriculum Research Bureau
of Teachers College, Columbia University. The
items were subsequently checked by specialists
in the field concerned, and by public school
teachers. They were then tried out in a number
of schools, and revised accordingly.

The tests carry the very interesting innova‐
tions of providing grade norms for both typical
schools, and for "superior curriculum" schools.
For the typical school group, the authors se‐
lected schools reporting an expenditure per
pupil of about $75, representing different geo‐
graphical areas. The "superior curriculum"
schools were those which had the outstanding
courses of study above referred to. Pupils in
the two groups of schools were equated for
chronological age and mental age, as well as
grade. One thousand cases, carefully selected
on the basis of the above criteria, were used
for each set of schools.

The presentation of differentiated norms is
to be highly commended. Not only does it

provide appropriate goals for different classes
of schools, but it makes a significant contri‐
bution in the direction of breaking down
the expectancy—of educators as well as lay‐
men—that the average accomplishment of
classes should be at a single place, namely, *the*
norm.

Hilda Taba, University of Chicago. Accord‐
ing to the statement in the manual of directions
this test attempts to give students an oppor‐
tunity to react to situations similar to those
they face in everyday life. In an effort to
achieve this purpose the authors describe a
series of so-called problem situations in the
areas of health, personal economics, family
and community relationships, and social and
civic problems. Under each of the descriptions
are several statements to which the students
respond by either agreeing or disagreeing with
them. The key designates each of these re‐
sponses as either right or wrong and the total
of right answers represents the score of social
competence. These scores, it is said, can be
related to grade norms of either the "superior
curriculum" or of the average schools. The test
claims the following uses: (1) Checking the
effectiveness of the school curriculum from a
new angle of appraisal. (2) Motivating in‐
struction through the presentation of practical
problems. (3) Providing individual diagnosis
and guidance, particularly providing evidence
on whether or not the students are applying
the materials learned in courses.

A closer examination of the test reveals
curious discrepancies between its stated nature
and function and its actual nature and function.
In the first place, one would expect a test of
judgments of a socially competent person,
especially one whose purpose it is to reveal
to what degree the materials learned are being
applied, to deal with problems demanding some
independent judgment on the part of the stu‐
dent. Actually many of the items are such that
rote memorization of statements suffices and
no analysis and interpretation in specific terms
are necessary. In other cases definitions are
asked to define such things as who is a good
scientist or a competent doctor. In still other
items the response represents expression of
opinion, such as whether or not improving
economic conditions would help in prevention
of crime and delinquency. The test then mea‐

sures different types of behavior, some of which has little direct relevance to social competence, and all of which certainly cannot be compounded without differentiation into a single score of social competence.

Secondly, the manual emphasizes the problem technique and its effectiveness in inducing a high degree of pupil participation. In too many cases, however, the right as well as the wrong conclusions about the situations have nothing whatever to do with the situation as described. The following exercise is a case in point. "Mr. and Mrs. Smith have three children: 18-year-old Jack, 16-year-old Sally, 13-year-old Mary. They have a car and own their home. All the children are in school. Indicate with which of the following statements concerning such families as the Smiths you agree and with which you disagree." The following statements are samples of the right answers: "Mr. Smith should always spend some time each week with his children no matter how tired he is. Sally should be encouraged to buy her own clothes. All three children should have a regular allowance, whether they work part-time or not. Sally's friends should include both boys and girls." All of these are generalized statements about desirable behavior in families in general and they have little necessary reference to the Smith family as described in the test.

In some other cases the "right" judgments are highly questionable by all relevant criteria. Thus, the answer called "right" to the question as to what vocation should be chosen by a boy who is underweight and has been out of school because of illness is that he should become a bricklayer.

Throughout the test the accepted judgments are those which involve either memorization of verbal generalities, as is especially true in the section on social-civic competence, or which offer platitudinous solutions, such as visiting the dentist twice a year, brushing the teeth and washing the hands as solutions to the problem of maintaining the best possible mental and physical health. Not much opportunity is given students to apply their own judgment, to reveal their own analysis of the problem or to apply what they know in any real sense.

In view of these facts, the test is not only irrelevant to its purpose but its use will promote uncritical and poor thinking, penalizing those students who are averse to respond with vague generalities or platitudes. And as to its motivation of instruction, let us hope that the teachers striving to develop intelligent and competent judgment will not take this test seriously.

Tests of the Socially Competent Person

SOCIAL STUDIES — SECOND MMY

Reviews by Howard R. Anderson, Clinton C. Conrad, Warren G. Findley, Kenneth E. Gell, J. R. Gerberich, Grace Graham, Lavone A. Hanna, Robert E. Keohane, W. C. McCall, S. P. McCutcheon, Wilbur F. Murra, Pedro T. Orata, Jacob S. Orleans, Anna Parsek, Roy A. Price, G. M. Ruch, Hilda Taba, Wallace Taylor, Marie E. Trost, R. M. Tryon, Margaret Willis, Edgar B. Wesley, and Ernest C. Witham.

[1614]
Beard-Erbe Social Science Tests. Grade 12; 1937; 1 form; 5¢ per test; 20¢ per specimen set; nontimed (40-50) minutes; Marshall Rust Beard and Carl H. Erbe; Cedar Falls, Iowa: Holst Printing Co.

Kenneth E. Gell, Head of the Department of Social Studies, Washington High School, Rochester, New York; and Special Lecturer in Education, The University of Rochester. The reviewer does not feel that this test compares favorably with certain other tests produced by members of the faculty of the Iowa State Teachers College.

This test seeks to measure understanding in the whole field of social science including the several histories. It attempts to do this in 45 minutes with 148 questions. The sampling is too meager for such a wide field, and because the questions are arranged according to type of question construction rather than type of information tested there is almost no diagnostic value. It seems that the most a score on this test can tell is the number a student gets right out of this particular sampling, rather than his true knowledge of the field supposed to be covered. Not only are all fields of the social sciences included, but also the various elements of a total understanding of them—events, terms, dates, personages, causes and results, and so forth. All of these are in a confused order.

Too many of the items seem poorly chosen for their basic importance; for example, the date of George Washington's birth. Other items tested seem unimportant because of the maturity or involved understanding of the subjects studied; for example, such terms as "amnesty," "mandamus," and "extroversion." It is doubtful if such terms *in a short sampling* are valid in testing high school students. The ratio of the field to be tested to the length of the test makes it very sketchy, and a further disadvantage is that that sketchiness is "spotty," thereby making the remaining parts even thinner; for example, there is an emphasis upon legal terms, persons from American history, technical economic terms, etc. The testing of chronology is by 9 simple order-of-event groups of three each, and by 10 specific date items; some of these chronological items are not well chosen. There are a few other scattered time items. Ten questions are used to test the qualifications and responsibilities of senators as compared with United States representatives, which seems undue stress on these offices in an effort to test United States government as such.

Too many completion items and simple matching items are used.

The test is arranged to correct the raw score for chance, and there is a conversion table to turn these raw scores into percentiles; but the percentiles are based upon too few cases to have great meaning (only 1608 cases were used) except in the institution where the test was standardized.

The reviewer cannot recommend this test because it is too sketchy and too "spotty" to be of reasonable validity, because it is not based upon enough cases to have real measurement reliability (this despite the reliability table cited), and because the test is not arranged to provide for diagnostic analysis.

For a review by Edgar B. Wesley, see 1144.

[1615]
Cooperative Test of Social Studies Abilities. High school; 1936-39; Experimental Forms 1936 and Q; 6¢ per test, 10 to 99 copies; 25¢ per specimen set; Form 1936: 90(95) minutes; Form Q: 80(85) min-

utes; form 1936: J. Wayne Wrightstone; Form Q: J. Wayne Wrightstone with the assistance of Robert E. Keohane, William M. Shanner, Wilbur Murra, and Margaret Seder; New York: Cooperative Test Service.

Roy A. Price, Dual Professor of Social Science and Education, Syracuse University. This test consists of four parts. The first part measures students' ability to obtain facts from tables, graphs, and maps, and how to use indexes and card catalogs, and knowledge of the sources to utilize in seeking certain types of information. The second part measures students' ability to organize material and to distinguish between relevant and irrelevant material. Part III measures the ability to interpret facts. The final part of the test measures the ability to apply generalizations.

We have long recognized the need for measuring instruments in the social studies which would make possible an evaluation of students' achievement other than in terms of the amount of information required. Lip service has been paid to other types of objectives but we have not been able to measure in any objective manner the extent to which these objectives were being achieved. The *Cooperative Test of Social Studies Abilities* is one of a number of extremely promising attempts to devise instruments which will meet this need.

This test not only attempts to make possible measurement of a number of skills but does so in an ingenious manner. Evidence of the reliability and validity of the tests is not available.

The chief weakness of the test, in my opinion, is that certain items seem to lack objectivity, i.e., that experts could not agree with the published scoring key. Other technical difficulties appear also in that: (a) the directions to some parts of the test are complicated and confusing; (b) some graphic materials included are so small as to make exact reading difficult; and (c) in a few instances the meaning is not clear because of wording. Another difficulty is that the paragraphs of subject matter which are introduced are somewhat advanced. When a student is asked to read such a paragraph and then fails to apply a generalization to a specific event given, we are not able to ascertain whether his difficulty arose from inability to read and interpret the paragraph correctly, or whether he is unable to apply the generalization. Similarly, in the section on relevancy of statements, the particular statement in question may be relevant but not listed as a reason. Thus the validity of such items may be placed in some doubt.

The test is valuable not only as a measurement of achievement but perhaps even more important as a diagnostic device. Use of such a measuring scale as this would make the diagnosis of pupil weaknesses and subsequent remedial exercises a much simpler problem. There can be no question that this type of testing is greatly needed and this instrument illustrates the possibilities inherent in this relatively new field of evaluation.

For a review by Howard R. Anderson, see 1146.

[1615.1]
Illinois State Normal University Social Science Test, 1938 Edition. Grades 10-13; 1938; the instruction sheet refers to this test as the *Cooperative Social Science Test;* 1 form; $3.50 per 100; 5¢ per test; 50(55) minutes; John A. Kinneman and Clarence Orr; Bloomington, Ill.: McKnight & McKnight.

[1616]
Melbo Social Science Survey Test. Grades 10-16 and adults; 1937; 1 form; out of print; nontimed (40-45) minutes; Irving R. Melbo; Bloomington, Ill.: Public School Publishing Co.

REFERENCES

1 MELBO, IRVING R. *Information of High School Seniors on Contemporary Social, Political, and Economic Problems and Issues.* Unpublished doctor's thesis, University of California, 1935.
2 MELBO, IRVING R. "Information of High-School Seniors on Contemporary Problems." *Social Studies* 27:82-6 F '36.

Howard R. Anderson, Associate Professor of Education, Cornell University. According to the introductory statement in the teacher's handbook, the purpose of this test is "to measure the extent and nature of the information of high school students, college students, and adults on the major contemporary social, political, and economic problems and issues in American life." The handbook further suggests that the test has four uses: (*a*) to determine extent of information about major problems and issues; (*b*) to do this for specific issues; (*c*) to determine gains in information by making retesting possible; and (*d*) to serve as a basis for subsequent study of selected issues. There also is an account of the research underlying the test, i.e., criteria for the selection and validation of items, reliability coefficients (Form A—.885; Form B—.860), data indicating the equivalence of the two forms, a table of item difficulty, and norms expressed in terms of deciles. It perhaps should

be noted that the data pertaining to item difficulty as well as the norms are based on the administration of the test to 5,474 high school seniors in the spring of the years 1934 and 1935.

The test itself consists of 56 true-false items and 44 four-response best-answer items. In structure these conform to rules for the construction of good objective-type test questions except that the meaning of certain questions is not clear. For example, exactly what is the point of Item 38? "Even before the depression the United States maintained the shortest school term of any western nation." (True) Obviously the federal government does not dictate the length of the school term in the various states. And which are western nations: Brazil and Argentine, or Great Britain, Germany, and Sweden? Does "term" mean average total time spent in school? Item 88 reads: "Approximately one-half of the tax dollar is expended for . . ." Which unit of government is to be considered—federal, state, local, or all three?

Some of the items, as Item 80, "The first state-wide unemployment insurance law was passed by the state of . . . ," are rather narrowly factual; and others, as Item 87, "The per cent of the total national income regularly given to private religious, educational or charitable organizations is about (*a*) 2 per cent (*b*) 4 per cent (*c*) 8 per cent (*d*) 12 per cent," call for rather fine distinctions. The years that have passed since the test was developed cause other items to tend toward obsolescence. For example, Item 62, "The proposed federal pure food and drug laws . . . "; Item 78, "The total tax bill (federal, state, and local) is about (*a*) 4 billions (*b*) 6 billions (*c*) 8 billions (*d*) 10 billions"; Item 82, "By the terms of the present farm bill . . . "; etc.

A few of the items seem to be keyed incorrectly despite the claims made for the validation of concepts. For example, Item 11 states that "About one-half of the total population live in the metropolitan areas." (True) The 1930 census figures indicate that 56.2 per cent live in communities of more than 2,500. Surely all of these cannot be described as metropolitan areas. Then Item 23 reads, "With the exception of labor laws, the last century has witnessed but little change·in the laws relating to marriage and children." (True) What about divorce and school attendance legislation?

The mechanical features of the test if considered from the viewpoint of the person who is to do the scoring are rather unsatisfactory. The teacher is provided with a key printed on both sides of a sheet of paper. The printing is not spaced so that this key can be cut into strips. Of course even a strip key requiring seven separate adjustments would be greatly inferior to the stencil keys supplied with many commercial tests.

R. M. Tryon, Professor of the Teaching of the Social Sciences, The University of Chicago. The subtitle of this test is "A Test of Information on Contemporary Problems and Issues in American Social, Political and Economic Life." The form under review is composed of 56 true-false items and 44 multiple-choice items. Its purpose is to measure both the extent and nature of the information on contemporary American life in the realms of politics, economics, and group activities possessed by groups of high school pupils, college students, and adults. Instead of testing information about affairs that are strictly contemporary, the test attempts to discover one's knowledge of established trends and broad movements. The author claims that it tests information relative to "currents of events" rather than "current events."

It would seem from the information in the handbook for the test that the author has given much attention to such technical aspects as validity, authenticity, reliability and norms. If a teacher desires a survey test, an inventory test, an achievement test or an instructional test, he could make use of this one in any or all of these capacities. Inasmuch, however, as the test is now three years old and the material used in determining its make-up is somewhat older, contemporariness is not its paramount attribute. In fact, the responses to many of the items today are not what they were three years ago. By confining the test chiefly to information about "currents of events" the author has limited the usefulness of his test and probably doomed it to a short and uneventful life.

For a review by Alvin C. Eurich, see 1150.

[1617]

Social Studies Test: National Achievement Tests. Grades 4-6, 7-9; 1937-39; 2 forms, 2 levels; $1.75 per 25; nontimed (35) minutes; Robert K. Speer and Samuel Smith; Rockville Centre, N. Y.: Acorn Publishing Co.

[1618]

Survey Test in the Social Studies: Cooperative General Achievement Test, Part I. High school and college placement; 1937-39; Forms N, O, and P; 6¢ per test, 10 to 99 copies; 1½¢ per machine-scorable answer sheet; 25¢ per specimen set; 40(45) minutes; Form O: H. R. Anderson, E. F. Lindquist, and J. E. Partington; Form P: Mary Willis and Charlotte Croon with the editorial assistance of Ronald Beasley, Robert E. Keohane, Robert L. Carey, Samuel McKee, Jr., Martin Y. Munson, J. Folwell Scull, Jr., and the Social Studies Department, Beaver Country Day School; New York: Cooperative Test Service.

Hilda Taba, Assistant Professor of Education and Research Associate, The University of Chicago. [Review of Form P.] As the title describes, this test surveys the achievement in social studies. The sampling of areas is quite broad and includes the following: Geography, Civics and American Government, the Contribution of Early Civilizations and the Middle Ages, the Rise of Modern European Nations, the Development of the United States, Economic Problems and Problems of Society. These sections are not scored separately, and only a total score is given on the whole test.

According to the accompanying handbook, this test is designed to measure "real or *reasoned* understanding of the information, ideas, relationships, and generalizations presented in the course of instruction" and "the ability to use these facts and ideas in the interpretation of movements, institutions, and practices," in contrast to "emphasis on memorization of unique or stereotyped textbook statements."

The test lives up fairly well to the first claim, namely, that of measuring reasoned understanding. Most questions deal with problems and generalizations significant either in their content or in their implications. With but few exceptions discrete and isolated facts, dates, and names are avoided. This is even true of the section on history. The phraseology is fresh and avoids successfully the textbook stereotype.

From the standpoint of construction, the statements are clear and precise. The "wrong" answers are plausible enough not to permit the guessing of the right responses by eliminating the obviously wrong ones. There are only a few items in which the alternative answers are too vague or too general to permit accurate judgment.

There is more doubt about the validity of the test in measuring the ability of students to apply information and ideas known to them in interpreting new problems. Even defining application rather loosely, namely, as including all questions which cannot be answered without a modicum of reorganization and synthesis of discrete facts and ideas learned, only about one-fifth of the 120 items can be said to call for this ability. Most of the items, while not purely descriptive and discrete, are nevertheless of the type which call more for memory than for interpretation and reorganization of ideas.

This test, along with others in the Cooperative test series, makes use of scaled scores. Raw scores can be converted into scaled scores of 1 to 100, in which the score of 50 represents the score of "average child in average school with the usual amount of instruction." This common scale facilitates the interpretation of scores considerably, both for groups and for individuals. Thus, the individual's scores from year to year on the same test, as well as his scores on different tests, can be easily compared. One wonders, however, to what degree of accuracy the "average child in an average school with an average amount of instruction" can be established, or by what criteria that average was established. Can, for instance, the "average amount" of instruction be determined by the number of years of study devoted to a given area, as was done in this case?

The test is supposed to help discover student needs, to facilitate advice concerning election of subjects, to diagnose causes of failure, to help in advising future scholastic activities of students, and to help appraise the quality of instruction. The authors of the test wisely advise caution in using the results from this test or other similar tests as a sole basis for educational guidance. They point out that a variety of other evidence is needed for adequate diagnosis for any of the purposes mentioned above. The users of this test should take this advice seriously. In spite of the fact that this test is called a survey test in social sciences, there are many other important outcomes of social science teaching not measured by this test which should be considered in making decisions about such matters as causes of failure, election of courses, or future academic career. And even when one assumes that achievement of intellectual understanding of content and mastery of information should be the main basis for educational guidance, the single score derived from the test is hardly diagnostic enough

to decide why a student has failed and whether he should take further work in history, economics, or other social science areas.

[1619]
Test of Critical Thinking in the Social Studies: Elementary School Series. Grades 4-6; 1938-39; 2 forms; $6.30 per 100; 20¢ per specimen set; 45(50) minutes; J. Wayne Wrightstone; New York: Bureau of Publications, Teachers College, Columbia University.

Warren G. Findley, Assistant Director, Division of Examinations and Testing, State Education Department, Albany, New York. The test consists of three 15-minute parts purporting to measure pupil growth in three aspects of critical thinking—namely, obtaining facts, drawing conclusions, and applying general facts. Part I, Obtaining Facts, is further subdivided into sets of questions involving reading tables, reading graphs, where to locate facts, and how to use an index.

It seems likely that this test will prove quite usable and helpful to classroom teachers. Its virtue resides in the fact that it provides a number of objective exercises related to significant skills in social studies in the elementary grades. In so doing, it gives concrete form to the newer goals of instruction in this area. Moreover, this virtue of the test proper is enhanced by inclusion in the test manual of practical, understandable suggestions to the teacher regarding instructional procedures to use with pupils who do poorly on the test. Without recourse to norms the teacher can pick out the weakest pupils for special assistance and otherwise apply information gained from test scores in the classroom situation.

All the above is said despite the large number of questions one must raise as to the test's reliability and validity as a measure of ability to do critical thinking and despite the presence of serious faults in the construction of several items. The test is far less useful than it might be and unless it is carefully revised, is certain to be superseded by other tests that will develop in this field.

The test items are poorly constructed. Several items contain specific determiners. The two false statements on the first page of Part II, Form A, both contain the word "only," while the true statements on the same page contain qualifiers like "some" and "many." Elsewhere in Part II, in which sets of four inferences follow each paragraph, two consecutive inferences will be mutually contradictory, so that the pupil gets credit for indicating as true that "bricks have many more lasting qualities than wood" and then indicating as false the statement that "bricks spoil rather quickly." In another set of four, two statements are identical except for vocabulary and both are contradicted by a third statement. In an item in Part I the examinee gains separate credit for responding first that in 1935 in Russia 12,500,000 goats were raised, and then responding that the country which raised 12,500,000 goats in 1935 is Russia. Such paired items are not merely inefficient; they render meaningless any reliability coefficients computed by the split-halves technique.

Statistical evidence of reliability is not given clearly enough to permit one to judge the reliability of scores on the parts of the test as indicators of pupil progress. One cannot find data from which to estimate the probable error of an individual score. Then, too, were reliability coefficients based on the 4,000 cases used for the norms or on the 64 cases used in estimating validity? Turning to the norms, how many pupils in each grade were used? Moreover, are the grade-scores above 7.0 based on seventh graders or derived by extrapolation from data accumulated on pupils in grades 4 to 6? The author states the limitations of norms and indicates that they should not be used for standards. This is well, but does not warrant omission of data necessary to determine the reliability of norms for interpretation of individual or group data.

Finally, one may raise questions concerning validity which for a test in this new area should be answered more fully than is done in the manual. The scores of the parts of the test, and even the responses to individual items, might well be correlated with independent criterions of the various skills covered by the test to show their validity and distinctness. Under the head of validity the author should also be asked to specify a clear working definition of "critical" thinking. Is the term well used if extended to cover all activity, such as reading tables and graphs, which is basic to the evaluative type of thinking, or is it better to restrict the term to evaluative thinking, inference, deduction, and the like? In either case should we not treat the reading of tables, charts, and graphs as similar in essential character to what is commonly called reading com-

prehension and hence either organize distinct tests of comprehension and critical thinking or else explain the presence of Part I in this test and the absence of ordinary reading comprehension material as due to the fact that reading comprehension tests are available to supplement the present test?

A basic defect of this test is that it is not built on a working definition of critical thinking which may be used to explain the inclusion in the "test of critical thinking" of whatever is used and the exclusion of other types of test exercise as either irrelevant or adequately represented by the material included in the test.

Pedro T. Orata, Special Consultant, Occupational Information and Guidance Service, United States Office of Education, Washington, D. C. Philosophers used to discuss at length the difference between appearance and reality. There is considerable need for the same kind of disputation in the field of "progressive" testing at the present time. *Test of Critical Thinking in the Social Studies* appears attractive as a title, but the validity of its content in measuring thinking, to say nothing of critical thinking, may well be questioned. What is thinking, and what does it mean to be critical? To what extent does this test measure either process?

In real life, thinking consists, as one writer puts it, of the finding and testing of meanings, with testing as the distinctive characteristic of being critical. *Test of Critical Thinking in the Social Studies* may have the first element, of *finding* meanings, in spots, but there is not a faint indication in any of the items in the test that would give evidence of the second element, the *testing* of meaning, which is really the test of critical thinking. Let us look at the tests to find out what processes are involved.

Part I, Obtaining Facts, is a verbal factual test, which requires the student to pick out certain specific facts from a group of facts according to precise directions. In each case the right answer to the question is given. All that is required is ability to match the answer with the fact given in the testing situation, viz., referring to the "Facts about some States" in Table III, Item 9, reading 91,058 in the column under *Population* after *Nevada* and matching it with the figure 91,058 in the test item that gives four possible answers.

Part II, Drawing Conclusions from Facts,

is a reading test, which requires one to compare one set of facts with another set of facts and to pick out those that correspond. The process consists of reading a paragraph and matching four statements with it in order to determine the extent to which each of them is, according to the facts, indicated in the paragraph—again a factual test requiring no interpretation or reinterpretation of meanings. The conclusions are *not* drawn; they are picked out from a given set of conclusions.

Part III, Applying General Facts, is more of the same, finding a fact that best explains another fact, both facts being given, along with other facts. The only differences between this part and Part II are that there are two columns instead of one and that the directions are more complicated. The principle is the same.

To sum the evidence: there is hardly any need for thinking in order for one to see that 91,058 is not 225,565; in like manner, the simple process of reading a sentence and determining whether or not it is given in a paragraph cannot be classified as a thinking process; and, again, the use of even the imagination is hardly necessary in order to know that "The invention of machines has caused the growth of factories" and not "In a new country the first settlers usually live near rivers or bays" "Explains big factories." In short, a 100 per cent factual test is not a test of critical thinking or of thinking of any other kind. While it is true that facts are needed in order for one to think at all, the mere possession of the facts is no evidence of ability to think.

Wrightstone is one of the few who have condemned paper-pencil tests severely on the ground that they merely test verbal information and book learning. His test is a paper-pencil test, which differs in no essential respect, except in name, from existing tests. In fact, we have better tests of the same kind rightly named.

Test of Critical Thinking in the Social Studies, like most other paper tests, suffers very much from unreality. Thinking is both creative and critical. In real life a thinking situation is of the nature of a puzzle. The thinker is confronted with a difficulty for which available data or information does not suffice. Hidden clues may exist, but they may not even suggest the answer. New material and new meanings must be introduced before

the solution will "dawn" upon one. One solution after another is tested before the right one is found. Not a single item in the test being reviewed qualifies for this kind of process. All the facts are there. All one has to do is to find the right pairs, and presto! one is said to have thought critically. Good reading ability is all that one needs to have a high score in the test. Why not call it a reading test?

In one of his Ford Sunday Evening Hour talks, Mr. W. J. Cameron said, in developing the topic, "Initiate—Don't Imitate," "Setting up another peanut stand on a corner where one peanut stand is already competently and completely serving the trade, that is not competition. It is not business expansion either." *Test of Critical Thinking in the Social Studies* is one more peanut stand on an overcrowded corner. Some years ago Wrightstone said that we needed new tests for new needs. We still do. The need will not be supplied until and unless we discard the old content and produce new material that really measures the power to think. There is no miracle in the change of names, and neither is there any gain by paying lip-service to progressive education and proceeding to make old-fashioned tests with a new set of names.

So much for the shortcomings. The following may be regarded as outstanding merits of the test: (*a*) focusing attention on a significant educational objective—the development of critical thinking; (*b*) breaking down the objective into areas for which evidence may be obtained; (*c*) suggesting a way of determining individual (if the test is in fact sufficiently reliable for such purpose) and group differences in three aspects of critical thinking; (*d*) presenting a new validation procedure; and (*e*) pointing the way toward using the test itself and the test results as a device for the improvement of teaching.

G. M. Ruch, Chief, Research and Statistical Service, United States Office of Education, Washington, D. C. Wrightstone has chosen for the purpose of this test, to divide thinking into three aspects: (*a*) obtaining facts, (*b*) drawing conclusions, and (*c*) applying general facts. The three parts of the test contain, respectively, 36, 32, and 27 exercises, or a total of 95. The working time is 15 minutes per section, or a total of 45 minutes, a seemingly adequate allowance.

Test of Critical Thinking in the Social Studies

The conception of the test includes as one element the logico-psychological analysis of the thinking process as formulated by Dewey and others. As another element may be mentioned the influence of progressive curriculum formulations in such states as New York, California, Colorado, and Virginia. The validation methods rightly distinguish between curricular and statistical analysis—despite the fact that the latter appears not to have been carried out. The curricular validation of this test has unique features. By means of a specially prepared interview, 64 pupils gave free-answer responses to the test elements. These were evaluated independently by an unstated number of (but apparently never less that three) judges or teachers. Space does not permit full descriptions of the validation of the three parts of the test; the methods differ from part to part, and the manual account is too compressed for the reader to feel sure of his comprehension of the exact methodology. The statistical validation is based largely (or entirely?) on the correlations of the test with the reading part of the *Modern School Achievement Test* and McCall's *Multi-Mental Scale,* and on the inter-part correlations. It is not stated whether the routine item-analysis techniques were applied; presumably not.

Reliabilities are reported for stepped-up split-halves and form vs. form methods. The population used is not adequately described, other than that it comprised pupils in grades 4-6. The reliabilities quoted are, therefore, considerably higher than may be expected when the test is applied to a single class despite the statement that "these scores may be reliably used for individual analysis."

Raw scores may be transmuted into both age and grade equivalents, part by part, and total scores. The norms are based upon 4,000 pupils in six states, tested in 1938. The age and grade equivalents are in close agreement with those of the *Modern School Achievement Test* and the *New Stanford Achievement Test;* agreement with the later is almost perfect.

The mechanical features of the test are better than average. Much waste space might have been utilized to advantage by larger type and extra leading in places. The use of 42-pica lines (about 7 inches) is objectionable in the intermediate grades according to many authorities. Scoring is objective, simple, and economical.

There is no question that this test has moved some distance in the right direction. Its title is overly ambitious; it might more aptly be called a "Test of Work Skills in the Social Studies." Part I calls for obtaining facts from tables, graphs, etc., and contains little that is not also taught in arithmetic or several other school subjects. Part II is fundamentally a reading comprehension test under a more pretentious caption. Part III lives up to the title of the test more nearly, and involves judgment, which is certainly one element in critical thinking.

The reader should be left with the feeling that Wrightstone has both complemented and supplemented our useful measures in the field of the social studies; if any critical statements in this review overshadow such a general impression, the net result has been unintentional.

Chicago Sch J 21:232 Mr-Ap '40. D(enton) L. G(eyer). This long-awaited measuring instrument comes to us after the expenditure of many thousands of dollars and several years of effort, and is by all odds the most successful attempt yet made to measure one of the major educational outcomes whose attainment we have so far been able only to hope for and guess at. Every teacher of the social studies in the elementary school ought to secure a copy of this test and make a study of it.

[1620]

Test of General Proficiency in the Field of Social Studies: Cooperative General Achievement Tests, Revised Series, Part I. High school and college; 1940; Form QR; 6¢ per test, 10 to 99 copies; 1½¢ per machine-scorable answer sheet; 25¢ per specimen set; 40(45) minutes; Mary Willis with the editorial assistance of Ronald Beasley, Wilson Colvin, John S. Custer, Edgar B. Wesley, and J. Wayne Wrightstone; New York: Cooperative Test Service.

REFERENCES

Cooperative Test Service. *The Cooperative General Achievement Tests (Revised Series):* Information Concerning their Construction, Interpretation, and Use. New York: Cooperative Test Service, 1940. Pp. 4. Gratis. Paper.

[1621]

Wesley Test in Political Terms. Grades 6-16; 1932; 4 forms; 40¢ per 25; 30¢ per specimen set, including the *Wesley Test in Social Terms;* nontimed (5) minutes; Edgar B. Wesley; New York: Charles Scribner's Sons.

REFERENCES

1 WESLEY, E. B. "Wesley Test in Social Terms," pp. 219-26; and "Terms in the Social Sciences," pp. 502-609. In *Tests and Measurements in the Social Sciences.* By Truman L. Kelley and A. C. Krey. New York: Charles Scribner's Sons, 1934. Pp. xiv, 633. $3.00.

Howard R. Anderson, Associate Professor of Education, Cornell University. These tests are "similar in nature" to the *Wesley Test in*

Social Terms, "but being brief and inexpensive are especially valuable for testing the achievement of an entire class." With this statement from the examiner's manual this reviewer agrees only in part.

The tests (there are four forms; each consisting of ten five-response best-answer statements) are brief and are made up of questions also found in the two forms of the *Wesley Test in Social Terms.* How a test so limited in its sampling can test "the achievement of an entire class" is not clear. For a test even of knowledge of political terms the sampling appears inadequate.

Norms are given for each of the four forms in terms of the average number of correct responses per grade from the eleventh through the sixteenth. These suggest that the forms are too short and too easy to be used to advantage in the last three grades.

[1622]
Wesley Test in Social Terms. Grades 6-16; 1932; 2 forms; $1.30 per 25; 30¢ per specimen set, including the *Wesley Test of Political Terms;* nontimed, (30) minutes. Edgar B. Wesley; New York: Charles Scribner's Sons.

REFERENCES

1 WESLEY, E. B. "Wesley Test in Social Terms," pp. 219-26; and "Terms in the Social Sciences," pp. 502-609. In *Tests and Measurements in the Social Sciences.* By Truman L. Kelley and A. C. Krey. New York: Charles Scribner's Sons, 1934. Pp. xiv, 633. $3.00.
2 BOLTON, F. B. "The Predictive Value of Three Kinds of Tests for a Course in United States History." *J Ed Res* 30:445-7 F '37.
3 WILSON, HOWARD E. *Education for Citizenship,* pp. 56, 96-7, 272. New York: McGraw-Hill Book Co., 1938. Pp. 272. $2.75. (London: McGraw-Hill Publishing Co., Ltd. 15s.)

Howard R. Anderson, Associate Professor of Education, Cornell University. The *Wesley Test in Social Terms* is described as a test to "measure the results of instruction as distinct from intelligence or *random information*" and "can be used (1) as a diagnostic test, (2) as a final examination in the social studies, (3) as a qualifying examination, and (4) in any situation in which accurate measurement in the social studies is desired." The parallel between the last claim and similar ones formerly advanced in behalf of certain patent medicines is palpable.

What is the formula? In this case 80 best-answer exercises which require that the student indicate which of five descriptions of a term is most apt, or which of five terms best fits a given description. (The research underlying the selection of these social terms is described in Kelley and Krey's *Tests and Measurements in the Social Sciences.*[1])

. The following items from Form A are more or less typical: "The county court house is located at the county (1) capital (2) capitol (3) court (4) metropolis (5) seat." "Utility is that quality of a good which makes it (1) beautiful (2) cheap (3) costly (4) desirable (5) unusual." Now to this reviewer it seems that even limited "intelligence" or "random information," or both, will suggest that "seat" complements "county" better than the other words, and that "desirable" brings to a happy ending the definition of utility commonly provided in economics textbooks.

Some of the other items also contain clues. For example, "A protective tariff is designed to . . . protect home industries"; "An injunction is a court order"; "Habeas Corpus is a . . . writ"; "A patroon is a . . . Dutch landlord in colonial New York"; etc.

Other questions call for information which scarcely seems related to instruction in the social studies. For example, "A sentinel is . . . a guard"; "An illegal act is contrary to . . . law"; "A notary is. . . an official"; "For purposes of consideration, ideas are classified into . . . categories"; "The condition of being related by blood to another constitutes an example of . . . consanguinity"; etc. That the keyed answer to "A gold certificate is issued by . . . the treasury" is correct seems doubtful.

Unquestionably instruction in the social studies will help a student answer these questions. But so will extensive reading and intelligence. The examiner's manual gives a correlation of only .391 between the *Otis Self-Administering Test of Mental Ability* and the *Wesley Test of Social Terms.* Later research seems to indicate a much higher correlation between intelligence and performance on this test. In the recent New York State Survey, Wilson[3] reports a coefficient of correlation of .70 between intelligence quotients and Wesley test scores.

The tentative norms provided in the examiner's manual are rather inadequate since they consist only of an average score for each of the grades 6 to 16. The scoring key also is unsatisfactory in that the answers to Form A are printed on one side and those for Form B on the reverse side.

[1623]
20th Century High School Civics Test. Grades 10-12; 1935; 1 form; 3¢ per test, 4 or more copies; 10¢ per sample test; 60(65) minutes; [Gale Smith]· Fowler, Ind.: Benton Review Shop.

Wesley Test in Political Terms

ECONOMICS

[1624]

Cooperative Economics Test. High school and college; 1933-39; 40- and 90-minute editions; 25¢ per specimen set of either edition; Form P: Howard R. Anderson and J. E. Partington with the editorial assistance of Robert L. Carey, Howard C. Hill, and E. F. Lindquist; New York: Cooperative Test Service.
a) FORMS 1933 AND 1935. Out of print; 90(95) minutes.
b) REVISED SERIES FORM P. 1939; 5¢ per test, 10 to 99 copies; 1½¢ per machine-scorable answer sheet; 40(45) minutes.

Edgar B. Wesley, Professor of Education, The University of Minnesota. [Review of Form P.] This test has several merits. The matching and the best-answer forms are, next to clear recall, the best that have been devised, and they appear here in their most perfected style. The test includes names, terms, principles, facts, and problem situations. It thus embraces a wide sample of the field of economics. There are few available tests in economics, and this is certainly one of the best, if not the best, one available. A little more help from a skeptically disposed economist would make it even better.

In spite of its merits this test presents a series of confusions. One cannot see how many items there are. Part I opens with Item 10 and Part II opens with Item 20. A patient sort of teacher could figure out the number of items. The argument for convenience of the makers, printers, and scorers is unconvincing. The test reminds me of the accounting system in some stores where the customer is detained while the clerks and the office fill out their records.

Part I is made up of two kinds of items, and Part II continues with the same kind of items which appear in the second part of Part I. Those who have had courses in the mechanics of test construction can probably find clues and run down the significance, but prospective users may not be so kindly disposed nor so sleuth-like minded.

This test illustrates another easily defended, but nonetheless unfortunate, principle of test construction. It is probably suited to high school students of economics, but it causes the advanced student of economics considerable irritation and stirs many misgivings. Is it not possible to make items which are scholastically sound and at the same time fitted to high school students? For examples: Item 31—Is it a fact that people are buying more trademarked goods? Item 37—Who can say what form of organization is most temporary? Item 38—Which comes first, investment or control? Item 45—Does the word *public* mean *official* or the opposite of private? Item 48—What economist could answer the question at the time the item was written? Item 50—Is there a correct answer? Item 56—The facts contradict the "normal conditions" specified in the introductory phrase. Item 40—The correct answer is trivial and negates the significance of the whole item.

On the title page the student is told that "directions for each part are printed at the beginning of the part," but at the beginning of Part II, the student is merely told to continue. The mystery of why there are two parts thus deepens, and the confusion is increased by shifting the numbering scheme. Why does the publisher not explain the effect of the mechanical scoring machine?—if that is the answer. In spite of these defects the test seems to be entirely valid and useful.

GEOGRAPHY

[1625]

Analytical Scales of Attainment in Geography. Grades 6-7; 1933; 1 form; 75¢ per 25; 20¢ per specimen set; (45) minutes; M. E. Branom and M. J. Van Wagenen; Minneapolis, Minn.: Educational Test Bureau, Inc.

Ernest C. Witham, Associate Professor of Education, Rutgers University. This test is made up of geography information, in the form of multiple-choice statements, which ranges over the whole world. This does not conform well to many courses of study, as some parts of the world are not studied intensively before the eighth grade.

There are 160 statements divided equally into four groups as follows: (a) Geography Vocabulary, (b) Human Geography, (c) Industries, and (d) Products. While most of the statements are well selected, the division into such sections is rather meaningless, because many of the statements fall just as logically into one category as into another. Many of the statements could have been interchanged with equal geographical justification. For example, the statement "The country which imports the most lumber is (1) Great Britain (2) Germany (3) France (4) United States (5) Italy," seems to fit Industries or Products, but it is

Item 36 under Human Geography. The statement "Shoes are generally made from the hides or skins of (1) horses (2) cattle (3) sheep (4) goats (5) hogs," fits equally well Industries or Products. It is Item 11 under the latter. The statement "The fat of the hog is called (1) tallow (2) gristle (3) oil (4) margarine (5) lard," is listed in the Geography Vocabulary group. Just where is the geography vocabulary significance in such a question?

Specific directions for giving and scoring tests are indispensable, but all superfluous directions, in the interest of clarity and economy, should be dispensed with. For example, it is no longer necessary that every test shall give directions for clearing the desks and providing each child with two well-sharpened pencils.

The raw score results on this test are converted into C-scores and they in turn into geography ages. This seems unnecessarily complicated for the average geography teacher.

In the folder of directions for administering and scoring the test, there is no mention of validity and reliability.

In spite of the strictures mentioned the test has real value, and if I were a teacher of geography I would use it in my classes.

[1625.1]

Fourth Grade Geography Test. End of the fourth grade; 1940; 1 form; 8¢ per test; 4¢ per manual; 20¢ per scoring stencil; 3¢ per class record sheet; 30(35) minutes; Zoe A. Thralls, George Miller, and Marguerite Uttley; Bloomington, Ill.: McKnight and McKnight.

[1626]

Wiedefeld-Walther Geography Test. Grades 4-8; 1931; 2 forms; $1.15 per 25; 20¢ per specimen set; 60(65) minutes; N. Theresa Wiedefeld and E. Curt Walther; Yonkers, N. Y.: World Book Co.

Anna Parsek, Teacher in the Sixth Grade, Public School No. 6, West New York, New Jersey. This nine-year-old test was one of the first of the standardized tests in geography which purported to go beyond the measurement of geographical information alone to include the measurement of "skills in the finding, evaluation, and use of facts."

The authors state that Part 1, consisting of Subtests 1, 2, and 3, "measures the extent to which three necessary study abilities and skills have become part of a pupil's thinking and behavior in the effective study of geography."

Subtest 1, Reading, consists of sixteen 4-sentence paragraphs requiring the pupil to select the one sentence which "helps best to answer" the question following the paragraph.

In many cases the correct answer is too obvious and in other cases, such as Items 11 and 13, there are two answers equally correct. In light of the authors' claims that this subtest measures "the ability to read *various types* [reviewer's italics] of geographical material and comprehend their meaning for use in geographical interpretation," Subtest 1 does not appear to be valid.

Subtest 2, Organization, purports to measure "the ability to recognize the worth of geographical material with relation to geographical problems." Again many of the correct-according-to-the-key answers appear to be no better than other responses considered incorrect. Multiple-choice questions of this sort do not necessarily test reasoning ability. The examinee is given no freedom to suggest hypotheses or to marshal and organize data. This type of question does not test ability to think reflectively. Casting questions into objective-when-scored-according-to-the-key form must necessarily be at the expense of the validity of a test measuring "organizing ability."

Subtest 3, Map and Graph Reading, is excellent—it really tests ability to read and interpret maps and graphs. However, the maps are too small for the exacting reading required. Because of this, more than one answer ought to be considered acceptable for Items 10, 20, and 24. This subtest is too difficult for fourth and fifth grade pupils. Although most of the graphs are good, the circle graphs are too small. Item 44 may be answered correctly in two ways; the key accepts only one answer as correct.

Part 2, Geography Information, is similar to many other tests. The map exercise is needlessly confusing. With both political and physical divisions numbered in the same way, one frequently is at loss as to which the number represents.

The time allowed does not appear to be sufficient for a test which urges the students *"not to hurry."* It is unfortunate that the authors failed to name the "seven of the newest series of geography texts" which served as the basis for the choice and grade placement of the test items. Since omitted questions are penalized as much as wrong answers, a premium is placed upon guessing.

For measuring factual information and the reading of maps and graphs in grades 6, 7, and 8, the test should be of value. The test appears

Analytical Scales of Attainment in Geography

to be too difficult for grades 4 and 5. The authors state the test will enable the supervisor to "get objective information on the phases of the subject that need most improvement, the grades in which learning should be improved, and what assistance each teacher needs for the improvement of her instruction." Even though the test is hardly valid for these purposes, many supervisors will—unfortunately—use the test as the authors recommend.

Marie E. Trost, Teacher of Geography and Science in Grades 7 and 8, School No. 7, Belleville, New Jersey. Though intended for use in grades 4 through 8, this test is too difficult for children in grades 4 and 5. However, children in grades 6 through 9 should find the test stimulating. After taking the test, my own eighth graders wanted me to give them another test of the same kind.

Although most of the questions in Subtest 1 (10 minutes), Reading, are well-chosen, a few are not. For example, Item 9 asks, "Why is such a small part of Canada farmed?" The key gives as the correct answer, "The population is only about one-twelfth that of the United States."

Items 15-19 of Subtest 2 (10 minutes), Organization, are very involved and are arranged in a confusing manner. This subtest might better have been combined with Subtest 1 and a test on how to use the index put in its place.

Subtest 3 (15 minutes), Map and Graph Reading, is the most difficult subtest. The time allowed is much too short. At least ten minutes more is necessary if accuracy rather than speed is to be tested. For example, my own eighth graders earned on an average ten points more when given fifteen minutes extra for Subtest 3. The maps should be much larger and the relief map should have clearer markings. The questions on the silk graph should have been placed on the same page as the graph. As it is, the page must be turned eight times in order to answer the last four questions based upon the graph.

Subtest 4 (5 minutes), Geographical Vocabulary, appears to be a satisfactory test.

Subtest 5 (10 minutes), Geographical Relationships, consists of three exercises in which a total of twenty statements of effect are to be matched with twenty out of twenty-seven statements of causes.

Subtest 6 (10 minutes), Place Geography,

includes questions equally divided between the Eastern and Western Hemispheres. In the limited space used the maps are well arranged. The test requires the pupil to have an accurate knowledge of locations.

The *Wiedefeld-Walther Geography Test* is not just another test of factual information. The answers are not so obvious that a child needs to do no careful thinking. The test covers most of the major geographic skills. The questions indicate careful analysis of geographic subject matter and its relative importance. A great deal of research has gone into the preparation of this well-organized test. However, the mechanical setup of the test would have been much better had a larger size page been used.

The scoring mechanics could have been improved. Eleven adjustments of the answer strips must be made. To get total scores for three of the subtests, we must turn pages twice. On an average, I was able to score a test in four minutes.

If given at the beginning of a term, this test would be of considerable help to the teacher wishing to organize her geography instruction so as to be of most value to her pupils. The test should also serve as a guide in making test questions. Although the test is quite difficult, if used properly, it should make a definite improvement in geography teaching. Although published in 1931, it is still a very good tool for evaluating pupil growth in a rather progressive program of geography teaching.

[1627]
World Geography Test: The Dominion Tests. Grade 8; 1938; 2 forms; 2¢ per test, 10 or more; 5¢ per sample-copy; 15¢ per manual; 30(40) minutes; Toronto, Canada: Department of Educational Research, University of Toronto.

HISTORY

[1628]
American Council European History Test. Grades 10-15; 1929; 2 forms; $1.50 per 25; 20¢ per specimen set; 90(95) minutes; Harry J. Carman, Walter C. Langsam, and Ben D. Wood; Yonkers, N. Y.: World Book Co.

S. P. McCutchen, Assistant Professor of Education and Research Associate, Bureau of Educational Research, The Ohio State University. It seems reasonable to assume that one may carefully study the testing program and draw inferences as to the objectives of the course in which the tests are being used. On this basis one would have to say that the teacher who uses the *American Council European History Test* subscribes to a reservoir or cold storage theory of education. The chief justification for the things taught would be the assumption that the student would need this knowledge at some later date, presumably when he becomes an adult, in order to explain what is happening in his then contemporary world. Overlooking the factors of motivation and of retention, assuming that the teacher has persuaded, forced, or cajoled the student to learn the data selected, and that the student will retain it in useful form until the time of its later utility, there is still the question of accurate prediction to investigate. This test seems to operate on an assumption of eternal verities in history which all people need to know, and assumes, therefore, that every teacher will teach all of the facts to all students. In the main the items selected call for little association or constructive thought. Students are asked to indicate the truth or falsity of such items as "The *cahiers* were salt taxes" and "The *Zollverein* was a German customs union"; they are expected to identify Suleiman the Magnificent with Turkey, Henry Stanley with African exploration, and Dr. Quesnay with the Physiocratic movement; they should know what James Watt invented and the religion of George Fox; they must exercise selectiveness in indicating that General Foch was not a peaceful man, and that Blücher was not a scientist or writer.

Only occasionally does the necessity for thinking arise and the association is usually historical. This item in the true-false section is an illustration: "Being a leading aristocrat and believing in a policy of 'blood and iron,' Bismarck was always strenuously opposed to all forms of legislation tending to improve the condition of the working man." The item slyly identifies Bismarck with aristocracy and forthright methods, and challenges the student's naive assumption that such a person could not possibly have the interests of the working man at heart. Truly, a mental biography of Bismarck is required in order to attain the correct answer, false, for this item. The test illustrates the difficulty of standardized instruments in keeping pace with the tempo of modern events. These items are in the true-false section: "All the so-called Great Powers except the United States and Russia are at present members of the League of Nations." (The key

indicates that the statement is true.) "True to tradition, Austria still has a very undemocratic constitution." (To fit the key, this should be marked false.)

Very few people concerned with secondary education today advocate the complete elimination of testing, but the use of this test for measuring achievement seems a rather clear indication that the teacher has abdicated and is willing to let someone who does not know the uniquenesses of the community, uniquenesses of the teacher, uniquenesses of the student group prescribe the curriculum. There is probably no better way to contribute to a docile acceptance of authoritarianism.

[1629]

American History Test. First, second semester : high school; 1938; 1 form, 2 parts; 3¢ per test, 4 or more copies; 10¢ per sample test; 40(45) minutes; Gale Smith; Fowler, Ind.: Benton Review Shop.
a) FROM THE DISCOVERY OF AMERICA TO 1850.
b) FROM 1850 TO PRESENT TIME.

[1630]

American History Test: National Achievement Test. Grades 7-8; 1937-39; 2 forms; $1.50 per 25; 5¢ per specimen set; nontimed (45-60) minutes; Robert K. Speer, Lester D. Crow, and Samuel Smith; Rockville Centre, N. Y.: Acorn Publishing Co.

Jacob S. Orleans, Associate Professor of Education, The College of the City of New York. The purpose of this test, as indicated by the authors, is to measure the pupil's ability to interpret major lessons in American history, his mastery of the time sequence of events, his knowledge of historical associations, and recognition of important facts. There can be no question that the content of this test tends to go beyond the more typical factual tests in American history that have been published in the past. However, despite the names of the four parts of the test, it still is largely factual and may not be an improvement over some of the better elementary school history tests that have already appeared.

The only item available on content validity appeared in a circular which stated that : "The tests are in close agreement with numerous city and state courses of study, widely used textbooks, and the judgments of scores of school administrators and teachers. In most cases, each test includes not only the important subject matter, but especially questions to measure the pupil's power to use the knowledge he has acquired." Analysis of the content of the test shows a fairly good distribution for the various periods of American history with perhaps **a** little overemphasis on the Colonial Period and the period prior to the Civil War. It is interesting to note that of the 114 items in the test, 21 deal with the 5 specific items of. States' rights, taxation without representation, the Monroe Doctrine, the Emancipation Proclamation, and the cotton gin. No information is available as to whether the authors made an analysis of the questions in terms of types of content such as social, economic, political, chronological, and the like.

No information was at hand concerning the statistical validity of the test.

The data provided for reliability indicate a reliability coefficient of .88 for grades 7 and 8. Presumably this means for the two grades combined. The norms show a variation of 36 points representing 20 months of achievement, or slightly over one-half month per point. Since the probable error of a pupil's score is 2.6, the probable error of a pupil's score is less than one and one-half months of achievement. It is interesting to note that a shorter history test contained in the National Achievement Test Battery has a higher reliability coefficient for grade 6 alone.

The scoring is done without a key for three of the four parts of the test. The scorer is given a key word. Any answer is correct if preceded by a letter which is part of that word. There are only three choices for the multiple-choice questions in Parts 1 and 4, without any correction for guessing in the scoring. It is possible that the pupils may be somewhat confused in Part 2 by the continuous shifting in alternate questions from determining which of four items comes first to which of the four items comes last.

Despite the title of Part 1, Lessons of History, only 14 of the 29 questions deal with the lesson to be learned from a given situation. The other 15 items are almost entirely factual. In the case of several of the questions in Part 1, the authors may have difficulty justifying some of their answers. For example, our refusal to enter the League of Nations may be just as indicative of the fact that we do not understand European affairs as that we are opposed to political agreements with European countries. Although Part 4 is labeled "Miscellaneous Problems," the questions are purely items of historical fact.

Grade norms by months are given for grades 7 and 8 only. Therefore, it is not possible to give a specific equivalent measure for the poorest seventh grade pupils or the best eighth grade pupils.

Although the pupil's score on the entire test is undoubtedly reliable it is questionable that scores on the individual parts have meaning for analytical purposes. The diagnostic purpose which the test is meant to serve can then hardly be on the basis of reliable measurement in any one of the four parts of the test.

Wallace Taylor, Assistant Professor of Education and Supervisor in Social Studies, Milne High School, State College for Teachers, Albany, New York. The claims for the test seem extravagant. It is doubtful that it measures "power to interpret major lessons in American History; the ability to analyze principles; or ability in tracing cause and effect." It does fulfill its claim to test for a recognition of facts even though some of the facts seem scarcely important enough to deserve inclusion. Part VII, Historical Associations, tests for names of men, several of whom are not very important, and in addition employs the device of supplying the first name which certainly has the effect of encouraging verbal association.

The section dealing with time concepts would be more valuable if there was a definite relationship between each of the events that are to be placed in order.

Too many of the items deal with political history. Understanding of the aspects of the life of the common man which the better teachers of junior high school American history commonly stress, is not sufficiently stressed. Also, items in which the pupil is asked to use historical principles in the explanation of present-day problems are lacking.

The items are generally free from the more obvious defects of specific determiners, grammatical inconsistencies, and clues, but in many instances the incorrect responses are so obviously wrong as to require very little discrimination in arriving at the correct answer. It is probable that many of these items test for general intelligence rather than American history.

The element of guessing would have been reduced by the use of four rather than three responses. The opportunity for guessing probably results in spuriously high scores.

The use of code words in scoring seems

unnecessarily complicated. Any device of this type may possibly have the effect of causing the pupil to spend time trying to figure out the code that may be used in answering the questions. There is no apparent advantage resulting from its use.

[1631]

Analytical Scales of Attainment in American History. Grades 7-8; 1932-33; 1 form; 75¢ per 25; 20¢ per specimen set; (45) minutes; Mary G. Kelty and M. J. Van Wagenen; Minneapolis, Minn.: Educational Test Bureau, Inc.

Wilbur F. Murra, Executive Secretary, The National Council for the Social Studies, Washington, D. C. This test is intended for diagnosis only. It supplements the general achievement test by the same authors which is published as the American history section of the *Unit Scales of Attainment.* It claims to diagnose relative attainments in each of the following categories: historical vocabulary, historical background, persons, and places and conditions. Each section consists of 30 or 40 five-choice multiple-choice items.

The individual items are almost completely free from technical flaws. Directions are commendably clear and succinct. Format is excellent. It would seem unfortunate, however, that there is a 45-minute time limit on a test of this kind. Certainly many slower pupils will be unable to complete all 140 exercises in that time, and accordingly their scores on the fourth section will not be accurate measures.

Content is adequately representative of conventional courses in junior high school American history, but it will be found less well suited for those newer courses which put more emphasis on social and economic history and problems of the twentieth century. Out of a total of 140 items, only 11 deal exclusively with the twentieth century and 13 others—particularly places and terms—touch the twentieth century in part. Of the 11 which are exclusively concerned with events since 1900, three deal with the Panama Canal, six with military and diplomatic events of the World War, one with the Nineteenth Amendment, and one with the Kellogg Pact.

In a diagnostic test each trait separately measured should be identifiable and clearly distinguishable from every other trait. This important criterion is far from satisfactorily met by the instrument here under review. Such a short-

coming is due in part to the inherent nature of achievement in the field of history, where separate elements are scarcely distinguishable. It is, nevertheless, a specific fault of the *Analytical Scale of Attainment in American History* that its section titled Knowledge of Places and Conditions contains a miscellany of exercises touching such matters as legislation restricting immigration, motives for early exploration and settlement, and the founding of Harvard College. The teacher may well be in doubt as to the meaning of any pupil's score on this section. The section headed Historical Background is very similar, as its broad title more candidly indicates. The Historical Vocabulary subtest appears to demand "historical background" information almost as much as other sections, although a minority of its items treat exclusively of word meanings. The section headed Knowledge of Persons is least open to criticism on this ground.

With such indefinite limits for each section, it is quite to be expected that there is much overlapping. This fault is most indefensibly evident when one finds that Item 27 in the subtest Knowledge of Historical Background is repeated in its *identical* form as Item 37 in the subtest Knowledge of Places and Conditions. (The item deals with the effect of the Russian Revolution on the World War.)

Perhaps the most distinctive feature of this test is its scheme for expressing results in terms of "C-scores." This feature, of course, it shares with all its companion tests in the "Analytical Scales" and "Unit Scales" series by the same publishers. It admittedly affords a more valid basis for appraising the gains made by a pupil or class over a period of time, although it seems to have no advantage over other simpler systems of norms for *comparing* the attainment of a pupil or class in respect to the four traits measured in this test—or for comparing any one of them with other tests in the "Analytical" and "Unit" batteries. But the special claims which the publishers make for the C-score (the reference to a mythical "absolute zero point" and the "consistent unit of measurement") seem to this reviewer to afford no essential help to teacher-interpretation of test scores, however serviceable they may be for more sophisticated statistical analysis.

A table of norms for the "history age" equivalent of each C-score is provided. Such norms, however, are certainly not valid for interpreting achievement in American History. School curricula being what they are, attainment in this field cannot be thought of as continuous with advancing chronological age (as reading ability may be, for example). The pupil gains in knowledge of American history while he is studying that subject and rarely otherwise. Dependable surveys have demonstrated that the typical fifteen-year-old actually knows *less* American history than the typical fourteen-year-old, for the latter has normally just completed the study of the subject in grade 8, whereas the former has practically never had any study of it in grade 9.

Margaret Willis, Assistant Professor of Social Science Education, University School, The Ohio State University. This test includes four sections, Historical Vocabulary and Knowledge of Historical Background, each with thirty multiple-choice questions, and Knowledge of Persons and Knowledge of Places and Conditions, each with forty. The directions for scoring claim that "Since these Scales are like yard-sticks with a task of known value in place of the inch mark at each unit distance, the C-scores measure amounts of abilities just as numbers of inches measure amounts of height or numbers of pounds measure amounts of weight." The class analysis sheet is set up with norms for each section so that the "history age" of a pupil may be determined in each classification and the "Class Median Pc. Av. or IQ." calculated.

Since these are rather extensive claims it is interesting to examine the nature of test items which can be equated so accurately. The questions may also be examined for distribution of items as between periods of history and between the various aspects of living. Since the catalog of the Educational Test Bureau in which this test was listed points out that "no teacher believes a child learns only that which he is taught in the classroom," it is fair to watch for questions which an intelligent child might answer from his out-of-school experiences. Another point to consider is the opportunity which is offered for the exercise of the critical faculty.

It is not always easy to tell the historical period referred to by any particular question since time identifications are generally hazy, but the test seems to be heavily weighted toward the more distant past. Among the 40 persons included in the third section, 11 were connected with discovery and exploration, and 11 more with military affairs of the Civil War or earlier. Of the remaining 18, 6 were inventors and the other 12 scatter over all other fields during the whole period of our national life. In the section Knowledge of Places and Conditions, more than half of the items are pre-revolutionary. In the whole test not more than three or four living men are mentioned and they are wrong answers.

Throughout the test both facts and language are handled uncritically. For example, "The process of rebuilding the South after the Civil War was called: reconstruction." Was the South *rebuilt* during reconstruction? Also this: "Which one of these was the more important agricultural crop in America during the period from 1870 to 1900? (1) potatoes (2) cotton (3) wheat (4) rice (5) tobacco." The key says the answer is wheat, but how can anyone say which crop was more important unless there is some agreed standard for judging importance? Certainly throughout large sections of the country cotton seemed more important to the people whose whole living depended upon it.

Certain questions either repeat or contradict each other. The identical question appears as Item 27 under Historical Background and Item 37 under Places and Conditions. Under Historical Background the first question has *all* the English colonists raising Indian corn as their chief food, while the nineteenth question has the southern colonies raising rice as one of their most important occupations. The seventeenth question puts "most of the labor unions in the United States" in the American Federation of Labor, a contention which is certainly debatable in 1939. Throughout the test there are similar examples of carelessness in definition, in English usage, or in editing.

The test seems to this reviewer an instrument designed to measure and standardize the least desirable kind of history teaching now current. It bears little discernible relation to any part of a child's world except that of his textbook. As a measure of "ability" it is meaningless. The catalog of the Educational Test Bureau argues for standardized tests because where locally constructed tests are used instead "there is too apt to be the 'vicious circle' of tests modifying the curriculum and the curriculum modifying the tests." If such a situation were really a vicious circle, it would still

Analytical Scales of Attainment in American History

be preferable to the standardization of an indefensible status quo.

[1632]

Bowman United States History Test. Grades 7-8 and 12; [1931]; 1 form, 2 parts (A and B); $1.00 per 25 of either part; 20¢ per specimen set; 45(50) minutes per part; Lela Gibson Bowman; Bloomington, Ill.: Public School Publishing Co.

Grace Graham, Department of History, Columbia High School, Columbia, South Carolina, and W. C. McCall, Director of the Personnel Bureau and Associate Professor of Education, The University of South Carolina. GENERAL CRITICISM. This test undertakes to measure both upper elementary grades and high school seniors. In view of the marked difference in the attainments of seventh or eighth graders and of twelfth graders, the difficulty, if not impossibility, of such a task should be immediately evident. As Samuel Adams said of the preamble to the Constitution, "I stumble at the threshold." Some items must certainly prove to be inoperative in both age groups. For instance, it seems inconceivable that any twelfth grader, or even any seventh grader, should fail to match "Discovered America in 1492" with Christopher Columbus. It seems equally unlikely that seventh graders should know Bryan as "a temperance advocate, an orator, and an unsuccessful candidate for president of the United States."

The Bowman test, it seems fair to say, is poorly balanced in content. Approximately 37 per cent of the items relate to the periods of Exploration, Colonization, and Revolution. Most of the textbooks of elementary classes devote only approximately 25 per cent of the space to these periods, although it is perhaps true that elementary teachers give nearly, if not as much as, 37 per cent of instructional time to these topics of American history. It is the writer's belief that in senior high school instruction the average time given to these topics is approximately 25 per cent.

Other fields of instruction generally regarded as essential parts of United States history courses are negligibly treated, if at all. Only four items of the total 282 relate to the period since the World War and only two items have to do with the Constitution. Scant reference is made to the development of American foreign policy, to causes and results of movements or happenings, to social and economic problems, such as labor, religion, tariffs, immigration, money and trusts.

One multiple-choice section is headed Causal Relationship but none of the items given except the sample exercise and one other express a causal relationship. The other questions require definite factual knowledge. Multiple-choice questions, when properly constructed, can stimulate more thought-provoking responses and make less appeal to memorization of factual information. To escape the stigma of being a test of memorized facts, the Bowman test might profitably have used the multiple-choice pattern to sound out concepts of various problems and to test for causes and results.

In the geographical sections, which include 48 per cent of the items of the entire test, the type of information called for is place geography exclusively, except for one section which requires knowledge of colonial possessions. Although this knowledge is necessary and desirable, certainly it does not represent 48 per cent of teachers' labors. The including of maps on which places are to be located is unusual and interesting. The items which ask for the states or countries in which cities are located tend to encourage drill teaching, reminiscent of the era when each child memorized states and their capitals. No items call for a knowledge of geographical influences on the lives of the people, or of products or natural resources. The chronological-relationships group of items rather than the identification of definite dates, as called for in another group, is more in line with current teaching.

The mechanical construction of this test invites scoring errors because the completion pattern makes scoring excessively laborious and also introduces the element of teacher opinion and generosity as to acceptance of misspelled answers. Scoring the section on geography is rendered doubly tiresome by the completion-fill-in arrangement together with the provision that pupils use letters instead of numbers to record identifications in one section. Due to the alignment of numbering of the sample exercises along with the test items, there is the added scoring danger of counting the sample-exercise answers in with the pupils' answers. The scoring "key" supplied by the publishers is nothing more than a condensed one-page list of correct answers. Scoring labors and errors could both be greatly reduced if the publishers would supply pasteboard stencil-type scoring keys throughout the test.

Analytical Scales of Attainment in American History

The author and publishers have failed to supply any information whatever about reliability of the test. Also, norms data ("standards," in the language of the test manual) are incomplete for the senior high school level and no information is given about the number of cases on which the table of seventh and eighth grade norms is based. In the language of the manual the norms are "tentative" and have apparently continued in that state since the test was published in 1931. In all fairness, it should be noted that the author reports an extensive and laborious investigation of curriculum content in American history and of examination questions used by teachers as a basis for item selection and validation in harmony with curriculum and teaching practices. The careful work done by the author suggests that the test content might well be used as a basis for a revised test designed for either junior high school or senior high school levels, reduced in content and modernized in mechanical respects.

CRITICISM OF SPECIFIC ITEMS. Four items in the identifications are poorly constructed in that they merely require memorized information concerning presidents, such as "was fourth president of the United States," and "was elected president in 1920." Identification of Calhoun as a "war-hawk from South Carolina" emphasizes a relatively unimportant part of his career. A few items are poorly worded, such as the multiple-choice question on the Monroe Doctrine and "The commander of the fleet at the battle of New Orleans was (a) McClellan (b) Farragut (c) Scott." Most students would identify the "battle of New Orleans" with 1812 rather than with the Civil War conflict. Two items test the discovery of America by Columbus for both identification of Columbus and for the date. Such items are a waste of testing space, especially since the information given in one item answers the other. Several of the items in the geographical section are ambiguous: the country owning Samoa, the state in which Chesapeake Bay is located. Others in the geographical section are unimportant, such as, the ownership of Staten Island and of the island of Yap.

[1633]

Cooperative American History Test. High school; 1933-40; 40- and 90-minute editions; 25¢ per specimen set of either edition; Form P: Howard R. Anderson, E. F. Lindquist, and Charlotte W. Croon; Form Q: Harry Berg, E. F. Lindquist, and Charlotte W. Croon with the editorial assistance of H. C. Hill, Tyler Kepner, Samuel McKee, Jr.. Elmer J. Thompson,

and E. B. Wesley; New York: Cooperative Test Service.
a) FORMS 1934 AND 1937. Forms 1933, 1935, and 1936 are out of print; 6¢ per test, 10 to 99 copies; 90(95) minutes.
b) REVISED SERIES FORMS N, O, P, AND Q. 1937-40; 5¢ per test, 10 to 99 copies; 1½¢ per machine-scorable answer sheet; 40(45) minutes.

REFERENCES
1 LINDQUIST, E. F. "The Form of the American History Examinations of the Cooperative Test Service." *Ed Rec* 12:459-75 O '31.

Margaret Willis, Assistant Professor of Social Science Education, University School, The Ohio State University. [Review of Form P.] This test consists of 100 multiple-choice questions arranged in a rough chronological order which helps the reader to keep his bearings without elaborate time identifications. It is divided into two parts, apparently in order to insure that the slow worker will spend a fair part of his forty minutes on the last thirty-seven questions which deal with the period from the Spanish-American War to the present. Approximately half of the questions deal with the period of American history to the close of the Civil War, and only the first twelve with pre-revolutionary times. This proportion reflects newer emphases in teaching as does also the character of the questions themselves. The rote learner and the uncritical thinker will do very badly on this test, for the wrong choices are set up to make a particular appeal to him.

The booklet of directions, the booklet of norms and the handbook describing the purpose, content and interpretation of the coöperative tests all are cautious in their claims for the tests, and give some excellent advice as to the limits of their usefulness. The teacher who keeps in mind those limits and pays thoughtful attention to that advice may find the *Cooperative American History Test* a helpful instrument.

For a review by Edgar B. Wesley, see 1014.

[1634]

Cooperative Ancient History Test. High school; 1933-39; 40- and 90-minute editions; 25¢ per specimen set of either edition; Form P: Howard R. Anderson, E. F. Lindquist, Wallace Taylor, and Charlotte W. Croon with the editorial assistance of R. H. McFeely, J. H. Price, and F. S. Somerby; New York: Cooperative Test Service.
a) FORMS 1934, 1935, 1936, AND 1937. Form 1933 is out of print; 6¢ per test, 10 to 99 copies; 90(95) minutes.
b) FORMS O AND P. 1938-39; 5¢ per test, 10 to 99 copies; 1½¢ per machine-scorable answer sheet; 40(45) minutes.

S. P. McCutchen, Assistant Professor of Education and Research Associate, Bureau of Educational Research, The Ohio State University. [Review of Form P.] Since the American Council on Education is still printing a *Cooperative Ancient History Test* one must assume that there are still courses in ancient history being offered on the secondary level. The writer finds difficulty in figuring out why this is so. Of course, there are preparatory schools which have found that some of the Eastern colleges will accept, even prefer, to have students offer entrance examinations in ancient history, and perhaps there are teachers who still preserve high school ancient history courses because of the changeless nature of the course and its complete remoteness from practical modern concerns. Such people, however, having perfected the routine of their year's work so that they no longer have to take thought as to change, ought to have also their tests worked out and not require the aid of the Council. However, the *Cooperative Ancient History Test* exists, and it exists in two parts. Part I, labeled "Historical Facts," contains sixty-eight items using the multiple-choice technique. The thought process required of the student seems to be simple memorization in which the student is aided by the suggestions from which he makes his choice. Part II is called "Historical Judgment." The implication seems to be that the student exercises some independence of thinking in using the data furnished. The presence of an answer sheet, however, seems to question this inference for there is only one "right" judgment, and it seems likely that in this section also the student will fall back on his memory of what the textbook's comment was. (What textbook *does* one use for ancient history nowadays?)

Finally, it seems somehow anachronistic to see these "truths" of ancient history susceptible to machine scoring.

For a review by Wilbur F. Murra, see 1015.

[1635]

Cooperative Modern European History Test. High school; 1933-40; 40- and 90-minute editions; 25¢ per specimen set of either edition; Form O: Howard R. Anderson and E. F. Lindquist; Form P: Howard R. Anderson, E. F. Lindquist, and Charlotte W. Croon; Form Q: Wallace Taylor, E. F. Lindquist, Mary Willis, and Charlotte W. Croon with the editorial assistance of Howard R. Anderson, Margaret Hastings, Martin Y. Munson, Jean Stoner, and Elmer J. Thompson; New York: Cooperative Test Service. *a*) FORMS 1934, 1935, 1936, AND 1937. Form 1933 is

out of print; 6¢ per test, 10 to 99 copies; 90(95) minutes.
b) REVISED SERIES FORMS N, O, P, AND Q. 1937-40; 5¢ per test; 1½¢ per machine-scorable answer sheets; 40(45) minutes.

Lavone A. Hanna, Research Associate, School of Education, Stanford University. [Review of Form O.] In advertising this test, the publishers claim that it requires "the evaluation and understanding of fundamental movements and institutions as well as of personages, locations, and specific events" and that the recency of construction "permits the introduction of much contemporary material." These claims are not justified by the items covered in the test.

The test is divided into two parts. Part I deals with historical personages, historical terms, geographic terms, dates and events. Part II is called historical judgment. The items are all of the single-choice, best-answer type with each item containing four possible responses. Factual information is all that is required to select the correct answer in the first part, which contains such items as: Item 36, "At a time of crisis one member withdrew from the (1) Triple Entente (2) Triple Alliance (3) Entente Cordiale (4) Dual Alliance"; and Item 7, "The Reign of Terror came to an end after the execution of (1) Carnot (2) Danton (3) Mirabeau (4) Robespierre." Historical judgment seems a misnomer for the second section which uses the same technique used in Part I substituting a group of four phrases for names, places, terms, and events. Certainly little historical judgment is needed in selecting the right answer in such questions as: Item 87, "The country which produced the largest number of famous musical composers in the nineteenth century was (1) France (2) Italy (3) Germany (4) England"; and Item 77, "The office of prime minister in England developed (1) under the Restoration (2) during the arbitrary rule of the Stuarts (3) when the Bill of Rights was passed (4) during the reign of George the First." The second claim of the test, that it contains much contemporary material, is not very valid when only nine items out of the hundred deal with events of the last ten years.

If one is concerned with testing the factual information which students possess, the test has considerable value for the facts covered are well chosen and most of them are necessary to an understanding of contemporary Europe. The mere knowing of these facts does not, however, produce understanding and if one is concerned with appraising the understanding which students have of basal European problems as well as those fundamental to an understanding of international relations or with evaluating the grasp which students have of important concepts in world affairs, the test has little or no value. No attempt has been made either to evaluate the ability of students to see the relationship between the present situation and past events. Another defect in the test is that it follows the practice of most history tests in emphasizing political events and problems at the expense of economic and social ones.

The test is set up for machine scoring but can be easily and quickly hand scored. The reliability of the test (.908) is high but is based on a single grade or semester of group study.

For reviews by A. C. Krey and S. P. McCutchen, see 1016.

[1636]

Cooperative World History Test. High school; 1934-37; Forms 1934, 1935, 1936, and 1937; 6¢ per test, 10 to 99 copies; 25¢ per specimen set; 90(95) minutes; H. R. Anderson and E. F. Lindquist; New York: Cooperative Test Service.

Kenneth E. Gell, Head of the Department of Social Studies, Washington High School, Rochester, New York; and Special Lecturer in Education, The University of Rochester. [Review of Form 1937.] This test is a good one for both measurement and diagnosis. It is arranged in three parts by type of information to be tested, rather than by type of question as in many new type examinations. Part I tests recognition of names of 39 historical personages by 5-choice questions; 60 historical terms and 15 geographical terms are also tested in the same way. All items in Part I are well chosen for their basic importance and are well spread throughout history from ancient to modern times. The choices offered have high validity to world history and thereby add a further element to the value of the test. Part II tests eight sets of dates and events by the system of placing three significant events into one of five time intervals, marked off by five other important events, trends or periods. In this way 24 date elements are measured not by specific dates, which are so apt to be forgotten later, but by their relation to other events and

periods in the course of civilized history. All items in Parts I and II are well spaced throughout history, are well chosen for their importance, and place reasonable emphasis upon the social and cultural development of man rather than upon political events alone. The arrangement of Parts I and II should tell the instructor not only how much a student knows of the items tested but also indicates where the learning or teaching has been weak; they test whether or not the student knows by whom and when history was made, and whether or not he is acquainted with historical terminology. This is a very important point for prospective users of this test to keep in mind.

Part III, Historical Judgment, is tested by 47 5-choice questions. These items are more semifactual on matters of cause and result than on pure judgment, but they are none the less valuable by increasing the scope of measurement and the validity and the reliability of the test.

In criticism it may be said that the test is a little light on the more recent period of history, and makes no effort to test the place of United States history in the development of world history—which may or may not be a disadvantage depending upon how the students to be tested have been taught.

The test is a 90-minute test of 185 questions, which is a sufficient sampling to measure one field. The test is arranged so that the raw scores may be corrected for chance or guess answers, and a table for conversion to "scaled scores" is provided whereby relative marks on this test may be compared with relative scores in other subjects when measured by other tests in this series. The high diagnostic value of the test within the subject tested is thereby augmented by a diagnostic tool as between subjects.

The validity and reliability of the test has been worked out with a sufficient number of cases to make it worth while. Excellent tables of norms by both grades and geographic areas are provided. Thus a student's score can be compared with those of his fellow students, and the class as a whole can be matched against the achievement of other classes.

All told this is a good test, and compares very well with other Cooperative tests which the reviewer has used with good success (the reviewer has not used this test).

For a review by R. M. Tryon, see 1017.

[1637]
Ely-King Interpretation Tests in American History. Grades 7-8; 1929; 2 forms; $1.50 per 25; 15¢ per specimen set; nontimed; Lena A. Ely and Edith King; Los Angeles, Calif.; California Test Bureau.

Clinton C. Conrad, Lecturer in Education and Associate Director of Practice Teaching, The University of California; and Vice-Principal of the University High School, Oakland, California. This test is prepared in two forms. It is designed "to test pupils' ability to interpret meanings and evaluate historical situations." Its content includes "civic attitudes, appreciations, interpretations, and a minimum of merely factual response"; it is "not related to any given text, but contains materials suited to standard eighth grade courses in American History." These quotations are taken from the leaflet describing the tests.

Norms for the test in its two forms were obtained by giving over one thousand tests in different schools to 500 pupils at the end of the eighth grade. No evidence of the reliability of the test is adduced. No time limit is set for the test, save in the instruction, "Sufficient time should be allowed for most of the pupils to finish all of the exercises."

Each form of the test provides 75 opportunities for response to multiple-choice (including true-false), matching, and completion questions. In about half the exercises simple causal and temporal relationships are to be defined by the pupil. "Civic attitude" presumably is displayed in the pupil's choice of reasons for voting against a candidate for school office whose qualifications are set forth in a rather naive problem question.

To the reviewer's mind, this test places a premium upon the pupil's recall of a list of standardized facts and equally standardized relationships. Some of the latter seem unduly simplified; thus the sinking of the Lusitania is given as the cause of America's (sic) entering the World War. The political aspects of history are heavily weighted in nine of the eleven sections of the test.

The test may have limited usefulness in "standard eighth-grade courses in American History" to ascertain whether pupils have achieved standard results.

Edgar B. Wesley, Professor of Education, The University of Minnesota. This test was copyrighted in 1929. If one were to judge by its shortcomings, one would estimate its date

as even earlier. The parts are not numbered; eight items constitute a true-false section; matching exercises involve only two possible answers; the cloudy device of cause-effect is tried; the true-false technique is applied to guessing as to which of two events occurred first; the word "always" appears in a true-false item; and a student problem situation is presented to call forth the proper attitudes. Altogether the prospective test user has a right to be discouraged; he may even be justified in resenting the continuation of tests which perpetuate the faults that could have been eliminated even ten years ago. Unless this test is revised it should be dropped from further consideration.

[1638]
Information Tests in American History. Grades 7-12 and teachers colleges; [1932]; 2 forms; 75¢ per 25; 20¢ per specimen set; nontimed (35) minutes; A. S. Barr and C. J. Daggett; Minneapolis, Minn.: Educational Test Bureau, Inc.

Roy A. Price, Dual Professor of Social Science and Education, Syracuse University. This test is available in two forms. Each form is composed of six subtests: 1, historical terms in contexts; 2, importance of events; 3, men-event relationship; 4, chronological facts; 5, causal relations; and 6, present-day problem relationships.

Although labeled *Information Tests in American History*, it is intended to measure not only information but also certain skills. For example, success in Test 1, Historical Terms in Contexts, depends more upon the ability to read and interpret verbal symbols than upon accumulated information about American history or the particular meaning of certain terms used.

No evidence of the validity or reliability of these tests is presented which is a serious hardship to those who would interpret the test scores. The percentile scores for junior high school, senior high school, and college levels are low. The relatively low achievement on the tests may be due to lack of objectivity in scoring. For example, in one item the student is expected to judge the "event which has been of the greatest importance in the political history of the United States," as among: the annexation of Texas, the Webster-Hayne debate, the Constitutional Convention, the Alien and Sedition Acts, and the first presidential election. The scoring key indicates that the annexation of Texas is the correct answer. It is understandable that some may have chosen the Constitutional Convention. In regard to Part I of the test, the same criticism holds true, i.e., that a board of experts would almost certainly disagree with several answers which are indicated as correct.

A number of the test items are based on insignificant events, and the wording of other items is confusing. The number of items included (55 on each form) is not sufficient to provide an adequate sampling of a student's knowledge of the field, and study of the items which are included leads one to question their validity in terms of measuring knowledge of significant phases of American development. However, the authors do point out that in addition to the use of a study on objectives of American history teaching by Miller, the "curricular validity is based on an analysis of over ten thousand examination questions in American History, gathered from all parts of the United States."

[1639]

Kansas American History Test. First, second semesters: high school and college; 2 forms, 2 levels; 50¢ per 25; 15¢ per specimen set; 40(45) minutes; Arthur Hartung, H. E. Schrammel, and C. Stewart; Emporia, Kan.: Bureau of Educational Measurements, Kansas State Teachers College.
a) TEST I. First semester.
b) TEST II. Second semester.

Wilbur F. Murra, Executive Secretary, National Council for the Social Studies, Washington, D. C. This is a test of slightly better than mediocre quality intended for measuring general achievement in the conventional senior high school American history course. It is published in two parts: Test I, covering the years before 1830, may be used at the end of the first semester; Test II covers the full range of American history with emphasis on the last century. Each test is available in alternate forms of supposedly equal difficulty. This latter feature commends itself as a distinctive advantage which does not pertain to many other tests in this field.

Each form of each test consists of 150 objective items, 75 true-false, 25 reverse multiple-choice, 35 matching, and 15 chronological order. The high proportion of true-false items is a serious shortcoming, this form being notoriously ill-adapted to testing understanding in any of the social studies. The complete absence of the best-answer form is equally to be deplored, as this form is certainly the most generally useful of all test forms in the social studies and has several distinctive advantages. The reverse multiple-choice form (in which the testee selects the one of four choices which is wrong), on the other hand, has peculiar advantages and it is well utilized in the Kansas tests, whereas few other history tests have as yet made use of it. The chronology items are also good, avoiding as they do the pitfalls which so commonly beset items of this kind. The first matching exercise is very poor: it is too long (20 choices to be made from among 31 alternatives), and it lacks homogeneity of both content and grammatical form.

Perhaps the most critical weakness of the test as a whole is the generally poor phrasing of the individual items. Frequently found, especially in the true-false items, are: phrases with ambiguous or elastic meaning, pat phrases and rhetorical expressions, grammatical inconsistency, needless negative statements. To be sure, a majority of the items are free from these technical objections, freer than three-fourths of all teacher-made tests, but not so free as a test published in 1938 should be. Certainly, the defects that appear reduce the reliability of the tests—to what extent it is impossible to say. The test manual states that "preliminary studies . . . yielded reliability coefficients between .75 and .90." If the true reliability of the test is near the lower end of this range, it is *too low* for a test which is 150 items in length.

As compared with such admirable instruments as the American history tests published by the Cooperative Test Service and those published for use in or by the Iowa Every-Pupil High School Testing Programs, the Kansas test will reward pupils more for their memorized verbalisms, less for their reasoned understanding. As compared with published tests in this field other than those mentioned, however, the Kansas test is clearly well above the average in this regard. The sequence of items within each section is in accordance with chronological order of content rather than the preferable order of increasing difficulty of items. The format is annoyingly, but not critically, crowded. For many teachers, this defect may be compensated for in the resulting economy.

Percentile norms are provided for each part of the test. Based on 10,451 pupil scores from 364 schools, these norms should aid materially in the interpretation of results.

Kansas Modern European History: Test II. High School; 1938; 1 form; 50¢ per 25; 15¢ per specimen set; 40(45) minutes; Alvin L. Hasenbank and H. E. Schrammel; Emporia, Kan.: Bureau of Educational Measurements, Kansas State Teachers College.

Clinton C. Conrad, Lecturer in Education and Associate Director of Practice Teaching, The University of California; and Vice-Principal of the University High School, Oakland, California. This test is designed to measure "the student's understanding of significant movements and events in relation to their social and economic consequences." It is intended for use in high schools and colleges which offer a one-year course in this subject. Form A, the only form now available, covers the period from the French Revolution to the present time. The items in the test were selected "from the basic content of several leading textbooks," and were validated by history teachers and supervisors and specialists in test construction. Percentile norms have been computed from 694 student scores. No evidence is given on the test's reliability.

The test is composed of three parts, made up respectively of 100 true-false, 30 multiple-choice, and 15 matching items. The inclusion of so many true-false questions is of course open to criticism. Some of the items are poorly worded (e.g., "Subjecting of races has been one of the chief troubles of the Balkan regions"); and in several (e.g., "Great Britain has always permitted workers to organize unions and to call strikes"), specific determiners aid the student in his choice of responses. The choice of items seems haphazard, rather than derived from the thoughtful study of the purposes and content of a well-planned course.

The validity of the test is open to serious question, for examination of the items shows a heavy stress upon the student's ability to respond correctly to items which measure only his knowledge of factual information, such as: (a) "Russia is the largest contiguous territory in the world under one flag"; (b) "Russia was defeated in the Crimean War"; (c) "Norway and Sweden separated peacefully in 1905"; and (d) "The Treaty of Versailles was drawn up in the year: (1) 1917 (2) 1919 (3) 1925 (4) 1922." Whatever the authors' avowed purpose, this is evidently a test of historical information which can hardly provide valid evidence of the student's "understanding of sig-

nificant movements and events in relation to their social and economic consequences."

Taylor-Schrammel World History Test. First, second semesters: high school; 1936; 2 forms, 2 levels; 50¢ per 25; 15¢ per specimen set; 40(45) minutes; Wallace Taylor and H. E. Schrammel; Emporia, Kan.: Bureau of Educational Measurements, Kansas State Teachers College.
a) TEST I. First semester.
b) TEST II. Second semester.

J. R. Gerberich, Director of the Bureau of Educational Research and Statistical Service and Associate Professor of Education, University of Connecticut. This test, intended for use as a measure of achievement in one-year World History courses, provides Test I for the period from prehistoric man to the uprisings of 1820 and Test II for the period from 1820 to the present. These two tests, according to the authors, essentially cover the content of the first and second semesters of a typical course in the subject.

Users of this test are largely left to draw their own conclusions concerning test validity and reliability, the sole statement concerning these important criteria, contained in the one-sheet, mimeographed Manual of Directions, being that, "The test items were selected from the basic content of several leading textbooks in the field. All items were carefully checked by history teachers and supervisors and by test construction specialists."

The test format is not good, for the type is small and the print is crowded. The directions are consistently in error in using "parenthesis" where "parentheses" should be used. Punctuation is sufficiently in error in occasional items to change the literal meaning from what appears to be the intended meaning. The sample for Part II of all tests gives a three-response multiple-choice item in which one of the three alternatives is ruled out by the application of grammatical principles, for "education" does not correctly follow the indefinite article "a."

Pupils are allowed to draw their own conclusions concerning whether or not to guess on true-false sections, yet those parts are scored without correction for chance. Alternatives in multiple-choice sections vary in number from three to five for different items in at least one of the tests. The matching test sets are unbalanced and use items of such mixed categories that intelligence can well be applied to them in such manner that a tremendously better-than-chance result would be obtained without knowledge concerning content, and in some cases start at the bottom of one column and finish at the top of the other column on the page.

Percentile norms are based on 10,261 pupils from 412 schools which cooperated in four nation-wide programs, presumably those administered by the Bureau of Educational Measurements, Kansas State Teachers College of Emporia.

Despite the weaknesses of these tests, some of which are pointed out above, the test items themselves appear to be superior to the general impression obtained from an examination of the tests. In the main, the items do, as the authors point out, place emphasis upon the "cultural and social phases of history." Vocabulary, concepts, dates, persons, events, and movements of historical significance are covered. There seems to be a considerable over-weighting of items from contemporary history in Test II, and occasional items are no longer pertinent.

All tests are timed for 40 minutes, yet Test II consists of 136 items as compared with 77 items for Test I. Part IV of Test II consists of items of a type not found in Test I and probably requiring more time expenditure on the part of the pupil than most of the other item types in either test. It would seem that Test II should have a time allowance from 50 to 75 per cent greater than that for Test I.

It is unfortunate that the authors have not exerted more care in the mechanical and technical setup of the test, that they have not provided adequate evidence concerning its validity and reliability, and that they have not provided more comprehensive and meaningful norms, for the test items themselves appear to be so constructed that they could be made the foundation for a much more satisfactory test of achievement in world history than the authors have published.

[1642]

Test of Factual Relations in American History.
Grades 10-12; 1936; 2 forms; 25¢ per specimen set; nontimed (100) minutes; Eugene S. Farley; Minneapolis, Minn.: Educational Test Bureau, Inc.
a) PERIOD I, 1000 TO 1763. 45¢ per 25; (15) minutes.
b) PERIOD II, 1763 TO 1783. 45¢ per 25; (10) minutes.
c) PERIOD III, 1783 TO 1840. 65¢ per 25; (25) minutes.
d) PERIOD IV, 1840 TO 1865. 45¢ per 25; (15) minutes.
e) PERIOD V, 1865 TO 1898. 45¢ per 25; (15) minutes.
f) PERIOD VI, 1898 TO 1930. 45¢ per 25; (20) minutes.

REFERENCES

1 FARLEY, EUGENE S. *A Test of Factual Relations in American History.* Unpublished doctor's thesis, University of Pennsylvania, 1934.

Robert E. Keohane, Instructor in Social Studies, The College, The University of Chicago. This test attempts "to measure relationships rather than isolated facts" for sixty topics in United States history to 1930. The topics used were selected by the so-called "objective" method of studying 7,000 examination questions used by teachers of United States history. Consequently, while the test may fairly represent the content of the more traditional courses, it is not well adapted to the needs of schools in which social and cultural history are strongly emphasized.

The pupil is expected to recognize the following items for each abstract topic: (a) a cause or purpose, (b) a fact or detail, (c) an effect or result, and (d) a related event. Historical personages are to be linked with (a) principles or significant facts, (b) position or occupation, (c) outstanding achievement, and (d) a related event. The topics are listed in groups of three. Five or six choices are offered in each of the four given categories. The pupil marks the number of the topic under the letter in front of the one correct answer in each category. In the reviewer's opinion, provision of a separate answer sheet for each pupil would combine economy with ease in scoring.

In a test such as this, oversimplification is perhaps to some extent unavoidable. The extremely complex character of historical causation is obscured, and the selection of *one* preceding condition as *a* cause is easily converted, in the pupil's mind, to its pre-eminence and *the* one true cause.

Failure to define rigidly "causes," "facts," and "related events," or at least to apply such definitions, results in a lack of consistency among the items placed in each category. Some of the topics are too general and others are poorly stated. A good verbal memory rather than real understanding is promoted by the use of slogans and conventional labels. There are several errors in spelling which careful proofreading would have corrected. In a very few cases two or more answers are equally correct, though usually the test secures rather fine discrimination between the one correct answer and the others which are good distractors. Some material of no real significance for understanding is included, and certain inaccuracies of fact and interpretation would call forth the criticism of subject specialists.

In spite of these serious drawbacks, this test may be useful in conventional courses in United States history, preferably in the senior high school (though the T-scores given are for twelve-year-old children). Often the correct answering of a question requires fine discrimination and a rather detailed fund of information, so much so, in fact, that the test often appears to test more for the latter than for the wider relationships involved. Use of this test will doubtless stimulate teachers to revise their own means of measuring such factual relationships as seem most important to them and may encourage the author to revise his work to meet legitimate criticisms.

For a review by Wilbur F. Murra, see 1024.

SOCIAL STUDIES — THIRD MMY

REVIEWS BY *Dorothy C. Adkins, Howard R. Anderson, Harry D. Berg, W. H. Cartwright, Robert A. Davis, Elaine Forsyth, J. R. Gerberich, Lavone A. Hanna, C. Robert Pace, Roy A. Price, Edwin H. Reeder, Frederick H. Stutz, Wallace W. Taylor, Agatha Townsend, Marguerite Uttley, Edgar B. Wesley, Ray G. Wood.*

[590]

★American History—Government—Problems of Democracy: Acorn Achievement Tests. Grades 9-16; 1942–44; Forms A, B; $2.00 per 25; 15¢ per specimen set; 40(45) minutes; Vincent McGarrett; Acorn Publishing Co.

Howard R. Anderson, Specialist for Social Sciences, U. S. Office of Education, Washington, D. C. Each form of this test includes 100 four-response multiple-choice questions grouped under five section headings: Part I, Growth of a National Spirit; Part II, The Growth of Democracy; Part III, The Constitution; Part IV, Foreign Policy; and Part V, Problems of Democracy. The author is Mr. Vincent McGarrett, Chairman, Social Studies, Andrew Jackson High School, New York City.

The following purposes of this test are given in the Teachers' Guide: "(1) to measure . . . mastery of the content of standard courses in American History, Government and Problems, (2) to indicate those areas . . . in which remedial teaching may be necessary, (3) to test the student's grasp of the bases of America's democratic way of life, and (4) to measure the student's ability to make sound inferences based on the relationships among historical personages and events."

The author, in discussing validity, states, "In the preparation of the test fifty or more items were evaluated for each section . . . The events measured . . . are common to American history syllabi in all sections of the United States. . . . The results correspond very closely to those obtained in the American History examination given by the University of the State of New York. The administration of this test in advance of official (Regents'?) examinations in American History will reveal with high fidelity those students who . . . will pass or fail. . . ."

The Teachers' Guide gives the reliability coefficient of the test as .94 when "obtained by the odd and even scores and the Spearman-Brown formula." On the class record form norms are provided on a month by month basis for grades 8 to 14. Norms for the five parts of the test are also provided for grades 9 to 14. These norms "are based on trials which included 5,120 students in various sections . . ."

This reviewer doubts that this test can be considered a satisfactory test for "standard courses in American History, Government and Problems." In some states these courses are fused in a two-year sequence in grades 11 and 12, but in other states the practice is to allocate two, one, and two semesters, respectively, to the three courses in question. This reviewer would classify 60 items as primarily American history (Parts I, II, and IV) and 20 items each as government (Part III) and problems of democracy (Part V).

The forms need revision to eliminate "dated" items, such as "An outspoken supporter of American aid to democracies at war with aggressor nations" and "The chief purpose of the United States in fighting the Axis."

The right answer to some of the questions is difficult to determine: "The Latin American nations which hesitated the longest to join the Axis are: (a) Brazil and Uruguay, (o) Mexico and Guatemala, (e) Argentina and Chile, (c) Peru and Colombia" and "Which of these is generally *not* a cause for crime? (f) the automobile, (k) divorce, (c) poverty (i) vocational training."

The peculiar sequence of letters in the responses to test items results from the fact that pupils are told to underline the right response to each item and the teacher is given a "code word" to help him score the tests quickly.

[591]

★Cooperative Community Affairs Test. Grades 9-12; 1941; Form R; $1.75 per 25; 25¢ per specimen set, postpaid; 30(35) minutes; Roy A. Price and Robert F. Steadman; Cooperative Test Service.

REFERENCES

1. PRICE, ROY A., AND STEADMAN, ROBERT F. Part 8, "Testing for Community Information," pp. 213-25. In *Utilization of Community Resources in the Social Studies.* Ninth Yearbook of the National Council for the Social Studies. Washington, D. C.: the Council, 1938. Pp. 229. Paper. $2.00. *

W. H. Cartwright, Assistant Professor of Education, Boston University, Boston, Massachusetts. This test deserves to be widely used. It is suited for use in any community. It is particularly adaptable to courses in community civics but can well be used in local history, American history, modern problems, or any other courses in the social studies curriculum

in which special attention is given to community study.

The test consists of 40 multiple-choice and 40 modified true-false items. The publishers provide no information regarding the validity or reliability of the test.

The items call for specific information about many phases of the community, including geography, government, population make-up, employment, health, welfare, etc. Since the answers vary from community to community, they are not to be found in ordinary textbooks. Hence, neither scoring keys nor norms are available. This means that the teacher will have to construct his own key to fit his own community. While constructing a key will require some effort, it should not tax the teacher who is giving adequate treatment to community affairs. This local adaptation will probably lend more validity to the test for use in the local situation. In those cases where making a key does prove a burden to the teacher, the experience gained should make him aware of the potential value of the community as a source of curricular material.

The test was originally prepared in connection with the Regents Inquiry into the Cost and Character of Public Education in New York State but has since been revised to make it suitable for use anywhere in the country. An account of the circumstances surrounding its original construction, as well as a very helpful discussion of the problems involved in testing for community information, may be found in the Ninth Yearbook of the National Council for the Social Studies (1).

J. R. Gerberich, Director, Bureau of Educational Research and Service, and Professor of Education, University of Connecticut, Storrs, Connecticut. The *Cooperative Community Affairs Test* is the only standardized test of its type known to the reviewer. No scoring key is supplied, for correct answers to its recognition items necessarily depend upon such factors as the location of the community, its population, its cultural offerings, its crime rate, and other local characteristics. Individual differences are probably as great among communities as among human beings, so no scaled scores and consequently no norms are or conceivably could be provided. Part I consists of 40 four-response multiple-choice items and Part II includes 40 items requesting yes, no, or indeterminate answers. The scoring formula of $R - \frac{W}{3}$ for the entire 80 items appears slightly, although not seriously, to overcorrect for chance. The test format is excellent.

Items in Part I deal primarily with such characteristics of the community as its settlement, source of name, location, climate, elevation, and water supply; such population factors as its size, geographical origins, occupational pursuits, family size, age, illiteracy, and birth and mortality rates; such cultural factors as newspapers, recreational areas, library loans, churches, and school costs; such financial characteristics as wages, total incomes, and rental rates; and such crime indices as traffic violations, reasons for arrests, and juvenile delinquency. Responses are well chosen and appear to provide for any degree of community eccentricity in their scope.

In Part II, 6 grouped items deal with laws or rules governing the people; 3 grouped items deal with their activities; 19 items in three groups are variously concerned with community institutions, practices, and services; 4 items in a sixth group compare incomes and taxes of today with those of five years ago; and 8 items in a seventh group compare the community with the United States in general. A very few items in this part appear unlikely to function well in both large urban and rural communities, such as those dealing with farmers' incomes and laws concerning factory sanitation. Although provision is made for responses to groups of items which do not apply to the individual community, no unambiguous way of responding to such scattered items as the above is evident. Complete disregard for these few items in the scoring in those communities where they seem inapplicable would have no more serious effect than to reduce the total scoring points by a small number, however.

It seems possible to the reviewer that the test fails to include certain rather important criteria of community culture about which high school pupils might be expected to have knowledge and understanding. Among these are book ownership and magazine subscriptions, telephones, bathtubs, radios, etc., in the home. It may be, however, that the limitation of pupil experience to homes essentially at one economic or social level would to some degree invalidate such items. It is possible also that certain types of individual differences, such as sex and occupational, might advantageously receive somewhat more emphasis.

The reviewer is impressed with the values to be obtained from the use of this instrument with high school pupils as a measuring instrument, as a teaching device, or both. Its validity for measuring knowledge and understanding of one's community seems evident. Furthermore, the test demands upon the part of some school official in any community which uses it a worth-while experience in the development of community understanding, for it would be a rare individual indeed who could correctly key the test for his community without rather extensive research.

Lavone A. Hanna, Associate Professor of Education, San Francisco State College, San Francisco, California. This test consists of two parts. The 40 items in Part I are of the multiple-choice type as, for example, "The average annual family income in my community is ( ) less than $600, ( ) $600 to $1200, ( ) $1200 to $2000, ( ) $2000 or more." Part II consists of seven incomplete statements followed by several clauses or phrases, each of which is to be checked according to whether it is correct (Y), incorrect (N), or very doubtful or unknown (?).

The test was originally constructed to be used in the New York Regents' Inquiry and was revised to make it suitable for nation-wide use. The questions call chiefly for factual information about a community, and some of the items need to be revised in light of recent trends in employment and living costs. The test has value as a teaching device in introducing a unit on community life or as an end-test at the close of such a unit. No key is supplied, as the answers depend upon the local community.

No statistical data as to the reliability or validity of the test are given, and there are no norms or scaled scores. Although it is intended that the answers be written in the test booklet, standard answer sheets could be used if machine scoring is preferred.

[592]

★Cooperative Social Studies Test for Grades 7, 8, and 9. Grades 7-9; 1941-47; IBM; Forms R, S, X; separate answer sheets need not be used; $2 per 25; 25¢ per specimen set, postpaid; 40¢ per 25 machine-scorable answer sheets; 15¢ per stencil for scoring answer sheets; 80(85) minutes; Form R: Agatha Townsend and Mary Willis; Form S: Mary Willis; Form X: Harry D. Berg and Elaine Forsyth; Cooperative Test Service.

,Robert A. Davis, Professor of Education, University of Colorado, Boulder, Colorado. [Review of Forms R and S.] The purpose of this test is to provide a survey of the pupil's information and knowledge in the broad field of the social sciences. Where the maturity of the student permits, the test provides a convenient and valid measure of his background of information and knowledge in this field.

Form R consists of three parts: Part I, Facts, Skills, and Applications; Part II, Terms and Concepts; and Part III, Comprehension and Interpretation. The total time for administration is 80 minutes distributed as follows: Part I, 40 minutes; Part II, 15 minutes; and Part III, 25 minutes. Form S, published one year later, is similarly constructed but differs slightly in that Part I is labeled Informational Background. This form consists of the same number of items and the same time allotments.

The items are of the multiple-choice non-reasoning type. Almost all items deal with the problem of measuring information which the learner has obtained from a wide range of source materials and experiences. Historical materials are made more realistic by occasional pictures and graphs, on the basis of which the learner selects a response appropriate to the illustrative matter presented. The materials for the test were gleaned from a wide variety of sources by members of the testing committee.

Range of scores is wide and results tend to follow a normal distribution. The test, however, is too difficult for some pupils, as shown by the relatively small percentage of questions answered by groups used in the standardizing process. Typical seventh grade students, for example, answered correctly about one question in four; ninth grade students answered approximately 44 per cent.

The test places a premium on speed. There are 150 items. The typical junior high school pupil needs approximately a third of his time to read the test. Owing to the difficulty of the material and the premium placed on speed, some seventh and eighth grade pupils may find the test too difficult. For the ninth grade, however, the test is more appropriate. The manual provides no information regarding validity on the basis of detailed item analysis. Reliability coefficients are not given, but the large number of items should assure high coefficients, particularly for the entire test.

Norms are based on approximately 5,000

junior high school pupils. Scoring is objective and scores are corrected for chance. Items may be answered either on the test booklet or on the answer sheet, which may be scored by machine. The use of the answer sheet is recommended since the scoring key for the test booklet is somewhat cumbersome. Raw scores may be converted to scaled scores. Percentile scores for individual students insure easy interpretation.

Edgar B. Wesley, Professor of Education, University of Minnesota, Minneapolis, Minnesota. [Review of Forms R and S.] These tests each consist of 150 items, 75 being devoted to information, 45 to terms, and 30 to comprehension. All items are of the multiple-choice type with five options in each. Both forms make use of maps, charts, and other illustrative material, thus insuring a high degree of accuracy in testing the skills required in interpreting such graphic devices. Somewhat curiously, the questions relating to the use of these graphic materials appear in the section on information rather than under comprehension and interpretation where they would seem to belong.

The first parts, devoted to information, deal for the most part with significant matters; the second sections are clear identifications of words; and the third sections are primarily reading items. Parts I and III are needlessly wordy and even Part II could be condensed and thereby enhance its clarity. In fact, wordiness is a burden to the pupils, a time consumer, and a bar to simple, direct measurement.

In Form R, Item 75 is unfortunate in its implications, for it refers to "free" camping grounds in our national parks, whereas any one who has ever been to one must have marveled at the high charge for admission. Item 68 underscores the false connotation of the word "true." The authors obviously meant "accurate." Option 4, assuming a good critical author, is of course the best answer, but the testmaker keyed option 3. In Part II, Item 8 perpetuates the confusing and needless word "barter," which in spite of all pedagogical efforts is and will stay dead.

In Form S, Item 9 asks how most Americans made their living in 1840. It is a pointless question from the standpoint of achievement; it might have validity in an intelligence test. Item 48 is probably correct, but it implies that city voters have access to information about candidates, an assumption that is contrary to fact. In Part II, Item 3, the phrase "freedom of the press" is inadequately if not erroneously defined. The phrase historically and legally refers to freedom from govermental restraint. Item 15 contains a curious reference to a primitive country as one that has not developed "its" civilization or industries, implying that civilization is there like a mineral ready to be exploited. Item 38 says the King of England is the "sovereign" and so he is, but the "prime minister," which is one of the options, exercises sovereignty. The item is unfortunate in its teaching if it teaches anything.

In spite of these minor criticisms, however, both forms of this test are excellent. They deserve wide use, for they are vastly superior to the typical test devised by the classroom teacher.

[593]
Illinois Teachers College Cooperative Social Science Test, 1942 Edition. College; 1938–42; 1 form; 10-99 copies, 7½¢ per test; 10¢ per single copy; 15¢ per manual, postpaid; 40(45) minutes; John A. Kinneman and Clarence Orr; McKnight & McKnight.

Harry D. Berg, Assistant Professor, Board of Examinations, Michigan State College, East Lansing, Michigan. This test "has been developed as the result of a need for a comprehensive test in the social sciences which can be administered within a reasonable period of time. . . . The test should prove helpful to teachers in senior high schools and to instructors of college freshmen classes who want to make an evaluation of student accomplishments." This is the rather vague fashion in which the publication of this particular test is justified. Whatever may be the express or implied purpose, about the best that can be said of the test is that it can be "administered within a reasonable period of time." Apparently the examination is intended to serve as a measure of general proficiency in the social sciences and as a placement device. If so, it is this reviewer's belief that it falls far short of its purpose. For the most part the test is made up of highly factual "popgun" matching and multiple-choice items which have been drawn with no apparent plan from the fields of government, economics, and history. The item "The last religious rites for the dying Catholic is: a. baptism b. celibacy c. Holy Eucharist d. extreme unction" is typical. Many of the items violate the most elementary rules of test construction, particularly those with regard to clues,

verbalism, and homogeneity of foils. The whole test gives evidence of hasty construction. This is evident even in the matter of proofreading—at least it would be kindness to account for the spelling of "counterfeiting" as "counterfitting" in this manner.

The test is divided into several parts, namely: definition of terms, classification of names, sequence of events, recognition of facts, number relationships, identification of persons, and identification of terms. Such a classification of items is of little value for diagnostic purposes since the nature of the content covered in each classification is basically similar. The authors state that "the validity of the items and the reliability of the test have been determined by the chance-halves techniques." The reliability of the test is .94 but how the validity of the test can be determined in this manner and what it is are obviously not explained. Before purchasing a test for this intended purpose it would be well for the prospective user to examine the generally superior Cooperative Test Service tests.

[594]
Social Studies Test: National Achievement Tests. Grades 4-6, 7-9; 1937–45; Forms A, B; $1.75 per 25; 15¢ per specimen set; 35(40) minutes; Robert K. Speer and Samuel Smith; Acorn Publishing Co.

Ray G. Wood, Director, Ohio Scholarship Tests and Instructional Research, State Department of Education, Columbus, Ohio. Since no manual accompanies this test, little or no information is had on the method of validation, reliability, or the specific purpose this test is to serve.

GRADES 4-6. The items of the two forms are apparently parallel, measuring the same functions. The norms, which are only the medians of the total scores, are reported for each month for grades 3.1 through 8.1.

These medians give helpful data for intergrade comparison of the total scores, but this reviewer believes that this test would be much more useful if norms were available for each of the five parts of this test and if several percentile values were given.

Part I, Human Relations, Part II, Life Situations, and Part III, Social Problems, test the student's attitude on several basic social problems by thought-type questions, while other general information is tested by objective-fact items. The results on these three parts of the test will depend largely upon the background students have in the fundamental principles of good citizenship. For example, a typical item of Part I is: "The right of free speech (i) means the right to insult the President (o) permits citizens to express political opinions (q) belongs only to labor unions." The pupils' reaction to this type of item will be governed by his sense of propriety as well as by his concept of the place and use of free speech in a democracy. A citizen will not necessarily be fined or jailed if he "insults the President," since there is no law against such action. The accepted principle of respect for the chief executive of these United States would be the basis for the individual's reactions to such items. A typical item of Part II is: "Clothing that keeps one warm in winter climates is usually made of (m) silk (z) cotton (t) wool." The validity of this type of item in a social studies test, standardized on a nation-wide scale, is questionable since it is purely factual. If a pupil lives in a *warm* winter climate, he may give "silk" or "cotton" for the answer and be correct as governed by his environment. The answer "wool" which is the one expected will be given by those who live in a cold winter climate.

Part IV, Products and Peoples, and Part V, The Meaning of Events, are made up of information items on political geography, history, and the Constitution.

Both forms of this test are scored by one key word. This is a unique scoring technique, but it could easily destroy the validity of the test results if pupils obtain this "key word."

GRADES 7-9. The objectives tested are: Part I, Human Relations; Part II, Life Situations: Part III, Social Interpretations; Part IV, Value of Products; Part V, Social Ideas; and Part VI, Miscellaneous Facts.

It is noted that the objectives tested in Parts I and II are the same as those tested in Parts I and II of the test for grades 4-6. The number and sampling of items for these two parts of this test and those for the lower grades are neither parallel nor comparable. If the two tests would have been parallel for these important objectives, growth or changes in ideals, attitudes, and information of pupils in the higher grades could have been compared with those of pupils in the lower grades in the particular community or area being tested.

An achievement test must be evaluated not only in terms of breadth of content, but it should also be judged by the kind of reaction

students make in answering the test items. While many of the items of this test evaluate the students' reaction to fundamental social concepts, many are limited to simple recall. For example, Item 7, Part I, Form B reads: "Among the following, the country that depends most upon its colonies for raw materials is (f) Poland, (g) United States, (o) England, (w) Turkey." By process of elimination and the knowledge that England has a great merchant marine, the student would be able to answer this item. Item II, Part VI, Form A, reads: "A great rubber product manufacturing city is (o) Cleveland, (a) Akron, (q) Pittsburgh, (u) Denver." These are typical of some of the rather superficial items appearing in the two forms of this achievement test.

Typical of the items of this test that test for broader social concepts is Item 8, Part II, Form A, which reads: "When discussing social problems with a friend, you should consider his ideas liberal if he (b) wishes mainly to preserve the status quo (things as they are), (t) advocates the wider distribution of wealth, (z) wishes to give people jobs because of their race or religion, (p) attacks the right to strike and defends the right to work." The student's reaction to this type of social studies item is much more meaningful for interpretation of a social consciousness than being able to recall the name of a "great rubber products manufacturing city."

Five of the six parts of this test are scored with one key word. This is an easy way to make and provide a key, but it would be disastrous to the validity of the results were the students to get information on this key word.

[595]
★Stanford Achievement Test: Social Studies Tests. Grades 4-9; 1940-42; an adaptation of the social studies sections of the *Stanford Achievement Test;* IBM; Forms DM, EM; separate answer sheets must be used; $1.90 per 25; 70¢ per 25 machine-scorable answer sheets; 20¢ per key; 35¢ per specimen set, postpaid; 30(35) minutes; Truman L. Kelley, Giles M. Ruch, and Lewis M. Terman; World Book Co.

Ray G. Wood, Director, Ohio Scholarship Tests and Instructional Research, State Department of Education, Columbus, Ohio. These tests are carefully constructed examinations and represent much time and thought on the part of the authors. Forms DM and EM are machine-scorable revisions of the social studies tests in the *Stanford Achievement Tests,* Forms D and E. The authors have spared no effort in studying results of administering Forms D and E and in revising them on the basis of the data obtained. Forms DM and EM are among the best social studies tests available, according to this reviewer's judgment.

It does seem, however, that Forms DM and EM would be of more use to the social studies teacher and the pupil concerned if the items of these forms were organized under specific objectives rather than in the present "scrambled" form. It would be better to have Test I, History, and Test II, Geography, deal specifically with history and geography respectively and then to have a Test III, General Social Studies, covering the other areas of the social studies rather than to have the items of these general social subjects interspersed within the two special subjects. This would necessitate scaling the items by specific objectives rather than by the test as a whole.

The 70 items of each of the two forms of this social studies test represent a sampling of a great amount of information. Most of the items are factual seeking, rather than problem solving or thought provoking. While the items of these two forms have been carefully and excellently selected, a truer and better evaluation of a student's social studies achievement would be had if his reactions to practical, current social problems were tested as fully as his knowledge of the factors requiring "facts and memory."

For reviews by Walter W. Cook and Ralph C. Preston of the entire battery, see 18.

[596]

Test of General Proficiency in the Field of Social Studies: Cooperative General Achievement Tests, Revised Series, Test 1. Grades 10-12 and college entrants; 1942-47; IBM; Forms S, T, X; separate answer sheets need not be used; $2 per 25; 25¢ per specimen set, postpaid; 40¢ per 25 machine-scorable answer sheets; 15¢ per stencil for scoring answer sheets; 40(45) minutes; Forms S and T: Mary Willis, Charlotte W. Croon (Form S), and the Committee on Social Studies Tests of the Educational Records Bureau: Ronald Beasley, Charles K. Cummings, Jr., W. Ainsworth Greene, Margaret Hastings, and Elsie Resor; Form X: Jeanne M. Bradford; Cooperative Test Service.

Harry D. Berg, Assistant Professor, Board of Examinations, Michigan State College, East Lansing, Michigan. [Review of Forms S and T.] The purpose of this particular test is to measure general proficiency in the social studies at the high school and college freshman level for diagnostic and placement purposes.

With this intent in mind it is natural that the publishers should wish to claim that power and the achievement of general objectives in the whole field are measured rather than the acquisition of specific information. The task of constructing such a test is admittedly great because of the problems involved in establishing the nature of aptitude and defining general objectives in the social studies, and then constructing items which will test for these. It is this reviewer's belief that the authors have succeeded reasonably well.

Part I, on terms and concepts, is essentially a test of social studies vocabulary and is drawn from the fields of government, history, economics, and geography. Since any of the items can be easily classified within any one of these fields, one is led to question the claim that general objectives are being tested for. It is true, however, that the selection was carefully made, that textbook definitions have been avoided, and that the terms and concepts are generally those which are useful in the daily life of citizens and for future work in the field of the social studies. It may be of value to know that the items were based on studies made by Kelley and Krey (*Tests and Measurements in the Social Sciences*) and that the difficulty of words was checked by reference to Thorndike's *Teacher's Word Book of Twenty Thousand Words.*

It is evidently in Part II, which deals with comprehension and interpretation, that the authors feel that power or aptitude is being measured. These items are concerned with paragraph comprehension and the interpretation of maps, graphs, and cartoons, and are essentially of a basic skills nature. Pupils are asked to generalize, to discern motives, and to draw conclusions. The items in this part are of the multiple-choice type commonly used for this purpose, but since no provision is made for separate scores on the various skills involved, the diagnostic value of the test is lessened.

As is the case with most Cooperative tests, extensive tryouts were given before the examinations were issued for general use. Norms in terms of percentiles and scaled scores are furnished. These are based on a large number of cases and are differentiated on a basis of high school year-levels so that growth may be measured.

For a review by John V. McQuitty of the complete battery, see 3.

Test of General Proficiency in the Field of Social Studies

ECONOMICS

[597]

Cooperative Economics Test. High school and college; 1939–42; IBM; Forms P, S; separate answer sheets need not be used; $1.75 per 25; 25¢ per specimen set, postpaid; 40¢ per 25 machine-scorable answer sheets; 15¢ per stencil for scoring answer sheets; 40(45) minutes; Form P: H. R. Anderson and J. E. Partington; Form S: Mary Willis; Cooperative Test Service.

For a review by Edgar B. Wesley of an earlier form, see 40:1624.

GEOGRAPHY

[598]

Emporia Geography Test. Grades 4-7; 1937; Forms A, B; 75¢ per 25, postpaid; 15¢ per specimen set, postpaid; 30(35) minutes; H. E. Schrammel, E. J. Calkins, Harold Bechtoldt, Forrest Frease, and LaVerna Wharton; Bureau of Educational Measurements, Kansas State Teachers College of Emporia.

Edwin H. Reeder, Professor of Education, University of Illinois, Urbana, Illinois. The most serious problems in either making or evaluating tests in geography arise from the same unfortunate situation, namely, that there is no agreement among theorists in education or among specialists in geography on the question of what geography is. There are at least three conceptions of the nature of geography which are current either in theory or in practice. The first of these is that the aim of geography is to produce students who know place locations, boundaries, products of countries and some facts about mathematical geography. From classroom observation one might well conclude that this aim is still the most clearly operative of any, although no theorist would accept it today as embodying the most important goals of geography teaching.

The second point of view is that geography is the study of how man and his natural environment are interrelated; in other words, that geography is human ecology. It is probable that this conception is held by the majority of theorists in elementary and secondary education. The third notion is that geography is a study of specific regions from the standpoint of the ways in which geographical factors are operative in them. This view is held by a group of university professors of geography. It denies that there are any general "principles of geography" and maintains that a statement of geographical relationships must always be made in terms of a particular region.

It seems obvious that a testmaker in geography should make a test which will be in harmony with his point of view of what geography is. But when one examines tests in the field, one has the feeling that the testmakers were apparently not clear in their own minds about the nature of the subject or how to test competence in it. That is certainly the case with the *Emporia Geography Test.* In their manual, the authors say, "It includes questions of facts, principles, information, causes and effects, map study, and numerous others."

The test certainly includes many questions of "facts, information and numerous others." In these respects the test is comprehensive, and in the opinion of the reviewer, the test items are well chosen and widely distributed in range of geographical location. The test will, therefore, be helpful to the teacher who wishes to know whether his pupils are acquiring a wide knowledge of place locations and geographical information.

In that sense, therefore, the test is in harmony with the first of the three statements of aims enumerated above, but as has already been noted, this statement of aims is not in line with progressive thinking with respect to the chief goal of geography teaching.

If one may judge from the statement quoted above from the manual of directions, the testmakers accept in part at least the concept of geography as a study of man's interrelationships with his natural environment, for they say that the test "includes map study" and "causes and effects." But the reviewer does not believe that ability in these fields is measured by the test. Certainly the map questions which constitute the first 20 test elements measure map remembering, not map study. No geographical reasoning is required to answer these questions.

With respect to "causes and effects," it would be well to examine a sample of a test item which is apparently designed to test a child's ability to reason. There are a number of these in the largest section of the test which consists of more than 70 true-false statements. Here is a sample, Item 21 from Form B: "A fertile soil makes agriculture the most important industry of New England." Let us suppose that a child marks this correctly as false. What can one conclude about the reason for which he marked it correctly? Was it because he knows that the New England States are in a region of old, worn-down mountains; and because he then reasoned from this fact that agriculture is not a very prosperous industry in such a geographical location? Or was it because he simply remembered that New England is more a manufacturing than an agricultural region? Does this test element test geographical thinking or geographical remembering? The answer is not clear. Since a teacher cannot know why a class of pupils marked a test well or poorly, how can he know what to do about it in his teaching?

A final word may be said which needs no elaboration. Many of the test elements are out of date. For example, Item 103 on Form A reads, "The League of Nations meets in 1. Geneva. 2. London. 3. The Hague. 4. Paris." If the test is to be used today, revisions should be made.

To summarize, if one wishes to know whether the pupils in his class are memorizing a large number of place locations and miscellaneous geographical information, the *Emporia Geography Tests* will be useful. If one wishes to know whether children are attaining the aim of geography which consists in becoming geographical thinkers and reasoners, the test will be of little assistance.

Agatha Townsend, Research Assistant, Educational Records Bureau, New York, New York. This test will probably be found satisfactory for use in schools following a standard curriculum in which geography is studied as a separate subject. The emphasis is on place and physical geography and on factual material in human geography. Only about 15 of the 120 items in Form A call for the application of principles or the exercise of judgment based on inferences from geographical information. In view of this limitation, the test will probably appeal less to schools with a combined social studies program, unless the purpose of testing is to measure acquisition of facts independent of other objectives of the program.

From the more technical standpoint, the test has several advantages. Two comparable forms are available. Public school percentiles for both midyear and end-of-year testing in grades 4 to 7 are provided. The reliabilities reported by the authors indicate that the test should distinguish satisfactorily among groups of pupils, though they are not so high as seems desirable for individual diagnosis.

The date of publication of the test (1937) should not necessarily be taken as evidence that it is too old for use today. In Form A, one item

referring to the League of Nations and one to World War without further identification and in Form B, an item dealing with Alsace-Lorraine are the only questions whose keyed answers might be in some doubt. On the other hand, omission of references to air transportation and similar developments of increasing current significance may put the test more markedly out of line with recent courses of study.

[599]

Fourth Grade Geography Test. Grade 4; 1940; also called *National Council of Geography Teachers Geography Test;* Form A; 8¢ per test; 4¢ per manual; 3¢ per class record sheet; 20¢ per scoring stencils; 30(35) minutes; Zoe A. Thralls, George Miller, and Marguerite Uttley; McKnight & McKnight.

REFERENCES
1. NATIONAL COUNCIL OF GEOGRAPHY TEACHERS, TESTING COMMITTEE. "Fourth Grade Geography Test." *J Geog* 39:269-73 O '40. *

Elaine Forsyth, Assistant Professor of Social Studies, New York State College for Teachers, Albany, New York. The general excellence of this test makes it stand out sharply from many others in the same field. It has an attractive format. The items are varied in type, with yes and no responses or multiple choices with from three to seven foils. Vocabulary is carefully graded. The subject matter tested is common to nine widely used textbooks. Adequate information is given on test reliability, discriminating power of items, and range of difficulty of items. Scoring is done by means of a stencil. Preparation of an answer sheet for machine scoring might increase the usefulness of the test.

The most important aspect of the test to potential users is what it attempts to measure. In contrast to the more usual questions on isolated facts, this test attempts to measure the child's understanding of relationships in the field of natural environmental conditions and in the area of man's reactions to these conditions. It also attempts to measure the child's ability to read maps, to read pictures and text, and to draw reasonable inferences from them.

Because of its centering on common subject matter and generally acceptable objectives, this test should serve as an excellent measure of achievement; because of its careful and thoughtful construction, it should prove especially useful for diagnosis of difficulties.

Agatha Townsend, Research Assistant, Educational Records Bureau, New York, New York. This test seems to have a number of features of format and content to recommend it. The quality of the printing is good. The pictures are clear; and the maps, of good size and well-marked. Schools considering the use of the test should judge it carefully in terms of the objectives of the teaching done in the geography course and in terms of the specific outcomes for which they wish to test. This test will not measure so efficiently as, for example, the *Emporia Geography Test* or the geography section of the *Metropolitan Achievement Test,* the retention of facts of place and physical geography. It is designed to measure the ability of pupils to apply factual knowledge to the interpretation of a reading passage, a picture, or a map. The facts required for the performance of the tasks include knowledge of climatic conditions, identification of the main features of regions of Europe and Africa, and general awareness of the adaptations made by man in living under various climatic and physical conditions. In general, the test seems well designed to measure the aims of most geography teaching included in social studies programs, and the content of the items is appropriate. Some teachers, however, might desire more reference to industrial development and commerce.

The authors report information favorable to the reliability and validity of the test; the selection of questions was based on acceptable techniques of item analysis. A limitation of the usefulness of the test in its present form is the lack of published percentile norms and comparable editions for retesting. In addition, some doubt may be cast on the effectiveness of the test from the point of view of item construction. No correction for guessing is provided, and the inclusion of two-, five-, and seven-choice items in a single total score raises the question of the relative weight which is actually given to each answer.

The general conclusion of this reviewer is that here is a promising test which merits further development. The authors might well give more attention to test construction techniques and attempt to produce forms somewhat more homogeneous as to the types of items included and the response methods used. Further study of the results might also clear up some of the questions which occur to the prospective user: What is the relation between acquisition of factual knowledge and ability to interpret a hypothetical situation? To what extent does this test measure abilities distinct from those measured in a reading comprehension test? Would pupils in a traditional geography class do as well on a test of this sort as pupils following a social studies course?

[600]
Geography Test: National Achievement Tests. Grades 6-8; 1936-39; Forms A, B; $1.50 per 25; 15¢ per specimen set; nontimed (35-45) minutes; Robert K. Speer, Lester D. Crow, and Samuel Smith; Acorn Publishing Co.

Elaine Forsyth, Assistant Professor of Social Studies, New York State College for Teachers, Albany, New York. The purpose of these tests, according to the authors, is "to test the pupil's understanding of geographical ideas and his mastery of facts." Of course, there may be differences in definition of what constitutes a geographic idea, but apparently the authors do not include in geographic ideas any concerning relationships. The items on all four forms require recall of fact. The skill factor is entirely neglected. There are no items requiring use of maps, pictures, graphs, or reading material.

The following comments and illustrations are based on all four forms. In many items the information called for is of questionable value: "In which of these countries do men kiss each other when they meet?" The vocabulary items ask for definitions which may or may not be of geographic importance: dirigible, gyroscope, latex, potash. Other items ask for the uses of ostriches, oysters and elephant tusks and the location of winter sports, ancient ruins, and beautiful paintings. Occasionally questions are so clumsily worded as to be difficult to read: "A country the vast areas of which make it difficult to conquer is ———" Actual errors in fact are promulgated by such a question as this: "Which country in North America is part of Great Britain?" Often incomplete and even incorrect generalizations must be marked by the child in order to answer the question at all.

The tests are scored by key and code word. There are no answer sheets. A table of grade norms is provided, but there is no information as to how it was derived. No information is given on the reliability of the test or the discriminating power of the items.

These tests have little to recommend them unless someone needs a measure of ability to repeat verbatim isolated, fragmentary, meaningless tidbits of information of the quiz-program variety.

Fourth Grade Geography Test

[601]

★Tate Economic Geography Test. Grades 9-16; 1940; Forms A, B; 90¢ per 25, postpaid; 15¢ per specimen set, postpaid; 50(55) minutes; D. J. Tate and G. A. Buzzard; Bureau of Educational Measurements, Kansas State Teachers College of Emporia.

Marguerite Uttley, Associate Professor of Geography, Iowa State Teachers College, Cedar Falls, Iowa. This test is designed for high school and junior college students. Reliability is stated as approximately .90. Percentile norms for the high school level are given, but they are based upon too few cases to be dependable. Form A was given to 259 students in 17 high schools, and Form B, to 145 in 11 high schools. The year of high school was not indicated. Another evidence that more scores need to be collected and considered is the difference in the median scores of the two forms. The items in the two forms of the test are well paired, yet the median score for Form A is 76 (50 per cent of the total of 150 items) and that for Form B is 96 (64 per cent of a total of 150 items).

The test has a wide coverage of subject matter. Form A includes 139 different place names and 68 different commodities. The test items are predominantly fact questions. Few of the questions require a consideration of such earth conditions as climate, surface and soil; and no attempt is made to introduce the important factors of density of population per square mile and standard of living. There in no provision for measuring skill in reading and interpreting maps, graphs, or tables of statistics.

Various types of test items are used. In the total of 150 items, 60 are true-false, 30 multiple-choice, 30 matching, and 30 names of places indicated on outline maps. On the whole, the test items are free from ambiguity and error. In only two cases in the 60 true-false questions do the determiners "only" and "entire" appear. One true-false question is debatable: Item 5 in Form A, "Mexico contains extensive lands suitable to agriculture." The key indicates the statement to be true. Mexico does have extensive areas of poor grazing lands, but only a small per cent of its total area is suitable for plow agriculture. Item 109 asks for Trinidad's chief export and the answer is asphalt. Asphalt undoubtedly was once the chief export, but recently Trinidad has exported more than six times as many dollars' worth of sugar as of asphalt.

The workmanship on the outline maps is faulty. Some of the numbers are so placed that it is difficult to determine which number indicates the city and which the country. For example, Item 5 on the map, Part IV of Form A, is named Malay peninsula in the key, but this reviewer reads 5 as Singapore and 17 as the Malay peninsula.

With a few corrections and the calculation of norms for specific years of high school and college from an adequate number of scores, the test can become a valuable instrument for measuring the retention of facts of economic geography.

[602]

Wiedefeld-Walther Geography Test. Grades 4-8; 1931; Forms A, B; $1.70 per 25; 35¢ per specimen set, postpaid; 60(65) minutes; M. Theresa Wiedefeld and E. Curt Walther; World Book Co.

Marguerite Uttley, Associate Professor of Geography, Iowa State Teachers College, Cedar Falls, Iowa. When the *Wiedefeld–Walther Geography Test* was published in 1931, it was an innovation in geography testing. Abilities in geography other than the retention of facts are measured. To this date the reviewer has found no other geography test which is as comprehensive and as useful for diagnosis of pupil difficulties.

In the manual the purpose of the test is stated, "Part 1 [Tests I-III] tests the abilities and skills needed in the study of geography. Part 2 [Tests IV-V] tests the control of geographical information, or knowledge of geographical facts."

TEST I, READING. Each paragraph is composed of four sentences and is followed by a why question. The answer is one of the four sentences, but in no case can a child match the wording of the question to the wording of the sentence. He must use his reasoning powers in order to select the right sentence. Test items are carefully arranged in order of difficulty.

TEST II, ORGANIZATION. A set of why questions is given. Beneath each are several statements. The child is directed to select the general statement which answers the question. Then he is to indicate the statement which does not explain the general statement. This is a noble effort to test a child's geographic mode of thinking, but adults have difficulty understanding the directions. Much depends upon the teacher's interpretation and how well she explains the example to the children. The median scores attained by various grades on this part of the test are considerably lower than on any one of the other five sections of the test.

TEST III, MAP AND GRAPH READING. Four maps of Spain are printed at the top of two facing pages: (a) temperature and rainfall for January, (b) for July, (c) relief and ocean depths, and (d) political. Twenty-two completion questions call for the reading of these maps. These questions cover remarkably well the reading of scale, directions, altitude, symbols for cities, isotherms, rainfall, latitude, and longitude. It is unfortunate that the temperature maps are built on data reduced to sea level. A geographer is concerned with actual temperatures on the plateau of Spain and not with the hypothetical map which shows temperatures at sea level. However, the sea-level isotherms do not interfere with the map questions in this test. A question on a cross section, two questions on pictures, and nineteen questions on graph reading complete this section.

TEST IV, GEOGRAPHY VOCABULARY. Technical and semitechnical geographical terms are tested not by definition, but by association with particular places or with type regions. Included in the list are a few foreign words which are relatively unimportant in a geographic vocabulary, for example, kayak, kufa, mantilla, sirocco, gauchos.

TEST V, GEOGRAPHICAL RELATIONSHIPS. Three unbalanced matching exercises comprise this part of the test. In the first column are human activity items to be matched with natural environmental items from the second column. In each exercise the list of natural environmental items is longer than that of human activity items.

TEST VI, PLACE GEOGRAPHY. Four clear outline maps have 54 well-chosen places indicated by numbers. Where the number refers to a city, a dot is plainly marked in the appropriate location.

It is regrettable that in the years since 1931 few testmakers in geography have profited by the notable pioneering of Wiedefeld and Walther and advanced the frontier in the measurement of the geographic mode of thinking.

For reviews by Anna Parsek and Marie E. Trost, see 40:1626.

[603]
World Geography Test: Dominion Tests. Grade 8; 1938; Forms A, B; 50¢ per 25; 23¢ per specimen set; specimen sets must be purchased to obtain the manual; 30(40) minutes; prepared by the Department of Educational Research, Ontario College of Education, University of Toronto; Vocational Guidance Centre.

Edwin H. Reeder, Professor of Education, University of Illinois, Urbana, Illinois. This test

Wiedefeld-Walther Geography Test

reveals a lack of clearness with respect to what it is supposed to measure. Each of the two forms consists of 75 multiple-choice questions, each with five choices. The great majority of the test elements require pure memory of facts in order to answer them correctly. To the extent that a teacher wishes to know whether his pupils are memorizing large numbers of facts about climate, products, boundaries, locations and the like, the test will be of use. It should be noted, however, that the tests are published in Canada and the test questions are rather heavily weighted for information about the British Commonwealth of Nations. About one third of the items deal with parts of this group of nations.

A very small number of questions in the tests under consideration attempt to test geographical reasoning. Item 61, Form B, will illustrate this attempt. It reads as follows: "Tasmania, unlike most of the states of Australia, always has sufficient rainfall. This is because (1) it is very mountainous, (2) it lies in the path of the Trades, (3) it is unsheltered by the mainland of Australia, (4) it lies in the paths of the Monsoons, (5) it lies in the path of the Westerlies." Even in these test elements, however, it seems safe to say that remembering facts is an ability more required to answer them correctly than is reasoning from cause to effect. (For this reviewer's general remarks on geography tests, *see* 598.)

HISTORY

[604]
Cooperative American History Test. High school and college; 1942-47; IBM; Forms S, T, X; separate answer sheets need not be used; $1.75 per 25; 25¢ per specimen set, postpaid; 40¢ per 25 machine-scorable answer sheets; 15¢ per stencil for scoring answer sheets; 40(45) minutes; Forms S and T: Mary Willis; Form X: Harry D. Berg; Cooperative Test Service.

REFERENCES
1. LINDQUIST, E. F. "The Form of the American History Examinations of the Cooperative Test Service." *Ed Rec* 12:459-75 O '31. *
2. TRAXLER, ARTHUR E. "Progressive Methods as Related to Knowledge of American History." *Sch & Soc* 57:640-3 My 29 '43. *
3. TRAXLER, ARTHUR E. "Some Data on the Cooperative American History Test," pp. 46-8. In *1943 Achievement Testing Program in Independent Schools and Supplementary Studies.* Educational Records Bulletin, No. 38. New York: Educational Records Bureau, June 1943. Pp. xiii, 53. Paper, lithotyped. $1.50. *

For reviews by Edgar B. Wesley and Margaret Willis of earlier forms, see 38:1014 and 40:1633.

[605]
Cooperative Modern European History Test. High school and college; 1947; IBM; Form X; sepa-

rate answer sheets need not be used; $1.75 per 25; 25¢ per specimen set, postpaid; 40¢ per 25 machine-scorable answer sheets; 15¢ per stencil for scoring answer sheets; 40(45) minutes; Frederick H. Stutz; Cooperative Test Service.

For reviews by Lavone A. Hanna, A. C. Krey, and S. P. McCutchen of earlier forms, see 38:1016 and 40:1635.

[606]

Cooperative World History Test. High school; 1947; IBM; Form X; separate answer sheets need not be used; $1.75 per 25; 25¢ per specimen set, postpaid; 40¢ per 25 machine-scorable answer sheets; 15¢ per stencil for scoring answer sheets; 40(45) minutes; Wallace Taylor; Cooperative Test Service.

For reviews by Kenneth E. Gell and R. M. Tryon of earlier forms, see 38:1017 and 40:1636.

[607]

★**Examination in American History.** Grades 11-14; 1944; IBM; Form SAmH-2-B-4 (usually called Form B); separate answer sheets must be used; $2 per 25; 40¢ per 25 machine-scorable answer sheets; 15¢ per scoring key; 25¢ per specimen set, postpaid; 120(125) minutes; prepared by the Examinations Staff of the United States Armed Forces Institute; published by the American Council on Education; distributed by Cooperative Test Service. (Also distributed by Science Research Associates: $2 per 25; 65¢ per 25 machine-scorable answer sheets; 50¢ per key; 50¢ per specimen set.)

REFERENCES

1. Townsend, Agatha. "The Reliability and Validity of the USAFI American History Test," pp. 53-58. In *1947 Achievement Testing Program in Independent Schools and Supplementary Studies.* Educational Records Bulletin, No. 48. New York: Educational Records Bureau, June 1947. Pp. xii, 66. Paper, lithotyped. $2.00. * (PA 22:463)

Howard R. Anderson, Specialist for Social Sciences, U. S. Office of Education, Washington, D. C. This examination is one of a number prepared by the Examinations Staff of the Armed Forces Institute as a means of measuring the educational achievement of service personnel and of reporting it to "educational institutions from which these men and women may wish to secure credit."

The test being reviewed is a two-hour examination and includes 150 multiple-response items. An answer sheet which permits machine scoring is provided; but if part scores are desired for diagnostic purposes, scoring stencils must be used.

The manual describes the procedure followed in the construction of these tests. In brief, examiners who were skilled both in teaching and in testing American history met with teachers to identify educational objectives. These were defined as behaviors, and appropriate exercises constructed. The test materials were tried out and revised, and the revised materials criticized

by content experts before final forms were constructed.

The test includes seven parts: Chronology (to 1789; 1789–1860; since 1860), Identification, Ideology, Interpretation and Generalization, and Comparison and Contrast. Percentile norms for both total and part scores at both high school and college levels are provided. The manual suggests that these norms are based on results obtained with average pupils and suggests that institutions which feel that their student body is markedly inferior or superior may wish to establish their own norms.

The test items are carefully prepared and effectively sample concepts which are usually included in general courses in American history taught at either the senior high school or the junior college level. The test therefore should be a valid measure of general achievement in this field.

[608]

★**Examination in Modern European History.** High school and college; 1945; IBM; Form MEH-1-B-4 (usually called Form B); no norms available; separate answer sheets must be used; $2 per 25; 40¢ per 25 machine-scorable answer sheets; 15¢ per scoring key; 25¢ per specimen set, postpaid; 120(125) minutes; prepared by the Examinations Staff of the United States Armed Forces Institute; published by the American Council on Education; distributed by Cooperative Test Service. (Also distributed by Science Research Associates: $2 per 25; 65¢ per 25 machine-scorable answer sheets; 50¢ per key; 50¢ per specimen set.)

Frederick H. Stutz, Assistant Professor of Education, Cornell University, Ithaca, New York. The purpose of this test is to measure achievement in modern European history at the high school or college level. A manual accompanying the test explains in detail procedures used in constructing subject-matter tests, establishment of test norms and the evaluation of achievement, and directions for administering, scoring, and interpreting scores. Because the general philosophy of the USAFI achievement testing program is well known and because the statistical data supporting the tests are available to test users, this review will be confined to a discussion of the strengths and weaknesses of the test itself.

As is true of others in the series, the *Examination in Modern European History* was produced by the cooperative work of examiners, teachers, and subject-matter specialists. An attempt is made to measure pupil attainment in terms of accepted educational objectives in the field. The test consists of 148 items and is to be administered in a time of two hours. Of the 148 items, 15 test chronological relationships, 31 are matching exercises, 41 are of the multiple-choice type, 32 are based on keys, and 29 are concerned with the interpretation of reading passages.

In general, the test is well planned and well constructed. Among the educational objectives measured are knowledge of historical information, understanding of concepts and developments, understanding of chronological and of cause-effect relationships, ability to read and interpret historical passages, and ability to recognize historical allusions. The items are rather well distributed over the period of modern European history. Greatest emphasis is given to the rise of national states and the achievement of political rights by the peoples of western Europe. Most of the items are so constructed that in answering them the pupil gives evidence of using or of not being able to use the type of thinking which the items are designed to measure. Of particular value are the questions based on historical passages. These questions test both the student's knowledge of history and his ability to read and understand an appropriate passage.

The test has certain apparent weaknesses. An examination of the 148 items reveals that 99 require knowledge of political or military history, while only 13 are directly concerned with economic developments and only 32 deal with social, cultural, and intellectual events or trends. In the light of modern historical scholarship and of recent testing practice, this distribution seems to give too much emphasis to the political and military aspects of history. Other shortcomings in the distribution of items are evident. Though the test was copyrighted in 1945, no coverage is given to events after 1940 and very light coverage to those of the period from 1935 to 1939. French history is the subject of 34 items, but developments in eastern Europe receive relatively little attention. Certain periods of European history, such as that from 1815 to 1848 and that of industrial and scientific changes, are neglected. Certain questions, such as those which require recognition of and differentiation of the programs and basic aims of Chartists, Utopian Socialists, and Scientific Socialists, may presume an understanding of nineteenth century history which most high school students do not possess.

The test is an excellent one. It is well conceived and well built. It could be strengthened by the inclusion of more items dealing with economic and social developments and by a somewhat better distribution of items over the period.

[609]
★Examination in World History—High-School Level. High school; 1945; IBM; Form SWH-1-B-4 (usually called Form B) ; separate answer sheets must be used; $2 per 25; 50¢ per 25 machine-scorable answer sheets; 30¢ per scoring key; 35¢ per specimen set, postpaid; 120(125) minutes; prepared by the Examinations Staff of the United States Armed Forces Institute; published by the American Council on Education; distributed by Cooperative Test Service. (Also distributed by Science Research Associates: $2 per 25; 65¢ per 25 machine-scorable answer sheets; 50¢ per key; 50¢ per specimen set.)

Dorothy C. Adkins, Chief, Test Development Unit, U. S. Civil Service Commission, Washington, D. C. This test of 198 items appears to be comprehensive in coverage. There is no reason for the reviewer, a nonhistorian, to question the emphasis on the different phases of world history. The chronological ordering of the items will appeal to many persons as preferable to possible alternative arrangements.

A general manual accompanying examinations prepared by the United States Armed Forces Institute describes the general procedures used in constructing subject tests. Norms determined on the basis of tryouts are made available on a separate page or leaflet printed for each specific test. Unfortunately such a leaflet was not available to this reviewer. No mention of reliability determinations is made in the general manual, but there seems no reason to doubt that a test of the length and general characteristics of this one could be demonstrated to be adequate in this respect.

The general manual states that the tests are so organized that attainment of each objective can be measured separately. Possibly this statement is true of the world history test, but its applicability is not apparent to this reviewer. It seems likely that this aim was sacrificed in order to achieve a more nearly chronological ordering. Another statement in the general manual is probably not applicable to the world history test—that norms are given for part and total scores—since the test does not appear to be organized in such a way as to yield meaningful part scores readily.

The general manual emphasizes that the subject tests measure more than memory of facts.

"It will be observed that numerous exercises represent problem situations, involving for their successful solution applications of knowledge and the functioning of critical reflective thinking." This is probably true of the world history test; yet it should be noted that mere inspection of an item often does not reveal whether it tests factual knowledge or "critical reflective thinking."

One form of item used throughout the test may cause annoyance to the subject and, in addition, can be criticized from the measurement point of view. In this type, a question is presented and several (usually four) statements are presented. Each of the statements is essentially to be judged as true (applicable) or false (inapplicable). The subject does not indicate as his response the number(s) or letter(s) corresponding to the true statement(s) but must reveal his answers by a code, such as (A) I and II; (B) I and III; (C) I and IV; (D) II and IV; (E) II, III and IV. This necessity for coding the response introduces an irrelevant and probably irritating factor. Further, there are 16 possible responses if all combinations of the four statements are considered. Hence a type of scoring ambiguity is introduced. It is recognized that this device was probably adopted primarily in the interests of reducing the chance factor in two-choice items. And it may be that the particular combinations of responses presented to the subject were selected on the basis of a statistical analysis of the item presented in a different form. This possibility gains some credence when it is seen that for some items only 4 of the 16 combinations are presented. This shifting from four alternatives to five in itself may be confusing to some subjects. A solution to the objection from the standpoint of scoring ambiguity alone would be to limit the number of statements presented for each item to two. Then a four-choice code (neither I nor II, I alone, II alone, I and II) would apply. This suggestion still does not eliminate the first objection to the requirement of coding. Coding could be avoided by having the subject check all applicable statements and then scoring them as one would score two-choice items. One might then wish to reduce the weight of items of this type. The basic data are a series of responses to essentially two-choice items. It is difficult to understand how the accuracy of measurement is increased by translating the basic responses through a code that does not allow for many possible combinations of responses.

A similar difficulty occurs in items on the chronological order of each event within its group of three events. The emphasis on order rather than on exact dates is desirable. But the common difficulty that arises in scoring arrangement items enters here. Apparently each item correctly indicated as first, second, or third within its group contributes one point to the score. Yet it may be argued that the person, for example, who assigns three events order 321 when their correct order is 123 gets one point although he is wrong on all of the relationships, while the person who gives the order 312 gets zero on all three, even though he indicates correctly that 1 comes before 2.

There is no entirely satisfactory solution to this problem if the tests are to be machine scored. The items can be recast into a form requiring the subject to indicate which of several events occurred first (or second, third, fourth, or fifth) or into a form requiring the subject to indicate (by A, B, C, D, or E) when a particular event occurred in relation to a sequence of (four) other events. It may be objected that these devices yield less information about the subject per unit time than the method used in the test. If machine scoring is not an important consideration, perhaps the best solution is to assign scores on each possible combination of events proportionate to its rank-difference correlation with the correct order of the events. Such a scheme does not lend itself to machine scoring. Another possibility that might be considered would be to treat each set of three events as a unit, giving a credit of one point for the correct sequence on all three and no credit for other responses. Although this solution would again result in assigning the same score (zero in this case) to different degrees of knowledge, it probably would work more equitably than the present plan if the number of items were large enough. As the test stands, some persons may believe that too much weight is given to the knowledge involved in the sets of items in question, Items 49-63, 83-94, and 164-187. Dichotomous scoring of each set of three would probably result in better weighting for these items.

Aside from the points made above, the item construction is technically very good. The test format is excellent and the directions clear. Scoring is entirely objective and may be done either by hand or by machine. The score is simply the number of right answers. Not correcting the scores for chance success is entirely appropriate if the time limit of two hours is sufficient to allow practically all subjects to complete the test.

Wallace W. Taylor, Professor of Social Studies; and Head of the Department of Social Studies, Milne School; New York State College for Teachers, Albany, New York. This examination, in general, compares favorably with the best achievement examinations in world history now in existence. The individual items are well constructed and are free from clues and irrelevant material.

The allocation of items among the various fields of world history leaves something to be desired. For example, there are virtually no items testing understanding of the Far East and Latin America. The examination would be appropriate for the type of world history taught before the war but hardly valid for the good courses being taught at the present time.

The proportion of items devoted to cultural, diplomatic, military, economic, and social history seems well balanced for the areas treated in the examination. However, the ancient and medieval period is stressed at the expense of the modern period. For example, 64 of the 198 questions are devoted to the ancient world through the Roman period, and there are only 25 questions on the period since World War I. Unless it is intended that this examination be used concurrently with a contemporary affairs test, that proportion is surely unwise.

Probably too great a stress is placed on chronological items, as this type comprises 25 per cent of the total. The time-interval technique used in the Iowa Every-Pupil tests is more effective as a means of testing the understanding of cause-and-result relationships than the rearrangement technique used in this examination.

There is also some question as to whether the use of three varieties of multiple-choice items in addition to the matching, true-false, and chronology types does not cause loss of time in reading directions and some confusion in the minds of students in transferring from one type of item to another.

With many teachers committed to a program of teaching basic study skills as an integral part of all social studies courses, it seems that subject examinations should include some items to help them evaluate the success of their work in teaching these skills. This examination does not include items of that sort.

[610]

Kansas American History Test. First, second semesters high school; 1938; Forms A, B; 2 levels; 90¢ per 25 of either level, postpaid; 15¢ per specimen set, postpaid; 40(45) minutes; Arthur Hartung, C. Stewart Boertman, and H. E. Schrammel; Bureau of Educational Measurements, Kansas State Teachers College of Emporia.
a) TEST I. First semester.
b) TEST II. Second semester.

W. H. Cartwright, Assistant Professor of Education, Boston University, Boston, Massachusetts. There are two tests, one covering the pre-Civil War period and designed as an achievement test for the first semester of high school American history and the other concerning the entire period since 1492. Each test has two forms. Each form contains 75 true-false items, 25 reverse multiple-choice items, 35 matching items, and 15 items, each requiring the selection from four events of the one which occurred first. Convenient scoring keys are provided, as is a table of percentile scores, computed from 22,087 student scores reported from 757 schools.

The test does not sample enough aspects of society. While more than 100 of the 600 items require specific knowledge of individuals, one looks in vain for the name of an architect, an artist, an educator, a labor leader, or a musician. None of the authors or poets of the national period are mentioned. The only woman included is Anne Bradstreet; the only captain of industry, John D. Rockefeller; and the only inventor, Eli Whitney, although the names of "Cooper's locomotive" and "Fulton's steamboat" are required.

Contrary to the statement of the authors that Test II "covers chiefly the period from the beginning of the Civil War to the present," approximately 60 per cent of the items in that test are based on the period before 1860.

Despite the use of reverse multiple-choice items, the test does not sufficiently require the use of mental processes other than memory. It is unfortunate that the authors have included no questions of the best-answer type, which is especially suitable for testing judgment, understanding, and ability to discriminate.

Half the test is made up of true-false items. Such items do not test ability to discriminate or understanding of relationships. Those which require judgment are too often controversial. For instance, the student is required to believe that the colonies were independent before the Declaration of Independence was adopted; that the powers of the Second Continental Congress were not related to the Declaration of Independence; and that the Indians of the Old Southwest did not constitute so great a problem as those of the Old Northwest.

The matching questions are poorly constructed from several points of view. The columns are too long, the response columns containing from 20 to 31 items. Not only does the student waste his time scanning the lists, but his selection becomes too much a function of the IQ. Half of the matching exercises are composed of a wide variety of items. It requires no knowledge of American history to relate "John Smith's account of life in Virginia" with "A True Relation of Virginia," when the word "Virginia" appears only once in each column or to select the answer for the "first case in which a Congressional act was held unconstitutional by the Supreme Court" when the only lawsuit listed in the response column is "Marbury vs. Madison."

A few errors of fact have crept into the test. Great Britain did not "grant" the colonies their independence. The grandfather clauses are not a constitutional method of restricting Negro suffrage. The Mayflower Compact was not an agreement among the Puritans.

Minor weaknesses exist which might have caught the eye of an editor. Occasionally one item gives the answer to another. Typographical errors are frequent, including at least ten misspelled words in Test I, Form A.

With these shortcomings, it is doubtful whether the test can serve in helping the teacher to do more than compare the achievement of his students with that of a great number of others.

For a review by Wilbur F. Murra, see 40:1639.

[611]

Kansas Modern European History Test. First, second semesters high school; 1938–40; Forms A, B; 2 levels; 90¢ per 25 of either level, postpaid; 15¢ per specimen set, postpaid; 40(45) minutes; Alvin L. Hasenbank, H. E. Schrammel, and B. A. Hamilton; Bureau of Educational Measurements, Kansas State Teachers College of Emporia.
a) TEST I. First semester; 1940.
b) TEST II. Second semester; 1938.

Frederic H. Stutz, Assistant Professor of Education, Cornell University, Ithaca, New York. The test is designed to measure achievement in modern European history and is to be used in high school and college classes studying the subject for one year. Test I covers the period from the discovery of America to about 1850, and Test II covers the period from 1850 to the present. The publishers indicate that the purpose of the test is to measure "the student's understanding of significant movements and events in relation to their social and economic consequences." Though relatively little information is available to the reviewer concerning validity, reliability, and interpretation of results, the manual of directions explains that the authors made a detailed study of the content of books in modern European and world history and that items were checked by teachers, supervisors, and test-construction experts. A brief statement of test reliability is presented. Percentile norms, derived from 1,095 student scores obtained from 44 schools in nationwide testing programs, make it possible to translate test scores into school grades.

Test I, to be administered in 40 minutes, consists of 37 groups of items containing a total of 160 responses. All responses are to be answered as either true or false. Of the 37 groups, 8 are concerned with historical information, 9 with dates, 11 with concepts, and 9 with personages. Test II, to be administered in 40 minutes, contains 145 items, of which 100 are of the true-false type, 30 of the multiple-choice variety, and 15 of the matching type.

The items written for this test are fairly well distributed over the period of modern European history. Certain of the items are well constructed and measure significant aspects of the subject. The test is so constructed that it can be easily administered and scored. Though the period of history covered by this edition of the test stops with the year 1938, it is presumed that later editions will bring the test up to date.

In general, however, the test does not attain the standards set by comparable achievement tests in this field. Too much attention is given to mastery of factual information, while relatively little emphasis is placed on understanding of concepts, developments, chronological and cause-effect relationships, etc. The test would be a better one if it attempted to measure understanding of history in terms of educational objectives rather than of acquisition of historical facts. Over 65 per cent of the total items deal with political and military history, and inadequate coverage is given to economic, social, and cultural developments. Shortcomings in the choice and construction of individual items tend to weaken the test. Though true-false questions have long been regarded as among the least successful types for social studies testing, they are used liberally in this test. Many of the chronology items test merely the ability to associate a single date with an event or person and do not require an understanding of chronological relationships. The matching items lack homogeneity and therefore allow the student to select correct responses from a rather narrow range of choices. In several instances the multiple-choice or completion items contain textbook expressions or other clues that enable the pupil to select the correct response without understanding the reason for his selection.

For a review by Clinton C. Conrad, see 40:1640.

[612]
★Kniss World History Test. High school; 1940; Forms A, B; $1.75 per 25; 35¢ per specimen set, postpaid; 50(55) minutes; F. Roscoe Kniss; World Book Co.

REFERENCES
1. KNISS, F. ROSCOE. *The Construction of an Achievement Test in Tenth Grade World History.* Unpublished doctor's thesis, Pennsylvania State College, 1937.
2. FOWLER, VICTOR M. *A Critical Analysis of the Kniss World History Test.* Unpublished master's thesis, Ohio University, 1944. Pp. 59. (*Abstracts of Masters' Theses . . . ,* 1945, p. 9.)

Dorothy C. Adkins, Chief, Test Development Unit, U. S. Civil Service Commission, Washington, D. C. This test of 130 items is presented in 6 parts: Factual Knowledge (25 items), Time Relationships (15 items), Contributions of the Past (20 items), Cause and Effect (20 items), Tying Past and Present Together (20 items), and Problems of Life (30 items). It is intended to cover the content of high school world history courses as commonly given in the 10th grade. The divisions grew from a survey of objectives of world history courses based on research in social studies, textbooks, courses of study, and opinions of high school teachers. There is no obvious one-to-one relationship between the six objectives elicited and the six divisions, several of which tap several of the objectives. Although this is not necessarily a criticism of the test, the manner of arriving at the divisions might have been elaborated upon in the manual.

The test, published in 1940, now seems out of date, at least to a person who is not a student of world history. In fact, the impression it leaves, in so far as timeliness of content is concerned, is that it was written very shortly after World War I, which, of course, is not identified as such in the test. Probably many schools will hesitate to use this test until a new revision is issued.

Some points related to the statistical data given in the manual are not entirely clear. Items for a preliminary form were gleaned from textbooks, courses of study, teacher-made tests, research studies, and teachers' judgments. "In all, 2,927 items were obtained from which the first experimental edition of the test was constructed." Unless the 2,927 items constituted the first experimental edition, the number of items it contained is not given. The tetrachoric r of each item was computed, based on 210 cases. We are not told what the criterion was. Presumably it was the score on whatever total number of items comprised the preliminary form. We are not told what the standard was for deciding when to eliminate or revise an "indiscriminatory" item nor how many or what proportion of items were so treated.

A second edition was constructed with the items arranged by difficulty (presumably as determined by the percentages of the 210 subjects who answered them correctly) and with the proportions of items on ancient, medieval, and modern history corresponding to the space allotted by textbooks. It is stated that "the revision was administered to 244 tenth-grade pupils completing the course in world history, and *the results indicated not only that the test was valid* [italics mine] but also that it was a reliable measure." How the validity was determined by the results is not indicated. The final form of the test is said to be essentially the same as this second revision. Does this mean Form A or Form B, or does it mean that both were culled from the second revision?

The reported data on test reliability seem to be satisfactory. For 150 cases selected at random from the "normative population" (apparently described later on as consisting of over 1,100 pupils, although one wonders why so few cases were selected), the interform reliability for total scores was .90; for the 244 cases taking the second experimental edition, the corrected split-half coefficient was .95.

Regarding the comparability of the two forms, it is stated that "to insure comparability of content, the items were distributed similarly among the various phases of history covered. . . . The forms were also balanced with regard to the difficulty of items, in terms of difficulty values determined experimentally. As a final check on equality, both forms . . . were administered simultaneously in the same classes, half of the pupils taking Form A and the other half Form B." The size of the group on whom the difficulty values were based is not stated. Presumably the group referred to as giving the final check on equality was the "normative population" of over 1,100. It is little short of amazing, then, to encounter in the next paragraph a statement to the effect that the distributions of total scores plotted on normal percentile charts revealed that Form A scores were five points lower than Form B scores *throughout the entire range of scores*. It will not be denied that different distributions of item intercorrelations could affect the variance and the shape of the distribution of total scores. Two tests composed of items of the same difficulty distribution could not emerge with means differing by five points except as a result of instability in the original index of difficulty. But if they did differ for a new and larger population, would not the normal course be to shift items between the forms in order to equate the difficulty? Then the finding that the five-point difference is uniform and constant throughout the entire range of scores appears inexplicable to me, unless it is accounted for by the presence in the harder form of five items that *no one* answered correctly or by the presence in the easier form of five items that *everyone* answered correctly. This hardly seems plausible. The table of percentile ranks (Table I) has an additional peculiar feature. The entire list of percentile ranks for one form is *exactly* the same as the list for the other, except for this constant five-point difference. That is, raw scores of 5 on Form A and 10 on Form B have a percentile rank of .8, raw scores of 6 on Form A and 11 on Form B a percentile rank of 1.2, and so on. For tests that correlate only .90 for the population on which the ranks were based, this exact similarity would be impossible except by remote coincidence.

The writer does not question that the content of the test represents with reasonable adequacy the coverage and emphasis of high school courses and textbooks in world history (aside from the previously noted deficiency with respect to up-to-dateness).

The test format is good, although one wonders why provision for recording answers on a separate sheet was not made.

Most of the parts consist entirely of four-choice items, although the first part is in completion form. The directions for scoring are satisfactory in most respects, but they do not indicate what the scorer is to do about the misspellings that almost certainly arise on Part I. The instructions call for correction for chance success in scoring the four-choice items, and the subjects are instructed not to guess without at least partial knowledge.

The phrasing of some of the items leads this reviewer to wonder whether the purpose of the test is to test or to teach. The cover page states, "This test is to help you appreciate and understand better the meaning of world history." Some of the questions lead to the reaction that undue effort was exerted to draw in a relationship or a comparison of little significance. This is especially true of many of the items in Part V, Tying Past and Present Together. Many of them do not test powers of judgment or analytical ability or understanding of relationships but only knowledge of one of the two facts included in the item. For example, consider the following premise and answer: "Legislators today face the same conditions that Turgot did before the French Revolution; namely, that when attempts are made to tax the privileged class they . . . suggest other ways of raising money." Why bring in Turgot? In another item, one needs no knowledge of the early Romans to know that the desired response is that they (like the early American settlers) "were industrious and frugal." A similar criticism applies to many other items in this part. In Part VI, Problems of Life, this reviewer would prefer questions stated more objectively and not directed toward pointing a moral. For example, in Item 22, Form A, the first sentence, "The world is constantly striving to reach the place where just and fair treatment will be given to all," is unnecessary.

A number of items need pruning; several have answers given away immediately by the similarity of their wording to that of the question (Examples in Form A: Item 20, Part V; Item 8, Part VI) and there is some undesirable overlapping which results in the answer of one question being given away by the statement of the problem in another or in two interrelated items (Examples in Form A: Items 12 and 20, Part IV; Item 2, Part I and Item 15, Part IV).

Kniss World History Test

Perhaps the items in Part II, Time Relationships, place too great an emphasis on knowledge of exact dates. Probably the modern trend in the teaching of history is to stress knowledge of the chronological sequence of events, and especially of related events, rather than exact dates.

With some editing of individual items, the addition of items on recent world events, correction of the unequal difficulty of alternate forms, and more attention to adequate description of the standardization and statistical procedures used, a revision of this test should be worth while.

Wallace W. Taylor, Professor of Social Studies; and Head of the Department of Social Studies, Milne School; New York State College for Teachers, Albany, New York. This world history examination was copyrighted in 1940. An examination of the test shows that the items were apparently prepared several years before that. An item on the Saar plebiscite is the only item referring to anything that happened in the thirties. There are only a few items dealing with events since the first World War. In its present form, the test is outdated and should not be used.

The division of the test into six sections with the intriguing titles of Factual Knowledge, Time-Relationships, Contributions of the Past, Cause and Effect, Tying Past and Present Together, and Problems of Life, is misleading. The only heading that is really descriptive is the one on Factual Knowledge. The section titled Time-Relationships requires little more than a straight memorizing of dates. The section titled Problems of Life is just another heading for factual items concerned with social and economic history.

Entirely too large a proportion of this examination is devoted to items of doubtful importance. There are no items on Latin America or the Far East.

It is my opinion that a teacher seeking a terminal examination for a world history course would do far better to use one of the tests of the Cooperative Test Service or of the United States Armed Forces Institute.

Ed Res B 20:263–4 D 17 '41. William J. Jones. A thoroughly objective, standardized information test of world history * For those who accept the assumption that history information can be standardized, it is a carefully constructed

instrument. The usual rigorous procedure of examining current research, analyzing courses of study (7 in all), studying textbooks (8 mentioned), and summarizing questionnaires returned by 100 teachers has been followed. The result is a 130-item test, most of which are multiple-choice items with a few completion and matching. It is divided into six parts as follows: factual knowledge, time relationships, contribution of the past, cause and effect, typing past and present together, and problems of life. Validity is claimed for the test because: first, it discriminates between "good" and "poor" students; second, it includes "only items that cover what is being taught in world history courses" (textbook and course of study analyses, and so forth); third, it was "subjected to the careful scrutiny and criticism of 80 nationally known specialists in the fields of history and education"; fourth, the items are arranged according to difficulty following a tryout with 210 eleventh-grade pupils; and fifth, the numbers of items in each of the three phases of history— ancient, medieval, and modern—were made to correspond to the percentage of space allotted by textbooks to these three epochs. A study of the content of the test, however, reveals that the test does not measure what it purports to measure. The six parts of the test are supposed to measure the following experimentally determined objectives: to study the development of civilization, to explain the present, to foster patriotism, to develop intelligent citizenship, to broaden the pupil's sympathies, and to increase in the pupil the powers of interpretation and judgment. To test these purposes, nonfunctional memoriter learning is called for in the test! Part II, for example, requires the student to match 24 dates with 15 events and yet it is labeled "Time Relationships." Part IV, by requiring the student to pick a "best" cause or effect out of four, may actually encourage thinking in a single causation pattern. The test purports to measure powers of interpretation and judgment, but the students are not required to solve any problems, apply any principles, explore any relationships, interpret any data, or formulate any generalizations. The test may have some value as an information inventory, however. *

Teach Col J 12:70 Ja '41. Waldo F. Mitchell. * The 130 items cover the range of history from the Egyptian civilization to the present generation. Each of the items deals with a significant event, happening, or idea. Each item is well stated. In only a few cases of the match list items could there be any doubt about the correct answer. A perforated cardboard key to be superimposed on the answered test pages makes the scoring of the test easy and rapid. * This test is probably the best standardized test in world history for high school. It covers the field and it is excellent in form and content.

[613]

★Survey Test in United States History. High school and college; 1943; an adaptation of the history test given by the New York Times in its survey of 7,000 college freshmen in 36 colleges; norms not available; $1.50 per 25, postpaid; sample test free; (60) minutes; Turner E. Smith & Co.

REFERENCES
1. "Are 'Educators' to Blame for the Poor Results Shown by the 'Times' Test?" Sch & Soc 57:560-1 My 15 '43. *
2. "How Do Senior College Students and Adult Groups Stand on the 'Times' Test?" Sch & Soc 57:654 Je 5 '43. *
3. " 'The New York Times' Again Investigates the Teaching of History." Sch & Soc 57:403 Ap 10 '43. *
4. ALLEN, JAMES E. "Another Explanation of the 'Times' Test Findings." Letter. Sch & Soc 58:238 S 25 '43. *
5. BOYD, PAUL P. "The 'Times' Test and Our Public Schools." Sch & Soc 57:620-3 My 29 '43. *
6. BROUDY, H. S. "History Without Hysteria." Sch & Soc 58:106-7 Ag 14 '43. *
7. DILLA, GERALDINE P. "The American History Situation in Few Words." Letter. Sch & Soc 58:309-10 O 16 '43. *
8. DUNBAR, WILLIS F. "Why Our Faces Are Red: A Comment on the 'Times' Test." Sch & Soc 58:265-8 O 2 '43. *
9. FRASER, HUGH RUSSELL. "Hugh Russell Fraser Replies to a Criticism." Letter. Sch & Soc 58:504-5 D 25 '43. *
10. FRASER, HUGH RUSSELL. "The 'Inside' Story of 'The New York Times' Test." Sch & Soc 58:82-4 Ag 7 '43. *
11. FRASER, HUGH RUSSELL. "A 'Red Herring' Across the Trail of the 'Times' Test." Letter. Sch & Soc 58:190-1 S 11 '43. *
12. HICKS, CHARLES ROGER. " 'The New York Times' Test." Letter. Sch & Soc 58:311 O 16 '43. *
13. READ, JAMES MORGAN. "History Versus the Social Sciences." Sch & Soc 58:149-51 S 4 '43. *
14. SHAW, ROBERT S. "What is History?" Letter. Sch & Soc 57:634-5 My 29 '43. *
15. STUMPF, WIPPERT A. "On Mr. Fraser's Defense of the 'Times' Test." Letter. Sch & Soc 58:348-9 O 30 '43. *
16. TRAXLER, ARTHUR E. "Progressive Methods as Related to Knowledge of American History." Sch & Soc 57:640-3 My 29 '43. *

POLITICAL SCIENCE

[614-5]

★Cooperative Test in American Government. High school; 1947; IBM; Form X; separate answer sheets need not be used; $1.75 per 25; 25¢ per specimen set, postpaid; 40¢ per 25 machine-scorable answer sheets; 15¢ per stencil for scoring answer sheets; 40(45) minutes; John Haefner; Cooperative Test Service.

[616]

★Examination in Civics. High school; 1944; IBM; Form SCv-1-B-4 (usually called Form B); separate answer sheets must be used; $2 per 25; 40¢ per 25 machine-scorable answer sheets; 15¢ per scoring key; 25¢ per specimen set, postpaid; 90(95) minutes; prepared by the Examinations Staff of the United States Armed Forces Institute; published by the American Council on Education; distributed by Cooperative Test Service. (Also distributed by Science Research Associates: $2 per 25; 65¢ per 25 machine-scorable answer sheets; 50¢ per key; 50¢ per specimen set.)

REFERENCES
1. "A Note on the USAFI Tests in Civics and Problems of Democracy," pp. 59-60. In 1947 Achievement Testing Program in Independent Schools and Supplementary Studies. Educational Records Bulletin, No. 48. New York: Educational Records Bureau, June 6, 1947. Pp. xii, 66. Paper, lithotyped. $2.00. *

Roy A. Price, Professor of Social Science and of Education, Syracuse University, Syracuse, New York. The United States Armed Forces Institute, created to provide off-duty education for service personnel, established an examinations staff at the University of Chicago. This staff undertook to build tests from which reports of educational achievement could be made to the educational institution from which service personnel wish to receive credit. It was hoped that in this manner "the danger of blanket credit for military experience such as that which was so frequently given after the last war would be avoided." Civilian forms of the tests which attempt to measure valuable and generally accepted educational objectives in various subjects are published by the American Council on Education for use by high schools and colleges.

The tests were prepared by specialists after meetings with teachers of various subjects. Attempts were made to define objectives in terms of behavior situations. The original exercises were tried out, revised, and then submitted to critics who were asked to check coverage in content and objectives, accuracy, and validity. Norms for the finished tests are available for whole and part scores. Users are urged to make careful analysis of the various parts of the tests so as to facilitate diagnosis of individual weaknesses as well as formation of judgments on total achievement. The authors warn against the uncritical acceptance of the norms as absolute standards and stress the importance of local norms and standards. Excellent directions for the administration of the test and the interpretation of test scores are also given.

The Examination in Civics is, in the judgment of this writer, the finest test yet published in this field. The test seeks to measure an understanding of behavior and function of governmental officers, and the usual mystical treatment of government as a structure removed from human behavior is entirely lacking. Coverage includes trends in government, individual rights, the federal government, administrative agencies, organization and functions of Congress, political parties, relation of federal, local, and state government, foreign relations, taxes, and government aid to and control of such groups as agriculture, labor, and industry.

Data on validity and reliability are not presented, but the care exercised in the construction of the test and the type of items used suggest that the test compares favorably with others. The writer would like to have had included in the tables of norms separate scores for the questions that purported to measure the several objectives, making possible a comparison between success in one skill and success in another. It is also hoped that in the very near future, there may be forthcoming comparisons between norms on this test and norms on comparable tests.

[617]

★Examination in Problems of Democracy—High-School Level. Grades 11-12; 1944; IBM; Form SPrD-1-B-4 (usually called Form B); separate answer sheets must be used; $2 per 25; 40¢ per 25 machine-scorable answer sheets; 15¢ per scoring key; 25¢ per specimen set, postpaid; 120(125) minutes; prepared by the Examinations Staff of the United States Armed Forces Institute; published by the American Council on Education; distributed by Cooperative Test Service. (Also distributed by Science Research Associates: $2 per 25; 65¢ per 25 machine-scorable answer sheets; 50¢ per key; 50¢ per specimen set.)

REFERENCES

1. WILLIAMS, JAY, AND ABRAHAM, HERBERT J. "Evaluating the Course in Problems of Democracy." *Social Ed* 9:167-72 Ap '45. *
2. "A Note on the USAFI Tests in Civics and Problems of Democracy," pp. 59-60. In *1947 Achievement Testing Program in Independent Schools and Supplementary Studies.* Educational Records Bulletin, No. 48. New York: Educational Records Bureau, June 1947. Pp. xii, 66. Paper, lithotyped. $2.00. *

Lavone A. Hanna, Associate Professor of Education, San Francisco State College, San Francisco, California. This test consists of 10 short passages which present different points of view on social problems; 5 are excerpts from editorials, 2 are statistical tables, and 3 are quotations from a discussion between two speakers. The questions based on these passages purport to test the student's ability to read correctly and his knowledge and understanding of the problems with which the passages deal. The problems included in the test have been well selected and cover topics usually included in a problems of democracy or American problems course, such as: crime, population trends, labor unions, housing, prices and production, education, pressure groups, "Americanism," internationalism, and democracy.

Although no norms are given for the test and no statistical data are furnished on their reliability or validity, the care with which the tests of the Armed Forces Institute were constructed recommends the use of this test. The manual

states that the examiners, specialists both in teaching and testing in the subject field, met with teachers to identify the educational objectives which students were expected to attain and the exercises were constructed to test these objectives. The exercises were then tried out on groups of students, and, on the basis of this tryout, some exercises were eliminated because they were not discriminating, were ambiguous, or were of inappropriate difficulty. The test was then submitted to critics who checked the test for comprehensiveness in coverage, for accuracy of material, and for the validity of the items. The test was then revised on the basis of these criticisms. The test seems to this reviewer to be superior to most tests of social competence, and it is hoped that norms will be made available.

[618]

★Mordy-Schrammel Constitution Test. High school and college; 1940-45; Forms A, B; 90¢ per 25, postpaid; 15¢ per specimen set, postpaid; 40(45) minutes; Francis E. Mordy and H. E. Schrammel; Bureau of Educational Measurements, Kansas State Teachers College of Emporia.

W. H. Cartwright, Assistant Professor of Education, Boston University, Boston, Massachusetts. This test is intended to measure knowledge of the Constitution and understanding of its application. It is designed for use in an elementary course in high school or college.

There are two forms of the test, each containing 65 true-false items, 35 best-answer items, and 25 matching items. Convenient scoring keys are provided, as is a table of percentile scores based on 3,277 cases representing 126 schools.

A desirable feature of the test is Part 3, consisting of 10 items requiring the exercise of judgment in applying principles of the Constitution or of famous court decisions.

It is unfortunate that more than half of the test is made up of true-false items. Most of these test only memory of fact. In a few other instances, the student can know and understand all the facts involved and yet not give the keyed answer. For instance, the president is required to be a natural-born citizen, therefore it is true that he must have been a citizen for fourteen years; the House of Representatives cannot seat anyone it pleases; and the members of the cabinet may or may not all be eligible for succession to the presidency.

The matching exercises are poorly constructed. They are somewhat too long, having from 18 to 20 items in the response column.

More important is the lack of homogeneity among the items. For too many stimuli one particular response is dictated by grammatical construction or similarity in nature. Thus, "kinds of cases at court" is matched with "civil and criminal," the only plural item in the response column, and "a tax on goods manfactured in the country" is matched with "excise tax," the only item in the response column which contains the word "tax."

In several of the best-answer items, the correct option is easily distinguished by reason of its length. Such items, like many of those in the matching exercises, require native intelligence or practice in taking objective tests rather than knowledge of the Constitution.

There are some cases in which the keyed answer is incorrect, and a few in which there is no correct answer. A national convention for amending the Constitution would be called by Congress, not by two-thirds of the states (Item 36, Form A), and a writ of habeas corpus is not "the right to demand immediate trial" (Item 104, Form A). The keyed answers to Items 17, 29, 39, 71, 85, and 98, in Form B, are at least questionable.

A minor criticism of the form of the test is that in several instances the incomplete statement or one of the options is isolated from the rest of the item in another column or on a different page. This causes needless confusion and irritation to the person taking the test.

Despite its shortcomings, the test can serve to measure knowledge of the Constitution and to compare the achievement of students of one school with that of other students in other schools.

[619]

Mordy-Schrammel Elementary Civics Test. Grades 7-9; 1935; Forms A, B; 75¢ per 25, postpaid; 15¢ per specimen set, postpaid; 30(35) minutes; Francis E. Mordy and H. E. Schrammel; Bureau of Educational Measurements, Kansas State Teachers College of Emporia.

C. Robert Pace, Associate Director, Evaluation Service Center, Syracuse University, Syracuse, New York. The two forms of this test, published in 1935, are now out of date and their continued use in junior high schools is not recommended until revised editions are published.

Many of the needed revisions in the test are technical and editorial in nature. For example, the reliability, based on 115 cases, is reported to be .80, a figure which is rather low for an achievement test of 93 items. The first 47 items on each form are true-false items; rephrasing these in multiple-choice form would increase the reliability. Several items in both forms are attitude test items. Pupils are expected to agree with such statements as: "One of the best methods of group control is public opinion"; "Washington, D. C., is one of the best-planned cities in the world"; and "The mayor-council form of city government is the best form." Items of this sort do not properly belong in an achievement test. Midyear and end-of-year norms are given in percentiles for grades 7, 8, and 9. At the 50th percentile the difference between midyear and end-of-year scores is not significant in any of the three grades. Nor is there a significant difference between the 50th percentile scores of grades 7 and 8 and grades 8 and 9. When the differences between midyear and end-of-year and between one grade and the next are merely chance differences, it is difficult to see how the test can provide a very precise measure of student's progress or of the efficiency of instruction. The manual includes a table for translating percentile scores into school marks. The practice of assigning marks "on the normal curve" is, at best, debatable and should not, in my opinion, be encouraged.

Beyond these technical and editorial criticisms, a serious question can also be raised regarding the content of the test. Most of the items are concerned with simple identification or definition. Injunction, referendum, franchise, suffrage, and petit jury are typical terms in one large group of definition items. Another large group calls for knowledge of such facts as: a president may not be arrested while he is in office; the smallest unit of society is the family; the chief source of government income is taxation; general election day occurs on the first Tuesday after the first Monday in November. The authors state that "the test items were selected from the common content of several leading text books in the field." A more valid blueprint for test construction would be obtained from a study of the major objectives of junior high school civics courses.

SOCIAL STUDIES — FOURTH MMY

REVIEWS BY *Elizabeth C. Adams, Dorothy C. Adkins, Howard R. Anderson, Frederic L. Ayer, Harry D. Berg, Edith M. Huddleston, Martha E. Layman, Edwin H. Reeder, Hilda Taba, Robert L. Thorndike, and Edgar B. Wesley.*

[662]

★College Entrance Examination Board Achievement Test in Social Studies. Candidates for college entrance; 1937–51; available only in College Entrance Examination Board Admissions Testing Program (see 526); 60(70) minutes; prepared by College Entrance Examination Board Committee of Examiners in Social Studies in cooperation with the Staff of Educational Testing Service: 1951 membership: Henry W. Bragdon (Chairman), William A. Aiken, Harry D. Berg, Paul A. Fullam, and Loretta E. Klee; program administered by Educational Testing Service for the College Entrance Examination Board. *

REFERENCES

1. WARE, CAROLINE F. "The Alternative History Examinations of the College Entrance Examination Board." *Soc Ed* 2:399–403 S '38. *
2. PARGELLIS, STANLEY, AND WARE, CAROLINE F. "The New C.E.E.B. Examinations in History." *Soc Ed* 3:478–84 O '39. *
3. WARE, CAROLINE F. "New College Entrance Examination Board Examinations in History." *Proc Middle States Assoc Hist & Social Sci Teach* 37:31–6 '39. *
4. CHAUNCEY, HENRY. "The Social Studies Test of the College Entrance Examination Board." *Social Ed* 8:253–7 O '44. *
5. STALNAKER, RUTH C., AND STALNAKER, JOHN M. "A Study of the Social Studies Achievement Test of the College Entrance Examination Board Taken by Girls From Independent Schools." *Ed Adm & Sup* 30:490–6 N '44. *
6. WEBER, CHRISTIAN O. "Old and New College Board Scores and Grades of College Freshmen." *J Am Assn Col Reg* 20:70–5 O '44. * (*PA* 19:570)

ROBERT L. THORNDIKE, *Professor of Education, Teachers College, Columbia University, New York, New York.*

This test is planned for administration to high school seniors close to the time of graduation as part of the information supplied to colleges to which they are applying for admission. For that reason, the focus of the test is on American history, with a secondary emphasis on general world history. However, the test items themselves range far beyond the traditionally taught history course. In fact, there was some thought on the part of schools surveyed in an appraisal of the test that it ranged too far from the standard course content, becoming, according to one critic, "more an aptitude than an achievement test."

Including, as it does in some editions, sections on relevance of arguments in favor of and against a proposition, interpretation of cartoons and reading passages, allocation of quotations to periods and authors, as well as a wide range of item types covering terminology, chronology, causation, and the like, the test does place heavy demands upon a variety of reading skills, as well as upon a wide range of background information. These skills are certainly important for college work. Whether the social studies test is the point at which they should be evaluated, rather than the verbal section of the *Scholastic Aptitude Test,* may, perhaps, be debated. One would anticipate that there would be rather substantial correlation between these two tests and that the social studies test might have, as a result, a somewhat limited unique contribution to make to the prediction of college success. However, the skills, over and above the knowledge, represented in the test are certainly important and worth représentation somewhere in the CEEB testing program.

The statistics with respect to both item and test characteristics indicate that the test is well suited for the group with which it is being used. The test is essentially a power test, and different forms all have reliabilities (split half) over .90. Item-test correlations average .40 or better, and the items seem to include very few "lemons." This is, of course, a reflection of the continuity of the Board's testing operation, whereby item analysis data are gathered from one testing and used as a basis for item selection for later forms of the test.

Though content-minded teachers may be somewhat unhappy about this test as an evaluation of the outcomes of their instruction, it appears to provide a technically competent evaluation of a range of significant knowledges and skills in the social studies area.

[663]

*Cooperative Social Studies Test for Grades 7, 8, and 9.** Grades 7–9; 1941–51; 4 scores: informational background, terms and concepts, comprehension and interpretation, total; IBM; Forms X ('47), Y ('48); Forms R, S out of print; no data on validity; no specific manual; no description of normative population; general Cooperative manual ('51); norms ['48]; $2.50 per 25; 50¢ per specimen set, postpaid; separate answer sheets may be used; 80¢ per 25 IBM answer sheets; 15¢ per stencil for scoring answer sheets; cash orders postpaid; 80(90) minutes; Harry Berg (X), Elaine Forsyth (X), and Eunice Ann Lloyd (Y); Cooperative Test Division, Educational Testing Service. *

HILDA TABA, *Professor of Education, San Francisco State College, San Francisco, California.* [Review of Forms S, X, and Y.]

This test is made up of multiple choice items of a fairly discriminating quality. Each of the

forms consists of three parts: information, terms and concepts, and comprehension and interpretation. It is quite difficult to tell what is sampled in each part. The general manual gives only directions for administering and scoring and leaves one uninformed as to how the item sample was secured or what the validity may be.

The information items in Forms S and X seem to cover a vast range: early American history, world history, English and European history, general geographic facts and principles, civics, and the use of sources. It is even more difficult to determine the sampling pattern used for terms and concepts in these two forms. The items seem to emphasize historic information, especially of the kind that requires memory of specific information. While the concepts in Form X seem more functional, perhaps because this form was constructed more recently than Form S, many are either specious or self-definitive. Perhaps least satisfactory, from a technical point of view, not from the point of view of purpose, is the section on comprehension and interpretation in Forms S and X. Some reading items can be answered correctly only with rather specific information outside the given data. Other items can be answered by eliminating the obviously wrong answers. Still others are so vague that the right answer can be chosen only by guessing. And there are some in which interpretation hinges on an understanding of a single metaphoric expression.

Form Y seems to be the most adequate form, especially for the type of general social studies courses now conducted in the junior high school. The historic information required is rather general and is addressed to trends instead of very specific isolated bits of information. The items dealing with skills in locating information seem rather functional. The concepts sampled in the second part are by and large those that are required in a thoughtful understanding of the social scene today. These items also require fairly refined judgment rather than knowledge of specific definitions acquired from texts. The items on comprehension and interpretation require not merely surface reading but also understanding. The selection of items includes questions not only on what is true according to data but also on what can and cannot be concluded from the data. This pairing is important, because the awareness of the limitations of data is almost as important in interpretation as is the recognition of truths revealed. Some other items are so constructed as to include systematically several connected and needed aspects of analysis, such as comparing, contrasting, predicting, and logical reasoning from assumptions to conclusions. It is evident that Form Y is constructed on the basis of sampling important aspects of behavior as well as of content. This does not seem to be true for Forms S and X.

For reviews by Robert A. Davis and Edgar B. Wesley of Forms R and S, see 3:592.

[664]

★History and Civics Test: Municipal Tests: National Achievement Tests. Grades 3–6, 6–8; 1938–49; a subtest of *Municipal Battery* (see 20); 3 scores: lessons of history, miscellaneous facts, total; 2 levels; no data on reliability and validity and no description of normative population in manuals; no norms for part scores; Form A manual ('38), Form B manual ('39); $1.25 per 25; 35¢ per specimen set of any one level; postage extra; 15(20) minutes; Robert K. Speer and Samuel Smith; Acorn Publishing Co. *
a) GRADES 3–6. 1938–49; Forms A ('48—except for minor changes, same as test copyrighted in 1938), B ('49).
b) GRADES 6–8. 1939–49; Forms A ('49—except for minor changes, same as test copyrighted in 1938), B ('48).

HARRY D. BERG, *Associate Professor, and Examiner of Social Studies, Michigan State College, East Lansing, Michigan.*

These tests are short form subtests of the *Municipal Battery* of the National Achievement Test series. Each test is divided into two sections for which subscores may be obtained. Part I is devoted to "lessons of history" and Part II to "historical" or "miscellaneous facts." The recommended testing time is 15 minutes, which is evidence that these are truly short forms. In the estimation of this reviewer, these tests have little to recommend them and might better be passed over in favor of such generally superior tests as the *Cooperative Social Studies Tests for Grades 7, 8, and 9,* or the *Progressive Tests in Social and Related Sciences.* The following are some of the specific counts on which the tests were found to be wanting: (*a*) Even as short forms the tests seem far too short. As a result, reliabilities are low despite the fact that tryouts were administered to relatively heterogeneous populations. This inadequacy is heightened by the fact that many of the items which are included are trivial in nature. (*b*) The tests have little diagnostic value as compared with others on the market. The two parts of each examination test for what is essentially the same thing—the retention of mere factual information. The difference between the two parts lies chiefly in the

use of multiple choice items in the one and true-false in the other. What could be gained from studying subscores under such circumstances is problematical. (*c*) The technique of having students select "lessons of history," while it sounds impressive, in its present application places a premium upon the retention of facts in some cases and leads to overgeneralizations in others. (*d*) No norms of any consequence are available. (*e*) Data with regard to validation are lacking. (*f*) The tests for grade levels 3–6 and 6–8 seem quite undifferentiated insofar as difficulty of content, nature of content, and vocabulary are concerned. From inspection it would seem that they could be used interchangeably. There are few technical flaws in the construction of individual items, so no criticism can be made on this score. However, this is faint praise since there are few opportunities to make technical errors on a typical true-false item such as "Lord Baltimore was a Protestant." Clues and differences between apparent and functioning content usually appear only when higher level objectives are being tested.

This reviewer claims no extensive knowledge of the elementary school curriculum, but he at least hopes that something more is being accomplished there in the area of the social sciences than the imparting of such discrete bits of information as "Abraham Lincoln was born on January 22," "John Cabot captured Montezuma," "the Indians did not eat meat or fish," or "Armistice Day comes once a year." (All of the preceding are from the true-false sections of the tests.) But validity is meaningful only in relationship to objectives. If there are teachers who are interested in testing for such data and that alone, then these tests could be considered for use.

[665]

★Introduction to Social Science: Achievement Examinations for Secondary Schools. High school; 1951; 1 form; no data on reliability and validity; no manual; Minnesota norms (median and quartile deviation) available; similar norms for other regions by special arrangement with publisher; 7¢ per test, postage extra; 60(65) minutes; edited by Walter W. Cook; prepared by a curriculum committee of high school teachers for use in the Minnesota State Board Achievement Examinations Program; Educational Test Bureau, Educational Publishers, Inc. *

[666]

★Social Studies Test: Acorn National Achievement Tests. Grades 7–9; 1946–50; 5 scores: human relations and life situations, products and places, social ideas and facts, application of knowledge, total; Forms A ('50), B ('48); mimeographed manual ['46]; Form

A norms ('50), Form B norms ('48); $2.25 per 25; 35¢ per specimen set; postage extra; 40(45) minutes; Lester D. Crow and Everett F. Augspurger; Acorn Publishing Co. *

EDGAR B. WESLEY, *Visiting Professor, Stanford University, Stanford, California; formerly Director of Social Studies, University High School, and Professor of Education, University of Minnesota, Minneapolis, Minnesota.* [Review of Form A.]

This 150-item test consists of four parts: human relations and life situations, products and places, social ideas and facts, and application of knowledge. All items except those in Part 4 are of the multiple choice form with four options in each. True-false items are used in Part 4. Since very little information is provided with the test, the user scarcely knows what the test is or what it is supposed to do.

The categories are neither clear nor discrete. Historical items are numerous in Part 1 and predominate in Part 3. Many of the errors which appeared in tests during the 1920's appear in this test. An examination of a few items in Part 1 will demonstrate the uncritical nature of this test. Item 2 uses "an" in the stem of the item, thus providing a clue to the correct option. Item 16 refers to the family as a "type of community." Item 23 uses a foil that is contrary to fact. Item 25 says "elections enables." Item 27 refers to the characteristics of frontiersmen as "conditions." Item 41 indicates that the Declaration of Independence is "important" because it is "famous." Item 49 gives the clue by making the correct option unusually long and explicit. Part 4 contains fabricated passages, and the items constitute a rather uncritical reading test.

While the content of many items is important, and a few (e.g., Items 18 and 19 in Part 1) are exceptionally good, the test as a whole is not up to a very high standard.

[667]
Social Studies Test: National Achievement Tests. Grades 4–6, 7–9; 1937–45; Forms A ('45), B ('45—except for minor changes, same as test copyrighted in 1939); 2 levels; no data on reliability and validity and no description of normative population in manuals; no norms for part scores; manuals ('45); $2. per 25 of any one level; 35¢ per specimen set of any one level; postage extra; 35(40) minutes; Robert K. Speer and Samuel Smith; Acorn Publishing Co. *
a) GRADES 4–6. 6 scores: human relations, life situations, social problems, products and peoples, meaning of events, total.
b) GRADES 7–9. 7 scores: human relations, life situations, social interpretations, values of products, social ideas, miscellaneous facts, total.

For a review by Ray G. Wood, see 3:594.

[668]
*A Test of General Proficiency in the Field of Social Studies: Cooperative General Achievement Tests, Revised Series, Test I. Grades 10–12 and college entrants; 1940–51; for complete battery, see 5; 3 scores: terms and concepts, comprehension and interpretation, total; IBM; Forms X ('47), Y ('48), Z ('51); Forms QR–T; out of print; no specific manual; no norms for part scores; general battery folder ('51); general Cooperative manual ('51); norms ['41]; $2.50 per 25; 50¢ per specimen set, postpaid; separate answer sheets may be used; 80¢ per 25 IBM answer sheets; 15¢ per stencil for scoring answer sheets; postpaid; 40(45) minutes; Jeanne M. Bradford (X) and Elaine Forsyth Cook (Y, Z); Cooperative Test Division, Educational Testing Service. *

REFERENCES
1. ARTLEY, A. STERL. *A Study of Certain Relationships Existing Between General Reading Comprehension and Reading Comprehension in a Specific Subject-Matter Area.* Doctor's thesis, Pennsylvania State College (State College, Pa.), 1942.
2. ACHARD, F. H., AND CLARKE, FLORENCE H. "You Can Measure the Probability of Success as a Supervisor." *Personnel* 21:353–73 My '45. *
3. ARTLEY, A. STERL. "General and Specific Factors in Reading Comprehension." *J Exp Ed* 16:181–6 Mr '48. * (PA 20:5122)

For a review by Paul L. Dressel of Forms T, X, Y, and QR of the complete battery, see 5; for a review by Harry D. Berg of Forms S and T, see 3:596; for a review by John V. Mc-Quitty of the complete battery, see 3:3.

[669]
*Understanding of Basic Social Concepts: Iowa Tests of Educational Development, Test 1. Grades 9–13; 1942–51 (first published as a separate in 1951); for complete battery, see 17; Form Y-2 ('51—same as 1949 edition); manual ('51); general manual ('51); $3.75 per 25; separate answer pads or answer sheets must be used; $1.95 per 25 answer pads; $3 per 100 IBM answer sheets; 50¢ per scoring stencil; $2.50 per 25 first semester ('46) or second semester ('48) profiles for any one of grades 9–12; $1 per 25 self-interpreting profiles for students ('51); 25¢ per school summary report ('44); 4¢ per pupil score sheet ('48); 50¢ per specimen set; cash orders postpaid; 55(60) minutes; edited by E. F. Lindquist; J. W. Maucker; Science Research Associates, Inc. *

For a review by Eric F. Gardner of the total battery, see 17; for reviews by Henry Chauncey, Gustav J. Froehlich, and Lavone A. Hanna of Forms X-1 and Y-1 of the complete battery, see 3:12.

ECONOMICS

[670]
*Economics Test: State High School Tests for Indiana. High school; 1934–50; Form B ['49]; Form A out of print; mimeographed; no data on reliability and validity; no manual; norms ['50]; 4¢ per test; 15¢ per specimen set; postpaid; 40(45) minutes; Richard H. Gemmecke; State High School Testing Service for Indiana, Purdue University. *

[671]

★**Economics: 20th Century Test.** 1 semester high school; 1950; 1 form; no data on reliability and validity; no norms—author recommends the use of local norms; 10 or more copies, 5¢ each, postage extra; 35¢ per specimen set, postpaid; 40(45) minutes; Benton Review Publishing Co. *

[672]

★**Graduate Record Examinations Advanced Economics Test.** Senior year college through graduate school and candidates for graduate school; 1939–51; available only in Graduate Record Examinations programs (see 527); 180(220) minutes; prepared by the Advanced Economics Test Committee appointed by Educational Testing Service: Joseph J. Spengler (Chairman), Mary Jean Bowman, Clark L. Allen, Kenneth E. Boulding, and Ben W. Lewis; Educational Testing Service. *

[673]

★**Hills Economics Test.** High school and college; 1940; Form A; $1.05 per 25; 20¢ per specimen set; postpaid; 40(45) minutes; John R. Hills and H. E. Schrammel (manual); Bureau of Educational Measurements, Kansas State Teachers College of Emporia. *

GEOGRAPHY

[674]

★**Economic Geography: Achievement Examinations for Secondary Schools.** High school; 1951; 1 form; no data on reliability and validity; no manual; Minnesota norms (median and quartile deviation) available; similar norms for other regions by special arrangement with publisher; 7¢ per test, postage extra; 60(65) minutes; edited by Walter W. Cook; prepared by a curriculum committee of high school teachers for use in the Minnesota State Board Achievement Examinations Program; Educational Test Bureau, Educational Publishers, Inc. *

[675]

*****Geography: Every Pupil Test.** Grades 4, 5, 6, 7; 1935–51; new form usually published each April and December; 4 levels; form December 1951; no data on reliability and validity; no manual; norms ('51); 2½¢ per test; 1¢ per answer key; postpaid; 40(45) minutes; Ohio Scholarship Tests, Ohio State Department of Education. *

[676]

★**Geography Test: Municipal Tests: National Achievement Tests.** Grades 3–6, 6–8; 1938–50; a subtest of *Municipal Battery* (see 20); 3 scores: geographic ideas and comparisons, miscellaneous facts, total; 2 levels; no data on reliability and validity and no description of normative population in manuals; no norms for part scores; $1.25 per 25; 35¢ per specimen set of any one level; postage extra; 20(25) minutes; Robert K. Speer and Samuel Smith; Acorn Publishing Co. *

a) GRADES 3–6. 1938–49; Forms A ('49—except for minor changes, same as test copyrighted in 1938), B ('49).

b) GRADES 6–8. 1938–50; Forms A ('50), B ('39).

Economics: 20th Century Test

EDWIN H. REEDER, *Professor of Education, University of Illinois, Urbana, Illinois.*

When testmakers attempt to devise an instrument which will evaluate the results of instruction in so broad and complicated a field as geography, they have indeed undertaken a very difficult task. When they try to make this evaluation with a test containing only 40 test elements to be answered by children in 20 minutes, they have, in the opinion of the reviewer, attempted an impossible task. It might be interesting enough to give this test to elementary school children, but the reviewer would be at a loss to know what conclusions might be drawn from the results. Any deductions about the quality of geography teaching which were drawn from children's scores on the tests would be of extremely doubtful validity.

The assumption on which the maker of a short test in a broad field must rest his case in defending its validity is that the individual test items are so significant for the total field of the test that knowledge of them is correlated very highly with the pupil's total knowledge of the field. When viewed in the light of the above statement, many of the items in the tests under discussion would be open to serious question. One item requires the pupil to know how houses are numbered; others, that he know "which state produces the most of ready-made clothing"; "what other continent has most nearly the same number of people as North America"; that handshaking is more common in the United States than in France, China, or India; that in 1938 Germany was "our greatest competitor for South American trade"; that Greece rather than Ireland, Finland, or Palestine has about the same area and population as Illinois; that the Kiel Canal connects the North and Baltic Seas. One item indicates in the given correct answer that "men kiss each other when they meet" in France. In addition to being of doubtful significance, the accuracy of the implications of this item would also be challenged by those who had spent some time in France. No doubt men do sometimes kiss each other in France, but certainly they do not do so as often as we—and they—shake hands.

While it is true that in a long test some of the items above might be defended, they become highly questionable in a test of only 40 items.

Some of the items would be objected to by any geographer on grounds of accuracy. In Form A of the test for grades 3–6, Part I, Item 17 indicates that Canada is "part of Great Britain"; and in Form B, Item 17, the correct answer implies 'that Canada "belongs to a European power." One Wonders what a Canadian would say about these items. He would certainly raise the question whether the testmaker had any conception of the meaning of "Dominion" or of "The British Commonwealth of Nations." In the test for Grades 3–6, Form A, Part II, Item 9 reads as follows: "Which of these countries has the most of an important product used in making automobile tires? Argentina, Brazil, China, Australia." The correct answer given in the key is, of course, Brazil. But no geographer would pay much attention to Brazil as a rubber producer, because it is at present producing less than two per cent of the word's rubber.

In conclusion, it may be reiterated that the giving of the tests in question might be a rather interesting exercise, but it is doubtful that valid conclusions could be drawn from the results with respect to the quality of instruction or learning in the field of geography.

[677]

*Geography Test: National Achievement Tests.
Grades 6–8; 1938–49; 6 scores: geographical ideas, locating products, uses of products and instruments, economic and human relations, miscellaneous problems, total; Forms A ('49), B ('48); no data on reliability and validity and no description of normative population in manuals; no norms for part scores; Form A manual ('49), Form B manual ('48); $2 per 25; 35¢ per specimen set; postage extra; nontimed (35–45) minutes; Robert K. Speer, Lester D. Crow (A), and Samuel Smith; Acorn Publishing Co. *

For a review by Elaine Forsyth, see 3:600.

[678]

★Modern Geography and Allied Social Studies.
Grades 6–10; 1949–50; 11 scores: trade routes and their products, causal geography (U.S.), causal geography (world), miscellaneous geographical facts, invention-power-transportation-communication, geographical vocabulary, world products (sources and uses), economic and human relations, place geography (U.S. and western hemisphere), place geography (Europe and Eastern hemisphere), total; Form A ('49); no norms for part scores; manual ['50]; 4-page map sheet ('49); $2.50 per 25; separate answer sheets must be used; 2¢ per answer sheet; 3¢ per map sheet; postage extra; 35¢ per specimen set, postpaid; nontimed (90) minutes; C. A. Gregory; C. A. Gregory Co. *

EDITH M. HUDDLESTON, *Supervisor of Test Development in Social Studies, Educational Testing Service, Princeton, New Jersey.*

A review of this test indicates that it lives up to the author's concept of it as a test in social science "with a heavily weighted core of Geography." The emphasis on causal relationships and basic principles, in addition to factual knowl-

edge, is to be warmly commended. There are a few individual questions to which the reviewer takes exception, but on the whole the material is sound. The coverage is well-suited to courses of study which emphasize Western culture and civilization, but unfortunately there is only one item on the Far East—an area which is receiving increasing emphasis in current curricula.

The manual presents a table for the conversion of raw scores into scaled scores. These data are derived from a pooled sample of 812 students in grades 6–10, drawn from seven school systems located in four states. The population is not described in further detail, and there is no indication of the number of students taken from each grade level. According to the manual, a particular scaled score "means the same for a sixth grade student that it does for a tenth grade student." This statement may be misleading, since the scaling does not correct for differences between grades. An identical scaled score for a sixth-grade and a tenth-grade student can mean the same for the two students only in the sense that it represents a comparable number of items answered correctly.

Raw-score means and standard deviations are given for grades 6-A, 6-B, 7-A, 7-B, 8-A, 8-B, 9-A, and 10-A. The grade means are quite close together, ranging from 57.61 to 71.44, with standard deviations varying between 18 and 19. Since no information is given as to the type of geography instruction which the students received in each grade, the grade norms are difficult to interpret. It would seem advisable for schools using the test to create their own norms, interpreting them in the light of their own courses of study.

The statements on correction for guessing are theoretically in error. The author makes the assumption that since there are 140 4-choice questions, a student may answer one fourth of the questions correctly by chance (the author computes one fourth of 140 as 36!); therefore, he states that the quantity 36 should be subtracted from all students' scores. The test user should be warned that according to any tenable theory, correction for guessing should be based on the number of wrong responses and the number of items attempted by the student rather than the total number of items in the test. The author does not state what use is to be made of the corrected scores, once they are obtained. Apparently he has not incorporated them in the conversion table.

Modern Geography and Allied Social Studies

The reliability of the test is reported as .92, computed on the basis of odd vs. even scores. The manual does not name the population used in obtaining the reliability, but presumably it is the above-discussed sample of students in grades 6–10. If this is true, the reliability could be expected to be lower within a single grade level.

The manual claims validity for the test on the basis of the wide usage of the textbooks consulted. If the test material was reviewed by experts in the field, the manual does not so state, and no validation on the basis of external criteria is reported.

Despite the limitations in statistical treatment, however, the test contains good material which individual teachers or principals may wish to evaluate in terms of local courses of study.

EDWIN H. REEDER, *Professor of Education, University of Illinois, Urbana, Illinois.*

This test is a praiseworthy attempt to make a comprehensive evaluative instrument in an important field of the school curriculum. The areas covered by the ten parts of the test indicate that the author has a broad conception of the curriculum content in the social studies.

While to some public school people the 90 minutes required to administer this test may seem excessive, the reviewer agrees with the author that any estimate of pupils' progress in so comprehensive a field as the social studies cannot be based on a shorter test.

A common criticism of most tests in the social studies is that they are purely factual and require mere memorization of data. This is not true of the test under discussion. While there are parts of the test that are highly factual, other parts require reasoning and judgment. A teacher who required only memorization of facts would be likely to find that his pupils would not do well on several parts of this test. It is, incidentally, unfortunate that no norms are given for scores on the individual parts of the test; such norms would greatly enhance its diagnostic value.

A reviewer can probably always find in any test elements which he believes to be worthless or positively objectionable. This is true in the present instance. For example, the reviewer doubts whether it is worthwhile for school pupils to know that the approximate capital investment of railroad companies to provide a job for each employee is $24,000; that Japan catches and consumes more fish than does Norway, Russia, or the United States; or that Texas is known

as the Lone Star state. He seriously objects to the use of the word "race" in referring to such peoples as Mongolians or Caucasians. No reputable anthropologist today accepts any such racial divisions. The most objectionable test element is Item 2, Part 3. The correct answer assigned to the question why farming is not done extensively in the Amazon basin is that "white men cannot endure the climate and compete with the dense vegetation and the natives are too ignorant and lazy to farm extensively." This reviewer doubts the geographic accuracy of the reason assigned in the first place, and categorically denies its human implications in the second. But the percentage of unimportant or objectionable elements in the test is, in the opinion of the reviewer, small.

The most serious defect in the test is that the testmaker in his multiple choice statements has made the correct answer the longest one in far too many of the elements. In 71 of the multiple choice items, the answers consist of more than one or two words. In 33 of these 71, the longest response is the correct one. Thus a testwise pupil could make a fairly good score simply by counting the words in the responses and marking the longest.

The last two parts deal with place geography and require the use of maps on which locations are designated. Without research on these two parts, the reviewer cannot be sure that his impressions are correct; but he believes that the maps are too indistinct and cluttered to be satisfactory testing instruments. He believes that the results on these two parts will prove to be a combination of the evaluation of the visual acuity, intelligence, and knowledge of place locations of the pupils; and he doubts that anyone will know without further research in what proportion these three elements operated in yielding a score.

In spite of the defects cited above, this reviewer believes that the test is well worth using and that it will be an evaluative instrument which will prove helpful to teachers and supervisors in improving instructional techniques.

HISTORY

[679]

★**American History: Achievement Examinations for Secondary Schools.** High school; 1951; 1 form; no data on reliability and validity; no manual; Minnesota norms (median and quartile deviation) available; similar norms for other regions by special arrangement with publisher; 7¢ per test, postage extra; 60

(65) minutes; edited by Walter W. Cook; prepared by a curriculum committee of high school teachers for use in the Minnesota State Board Achievement Examinations Program; Educational Test Bureau, Educational Publishers, Inc. *

[680]

*American History: Every Pupil Test. Grades 7–8, 11–12; 1931–51; new form usually published each April and December; 2 levels; no data on reliability and validity; no manual; norms ('51); 2½¢ per test; 1¢ per answer key; postpaid; 40(45) minutes; Ohio Scholarship Tests, Ohio State Department of Education. *
a) GRADES 7–8. 1935–51; 3 tests: To 1770 A.D. (form December 1951 and April 1952), 1770–1860 (form April 1951 and December 1951), 1860 and on (form December 1951 and April 1952).
b) GRADES 11–12. 1931–51; form April 1951.

REFERENCES

1. BROWN, NELSON. A Critical Analysis of the Ohio Every Pupil Tests in American History for the Years 1929–1941. Master's thesis, Ohio University (Athens, Ohio), 1941. Pp. 79. (Abstracts of Masters' Theses...., 1941, p. 6.)
2. FINCH, JOHN F. A Study of the Effects of the Ohio Every Pupil Tests Upon the Teaching of American History. Master's thesis, Ohio University (Athens, Ohio), 1950. Pp. 159. (Abstracts of Masters' Theses...., 1950, pp. 34–5.)

[681]

*American History Test: National Achievement Tests. Grades 7–8; 1937–49; 5 scores: lessons of history, time concepts, historical associations, miscellaneous problems, total; Forms A ('49), B ('45); no data on reliability and validity and no description of normative population in manuals; no norms for part scores; manuals ('45); $2 per 25; 35¢ per specimen set; postage extra; 40(45) minutes; Robert K. Speer, Lester D. Crow, and Samuel Smith; Acorn Publishing Co. *

For reviews by Jacob S. Orleans and Wallace Taylor, see 40:1630.

[682]

*American History Test: State High School Tests for Indiana. First, second semesters high school; 1934–51; 2 levels; mimeographed; no data on reliability and validity; no manual; norms ['51]; 4½¢ per test; 15¢ per specimen set; postpaid; 50(55) minutes; Easdale Pickett; State High School Testing Service for Indiana, Purdue University. *
a) FIRST SEMESTER. Form B ['48]; Form A out of print.
b) SECOND SEMESTER. Form O ['48]; Form N out of print.

[683]

*American History: 20th Century Test. First, second semesters high school; 1938–48; 2 levels; Form A ('48); no data on reliability and validity; no norms—author recommends the use of local norms; manuals ('48); 10 or more copies, 5¢ each, postage extra; 35¢ per specimen set, postpaid; 40(45) minutes; Gale Smith; Benton Review Publishing Co., Inc. *
a) TEST I, FROM DISCOVERY OF AMERICA TO 1860. First semester.
b) TEST II, 1860 TO PRESENT. Second semester.

[684]

*Cooperative American History Test. High school and college; 1932–51; IBM; Forms X ('47), Y ('50—same as test copyrighted in 1948), Z ('49); Forms 1932–37, N–T out of print; no data on validity; no specific manual; general Cooperative manual ('51);

high school norms ['37]; college norms ['44]; $2.50 per 25; 50¢ per specimen set, postpaid; separate answer sheets may be used; 80¢ per 25 IBM answer sheets; cash orders postpaid; 40(45) minutes; Harry D. Berg; Cooperative Test Division, Educational Testing Service. *

REFERENCES

1–3. See 3:604.
4. MOSER, W. E., AND MUIRHEAD, JOSEPH V. "Age of Military Enlisted Men as Factors in Tests of General Educational Development and American History." J Ed Res 43:303–6 D '49. * (PA 24:3896)
5. MOSER, W. E., AND MUIRHEAD, JOSEPH V. "School Grade Last Completed by Military Enlisted Men as Factors in Tests of General Educational Development and American History." J Ed Res 43:221–4 N '49. * (PA 24:3877)

DOROTHY C. ADKINS, *Professor of Psychology and Chairman of the Department, The University of North Carolina, Chapel Hill, North Carolina.* [Review of Forms X, Y, and Z.]

This test is designed to test achievement in American history at the end of a high school or elementary college course. It is divided into two parts with time allowances of 25 and 15 minutes. However, a subject who completes the first part before the time is up can go on to the second part, and one who finishes the second part can return to the first. Thus, the purpose of the two-part division is not to insure that all subjects spend the same amount of time on either part. The general nature of the content of the two parts reveals no striking difference, all the items are five-choice items, part scores are not obtained, and the same scoring formula is applicable to both parts. Thus, the reason for the separation, with the inconvenience in administration of the test, is too subtle for this reviewer to grasp.

The technical quality of the items is high. This reviewer is not competent to judge the content, but the test appears to be up to date and comprehensive.

The materials accompanying the test do not contain information on the estimated reliability coefficient of the test, but they do give the standard error of measurement in terms of scaled scores, based on the parallel forms method.

The test can be used with separate answer sheets, either hand scored or machine scored, or the answers can be recorded in the test booklets. It is curious that the directions for scoring the Cooperative tests when the answers are recorded on the booklets and when separate answer sheets are used are not consistent. The directions for scoring when answers are recorded on the booklets contain the following provision: "When two answers are given for any item, the item should be marked as an omission, provided that one of the answers given is the correct answer; but if both answers are wrong, the item should be marked and counted as a wrong answer." The scorer is left in doubt as to the correct procedure if more than two answers are marked. Perhaps, however, this contingency is so rare when answers are marked on the booklets that no instruction is needed. A subject who marked only the right answers for 50 items, only a single wrong answer for each of 15 items, two answers including one right and one wrong for 10 items, and two wrong answers for 10 items would get a score of $50 - 25/4 = 44$. The directions for scoring separate answer sheets, however, call for counting all marks even where there is more than one for an item, counting the number of blackened spaces appearing through the rights key, and subtracting the latter (the number right) from the former to get the number of wrong answers. The subject above, who marked 105 answers, including 60 right answers, now gets a score of $60 - 45/4 = 49$. (By the more common scoring procedure of counting as wrong any item in which more than one answer is marked, the subject's score would be $50 - 35/4 = 41$.) This reviewer fails to see any sound basis for the variant scoring instructions in the two instances. ,

As is done for most Cooperative tests, tables of scaled scores for the several forms of the American history test, and percentile norms are available.

MARTHA E. LAYMAN, *Associate Professor, Board of Examiners, Michigan State College, East Lansing, Michigan.* [Review of Forms X, Y, and Z.]

Each of the three forms consists of 85 five-option multiple choice items to be administered in 40 minutes of working time. Though the items are not classified according to objectives, the experienced teacher of American history can easily recognize that the authors have included items designed to test knowledge of historical facts; understanding of cause and effect relationships, trends, and developments; and ability to recognize chronological relationships, interpret historical maps, and locate historical information.

The major emphasis is on political and diplomatic history. Economic and social history are covered to a lesser extent, but intellectual and cultural history have been given very little attention. For example, approximately 60 per cent of the items in Form X deal with political and

diplomatic developments, about 35 per cent are designed to test the student's understanding of economic and social events and trends, while the remaining 5 per cent are devoted to cultural and intellectual history and to testing the ability of the student to locate historical information. Though the sampling is probably an accurate reflection of the amount of attention given these factors in the average American history course, this test would not meet the needs of teachers who consider the history of American ideas as meriting a considerable amount of emphasis.

About one half of the items deal with events preceding 1860, while the remaining items are about equally divided between the period 1860 to 1900 and developments of the twentieth century. It is surprising that though Form Z was published in 1950 only two of the items deal with the post-World War II era. Schools stressing current trends and developments in American history classes would find it necessary to supplement this examination with a test of contemporary affairs.

This examination shows evidence of unusual care and technical skill in item construction. It is undoubtedly one of the best, if not the best of the commercial tests in American history.

For a review by Margaret Willis of Form P, see 40:1633; for a review by Edgar B. Wesley of Form 1937, see 38:1014.

[685]

*Cooperative Ancient History Test. High school; 1933–51 ; 3 scores : historical facts, historical judgment, total; IBM; Forms O ('50—same as test copyrighted in 1938), P ('51—same as test coyrighted in 1939) ; Forms 1933–37 out of print; no data on validity; no specific manual; general Cooperative manual ('51) ; norms ('37) ; $2.25 per 25 ; 50¢ per specimen set, postpaid ; separate answer sheets may be used ; 80¢ per 25 IBM answer sheets ; 15¢ per scoring stencil ; cash orders postpaid ; 40(45) minutes ; Howard R. Anderson, E. F. Lindquist, Wallace Taylor (P), and Charlotte W. Croon (P) ; Cooperative Test Division, Educational Testing Service. *

For a review by S. P. McCutchen of Form P, see 40:1634; for a review by Wilbur F. Murra of Form 1937, see 38:1015.

[686]

*Cooperative Modern European History Test. High school and college; 1932–51 ; IBM; Forms X ('47), Y ('48) ; Forms 1932–37, N–Q out of print; no data on validity ; no specific manual; general Cooperative manual ('51) ; norms ('37) ; $2.50 per 25 ; 50¢ per specimen set, postpaid ; separate answer sheets may be used ; 80¢ per 25 IBM answer sheets ; 15¢ per stencil for scoring answer sheets ; cash orders postpaid ; 40 (45) minutes ; Frederick H. Stutz ; Cooperative Test Division, Educational Testing Service. *

For a review by Lavone A. Hanna of Form O, see 40:1635; for reviews by A. C. Krey and S. P. McCutchen of Form 1937, see 38:1016.

[687]

*Cooperative World History Test. High school; 1934-51; IBM; Forms X ('47), Y ('48), Z ('49); Forms 1934-37 out of print; no data on validity; no specific manual; no description of normative population; general Cooperative manual ('51); revised norms ('49); $2.50 per 25; 50¢ per specimen set, postpaid; separate answer sheets may be used; 80¢ per 25 IBM answer sheets; 15¢ per stencil for scoring answer sheets; cash orders postpaid; 40(45) minutes; Wallace Taylor (X, Y) and Frederick H. Stutz (Z); Cooperative Test Division, Educational Testing Service. *

For a review by Kenneth E. Gell of Form 1937, see 40:1636; for a review by R. M. Tryon of Form 1937, see 38:1017.

[688]

★Crary American History Test: Evaluation and Adjustment Series. Grades 9-13; 1951-52, c1950-52; IBM; Forms AM ('51), BM ('52); manual ('51); $2 per 25; separate answer sheets must be used; 80¢ per 25 IBM answer sheets; postage extra; 35¢ per specimen set, postpaid; 40(50) minutes; Ryland W. Crary; World Book Co. *

EDGAR B. WESLEY, *Visiting Professor, Stanford University, Stanford, California; formerly Director of Social Studies, University High School, and Professor of Education, University of Minnesota, Minneapolis, Minnesota.*

This test consists of two 90-item forms. The manual provides rather complete information— nature and purpose, development, validity, reliability, standardization, item difficulty, directions for giving, scoring, and interpreting, and suggestions on individual and group guidance. All the customary data are furnished and the user can proceed with a clear understanding of what to do and what to expect.

This test is excellent, perhaps the best one available on American history at the secondary level. In fact, its merits are numerous and its faults curable. Only by a narrow margin does it fail to be outstanding.

The author consulted most of the obvious sources for determining content, and he has demonstrated how to measure information, skills, interpretations, understandings, and reasoned inferences. The user is thus assured that he has a test which measures more than information alone, for it emphasizes knowledge and synthesized understandings rather than minute details.

The test deserves some criticisms. One sentence in the directions for the first section is confusing, in fact, almost unintelligible. "Notice that all letters (a, b, c, d, e, f, g, and h) are not

given for each item." The testee will look down the page and see that all the items do contain all these letters. If he is a detective he will discover that the shortage of letters is on the answer sheet and not in the test. This confusing and needless distraction can be easily cured. This sentence and the one that follows are utterly unnecessary. Delete them.

The author lists the five aspects of history with which the test deals and states the number of items under each aspect: 28 factual, 16 skill, 8 interpretation, 26 understanding, and 12 inference. Unfortunately the reader can not figure out, except approximately, which items the author thinks belong to each of these categories. Thus the classification becomes merely an assertion, the correctness of which the reader can not check.

The author cites five sources from which the content was derived. They are worthy and useful sources, deserving attention and utilization. There is one curious omission. One can only speculate as to why he ignored *American History in Schools and Colleges.*[1] This report is the only one ever written in the field of the social studies that had the combined support of national historical associations and the National Council for the Social Studies. It contains the only official list of specific minima in American history that was ever agreed upon by a national committee. Furthermore, it contains the test which was administered all over the country to all kinds of groups to demonstrate the difference between ancillary facts and permanent outcomes. Surely this report deserved at least a casual examination by the author of this test.

A few items deserve comments. Item 1, Form AM, declares that the first representative assembly in America met in 1619. Spanish agencies, representative in nature, had been meeting for years before this date. Changing "America" to "English colonies in America" would remedy the inaccuracy. Item 42c, Form AM, says that the public school system was accomplished by local control and support. State aid and legislative controls make a mockery of this popular shibboleth. Item 55e, Form BM, is so neat as to deserve special praise. The association of the Cross of Gold speech with the election of McKinley is a touch of zetetic genius. This whole section

1 *American History in Schools and Colleges.* The Report of the Committee on American History in Schools and Colleges of the American Historical Association, the Mississippi Valley Historical Association, and the National Council for the Social Studies (Edgar B. Wesley, Director of the Committee). New York: Macmillan Co., 1944. Pp. xv, 148. *

(Items 53–57 and in Form AM, Items 47–50), is admirable in its searching use of association. Item 67, Form BM, asking for the fur-trading capital of the United States, is comparatively picayunish.

The section in each form made up of Items 59–66 in Form AM and Items 68–77 in Form BM consists of a reading test. In the opinion of this reviewer, this section is the weakest in the test, for it requires little discrimination or alertness. The fault is not in the idea but in the selection of the passages.

Items 67–87, Form AM, and Items 78–104, Form BM, are multiple choice items, the correct answers to which are incorrectly referred to as *best*. When an item deals with information there is a *correct* answer but not a *best* answer, for a *best* implies degrees of correctness.

Consider a few of the specific items. Item 68d, Form AM, asserts that the "industrial resources" contributed most to the Northern victory, which is about as logical as saying the hind wheels are more important than the front ones. Item 71, Form AM, and Item 82, Form BM, deal with groups of Presidents who increased or did not increase the "influence" of the executive branch. Harding, who was among the "least," followed Wilson who was among the "most." Why not be more precise and talk about strong and weak executives instead of a nebulous and disconnected "influence"? Item 79, Form AM, deals with the alleged reason why Theodore Roosevelt opposed Wilson's administration. All the options are unrealistic. Questions that involve motives are seldom desirable in a test.

Items 80 and 84, Form BM, are thinly disguised questions of dates. A simple completion would be a more economical method of testing. Item 83, Form BM, asks why the United States abandoned isolationism. The answer is pseudo-philosophical, nebulous, and unconvincing. Item 85, Form BM, deals with Lincoln's stand on slavery. When, as authorities agree, the candidate himself was equivocal, why ask high school students to be clear? Item 87, Form BM, should include the saving phrase "principal effect of those listed." Item 88, Form BM, is trivial and erroneous. The significance of the Kentucky and Virginia Resolutions is utterly obscured by tying them to the question of freedom of the press. Item 94, Form BM, states that a third party was "significant" in 1924. While this is possibly true, it is a fine point. Item 98, Form BM, deals with mercantilism. Should not this old skeleton be left to dangle in the musty past? Item 103, Form BM, asks what "territory" was last acquired. The word "area" should for obvious reasons be substituted.

The last section of the test (i.e., Items 88–90, Form AM, and Items 105–7, Form BM) is confusing. The items look like puzzles. Surely less complicated techniques could be used to achieve results.

The author is least successful with the multiple choice form. It should never be used to ascertain the presence or absence of specific information. Obviously there are more economical forms for that purpose. The multiple choice form is most useful when recognition, or still better, discrimination, is required. It can be most appropriately used when the situation allows shades or degrees of truth in all the options.

The virtues of the test far outweigh its defects. It is unfortunate that a description of its shortcomings requires more space than the enumeration of its good qualities. The reviewer regrets this inevitable disproportion, but it should not lead any reader to conclude that the final evaluation is unfavorable. It is, as stated at the beginning of this review, a challenging, reasonable, and practical test—one that deals with ideas rather than catalogic facts.

[689]

★Cummings World History Test: Evaluation and Adjustment Series. Grades 9–13; 1951–52, c1950–51; IBM; Forms AM ('51), BM ('52); manual ('51); $2.50 per 25; separate answer sheets must be used; 80¢ per 25 IBM answer sheets; postage extra; 35¢ per specimen set, postpaid; 40(50) minutes; Howard H. Cummings; World Book Co. *

DOROTHY C. ADKINS, *Professor of Psychology and Chairman of the Department, The University of North Carolina, Chapel Hill, North Carolina.*

This test is one of a series intended for high school use and referred to as the Evaluation and Adjustment Series. The test is available in two forms, each of which contains 80 items.

This reviewer, who is not a historian, will confine herself largely to technical aspects of the test.

The test uses separate answer sheets which may be scored either by hand or by machine. The front page of the test booklet is devoted to directions and sample items. The general format is good, with one exception worthy of comment. Instead of following the usual procedure of designating the answers to the items (all of which have five choices) by 1, 2, 3, 4, 5 or A, B, C, D,

E, the author alternates the first five letters of the alphabet with the second five in the matching exercises in Part A and the first five numbers with the second five in the items of Part B. Thus the responses to Item 46 are designated by 1, 2, 3, 4, 5, and those for Item 47 by 6, 7, 8, 9, 10. Such a practice forces one who wishes to use the test with answer sheets to purchase the specially printed answer sheets rather than to use the standard ones that are doubtless less expensive. It would also seem to have the disadvantage of leading to confusion on the part of the subject.

The manual accompanying the test reports that the objectives and the content of the test were based upon representative textbooks, courses of study from representative schools, statements of objectives by teachers in curriculum studies, and the Twentieth Yearbook of the National Council for the Social Studies.[1] Part A consists of 15 sets of 3 items each, each of the 3 items to be matched with one of 5 alternatives. The sets consist of factual items on historical events, dates, places, and leaders. Part B consists of 35 five-choice items distributed as follows: ancient history, 5; medieval Europe, 5; modern Europe, 12; World War I, 7; World War II, 6.

The 80 items for each form were selected from preliminary forms of 100 items each. It might have been advisable to start with a somewhat larger number of tryout items. The experimental forms were administered in 1949 to about nineteen hundred students in 17 high schools in 7 states. Item difficulty values and item-test correlations were approximated by averaging the percentages passing each item in upper and lower 27 per cents and by means of the Flanagan tables based on upper and lower 27 per cents, respectively. The size of the sample on which the item-analysis data were obtained does not appear to be stated in the manual. It is reported that the mean difficulty index for each form is .44 and that the items were so selected that the two forms are precisely balanced with respect to distribution of item difficulties. As a matter of fact, the two distributions of difficulty values are not identical, as this statement would seem to imply; on the other hand, there is no reason why they should be exactly the same. It is also reported that "the items in the two forms were balanced

with respect to validity indices" (item-test correlations), although elsewhere it is stated that the mean validity index of the items in Form AM is .50 and in Form BM, .41. One may wonder why it was not possible to select the items in such a way that these means would have been much closer.

The manual reports corrected split half reliability coefficients of .91 and .94 for samples of 160 and 161 students, but does not specify which form was used. With further respect to the equivalence of the two forms, the manual reports that they are comparable in content in the sense that their items cover the various aspects of the field in about equal proportions. It is also reported that as an additional check on equivalence, both forms of the test were given to the same group in counterbalanced order. It was found that the two forms were almost directly comparable at all points along the scale. At this stage the reader can legitimately expect to learn the correlation between the two forms, since they had been given to the same group, as the clinching argument for their equivalence. But the manual neglects this point.

The manual contains sections on "General Directions to the Examiner," "Specific Directions for Administering," "Directions for Scoring," "Interpretation of Results," and "Using the Test Results," all of which seem adequate. The norms were based on 3,587 students in 47 schools distributed over 24 states. The median chronological age of this group was 16 years and 1 month and their median IQ, based on the *Terman-McNemar Test of Mental Ability,* was 104. The raw scores on the Cummings test are converted to a scale of normalized standard scores with a mean of 104 and a standard deviation equal to that of the IQ of the standardization sample, 13.5. Percentile norms are also provided.

Brief consideration will be given to the quality of the items as revealed by inspection from a technical standpoint. Some of the sets of matching items suffer from the disparate character of the alternatives from which choice is to be made. Thus, one is to match "the head of a diocese which consists of a number of parishes of the Roman Catholic Church" with one of the following alternatives: bishop, Brahman, hoplite, mandarin, and tribune. The student surely would not have to be well acquainted with the hierarchy of the Roman Catholic Church to make the correct choice. Some of the items have undesirable

1 National Council for the Social Studies. *Improving the Teaching of World History:* Twentieth Yearbook, 1949. Edited by Edith West. Washington, D.C.: the Council, 1949. Pp. xii, 275. Paper, $2.50; cloth, $3.00. *

Cummings World History Test

overlapping in that a part of one item may help to indicate the answer to another (e.g., Items 22 and 74 and Items 46 and 51 in Form AM). In Form BM, one may note that Items 41 and 61 both depend on understanding that the term bourgeoisie refers to the middle class in European society. It may also be noted that some of the items in one form are essentially duplicated in the other, so that there may be some direct memory effect from one to the other. Some of the negative items reflect the problem of the item constructor who can think of four related statements that are true or four results that did stem from one cause but cannot think of a plausible but unacceptable alternative to include as the answer. Thus, in some cases the answers to the negative items seem to be so far afield that they would stand out at once as the answers, even for persons with little discriminatory knowledge of the subject matter in question. On the whole, however, the quality of the individual items is probably above the average for that of most standardized tests in the field of history.

HOWARD R. ANDERSON, *Chief for Social Sciences, Division of Higher Education, Office of Education, Federal Security Agency, Washington, D.C.*

A 7-page manual contains information about the nature and content of the test and its development, the reliability and equivalence of the two forms, general directions to the examiner and specific directions for administering the test, and directions for scoring, interpreting, and using the test results.

The manual states that this test "measures not only factual knowledge of world history, but also understanding of the great movements and social trends....in civilization." Part A includes 45 matching-type items (events, dates, places, leaders), and Part B, 35 five-response multiple choice items. The 80 items were selected from a total of 100 included in a preliminary test administered to students in 17 high schools in 7 states. Difficulty and validity indices were computed for the items in the two preliminary forms. The mean validity index of items in Form A is .50, and in Form B is .41. The mean difficulty of items in both forms is 44. Corrected split half reliability coefficients of .91 and .94 are reported for the two forms, and the standard error of measurement is given as 3.0. Many precautions have been taken to insure the equivalence of the two forms.

Cummings World History Test

End-of-year percentile norms, derived from the administration of the test to 3,587 students in 47 schools representing 24 states are provided. The median age and median IQ of these students are stated. Raw scores on this test are converted to a scale of normalized standard scores which relate them to scores on the *Terman-McNemar Test of Mental Ability.* Suggestions are provided for using test results in evaluating individual and group achievement, and in guidance.

The matching-type items generally are more narrowly factual and in other ways inferior to the multiple choice items. In Form A, for example, Item 6 in Part A requires the student to select "a great Russian novelist of the 19th Century" among Alexander, Cromwell, Demosthenes, Pitt, and Tolstoy. In Form B, a similar item calls for the student to identify in this list (Ebert, Gandhi, Lenin, Marx, Smuts) the man who "led the movement for independence in India." There is a need to include in the test a few items dealing with important developments since World War II.

This world history test, as the manual admits, cannot be used to furnish "analytical measures of....mastery of various aspects of the subject." It does have value in providing "a valid, objective measure of achievement....for the individual student" and as a "predictor of what he is likely to do in the future, particularly in closely related fields."

[690]
★**Graduate Record Examinations Advanced History Test.** Senior year college through graduate school and candidates for graduate school; 1939–51; available only in Graduate Record Examinations programs (see 527); 180(220) minutes; prepared by the Advanced History Test Committee appointed by Educational Testing Service: Edward C. Kirkland (Chairman), Philip Davidson, Edgar E. Robinson, Joseph R. Strayer, and Alice Felt Tyler; Educational Testing Service. *

[691]
★**Indiana History.** Grades 7–8; 1950; 1 form; no data on reliability and validity; no manual; no norms—publisher recommends use of local norms; 4 or more copies, 5¢ each, postage extra; 35¢ per specimen set, postpaid; 40(45) minutes; M. Vigil Schneider; Benton Review Publishing Co., Inc. *

[692]
★**Modern World History: Achievement Examinations for Secondary Schools.** High school; 1951; 1 form; no data on reliability and validity; no manual; Minnesota norms (median and quartile deviation) available; similar norms for other regions by special arrangement with publisher; 7¢ per test, postage extra; 60(65) minutes; edited by Walter W. Cook; prepared by a curriculum committee of high school teach-

ers for use in the Minnesota State Board Achievement Examinations Program; Educational Test Bureau, Educational Publishers, Inc. *

[693]

★**Understanding of American History, 1940 Revision.** Grades 8–12; 1922–40; 5 scores: character judgment, historical vocabulary, sequence of events, cause and effect relationships, total; 1 form, '40; manual ('40); $2.40 per 100, postage extra; 12¢ per specimen set, postpaid; nontimed (25–40) minutes; Luella Cole and R. C. Richards; Public School Publishing Co. *

ELIZABETH C. ADAMS, *formerly of the Social Studies Section, Test Development Department, Educational Testing Service, Princeton, New Jersey.*

There is little to commend in this test. Its title is deceptive (at least, no historian or history teacher of the reviewer's acquaintance would concede that most of the items measure anything but memorization); its appearance is displeasing; and it is a time-waster for the teacher.

On each of the four 5½ × 9 inch pages are crowded 26 multiple choice items. The student underlines the correct choices in the booklet. Since the choices are not aligned vertically, scoring is laborious. Answers are printed in four columns in the manual—the columns cannot be separated into strips for convenient use without destroying the class record sheet on the reverse side! Few teachers can afford the time which scoring this test requires; and if they have the time, they may better spend it in analyzing their students' work on a better test which is more easily scored.

The manual contains the customary directions for administration and statements on reliability and validity. The validity is based on correlations with teachers' grades and with other tests, and on a textbook survey. The date of the survey is not mentioned, but the date of original publication of the test and the type of test item included lead one to suspect that it was made around 1920. Norms consist only of median scores for October and May testing in grade 8 and in high school. There are no other percentiles and no system of standard or scaled scores. Few teachers will consider these norms adequate.

In evaluating a subject matter test, one must necessarily consider the points just mentioned as secondary in importance to the subject matter coverage. The content of this test may have been appropriate when the test was first published, but it bears no recognizable relation to the contemporary history curriculum as discussed, for

example, in the Seventeenth Yearbook of the National Council for the Social Studies. Little attention is given to understanding, and the facts tested are those which can be put into pat phrases. Large-scale historical developments are ignored in favor of the Battle of Buena Vista and the Ironclad Oath.

Test 1, Character Judgment, deserves to be condemned on both educational and scholarly grounds as perpetuating the tendency to label a character with an adjective and dismiss him. In one item, the student must judge whether Benjamin Franklin was emotional, retiring, prudent, or blunt. Is "prudent" the only word which can be found to describe one of our most original and farsighted founding fathers? When a test can devote so little attention to any one figure, let the recognition be consistent with his stature. Unfortunately, this item is typical of the items in Test 1. In Test 2, Historical Vocabulary, the items are much more significant. But in Item 26 the student must select "corporation" as the word most similar in meaning to "trust"! We may hope that no teacher will allow his students to retain such an indefensible misconception.

Each item in Test 3, Sequence of Events, requires the student to select which one of four events came first. Test 4, Cause and Effect Relationships, requires the student to select from four events the one which is the result of the other three. It is sound in conception, and a number of the items do involve some exercise of reason. Other items, however, require only that the student call up such things as the proverbial "three causes of the Revolution" and "three reasons for the growth of sectionalism" which used to be, and in some cases still are, standard textbook phrases.

Certain items contain outdated phrases—"the World War," for instance. On the side of omissions, the test, most recently revised in 1940, perforce includes no items dealing with World War II or with American politics since 1940. There is almost nothing on race problems, labor relations, geographical influences on history, or the whole question of the government in economic life. Questions on sectionalism and the Civil War abound; questions on the development of the Constitution are totally lacking.

The reviewer sees no reason why this test should be used. The *Cooperative American History Test* has much better constructed items; both it and the *Crary American History Test* have better factual coverage. These two tests approximate the contemporary course of study much more closely than does the Cole-Richards test; they have better norms; and they are more economical of the teacher's time.

[694]

*World History: Every Pupil Test. High school; 1933–51; new form usually published each April and December; form December 1951; no data on reliability and validity; no manual; norms ('51); 2½¢ per test; 1¢ per answer key; postpaid; 40(45) minutes; Ohio Scholarship Tests, Ohio State Department of Education. *

[695]

★World History Test: Acorn National Achievement Tests. High school and college; 1948; 6 scores: social studies terms, world geography, contributions of world peoples to civilization, political history, economic-social-cultural history, total; Form A; no norms for part scores; $2.50 per 25; 35¢ per specimen set; postage extra; 40(45) minutes; Vincent McGarrett and Edward H. Merrill; Acorn Publishing Co. *

[696]

*World History Test: State High School Tests for Indiana. First, second semesters high school; 1934–51; 2 levels; mimeographed; no data on reliability and validity; no manual; 4½¢ per test; 15¢ per specimen set; postpaid; 40(45) minutes; Donald P. Knott (C), Paul C. Baker (C), Lawrie F. Davis (O), Harold Hargrave (O), and Frankie Jones (O); State High School Testing Service for Indiana, Purdue University. *
a) FIRST SEMESTER. Form C ['50]; Forms A, B out of print; no norms.
b) SECOND SEMESTER. Form O ['48]; Form N out of print; norms ['51].

[697]

★World History: 20th Century Test. First, second semesters high school; 1937–49; 2 levels; Form A ('48); no data on reliability and validity; no norms—author recommends the use of local norms; manuals ('49); 10 or more copies, 5¢ each, postage extra; 35¢ per specimen set, postpaid; 40(45) minutes; Gale Smith; Benton Review Publishing Co., Inc. *

POLITICAL SCIENCE

[698]

★American Civics and Government Tests for High Schools and Colleges. High school and college; 1930–49; Forms A ['49], B ['49]; 90¢ per 25, postage extra; 12¢ per specimen set, postpaid; 40(50) minutes; F. A. Magruder, R. J. Clinton, and M. M. Chambers; Public School Publishing Co. *

[699]

★American Government and Citizenship: Every Pupil Test. Grades 11–12; 1935–51; new form usually published each April and December; form April 1951; no data on reliability and validity; no manual; norms ('51); 2½¢ per test; 1¢ per answer key; postpaid; 40 (45) minutes; Ohio Scholarship Tests, Ohio State Department of Education. *

ELIZABETH C. ADAMS, *formerly of the Social Studies Section, Test Development Department,* *Educational Testing Service, Princeton, New Jersey.*

This test is unprepossessing in appearance, uninspiring in content. Whether it was carefully standardized cannot be determined from the brief statement on construction of the test; the point is more or less irrelevant, since it would hardly be good economics to spend much on a standardization program for a test so mediocre in conception.

The items in Part I are multiple choice; the choices are strung across the page and the items are crowded together. Part II contains matching items. Answers for both parts are written in parentheses in a column on each page, so the scoring is reasonably easy. Booklets are expendable, since no provision is made for using separate answer sheets. The manual consists of one sheet bearing instructions, descriptive information, and norms. The latter are in the form of end-of-course percentiles for high school and college. They are stated in the reverse of the customary fashion; i.e., the highest score is listed as "1% equals or exceeds score" instead of "99th percentile." This will make for confusion when the students' ratings are entered on cumulative record cards. The college scores are very little higher than the high school scores. This may only indicate, of course, that the high school government course teaches as much as does the college course. However, the high school population is so much more heterogeneous in ability that one would expect more than 3 raw score points difference in median scores.

The test is strictly factual despite the authors' statement that an effort was made to select items which test understanding. In each form there are one or two "thought" questions, but that is all. Now let it be agreed that a knowledge of the facts of American government is vital to effective citizenship and that such knowledge should be tested. But the kind of facts tested here are nearly all of the definition type or the "five functions of the legislative branch" type—the kind of knowledge which can be put into test questions by any teacher at the rate of perhaps 30 an hour. Why buy a standardized test for the purpose?

More serious than what the test includes is what it neglects: many processes which are of tremendous importance in American political life but which cannot be put into one-word answers. For example, there is no mention of the dilemma posed by the need to preserve civil liberties and at the same time protect the state against·those who would destroy it. The concepts of administrative legislation and judicial review—the wide power of agencies to make rulings and of courts to determine the meaning of the Constitution for any given generation—are not dealt with. Nor is there any emphasis on the responsibility of the individual for securing good government. The basic differences between the philosophy of democracy and the philosophy of totalitarianism are not covered, and there is no mention of the questions brought up by American participation in international organizations. These are points which alert teachers think important. They are also topics which make the course come to life for the student. In effect, I should say, this test is a partner of certain textbooks in rendering the study of American government dry, dead, and repulsive to countless students. Can anything be more subversive? Teachers may better use the *Cooperative American Government Test,* which contains much more penetrating items and puts life into the subject.

[700]

★**Civic Vocabulary Test.** Secondary school (high school); 1951; 1 form; no norms; preliminary mimeographed manual; 2s. 6d. per 10; 3d. per single copy; 9d. per manual; cash orders postpaid within Australia; nontimed (10–30) minutes; S. A. Rayner; Australian Council for Educational Research. *

REFERENCES
1. RAYNER, S. A. *The Special Vocabulary of Civics.* Foreword by Alice Hoy. A.C.E.R. Research Series, No. 65. Published for the Australian Council for Educational Research. Melbourne, Australia: Melbourne University Press, 1951. Pp. x, 105. Paper. *

[701]

*Civics: 20th Century Test.** First, second semesters high school; 1935–49; formerly called *The 20th Century High School Civics Test;* 2 levels; Form A ('48); no data on reliability and validity; no norms—author recommends the use of local norms; manuals ('49); 10 or more copies, 5¢ each, postage extra; 35¢ per specimen set, postpaid; 40(45) minutes; Gale Smith; Benton Review Publishing Co., Inc. *

[702]

*Cooperative American Government Test.** High school; 1947–51; IBM; Forms X ('47), Y ('48); no data on validity; no specific manual; general Cooperative manual ('51); norms ('48); $2.50 per 25; 50¢ per specimen set, postpaid; separate answer sheets may be used; 80¢ per 25 IBM answer sheets; 15¢ per scoring stencil; cash orders postpaid; 40(45) minutes; John Haefner; Cooperative Test Division, Educational Testing Service. *

FREDERIC L. AYER, *Head, Division of Evaluation and Research, Citizenship Education Project, Teachers College, Columbia University, New York, New York.* [Review of Forms X, Y.]

This test is a comprehensive examination of the ability to learn and retain facts about the structure, mechanics, and history of government in the United States. It covers adequately the content of most textbooks on American government and should be particularly useful to those who are interested in determining how well students have assimilated the atoms of truth which make up the factually oriented course.

Although the tests are listed by the publishers as high school forms, the norms supplied are based on data for twelfth grade students only. Students of grades 9 through 12 to whom this reviewer administered the tests found great difficulty with the vocabulary used in many of the items ("negotiate," "significant weakness of a unicameral....legislature," "His Superfluous Excellency," to mention a few).

Occasional items are introduced which require the selection of the poorest choice (e.g., "Which of these is *not* essential to a democracy?"), a technique that in the context of items calling for the *best* choice often throws respondents off the track. Mixed in with straight recall items are many which appear to require a high discriminative judgment, often based on much more complete information and wider experience than students might be expected to have. ("Which is the most serious governmental problem facing metropolitan areas like New York and Chicago?" "Which is the most serious practical objection to the principle of 'separation of powers'?" "What is considered [*sic!*] the greatest advantage of the 'office column' type of ballot?")

Other items commendably require the application of facts to a specific situation—the methods of practical politics—rather than a mere knowledge of facts ("Sam Spellbinder, the leading orator of his party, is most likely to be given what job in the national nominating convention?" "The job of a typical precinct captain.... is to 'deliver the vote' * How is he usually paid?" In connection with a map of a gerrymandered state, "In whose favor has the imaginary state of Pandemonium been gerrymandered?") There are, however, only about four or five items of this type in each form.

Two professors of political science at Columbia University who checked the key voiced serious disagreement with the choices given as correct. On some items they disagreed both with each other and with the key; on others their opinion was that none of the choices represented a correct response. For a few items they stated flatly that the "correct" response was wrong. Part of this confusion occurs with those items which deal with problems concerning jury trials and other situations in which the law is not the same in all states; part is accounted for by "dated" items—problems which were serious in 1947–48 and have now either been solved or are overshadowed by still more serious problems of government. It would probably be advisable for those using this test to prepare their own keys to be consistent with the state laws and text materials applying in the local situation.

No specific manual is issued for these tests; the manual supplied gives only general instructions for test administration and interpretation of scaled scores. No data are given as to reliability or comparability of forms, or to specific statistical validity studies.

The authors have made an enviable attempt to cover the field of course material in American government. They have succeeded in sampling adequately the body of knowledge contained in many different kinds of government courses. A more effective approach might have been to limit the coverage to either knowledge background or political reasoning based on knowledge, or to divide the forms into subtests covering these areas. This would permit teachers to measure directly the success of either the historical or the problems type of course.

The reviewer would recommend the test for use in classes where the emphasis is on the teaching of facts about American government. It does not appear to be applicable, however, to courses such as those titled Problems of Democracy and is not recommended for students below the twelfth grade unless they have exceptional reading ability.

[703]

★**Graduate Record Examinations Advanced Government Test.** Senior year college through graduate school and candidates for graduate school; 1939–51; available only in Graduate Record Examinations programs (see 527); 180(220) minutes; prepared by the Advanced Government Test Committee appointed by Educational Testing Service: V. O. Key, Jr. (Chairman), Albert Lepawsky, Carl B. Swisher, John A. Vieg, and Ruth G. Weintraub; Educational Testing Service. *

[704]

*Junior High School Civics Test: State High School Tests for Indiana.** Grades 7–9; 1934–46; 2 levels; mimeographed; no data on reliability and validity; no manual; norms ['47]; 4½¢ per test; 15¢ per specimen set; postpaid; Florise Hunsucker; State High School Testing Service for Indiana, Purdue University. *
a) FIRST SEMESTER. Form A ['46].
b) SECOND SEMESTER. Form N ['46].

[705]

★**Patterson's Tests on the Federal Constitution.** Grades 9–14; 1927–37; 3 tests (labeled Forms A, B, and C); 1 form, '37; no data on reliability and validity; no norms; manual ['27]; 10 or more copies, 5¢ each; 25¢ per specimen set; cash orders postpaid; Raymond G. Patterson; Palmer Co. *
a) FORM A, FUNDAMENTAL FACT TEST. Nontimed (25) minutes.
b) FORM B, COMPLETION TEST. Nontimed (35) minutes.
c) FORM C, MATHEMATICAL TEST. Nontimed (25) minutes.

[706]

★**Senior High School Civics Test: For a One-Semester Course: State High School Tests for Indiana.** 1 semester high school; 1949; Form B; mimeographed; no data on reliability and validity; no manual; norms ['49]; 4½¢ per test; 15¢ per specimen set; postpaid; 40(45) minutes; Meribah Clark; State High School Testing Service for Indiana, Purdue University. *

[707]

*Senior High School Civics Test: State High School Tests for Indiana.** 1, 2 semesters high school; 1934–47; 2 levels; mimeographed; no data on reliability and validity; no manual; norms ['47]; 4½¢ per test; 15¢ per specimen set; postpaid; 40(45) minutes; Meribah Clark (A) and Olis G. Jamison (N); State High School Testing Service for Indiana, Purdue University. *
a) FIRST SEMESTER. Form A ['47].
b) SECOND SEMESTER. Form N ['47].

SOCIOLOGY

[708]

*Black-Schrammel Sociology Test.** High school; 1936–37; Forms A ('36), B ('37); manual ['37]; $1.05 per 25; 20¢ per specimen set; postpaid; 40(45) minutes; William A. Black and H. E. Schrammel; Bureau of Educational Measurements, Kansas State Teachers College of Emporia. *

[709]

★**Graduate Record Examinations Advanced Sociology Test.** Senior year college through graduate school and candidates for graduate school; 1939–51; available only in Graduate Record Examinations programs (see 527); 180(220) minutes; prepared by the Advanced Sociology Test Committee appointed by Educational Testing Service: Wilbert E. Moore (Chairman), Theodore Abel, Everett C. Hughes, Edward P. Hutchinson, and Logan Wilson; Educational Testing Service. *

REPRINTED FROM *The Fifth Mental Measurements Yearbook*

SOCIAL STUDIES—FIFTH MMY

REVIEWS BY *Howard R. Anderson, Harry D. Berg, Donald T. Campbell, Robert H. Ferrell, James A. Field, Jr., Wayne A. Frederick, Richard E. Gross, John H. Haefner, David K. Heenan, David R. Krathwohl, Christine McGuire, John Manning, I. G. Meddleton, Raymond C. Norris, S. A. Rayner, Douglas E. Scates, Frederick H. Stutz, Ralph W. Tyler, and M. J. Wantman.*

[785]

*American History—Government—Problems of Democracy: Acorn Achievement Tests.** Grades 9–16; 1942–53; 6 scores: growth of a national spirit, growth of democracy, the Constitution, foreign policy, problems of American democracy, total; Forms A ('53, identical with test copyrighted in 1942 except for minor changes), B ('44); directions sheets (A, '42; B, '44); teachers' guide ['44]; $3.50 per 25 tests; 50¢ per specimen set; postage extra; 40(45) minutes; Vincent McGarrett; Acorn Publishing Co. *

RICHARD E. GROSS, *Associate Professor of Education, Stanford University, Stanford, California.*

The reviewer agrees with the remarks made by Howard R. Anderson in *The Third Yearbook* (see 3:590) and wishes to underscore and extend these. Time has made even more of the test items outdated.

While the Teachers' Guide claims that the test does *not* include current events items, many items, even in the history sections, reflect the fact that the test has never been seriously revised. Items which discuss the "ever-normal granary" concept and wartime priorities in the present tense are typical examples; one item refers to the Second World War, as follows, without any concluding date—(1939–   )!

All items are of the multiple choice type. Although this type of item can be used fruitfully to reveal depth of understanding of cause and effect relationships and ability to differentiate between lesser and more important events or long term and short term results and to assess problem-thinking, the great bulk of items in this test remain of a purely informational nature. In addition, a number of items are concerned with events of minor importance, such as one which attempts to ascertain the correct order in which the departments of the United States Cabinet were established and another which requires the testee to indicate whether it was Henry Morton, Edwin Booth, John Drew,

or Otis Skinner who was not a star in the American theatre.

The reviewer tends to be most critical of the items lumped together in the problems of democracy section. Many of these are especially outdated, like the question which asks the testee to select from among Alben Barkley, Hamilton Fish, Martin Dies, and Carter Glass the member of Congress who has been chairman of an un-American activities committee. The same items are often concerned with relatively unimportant information, like the population of various American cities or states in terms of the 1940 census.

The tests contain the usual share of poor and ambiguous items, like the following:

15. Who of these favored free enterprise?
    a. Harry Truman
    n. Dwight Eisenhower
    c. Franklin Roosevelt
    r. Dean Atcheson [sic]
18. American policy since 1939
    d. has been consistently in agreement with Jefferson's foreign policy
    f. was opposed to the Monroe Doctrine
    s. reversed the attitude taken by the U.S. toward China after the close of the Boxer Rebellion
    b. has differed from Washington's foreign policy

Some items are so carelessly constructed as to penalize the able student. For example, the testee is given the names of Marion Anderson, Booker T. Washington, William C. Handy, and Dred Scott and asked which *is* a figure important in the field of Negro education. The word "is" might here lead a bright student who knows that the latter three are dead to select Marion Anderson as the correct answer. Finally, no test supposedly having gone through at least one revision should include spelling errors like "Gasden" in an item referring to the Gadsden Purchase.

The reviewer does not believe the test to be adequate for use in American history classes, and it is certainly not satisfactory for use in civics and problems of democracy classes.

Teachers will do far better to use up-to-date, separate, specific tests available in each of these areas, such as the *Crary American History Test* and the *Peltier-Durost Civics and Citizenship Test*.

For a review by Howard R. Anderson, see 3:590.

[786]

*College Entrance Examination Board Achievement Test in Social Studies. Candidates for college entrance; 1937–58; for more complete information, see 599; IBM; 60(80) minutes; program administered by Educational Testing Service for the College Entrance Examination Board. *

REFERENCES

1–6. See 4:662
7. BRAGDON, HENRY W. "College Entrance Board Social Studies Test." *Social Ed* 16:369–72 D '52. *
8. NEWMAN, SIDNEY H.; FRENCH, JOHN W.; AND BOBBITT, JOSEPH M. "Analysis of Criteria for the Validation of Selection Measures at the United States Coast Guard Academy." *Ed & Psychol Meas* 12:394–407 au '52. * (*PA* 27:6159)
9. COLLEGE ENTRANCE EXAMINATION BOARD. *Social Studies: A Description of the Social Studies Test of the College Entrance Examination Board.* Princeton, N.J.: the Board, 1953. Pp. 24. *

RALPH W. TYLER, *Director, Center for Advanced Study in the Behavioral Sciences, Stanford, California.* [Review of Form FAC.]

The test is one of 13 in the battery of achievement tests of the College Entrance Examination Board. As an achievement test it should measure the extent to which the high school student has attained the major objectives of the social studies. As part of the battery used for college admission purposes it should emphasize the most significant intellectual tasks of this field because of its influence upon teaching and learning of high school students. The test does avoid exercises which require only rote memorization but it falls far short of reflecting the best in the social studies.

In the first place it does not cover the social studies but deals only with history, primarily, but not solely, United States history. In the 100 items in the test, concepts, generalizations, and problems dealt with in the contemporary social sciences are not included as such, except for a group of six items on international trade and balance of payments. The effort of teachers of the social studies to help students to understand some of the major concepts useful in interpreting and analyzing important social problems, and to use valid generalizations in predicting possible consequences of courses of action employed to grapple with these problems is not reflected in the exercises. The test also fails to include items requiring the student to identify or to use dependable sources of information about social phenomena.

Even as a history test it is not a well organized selection of exercises appropriate for appraising the extent to which high school students have attained the commonly recognized objectives of history. It samples three objectives but does not touch upon three other important ones. In this reviewer's opinion, the best exercises in reflecting the aims of history teaching are those requiring the student to explain the meaning and implications of certain important policies and movements, such as "dollar diplomacy," the British Labor Party, the TVA, and the Protestant Revolution. Twenty items are of this sort. Twenty items are also devoted to identifying major historic persons in terms of the policies they supported or viewpoints they held. Most of the remaining items sample the students' knowledge of historic events. Almost all the items in the test require the student to go beneath the label of doctrines, movements, or slogans to more significant knowledge of their content. This is commendable. However, the failure to test for understanding of the long-time development of major issues, policies, or practices and the omission of exercises dealing with the great debates of history are serious weaknesses. Even more serious in this reviewer's opinion is the lack of testing for elementary understanding of history as an intellectual discipline. A test which treats all historic matters as matters of fact without touching on the problems of "constructing" history is contributing to the intellectual confusion of our time.

The test is well edited and has good typography. The manual reports a reliability coefficient of .92. The time limit of 60 minutes is a bit short for the 100 items so that the high reliability may be partly due to the speed factor. The test is an improvement over history tests of earlier years but it is still inadequate for the needs of high school social studies.

For a review by Robert L. Thorndike of an earlier edition, see 4:662.

[787]

*Cooperative General Achievement Tests: Test I, Social Studies. Grade 12 and college entrants; 1937–56; manual uses the subtitle *A Test of General Proficiency in the Field of Social Studies;* 3 scores: terms and concepts, comprehension and interpretation, total; IBM; Forms XX ('53, revision of Form X), YZ ('51, revision of Forms Y and Z); no norms for part scores; high school norms same as those published in 1938; separate answer sheets must be used; $2.95 per 25 tests; $1 per 25 IBM answer sheets; 25¢ per scoring stencil; 35¢ per battery manual ('56); $1 per specimen set; postage extra; 40(50) minutes; Jeanne M. Bradford (XX); Cooperative Test Division, Educational Testing Service. *

For a review by Harry D. Berg of earlier forms, see 3:596. For a review by Max D. Engelhart of the complete battery, see 6; for a review by Paul L. Dressel of earlier forms, see 4:5; for a review by John V. McQuitty, see 3:3.

[788]

★**The Greig Social Studies Test.** Grades 6–8; 1957; for Catholic schools; IBM; 1 form; $3.20 per 25 tests; separate answer sheets may be used; $1.40 per 35 IBM scorable answer sheets; 12¢ per scoring stencil; 50¢ per specimen set; postage extra; 40(50) minutes; Mary E. Greig; Scholastic Testing Service, Inc. *

DAVID R. KRATHWOHL, *Research Coordinator, Bureau of Educational Research, and Professor of Education, Michigan State University, East Lansing, Michigan.*

This test is intended "to measure the extent to which pupils in Catholic Elementary Schools have achieved the important objectives of courses in American History, Civics, and Geography offered at the sixth, seventh, and eight grade levels." The manual claims that both curriculum and test emphasize not only acquisition of factual knowledge, but also higher types of learning.

The development of an outline based on a review of test and curriculum materials from Catholic sources preceded the construction of a 125-item experimental test from which 100 four-choice items were selected for the final form. Selection of items was determined by the test outline, difficulty indices, and validity indices. According to the outline, approximately two thirds of the items might be expected to call for learning beyond the memorization of facts. This is very far in excess of the proportion of items the reviewer would so classify. Proper classification of the behaviors elicited by a test item requires a knowledge both of pupil background and of the nature of the item; judged solely by the latter criterion, however, very few of the items appear to test other than factual acquisition. For example, the statement on content says that "numerous items....are aimed at an interpretation of historical information and at reasoned inferences based on knowledge of the historical process," and the test outline indicates that 9 per cent of the items

can be classified as "reasoned inferences." The publisher graciously sent the reviewer a classification of the items. According to the classification, these items are examples of "reasoned inferences":

74. An agency set up by the federal government to give work in the forests to young men was
   a. the F.H.A.   c. the T.V.A.
   b. the W.P.A.   d. the C.C.C.
75. The main purpose of the Kefauver Committee was to investigate
   a. slums   c. housing
   b. excessive taxes   d. crime

It is difficult to understand on what bases these may be considered "reasoned inferences."

Split-half reliabilities are reported as follows: grade 6, .90; grade 7, .90; and grade 8, .93. Comparable Kuder-Richardson (formula 21) reliabilities are .92, .90, and .90, respectively. These estimates of reliability may be inflated by a speed factor at the sixth grade level. The standard errors of measurement are also given for each grade.

Norms are based on scores by 4,320 pupils in 20 schools in 7 well diversified states. A check of these norms against the results of 1,750 eighth graders from all the schools of a midwest diocese showed "substantial agreement" between the two. The norms tables give percentile equivalents for each raw score for each of grades 6–8. The norms show a marked progression in median raw score from grade to grade, successive medians for grades 6, 7, and 8 being 19.7, 30.8, and 48, respectively.

Since the test consists of 100 four-choice items and there is no correction for guessing, a chance score for a completed test is 25. The percentile equivalent for this score is 64 for grade 6, 31 for grade 7, and a reasonable 4 for grade 8. Thus, on the basis of the norms provided, about two thirds of the sixth graders who complete the test can be expected to score below chance. In view of the high reliability coefficients, it seems more likely the tests are speeded, at least for sixth graders. Introducing a speed factor into an achievement test of this type would be questioned by most teachers.

The test is printed in an acceptable format on strong paper. The directions for both administration and scoring appear to be clear and straightforward. The instructions for interpretation are written sensibly and in a manner understandable to the unsophisticated user. Only the total score is interpreted since the test is not diagnostic except as a teacher makes her own question by question analysis.

The authors are to be commended for developing a test manual along the lines of the standards for test users adopted by APA, AERA, and others. The test items are devoid of obvious flaws. But the test as a whole appears to be much more heavily oriented toward measurement of factual knowledge than higher mental skills despite the manual's claim to the contrary. Its use with the lower grades in its intended range appears questionable on the basis of the norms. Since only six out of the 100 items would be considered colloquial to the Roman Catholic curriculum, other social studies tests might fit the curriculum as well, or if the orientation is toward objectives other than memorization of information, better. The Catholic school teacher will do well to consider carefully alternative measures in this field.

[789]

*Introduction to Social Studies: Achievement Examinations for Secondary Schools. High school; 1951–53; title on Form 1 is *Introduction to Social Science;* Forms 1 ('51), 3 ('53) ; no specific manual; no data on reliability; norms: Forms 1 ['52] ; 3 ('53) ; 10¢ per test, postage extra; (60–90) minutes; Kenneth D. Seeling (3) ; Educational Test Bureau. *

[790]

History and Civics Test: Municipal Tests: National Achievement Tests. Grades 3–6, 6–8; 1938–55; subtest of *Municipal Battery;* 3 scores: lessons of history, historical facts, total; 2 forms; 2 levels; directions sheets (A, '38; B, '39) ; no data on reliability; no norms for part scores; $1.75 per 25 tests; 50¢ per specimen set of either level; postage extra; 15(20) minutes; Robert K. Speer and Samuel Smith; Acorn Publishing Co. *
a) GRADES 3–6. Forms A ('48, identical with test copyrighted in 1938 except for minor changes), B ('49, identical with test copyrighted in 1939 except for minor changes).
b) GRADES 6–8. Forms A ('49, identical with test copyrighted in 1938 except for minor changes), B ('55, identical with test copyrighted in 1939 except for minor changes).

HOWARD R. ANDERSON, *Professor of Education, and Dean, University School of Liberal and Applied Studies, The University of Rochester, Rochester, New York.*

Each of the two forms for grades 3–6 includes 70 items—10 four-response multiple choice questions in Part 1, and 60 true-false questions in Part 2. The title "Lessons of History" seems pretentious for the shorter section. Consider these "lessons" tested for in Form A : Item 2, The Indians lost America because they "did not have a common government." Item 3,

Greig Social Studies Test

From reading about wampum, we learn that "dollars and cents were not the first kinds of money." There must be other reasons why the Indians lost. And the reviewer doubts that any reasonably bright youngster, even though he had never heard about wampum, would believe that our monetary system was the first in the world.

The true-false statements are, for the most part, factual; for example, "Indian women were called 'braves' " and "The Pilgirms came to America from Russia." In Form A seven items mention Washington; five, Franklin; four, the Civil War; and three each, Lincoln, War of 1812, and Indians. Of course the item "In Franklin's time, most people travelled by steamboat" also calls for time judgment. About one half the items deal with the period before 1789, about one fourth with the period since 1865.

The two forms for grades 6–8 are similar to the tests just described. Part 2, however, has been given the more accurate title "Miscellaneous Facts." Whereas Part 2 in Form B contains 60 true-false items, there are only 48 such items in Form A. In Form B there are seven items on World War I, and about twice as many items for the period since 1917 as in Form A. About one fourth of the items deal with the period before 1789, and just over half with the period since 1865.

In Form A one might have difficulty discovering the "lesson of history" to be learned in Item 1. The stem reads, "From reading about Andrew Jackson we learn"; two of the responses are "he refused to enforce unpopular laws" and "he enforced laws he did not like." There is reason to think he did both. In this same form a true-false statement reads, "Misplaced persons in Europe were not admitted to the United States after World War Two." Another item in this form probably will give pupils more trouble: "To become a naturalized citizen, an illiterate alien must be at least 30 years old." Fortunate is the youngster who marks it false because the age restriction seems implausible, and who does not puzzle over immigration restrictions and whether an illiterate alien can qualify for citizenship.

Unless teachers actually teach the type of information tested for in this test, there is little reason why they should use it. Certainly there are superior tests, among them the social studies test included in the STEP program of the Educational Testing Service.

For a review by Harry D. Berg, see 4:664. For a review by J. Murray Lee of the complete battery, see 18; for a review by Ralph C. Preston, see 4:20; for reviews by A. M. Jordan and Hugh B. Wood of the complete battery for grades 6–8, see 40:1191.

[791]

*The Iowa Tests of Educational Development: Test 1, Understanding of Basic Social Concepts.** Grades 9–13; 1942–58; IBM; Forms X-3S, Y-3S ('52); examiner's manual ('58); battery manual ('54); pupil profile leaflet, fourth edition ('58); profile card (no date); separate answer sheets must be used; $3 per 20 tests; $5 per 100 IBM answer sheets; 50¢ per scoring stencil; $3 per complete specimen set; postage extra; 55(65) or 40(50) minutes; prepared under the direction of E. F. Lindquist; Science Research Associates. *

For reviews by J. Murray Lee and Stephen Wiseman of the complete battery, see 17; for a review by Eric F. Gardner of earlier forms, see 4:17; for reviews by Henry Chauncey, Gustav J. Froehlich, and Lavone A. Hanna, see 3:12.

[792]

★Sequential Tests of Educational Progress: Social Studies. Grades 4–6, 7–9, 10–12, 13–14; 1956–57; IBM; Forms A, B ('57); 4 levels; manual ('57); battery directions ('57); battery technical report ('57); no data on reliability of Form B; separate answer sheets must be used; $3.95 per 20 tests; $1 per 20 IBM scorable answer sheets; 45¢ per scoring stencil; $1 per manual; $1 per battery technical report; $1.25 per specimen set of any one level; postage extra; 70(90–100) minutes; Cooperative Test Division, Educational Testing Service. *
a) LEVEL 4. Grades 4–6; Forms 4A, 4B.
b) LEVEL 3. Grades 7–9; Forms 3A, 3B.
c) LEVEL 2. Grades 10–12; Forms 2A, 2B.
d) LEVEL 1. Grades 13–14; Forms 1A, 1B.

RICHARD E. GROSS, *Associate Professor of Education, Stanford University, Stanford, California.*

These tests are not conventional instruments which attempt to measure the results of any separate subject matter course. While test items are drawn from the areas of history, geography, economics, government, and sociology, they tend to call for the application of one or more skills or of knowledge of the field rather than for the recall of information.

The geographically oriented map problems are particularly good; in some instances care is taken to avoid answers which depend only upon memory by providing maps of imaginary islands or areas where the testee must use his knowledge and skills. The pictorial items are perhaps least satisfactory and, as is true of other items, assume a rich background on the part of the testee. In several, such as the picture at the top of page 13 of Form 2B, the important details (here, terracing) are so small as to make it difficult and time-consuming for even the bright and perceptive student to figure out the correct answers. Others query the testee about pictures which involve too much conjecture; in Part 1 of Form 3A, for example, Item 30 asks the testee to differentiate between the limitations in location of four factories depicted. Just because a river is shown adjacent to the buildings of factory 1 does not mean that that factory has to be near a flow of water; factory 4 might well be more dependent upon the huge power sources hinted by its belching chimneys. A more understandable picture could certainly have been selected to cover the questions on the 1930 depression in Part 2 of Form 2A; the right answers to these questions are debatable, to say the least. This part also presents a reproduction of a newspaper column showing the transactions of the New York Stock Exchange on a given day. Here no explanation is presented as to legends used in the table and a student unfamiliar with the terminology and abbreviations would be penalized in answering Items 21 and 23. The great bulk of items, however, is very well conceived, and with all the practical screening that the test items have had, the reviewer could find few with which to quibble. He feels that Item 24 in Part 2 of Form 2B, in which the organization of an army is described as similar to that of a business organization, is overdrawn. He also believes that a testee living in New York would have considerable advantage over a Floridian or a Nebraskan in answering Item 9 in Part 2 of Form 3A, which concerns the Erie Canal and travel time thereon. Aside from a few such points, the test items are far superior to those the reviewer has found in a number of other instruments that often have too many poorly constructed or ambiguous items and too many items that are limited primarily to informational assessment.

The reviewer feels strongly that many of the social science competencies necessary to do well on these tests are being neglected in too many schools across the country. In his opinion, if tests like these are used often enough in such situations, they may serve a significant purpose in upgrading instruction and promoting needed alterations in curricular emphasis. Therefore, in addition to their valuable evaluation role, these tests promise to make a real contribution towards improved and more functional social studies programs.

S. A. RAYNER, *Assistant Registrar, The University of Queensland, Brisbane, Australia.*

The *Sequential Tests of Educational Progress: Social Studies* represent the most commendable attempt known to this reviewer to apply modern doctrines of measurement in the preparation of social studies tests. The improvement over earlier tests in this field lies principally in the quality of the norms and in the comprehensive information in the manual and accompanying publications.

GOALS. The tests aim to measure development in seven skills and eight areas of understanding "which effective citizens should possess." As a check on whether such claims are justifiable, each item in Form 2B (intended for grades 10–12) was classified according to the principles in Bloom's *Taxonomy of Educational Objectives*. This analysis showed that at least three quarters of all items involve "translation," i.e., the ability required to explain a picture, a cartoon, a statistical table, a graph, and so on, or the ability to select a particular example of a general principle; the other items required the ability to interpret data. Very few items depended principally on knowledge or memory. However, although the STEP tests depend on both knowledge and skills, they do not primarily measure the higher mental processes.

Since the general goal of all the tests is to measure "the broad outcomes of general education rather than the relatively narrow results of any specific subject matter course," the tests draw on problems from many areas in history, geography, economics, government, and sociology; generally the questions involve an application to American affairs. Since each test contains only 70 items, it obviously cannot provide a reliable measure of any of these areas of knowledge.

FORMAT. Each test is attractively presented. The space in the test booklet is used economically but effectively. The uniformity of time limits, instructions, and answer sheets, which permits different forms of STEP to be administered to one group at the same time, is a practical advantage that will commend itself to the tester. One minor blemish is that the coloured dots which enable the marking stencil to be oriented rapidly on the answer sheet have not been placed correctly. This should be corrected in later printings.

NORMS. Improved sampling techniques are among the commendable features of the STEP norms. It has been realized that the adequacy of the standardization programme depends on the number of sampling units (in this case, school districts or colleges) rather than on the number of testees; for example, by selecting only two students per grade in 120 colleges and by stratifying the colleges by region and type, the sample of some two hundred students in each grade should provide more reliable norms than would a far larger sample of students drawn from a few colleges.

The norms draw attention to the importance of taking account of standard errors in the interpretation of scores. By showing that a given raw score indicates a relatively wide band on the percentile scale, the authors may discourage test users from regarding small differences in test scores as meaningful.

A third merit of the STEP norms is the attempt to convert scores on all tests to a common scale. However, there is no empirical evidence to show whether there is close agreement between the scale scores of students who have taken the tests at two levels.

RELIABILITY. The Kuder-Richardson estimates of internal consistency do not provide a satisfactory estimate of reliability for these tests. If the equation of scores between grades 4 and 13 implies a long term consistency in development, there is an obligation on the publishers to provide estimates of stability reliability.

VALIDITY. No evidence is provided on validity. The most satisfactory type of evidence would be agreement with the scores on another test prepared independently from the same specifications by experts of equal calibre. In lieu of this, each user must determine for himself how closely the test items appear likely to measure his own objectives. The publishers' promise to relate test scores to suitable criterion measures may be difficult to implement since the test itself may be the best available measure of such a criterion.

Correlations are reported between each form of STEP and the *Cooperative School and Col-*

lege Ability Tests (SCAT). The correlations range from .73 to .89, with a median of .80. Coefficients of this magnitude must raise the question of whether the STEP tests are measuring development in the social studies or whether they are virtually measures of general ability. The coefficient of .82 for Form 2B in grade 12 is, by Australian standards, incredibly high.

Form 2B was selected for an intensive check on the validity of individual items. In Part 1, the meaning of the first cartoon is not clear and there does not seem to be any particularly good answer to Item 2. To answer Item 14 correctly a student should have read the background statement carelessly, have been unfamiliar with Einstein's history, or have been ignorant of the geography of Europe; there is certainly no correct answer to the item as it stands. In Part 2 the analogy between an army and a modern business organization (Item 24) does not seem close enough to be worth making. The other items appear to cover a wide area and to provide a searching test.

OVERSEAS USERS. Few United States social studies tests would be suitable for use in Australian or English schools because of the many American references. If the tests were to be adapted for another country, most changes would be needed in the level 4 tests and fewest in the level 1 tests. Even at present, the level 1 tests appear to be within the range of an Australian undergraduate majoring in history.

EVALUATION. A specimen set of this series would be very suitable for use in a course in educational measurement since the tests and manual represent an admirable attempt to meet the specifications prescribed for attainment tests by leaders·in the measurement field. The tests themselves contain minor blemishes which are probably due to the speed with which they were constructed. If they can be revised after use for a year or two and if additional information can be provided on them, they should become far superior to any social studies tests at present available.

RALPH W. TYLER, *Director, Center for Advanced Study in the Behavioral Sciences, Stanford, California.*

This series is constructed to provide samples of the student behavior defined as the objectives of social studies instruction by leading teachers in this field. By focussing on similar kinds of behavior throughout the four levels and by using overlapping scales, the tests furnish a means for assessing progress students are making in the development of these abilities and skills from the fourth grade through the sophomore year in college. They are a helpful attempt to meet a long standing and important need in the social studies.

They were planned to test the abilities involved in reading and interpreting social studies materials—maps, charts, graphs, cartoons, pictures, diagrams, and the printed word. The exercises require several kinds of behavior in interpreting these materials, such as to identify main points and central issues, to compare and contrast underlying assumptions, biases, and motives, to distinguish fact from opinion, to assess the adequacy and relevance of data, to apply appropriate outside information, and to use relevant concepts from the social sciences in analyzing, criticizing, and drawing conclusions. To lessen the influence of variations in specific content treated in different social studies courses, each exercise provides some necessary specific data and requires the student to recall and use some concepts and generalizations commonly treated in social studies courses throughout the country. Each test contains only 70 items so that it is not possible to get a reliable measure of each of these abilities and skills, but the total score is reliable enough (the reported coefficients of reliability range from .93 for level 4 to .84 for level 2) to give a useful measure of relative student achievement of the complex of abilities and skills which are common aims of the social studies. The provision of norms on a single scale for the four levels provides a beginning for measuring student progress. These norms are derived from cross-sectional samples rather than from repeated testing of the same students. Hence, they serve as approximations only to norms which may later be worked out on the longitudinal basis.

In the future development of these tests there are four steps to be taken to increase their validity. Exploration of new forms of items is needed to provide greater flexibility in testing more directly these abilities and skills. The more mature abilities required for problem solving, such as the ability to predict the probable consequences of social policies and courses of action, should be identified and become part of the specifications for test construction. A comprehensive list of the basic concepts useful in understanding social phenomena and analyzing social problems needs to be definitely identified so as to serve to specify the content for the tests. Finally, the senior high school and the college level tests should include exercises testing the students' understanding of the nature of the social sciences, the kinds of problems with which they deal, the kinds of methods they use, and the kinds of knowledge they produce. These developments are essential to provide tests appropriate for the sophisticated students in this field.

This reviewer has long urged the construction of tests which are built to appraise directly the students' attainment of objectives actually sought by good teachers and the more extended use of such tests to take the place of tests which are based only on an analysis of common content of textbooks and courses of study. This is necessary both to obtain a valid measure of student achievement and also to focus the attention of students and teachers upon the important educational aims rather than upon memorization of course content. Tests exert a powerful influence on teaching and learning. Slowly testmakers are moving in this direction. The STEP tests are a fine contribution to this essential improvement in education.

For reviews by Robert W. B. Jackson and Wilbur L. Layton of the complete battery, see 24.

[793]

★Shearer Social Studies Test. Grades 7–9; 1952; Forms A, B; mimeographed manual; $1.20 per 25 tests, postage extra; 25¢ per specimen set, postpaid; 40(45) minutes; Lois Shearer; Bureau of Educational Measurements. *

REFERENCE
1. SHEARER, LOIS M. *The Construction and Standardization of a Social Studies Test.* Master's thesis, Kansas State Teachers College (Emporia, Kan.), 1952.

RAYMOND C. NORRIS, *Associate Professor of Psychology, George Peabody College for Teachers, Nashville, Tennessee.*

This test was developed to measure the understanding junior high school students have of material generally included in seventh, eighth, and ninth grade social studies. To assure more than local applicability, the author based her items on "leading text books of recommended or preferred lists in a number of states." Each form consists of 60 true-false, 40 matching, and 48 multiple choice items with the follow-

ing percentage distribution: history, 60; geography, 25; civics, 9; and citizenship, 6. Although prospective users should examine the test item by item to determine its relevance to their local curricula, it would have been helpful if the author had listed the texts or even the state lists used to assure content validity. It would have been helpful also if she had indicated the manner in which these materials were used to assure curricular validity.

Both split-half and parallel-forms reliability estimates appear high. For a group of 97 undescribed individuals the split-half coefficients for Forms A and B, respectively, were .91 and .89. For the same 97 subjects the correlation between scores on the two forms when administered within a week of each other was .86.

Percentile-within-grade norms are provided for the middle of the seventh, eighth, and ninth grades and for the end of the seventh and eighth grades. The normative sample is described only as consisting of the 1,553 pupils who participated in the Nation-wide Every Pupil Testing Programs of 1952.

Inspection of the test items and of the reliability data suggests that the test may be better than one might gather from the sketchy description of the method of development and of the norm groups.

[794]

★Social Studies: Every Pupil Scholarship Test. Grades 7–8; 1935–58; new form usually issued each January and April; norms available following testing program; no data on reliability; 4¢ per test; 4¢ per scoring key; postage extra; 30(35) minutes; Bureau of Educational Measurements. *

[795]

★Social Studies: Midwest High School Achievement Examinations. High school; 1955–57; title on Form B is *Social Science XII*; Forms A ('55), B ('57); no specific manual; no data on reliability; norms: [A, '55; B, '57]; 10¢ per test, postage extra; Form A: 60(65) minutes; Form B: 90(95) minutes; Lola Faye (A) and Kopple C. Friedman (B); Educational Test Bureau. *

[796]

*Social Studies: National Teacher Examinations. College seniors and teachers; 1940–58; for more complete information, see 538; IBM; 80(90) minutes; Educational Testing Service. *

For reviews by William A. Brownell, Walter W. Cook, and Lawrence G. Derthick of the entire series, see 538; for a review by Harry N. Rivlin of an earlier edition, see 4:802.

[797]
★Social Studies: Teacher Education Examination Program. College seniors preparing to teach secondary school; 1957; for more complete information, see 543; IBM; 80(95) minutes; Educational Testing Service. *

For a review by Walter W. Cook of the entire series, see 543.

[798]
*Social Studies Test: National Achievement Tests. Grades 4–6, 7–9; 1937–57; 2 forms; 2 levels; directions sheets ('45); no data on reliability; no norms for part scores; $2.75 per 25 tests; 50¢ per specimen set of either level; postage extra; 35(40) minutes; Robert K. Speer and Samuel Smith; Acorn Publishing Co. *
a) GRADES 4–6. 6 scores: human relations, life situations, social problems, products and peoples, meaning of events, total; Forms A, B ('55, identical with tests copyrighted in 1945 and 1939, respectively, except for minor changes).
b) GRADES 7–9. 7 scores: human relations, life situations, social interpretations, values of products, social ideas, miscellaneous facts, total; Forms A ('57), B ('45), identical with tests copyrighted in 1945 and 1939, respectively, except for minor changes).

For a review by Ray G. Wood, see 3:594.

[799]
*Stanford Achievement Test: Intermediate and Advanced Social Studies Test. Grades 5–9; 1940–54; same as the social studies sections of Stanford Achievement Test; IBM; Forms JM ('52), KM ('53), LM ('53); manual ('54); separate answer sheets must be used; $2.35 per 35 tests; $1.25 per 35 IBM answer sheets; 20¢ per machine scoring stencil; postage extra; 35¢ per specimen set, postpaid; 30(35) minutes; Truman L. Kelley, Richard Madden, Eric F. Gardner, Lewis M. Terman, and Giles M. Ruch; World Book Co. *

HARRY D. BERG, *Professor, Office of Evaluation Services, Michigan State University, East Lansing, Michigan.*

The present test is a separately published edition of that portion of the *Stanford Achievement Test* devoted to the measurement of social studies growth in grades 5 to 9. The general content of the items is divided quite equally over the areas commonly designated as history, geography, and civics or social problems. The specific item content and difficulty are based upon an extensive national survey of texts and courses of study used in the elementary school. In the latter connection, it may be significant to note the authors' comment that "despite frequent statements to the contrary there is, in fact, widespread agreement concerning much of the content of the elementary Social Studies curriculum." It is hoped that this is true, since the validity of a test using national norms is dependent in a large measure upon a considerable degree of uniformity in instruction.

Alternate forms of the test are available, each form containing about 100 brief multiple choice items. It is expected that all or nearly all pupils will be able to finish in the allotted time (30 minutes); thus the test is intended as one one of power rather than of speed.

All aspects of test making, administration, and interpretation have been handled in so adequate and professional a manner that this reviewer has only one issue to raise, but that is a rather fundamental one. It concerns the requirements of the items or the question of what constitutes social studies growth. The authors, who frankly state that "the items in the test measure primarily social studies content or information," are also "well aware of the many other objectives of social studies instruction in the grades." Factual information is important, measureable growth does occur with regard to it, and there is probably a high correlation between such growth and other objectives. But some prospective users may well wish a test which more directly measures growth in terms of understanding, critical thinking ability, and skills. A comparison might be made between the items on this test and those in social studies tests of the *Iowa Tests of Educational Development* and the recently published *Sequential Tests of Educational Progress*. These tests also attempt to measure social studies growth, but with different emphases.

However, assuming that he feels that the kind of growth measured in the Stanford test is significant, the user will have available to him a very excellent set of norms for measuring that growth. Three kinds of norms are provided: modal-age grade norms for the interpretation of individual scores, total-group grade norms for the interpretation of group averages, and within-grade percentile norms. An especially useful adjunct to the norms is the provision of standard errors of measurement. These factors and others make this examination, within the scope of its content, one of the finer products of the test builder's art.

For a review by Ray G. Wood of the previous edition, see 3:595. For a review by N. L. Gage of the complete battery, see 25; for reviews by Paul R. Hanna (with Claude E. Norcross) and Virgil E. Herrick of the previous edition, see 4:25; for reviews by Walter W. Cook and Ralph C. Preston, see 3:18.

ECONOMICS

[800]

*The Graduate Record Examinations Advanced Tests: Economics.** College seniors and graduate students; 1939–57; for more complete information, see 601; IBM; 180(200) minutes; Educational Testing Service. *

For a review by Harold Seashore of the entire series, see 601.

GEOGRAPHY

[801]

*Coordinated Scales of Attainment: Geography.** Grades 6, 7, 8; 1946–54; subtest of *Coordinated Scales of Attainment;* IBM; Forms A ('46), B ('49); 3 levels; directions for administering ['52]; battery manuals (A, '54; B, '49); separate answer sheets must be used; $1.90 per 25 tests; $1 per 25 IBM scorable answer sheets; 10¢ per scoring stencil; 50¢ per specimen set; postage extra; (20) minutes; Mendel E. Branom; Educational Test Bureau. *

For a review by Alvin W. Schindler of the complete battery, see 4:8; for reviews by Roland L. Beck, Lavone A. Hanna, Gordon N. Mackenzie (with Glen Hass), and C. C. Ross of batteries 4–8, see 3:6.

[802]

*Economic Geography: Achievement Examinations for Secondary Schools.** High school; 1951–53; Forms 1 ('51), 3 ('53); no specific manual; no data on reliability; norms: Forms 1 ['52], 3 ('53); 10¢ per test, postage extra; [60–90] minutes; Helen Haberman (3); Educational Test Bureau. *

[803]

★Economic Geography: Midwest High School Achievement Examinations,** High school; 1952–55; Forms A ('55), B ('52, identical with Form 2 of *Economic Geography: Achievement Examinations for Secondary Schools*); no specific manual; no data on reliability; no norms; 10¢ per test, postage extra; 60(65) minutes; Helen Haberman (A); Educational Test Bureau. *

[804]

*Geography: Every Pupil Scholarship Test.** Grades 5–7; 1933–58; new form usually issued each January and April; norms available following testing program; no data on reliability; 4¢ per test; 4¢ per scoring key; postage extra; 30(35) minutes; Bureau of Educational Measurements. *

[805]

*Geography: Every Pupil Test.** Grades 4, 5, 6, 7; 1935–58; new form usually issued each December and April; 4 levels; norms available following testing program; no data on reliability; 3¢ per test; 1¢ per scoring key; cash orders postpaid; 40(45) minutes; Ohio Scholarship Tests. *

[806]

*Geography Test: Municipal Tests: National Achievement Tests.** Grades 3–6, 6–8; 1938–52; subtest of *Municipal Battery;* 3 scores: geographical ideas and comparisons, miscellaneous facts, total; 2 forms; 2 levels; no data on reliability; no norms for part scores; $1.75 per 25 tests; 50¢ per specimen set of either level; postage extra; 20(25) minutes; Robert K. Speer and Samuel Smith; Acorn Publishing Co. *
a) GRADES 3–6. 1938–52; Forms A ('52, identical with test copyrighted in 1938 except for minor changes), B ('49, identical with test copyrighted in 1939 except for minor changes); directions sheet ('38).
b) GRADES 6–8. 1938–51; Forms A ('50), B ('51, identical with test copyrighted in 1939 except for Item 8, Part 1); directions sheets (A, '50; B, '39).

For a review by Edwin H. Reeder, see 4:676. For a review by J. Murray Lee of the complete battery, see 18; for a review by Ralph C. Preston, see 4:20; for reviews by A. M. Jordan and Hugh B. Wood of the complete battery for grades 6–8, see 40:1191.

HISTORY

[807]

*American History: Achievement Examinations for Secondary Schools.** High school; 1951–53; Forms 1 ('51), 3 ('53); no specific manual; no data on reliability; norms: Forms 1 ['52], 3 ('53); 10¢ per test, postage extra; [60–90] minutes; M. J. Haggerty (3); Educational Test Bureau. *

[808]

*American History: Every Pupil Scholarship Test.** High school; 1926–58; 2 tests; norms available following testing program; no data on reliability; 4¢ per test; 4¢ per scoring key; postage extra; 40(45) minutes; Bureau of Educational Measurements. *
a) AMERICAN HISTORY TO 1865. New form usually issued each January.
b) AMERICAN HISTORY SINCE 1865. New form usually issued each April.

[809]

*American History: Every Pupil Test.** Grades 7–8, 11–12; 1931–58; 2 levels; norms available following testing program; no data on reliability; 3¢ per test; 1¢ per scoring key; cash orders postpaid; 40(45) minutes; Ohio Scholarship Tests. *
a) GRADES 7–8. 1935–58; new form usually issued each December; 2 tests: To 1840 A.D., 1840 and on.
b) GRADES 11–12. 1931–58; new form usually issued each December and April.

[810]

★American History: Midwest High School Achievement Examinations.** High school; 1955–57; Forms A ('55), B ('57); no specific manual; no data on reliability; norms: [A, '55; B, '57]; 10¢ per test, postage extra; Form A: 60(65) minutes; Form B: 90(95) minutes; M. J. Haggerty (A) and Peter Otterness (B); Educational Test Bureau. *

HOWARD R. ANDERSON, *Professor of Education, and Dean, University School of Liberal and Applied Studies, The University of Rochester, Rochester, New York.*

Stanford Achievement Test: Intermediate and Advanced Social Studies Test

The series manual states that the purposes of the examinations are "to motivate efforts of accomplishments by the students" and "to stimulate thinking ability based on mastery of contents resulting from efforts of work."

The American history test includes 150 items. There are 40 five-response, 65 four-response, and 15 three-response multiple choice items plus two matching exercises of 15 items each. Most of the questions deal with persons, events, dates, places, and things. For example, the pupil is expected to match "Cross of Gold," "Polar Bear Garden," "Swamp Fox," "The Fur Lord," and "The Raven" with Bryan, Seward, Marion, Astor, and Houston, respectively.

The only norms provided for this test are 25th percentile, median, 75th percentile, and perfect scores. The series manual contains the surprising statement that norms for all tests "are printed on one sheet to show variation of accomplishment from subject to subject." Surely there must be other reasons why the median on the 150-item American history test is 76 whereas the median on the 114–item world history test is 61.

The series manual states, "The scoring keys are as specific as possible." This statement does not guarantee accuracy. To illustrate: For Item 2, Renaissance is keyed as the name by which "the five centuries following the extinction of the Roman Empire" are known. For Item 39, Dag Hammarskjold is listed as the "U.N. general assembly president."

In some cases it is difficult or impossible to figure out how the author identifies the right answer in the responses provided. Thus, in Item 26 he gives Vicksburg, not Gettysburg, as the "high water mark of the Confederacy." In Item 62 he holds that sailboats had nothing to do with westward expansion although thousands went to California by clipper ship during the gold rush.

A few items in this test contain misleading or wrong information in the stem. For example, the stem of Item 3 states that the capture of Constantinople by the Turks closed "the connection between oriental and occidental trade routes." Items 31 states that the "Pan American Congress was inaugurated in 1889"; actually the first meeting was held on October 2, 1890.

This examination appears to have been hastily prepared and carelessly edited. It seems unlikely that its use will "stimulate thinking ability" in American history. It would be unfortunate if teachers were misled into believing that the items included in this test identify the "contents" to be mastered by their pupils.

[811]

*American History Test: National Achievement Tests. Grades 7–8; 1937–56; 5 scores: lessons of history, time concepts, historical associations, miscellaneous problems, total; Forms A ('56, identical with 3 forms copyrighted in 1939, 1944, and 1949 except for minor changes), B ('45, identical with test copyrighted in 1938 except for minor changes); no data on reliability; no norms for part scores; directions sheets (A, '45; B, '38); $2.75 per 25 tests; 50¢ per specimen set; postage extra; 40(45) minutes; Robert K. Speer, Lester D. Crow, and Samuel Smith; Acorn Publishing Co. *

For reviews by Jacob S. Orleans and Wallace Taylor, see 40:1630.

[812]

★College Entrance Examination Board Advanced Placement Examination: American History. High school seniors desiring credit for college level courses; 1956–58; for more complete information, see 600; 3 scores: objective, essay, total; IBM in part; 2 parts; 180(200) minutes; program administered by Educational Testing Service for the College Entrance Examination Board. *

JAMES A. FIELD, JR., *Professor of History, Swarthmore College, Swarthmore, Pennsylvania.* [Review of Form FBP.]

This examination is designed to test advanced high school work in American history at a level described in the prospectus of the Advanced Placement Program as "equivalent to.... an introductory college course." It is made up of three parts: an objective section taking 45 minutes and counting 25 per cent of the total score, a discussion (for 20 minutes and 15 per cent) of an interpretation of an historical event, and two 50-minute essays amounting together to 60 per cent of the total. Fifteen minutes are given for review of the written work.

The objective section contains 75 multiple choice items of ingenious and demanding nature. Thirty-five consist of questions to be answered, incomplete statements to be completed, or statements to be placed in context; 17 present quotations for identification by name, meaning, or origin; there are 10 map questions; 13 questions involve the exegesis of three documents, one of which is a cartoon. Quite properly a number of the questions call for a fairly sophisticated discrimination, but only two or three seem to contain undesirable ambiguities.

For the essay on historical interpretation the student is offered a choice of one of four subjects ranging from the very general to the particular. By all odds the hardest was one concerning individual motivation; this was attempted by many of the better students (as judged by their scores on the objective section) with results, costly to them, which raise the question of how to avoid penalizing ambition and enterprise.

The booklet describing the Advanced Placement Program lists 16 topics (e.g., The Westward Movement, Divisive Forces in American History) as a guide to study. These are thoroughly covered in the 14 essay subjects offered in the examination, yet there are problems of emphasis. The favorite subjects of the examiners, as shown both here and in the objective section, lie in the areas where economics and politics interact, in the relations between farmer, labor, business, and the federal government. The period of the industrial revolution is sliced all ways for the essay writer, but there is no chance to discuss the antebellum South, slavery, territorial expansion, manifest destiny, or the causes of the Civil War. The student with an interest in the history of foreign relations would have some difficulty bringing his information to bear. Intellectual history is (perhaps properly) slighted.

This emphasis on the period of industrialization seems excessive. Complete ignorance of all that happened before 1860 would cost the candidate a mere 8 per cent of his possible score, and this only in the objective section where 20 of the 75 items concern the antebellum period. In comparison there are 35 items on the period from 1861 to 1919 and 15 on the years since the First World War; the three documents which form the basis for 13 questions all fall between 1875 and 1912. Although the short essay on interpretation offers a 50-50 choice, the long essays are weighted about two to one against the earlier time: 5 of the 14 topics call for postbellum information only, 3 permit and 5 require some antebellum information, and a single essay subject is restricted to the period before the election of Lincoln.

This disproportion appears to have been noted by the readers of the examinations, and may consequently be corrected in future editions of the test. In all other respects the examination seems generally of high quality.

CHRISTINE MCGUIRE, *Assistant Professorial Lecturer in the Social Sciences, and Examiner, The University of Chicago, Chicago, Illinois.*

The Advanced Placement Program, as described in the booklet provided for prospective users, is an exceedingly interesting development, designed to encourage high schools to develop college level courses for superior students and to furnish colleges with reliable information on the basis of which they can consider for credit and advanced placement students who have taken such courses.

The description of the examination for the American history course makes clear that students will be expected to demonstrate "a thorough grounding in facts....[and understanding] of their contexts, their causes and results and their significance....[the ability] to read historical material analytically and critically, and.... to express themselves in good English." Illustrative items of both an objective and essay type are provided.

Unfortunately, the examination does not measure the student's achievement of these objectives. One fourth of the total test time is devoted to objective questions. These are excessively concrete, lack any consistent development of an idea or institutional form, and are usually very simple. In short, they test primarily the recall of often quite trivial information. For example, one question on a desegregation case merely refers to another case, but not to the principles of the recent decision, especially the introduction of modern psychological and sociolgical data as a basis for deciding public policy, nor to the role of equality as a value in modern America, nor to this value historically, nor to the processes by which values may be changed. In short, the item does not touch on the significance of the issue or of the decision. Again the "correct" answer to one question about Calhoun's "theory of concurrent majority" fails to address the major issue of popular government with which the theory was concerned and actually perverts the concept in its oversimplification. Similarly, the role of religion is dealt with by questions requiring the identification of the denomination of certain religious leaders rather than in terms of its or their significance historically, politically, or socially under the conformist pressures of an egalitarian society.

The conscientious teacher will try to shape his course so as to avoid placing his students at any serious disadvantage. Consequently, a test like this might very well lead to an excessive preoccupation with specifics at the sacrifice of abstract ideas and important skills.

The essay portion of the test does little to correct this tendency. Though some of the questions are excellent in requiring a thoughtful analysis or interpretation, the choice among a series of alternatives is so wide and the variation in quality is so great that narrow concentration in preparation in one or a few areas will certainly suffice. Nor are the standards employed in grading the essays reassuring in this connection. In the longer essays 25 per cent of the grade was based on mechanics of English and organization and another 25 per cent was determined by the accuracy, relevance, and sufficiency of the facts cited. Secondly, the passing standards even for these quite ordinary qualities seem to this reviewer to be exceedingly low.

The data supplied for the interpretation of test results are seriously inadequate. Though the usual data are reported for reliability, means, percentiles and the like, it is impossible to judge the significance of these data in the absence of information about the characteristics of the groups on which they were calculated. Further, it is not clear that the precautions to assure reliable grading of the essays were actually adequate in view of the rather large variations in the mean essay scores of students choosing to write on different questions and of the quite low intercorrelations of essay parts. Data on student performance on each item of the objective section are, necessarily, unavailable to teachers as a result of the agency's policy in not releasing specific items.

Though the program for which this test was designed is indeed a laudable one and certainly to be encouraged, the current form of the test is inadequate for judging whether or not students have achieved the stated objectives and hence is inadequate as a basis for granting college credit in American History. Unfortunately, no alternative tests are currently available for this specific type of collaboration between school and college.

[813]

★College Entrance Examination Board Advanced Placement Examination: European History. High school seniors desiring credit for college level courses; 1956–58; for more complete informa-

tion, see 600; 3 scores: objective, essay, total; IBM in part; 2 parts; 180(200) minutes; program administered by Educational Testing Service for the College Entrance Examination Board.

[814]

Cooperative World History Test. High school; 1934–49; IBM; Forms Y ('48), Z ('49); no specific manual; general Cooperative manual ('51); norms ['49]; $2.95 per 25 tests; separate answer sheets may be used; $1 per 25 IBM answer sheets; 25¢ per scoring stencil; postage extra; 40(45) minutes; Wallace Taylor (Y) and Frederick H. Stutz (Z); Cooperative Test Division, Educational Testing Service. *

DAVID K. HEENAN, *Assistant Professor, Office of Evaluation Services, and Examiner in the Humanities, Michigan State University, East Lansing, Michigan.*

The *Cooperative World History Test* is designed to furnish information about the capabilities, achievements, and competence of the student in the subject and to check the effectiveness of the materials, curriculum, and teaching methods used in a given class or school. The test contains 85 items covering the social, economic, political, and cultural aspects of world history from the prehistoric age to post-World War II. At best the items "spot check" the student's knowledge of details in a very broad field. At first inspection some of the items appear superficial and petty, but closer analysis reveals that a student who relies on rote memorization alone will not score well. Consequently, the tests should measure, at least by indirection, the extent to which the broad objectives of the world history course have been attained.

The manual supplied with the tests contains detailed instructions for administering and scoring the test and suggestions for recording and interpreting test results. Percentile norms based upon the results of 1,293 tenth grade and 281 eleventh grade students are provided separately.

Some parts of the test should be reviewed and revised. This is particularly true of the materials dealing with the United Nations and events during and immediately following World War II. Several items call for knowledge of specific facts which were receiving greater attention in the study of current events at the time the tests were written than they are at the present time: e.g., "Which of these agencies provided for in the United Nations Charter had no counterpart in the League of Nations organization? (Military Staff Committee)" and "Which of the following books was

Cooperative World History Test

written as a result of the invention of the atomic bomb? (*One World or None*)" In the latter item the other foils are *The Power and the Glory, The Cornerstones of Peace, Mein Kampf,* and *One World,* all conceivably more familiar immediately after the war than they are now.

But the most striking weakness of the test (especially of Form Y) is the subject matter used in testing cultural history. One item reads: "The influence of ancient Egyptian architectural design may be seen in the (Washington Monument)." The fact that the Washington Monument is an obelisk does not necessarily mean that it was influenced by the Egyptian architectural style; more likely it was influenced by the Renaissance or Baroque designs. This is an example of some of the superficial questions on an important field. The item could be improved by asking for a comparison of the Greek style with a Greek revival building of 19th century America. Another item asks: "In which of the fine arts has there been *least* change since the Renaissance? (Sculpture)" This involves a judgment which most people are not equipped to make. The only way that one could answer this item is to accept the opinion of the writer of the textbook being used or conclude that all sculpture ended with the work of Auguste Rodin.

Other items involving judgment could be improved. One item, for example, asks, "Which of the following best explains the chief weakness of the political reform movement in western Europe around 1750? (Political power was not in the hands of the people.)" This type of item calls for the expected answer of a democratically oriented student and is not really a valid test of knowledge.

With some slight revisions this test would be a first-rate instrument for measuring the student's knowledge of world history. As it now stands, it is as good as any test the reviewer has seen in this field. Form Z, the more recent form, appears to contain fewer of the faults described above than does the older Form Y.

For a review by Kenneth E. Gell of an earlier form, see 40:1636; for a review by R. M. Tryon, see 38:1017.

[815]
Coordinated Scales of Attainment: History. Grades 4, 5, 6, 7, 8; 1946–54; subtest of *Coordinated*

Cooperative World History Test

Scales of Attainment; IBM; grades 4, 7: Forms A ('46), B ('49); grades 5–6, 8: Forms A, B ('49); 5 levels; directions for administering ['52]; battery manuals (A, '54; B, '49); separate answer sheets must be used; $1.90 per 25 tests; $1 per 25 IBM scorable answer sheets; 10¢ per scoring stencil; 50¢ per specimen set; postage extra; (20) minutes; Edgar B. Wesley; Educational Test Bureau. *

For a review by Alvin W. Schindler of the complete battery, see 4:8; for reviews by Roland L. Beck, Lavone A. Hanna, Gordon N. Mackenzie (with Glen Hass), and C. C. Ross of Batteries 4–8, see 3:6.

[816]
Crary American History Test: Evaluation and Adjustment Series. Grades 9–13; 1950–54; IBM; Forms AM ('51), BM ('52); manual ('51); expectancy chart ['54]; separate answer sheets must be used; $3.60 per 35 tests; $1.40 per 35 IBM answer sheets; postage extra; 35¢ per specimen set, postpaid; 40(50) minutes; Ryland W. Crary; World Book Co. *

REFERENCES
1. TOWNSEND, AGATHA. "A Review of the Crary American History Test." *Ed Rec B* 61:67–71 Jl '53. * (PA 28:4864)
2. COWNE, LESLIE. "Reliability of the Crary American History Test, Form Bm, and Correlation of Scores With School Marks." *Ed Rec B* 63:81–5 Jl '54. * (PA 29:4684)

FREDERICK H. STUTZ, *Professor of Education, Cornell University, Ithaca, New York.*

This test appears to be excellent in design and construction. The 90 items in each form have been selected to represent those aims of the study of American history which are accepted as standard by authoritative groups such as the National Council for the Social Studies. The test is designed to measure mastery of information, skills, understandings, and ability to interpret historical materials. There is a suitable emphasis on nearly all of the major aspects of the development of the American nation. There is an informative manual which explains the development of the test and its administration and uses, and which seems to be accurate and complete.

Though this is a good test, a teacher will want to use it as only one part of the evaluation process. For example, students will need to show power in answering essay questions as well as in handling the types of questions found in a test of this type. The test has two minor weaknesses. Though aspects of social and intellectual history are dealt with, little attention is given to developments in literature, the arts, and education. The map questions and certain of the matching questions may pose reading and identification problems of an unnecessary sort.

The test is a well designed and constructed

measure of the achievement of objectives in a course in American history. It should be a valuable instrument to be used with average or above average students in courses in the upper years of the high school.

For a review by Edgar B. Wesley, see 4:688.

[817]

*Cummings World History Test: Evaluation and Adjustment Series. Grades 9–13; 1950–54; IBM; Forms AM ('51), BM ('52); manual ('51); expectancy chart ['54]; separate answer sheets must be used; $4.15 per 35 tests; $1.40 per 35 IBM answer sheets; postage extra; 35¢ per specimen set, postpaid; 40(50) minutes; Howard H. Cummings; World Book Co. *

REFERENCE

1. TRAXLER, ARTHUR E., AND TOWNSEND, AGATHA. "Some Data on the Results of the Cummings World History Test Among Independent School Pupils." *Ed Rec B* 59:77–8 Jl '52. * (PA 27:2997)

For reviews by Dorothy C. Adkins and Howard R. Anderson, see 4:689.

[818]

*The Graduate Record Examinations Advanced Tests: History. College seniors and graduate students; 1939–56; for more complete information, see 601; IBM; 180(200) minutes; Educational Testing Service. *

ROBERT H. FERRELL, *Assistant Professor of History, Indiana University, Bloomington, Indiana.* [Review of Form EGR.]

This test requires both generalization and narrow factual knowledge, and the ingenious combination of these two requisites within one examination is a tribute to the skill of the Educational Testing Service. Especially well chosen are the quotations which students must read and interpret. Such intellectual exercises offer as acceptable a measurement of students' skills as do the usual essay examinations. The map questions seem difficult, and the choice of country on which they are based somewhat unfortunate—that country's history no longer has the importance it once had. And to pursue this matter of relevance, it does appear that the test is a little too traditional not merely in choice of the above mentioned country for map questions but also in its slighting of the history of a nation with which the United States presently is enjoying some serious relations. Too, there should be more questions on ancient history and modern European history before the 20th century. American history is given more attention than it should have, judging from the history curricula in most colleges today. The chief comment of the reviewer, in an adverse sense, is that the test needs grammatical tightening. The language of some of the questions is unduly loose. For example, some questions contain a string of prepositional phrases, making it necessary for the student to read the question two or three times to find his way through the turgidity. There are bumbling expressions, one question inquiring about a "direct outgrowth"—whatever that is; another asking about something which "originally drew" the United States toward a course of action—seeming to mean that one can draw both originally and secondarily. An easy improvement in the style of the questions would be to eliminate passive verbs; there are entirely too many in these questions, and they require the student to turn a sentence upside down to get its sense.

Perhaps the reviewer should also enter a comment about some of the explanatory material which accompanies these tests: the Handbook for Deans and Examiners, the Supervisor's Manual, the Manual of Directions to Examiners. This material is mostly an elucidation of the obvious, or an impossible effort to answer every conceivable question—which may while away the time of a bored supervisor but will make little impression upon most individuals sincerely anxious to discover the mechanics of the testing. There is also a considerable amount of gratuitous advice in these manuals, such as: "Proctors should at all times give strict attention to their duties. *They should not read or engage in conversation while an examination is in progress.*" And again: "Your manner during the testing should be firm but pleasant." These remarks seem unnecessary when directed to a university audience.

Having said all this, the reviewer must repeat that taken as a whole the test is well done. Admittedly it is only one of several factors on which one can judge a student's promise; but, considered along with health, working habits, financial condition, and the like, it ought to assist greatly the graduate faculties in choosing for admission and scholarships the most attractive of each year's candidates.

For a review by Harold Seashore of the entire series, see 601.

[819]

*History: Every Pupil Scholarship Test. Grades 5–6, 7–8; 1933–58; new form usually issued each January and April; 2 levels; norms available following testing program; no data on reliability; 4¢ per test; 4¢ per scoring key; postage extra; 30(35) minutes; Bureau of Educational Measurements. *

[820]

★Kansas United States History Test. 1, 2 semesters in grades 7–8; 1957; IBM; Form A; 2 levels; $1.20 per 25 tests; separate answer sheets may be used; 85¢ per 25 IBM answer sheets; 30¢ per scoring stencil; postage extra; 25¢ per specimen set, postpaid; 30(35) minutes; Shirley Meares and M. W. Sanders; Bureau of Educational Measurements. *

WAYNE A. FREDERICK, *Social Studies Department, Isidore Newman School, New Orleans, Louisiana.*

The manual for this test states that the items cover "knowledge of facts, as well as the application of information and reasoning." Basically, the test measures only the retention of factual data. There are very few, if any, items which test the student's ability to reason from historical concepts, and none which measure his ability to apply historical concepts.

As a test of factual knowledge the items certainly cover the subject matter. All the important periods in United States history are covered. However, very little attention has been given to the significance of historical concepts. For example, the state in which Abraham Lincoln spent his boyhood years has relatively little significance as compared with the status granted California by the Compromise of 1850. Further, the significance of Lincoln's childhood does not rest on the fact that it was experienced in a certain frontier state, but that it was experienced in a frontier society of the Northwest Territory.

The manual indicates that the test may be used as a determinant of pupil achievement and as a check on the efficiency of instruction. Achievement should be measured not only in terms of identifying historical concepts, persons, and events, but also in terms of understanding historical relationships and of interpreting new historical data based on known concepts. In these two respects the test fails to measure pupil achievement and, consequently, the quality of instruction. The few items which test historical relationships do so only within a very narrow frame of reference. Test 2 includes more items of this type than does Test 1, but the items demand only a simple identification—recall ability, rather than the thinking abilities involved in seeing means-end and cause-effect relationships. No item in either test measures understanding of broad generaliza-

tions or the ability to interpret, analyze, or evaluate historical data.

A few minor points of criticism are as follows: (*a*) The type is much smaller in size than what seventh and eighth graders are accustomed to reading in their textbooks. (*b*) A few items are stated in terms of historical myths and not in terms of historical facts. (*c*) Several items have options which are neither pertinent to the concept nor parallel in construction.

Because the *Kansas United States History Test* measures only the student's ability to recall specific historical data in a direct and narrow frame of reference, it is not useful for the purposes for which it is intended.

JOHN MANNING, *Associate Professor, Department of Humanities, and Office of Evaluation Services, Michigan State University, East Lansing, Michigan.*

Each form consists of 65 four-option items of the multiple choice type. The items cover "knowledge of facts as well as the application of information and reasoning." They are said to survey "the most important subject matter commonly presented by a number of leading elementary textbooks and courses of study," and to be proportional to the amount of content and the emphasis given in these sources.

Coefficients of reliability for Test 1 are given as ranging from .71 to .86; for Test 2, from .70 to .80. Although the manual is reasonably complete in regard to statistical information, more information on reliability would be helpful. The manual would be improved further by giving a more adequate description of the normative population. Users of tests are entitled to have an accurate and detailed description of the group upon which a test is standardized.

It is to be regretted further, that only half a dozen or so items in Test 1 appear to measure reasoning ability, while the remaining items test knowledge of facts almost exclusively. About 18 items present choices of place names exclusively, and another 25 or more items involve choices from names of persons, etc. The proportions appear to be approximately the same in Test 2. Since the test constructors do not list the textbooks and courses of study which were used as source material, it is difficult to estimate whether more items involving cause and effect relationships, critical judgment, and cultural trends could have been validly included. In any event, more items of these latter types would be highly desirable.

The test itself shows evidence of care and technical skill in the construction of the items. For practical purposes, it appears to fulfill the purpose for which it was designed, that is, to test "the most important subject matter commonly presented by a number of leading elementary textbooks and courses of study."

Regrettably, it is probable that the sampling is a fairly accurate reflection of the amount of emphasis actually given to these factors in the average course in American history in grades 7 and 8.

[821]

*Modern World History: Achievement Examinations for Secondary Schools. High school; 1951–53; Forms 1 ('51), 3 ('53); no specific manual; no data on reliability; norms: Forms 1 ['52], 3 ('53); 10¢ per test, postage extra; (60–90) minutes; Lola Fay (3); Educational Test Bureau. *

[822]

★Modern World History: Midwest High School Achievement Examinations. High school; 1955–57; title on Form A is *World History;* Forms A ('55, revision of Form 2 of *World History: Achievement Examinations for Secondary Schools*), B ('57); no specific manual; no data on reliability; norms: [A, '55; B, '57]; 10¢ per test, postage extra; Form A: 60(65) minutes; Form B: 90(95) minutes; Lola Faye (A) and Don Estenson (B); Educational Test Bureau. *

[823]

*World History: Every Pupil Scholarship Test. High school; 1926–58; new form usually issued each January and April; norms available following testing program; no data on reliability; 4¢ per test; 4¢ per scoring key; postage extra; 40(45) minutes; Bureau of Educational Measurements. *

[824]

*World History: Every Pupil Test. High school; 1933–58; new form usually issued each December and April; norms available following testing program; no data on reliability; 3¢ per test; 1¢ per scoring key; cash orders postpaid; 40(45) minutes; Ohio Scholarship Tests. *

[825]

*World History Test: Acorn National Achievement Tests. High school and college; 1948–57; 6 scores: social studies terms, world geography, contributions of world peoples to civilization, political history, economic-social-cultural history, total; no norms for part scores; Form A ('48); directions sheet ('57, identical with sheet copyrighted in 1948); $3.50 per 25 tests; 50¢ per specimen set; postage extra; 40(45) minutes; Vincent McGarrett and Edward H. Merrill; Acorn Publishing Co. *

JOHN MANNING, *Associate Professor, Department of Humanities, and Office of Evaluation Services, Michigan State University, East Lansing, Michigan.*

The test is divided into five parts. The first part presents 10 four-option multiple choice items on terms commonly used in social studies. Some of these items appear to lack a certain amount of accuracy and discrimination. For example, the student is asked to define imperialism as a policy of "trying to add to the lands over which a nation rules," and plebiscite as a "vote of the people." The "gimmick" (used also in Parts 3, 4, and 5) of keying the items to and designating the options by the letters of a code word would seem to pose a definite problem in security and reliability.

The second part of the test consists of 15 assertive sentences to be matched with 15 geographic locations designated by letters of the alphabet scattered over an outline map of the world. The map itself is poorly drawn and the designated places are far from accurately located. A better testing situation could be secured by the use of heavy and clearly marked arrows running from the top of the page to each location and lettered in sequence across the top of the page. Technically, the items could then be improved by offering as options four or five letters for each of the items, instead of forcing the students to consider all 15 letters in connection with each of the sentences.

Part 3 consists of 25 items revolving around "contributions of world peoples to civilization." A number of these items, however, stress persons rather than contributions of peoples, such as "United States Senator Taft and Representative Hartley were co-sponsors of a law which was related to the same field as a bill sponsored by (Wagner-Connally)," and "Shadrach, Meshach and Abednego had reason to dislike (Nebuchadnezzar)." A number of items have either a stem that appears inaccurate (such as, "The democracy of the modern American town meeting is very much like that of....") or an answer that is not very carefully defined (such as, "As a bi-product [sic] of the development of the atomic bomb, scientists now have (a method of diagnosing diseases hidden within the body)"). In the latter item a word like "tracing" or "studying" would be preferable to "diagnosing."

Part 4 consists of 25 items designated as "political history," and Part 5 of 25 questions on what is termed "economic, social and cultural history." Several items in these sections are in need of improvement both technically and historically. Whether or not "The reference in the American Declaration of Independence to 'life, liberty, and the pursuit of happiness' stems from the writings of (Locke)," is an open question; it would be preferable to substitute "is similar to" for "stems." The item, "Jupiter held the same place among the gods of the Romans as the Greeks gave to (Zeus)," could be improved by substituting, "To which god did the Greeks allot a similar place as the Romans allotted to Jupiter?" One would be in a better position to appraise the validity of the content of the items if some indication were given of the text(s) or course(s) of study around which the items were constructed. Such an item as, "The contribution of Pindar to Greek literature was paralleled in Roman literature by the work of (Horace)" has little value *unless* the pupils have read some of the Greek or Roman literature involved. A question on the Bayeaux Tapestry is a little esoteric in a test designed for students in American high schools as well as those in college.

The sheet of directions gives a table of norms based on approximately 5,000 students "in schools in the East, Central, West and Southern sections of the United States," for grades 9 through 12, and for college. The sheet does not mention the stage in their college careers at which the college students took the test or the proportion of college to high school students. Neither does it say *when* the norms were established (In 1948, the original copyright date?).

The amount of attention given to geography and economic, social, and cultural history as well as political history is commendable. This test probably has served its purpose in the past, but it now needs technical revision. Up-to-date reliability and validity data should be added to (or clarified in) the directions sheet. Separate norms should be given for the separate parts of the test. Additional items involving judgment need to be added.

POLITICAL SCIENCE

[826]
*American Civics and Government Tests for High Schools and Colleges, Revised Edition. High school and college; 1930–54; Forms A, B ['54, same as forms copyrighted in 1949 except for minor changes]; directions sheet ['49]; reliability, validity, and normative data based on 1949 forms; $2 per 25 tests; 30¢ per specimen set; postpaid; high school:

40(50) minutes; college: 35(45) minutes; F. A. Magruder, R. J. Clinton, and M. M. Chambers; Public School Publishing Co. *

[827]
*American Government and Citizenship: Every Pupil Test. Grades 11–12; 1935–58; new form usually issued each April; norms available following testing programs; no data on reliability; 3¢ per test; 1¢ per scoring key; cash orders postpaid; 40(45) minutes; Ohio Scholarship Tests. *

For a review by Elizabeth C. Adams of an earlier form, see 4:699.

[828]
*American Government: Every Pupil Scholarship Test. High school; 1930–58; new form usually issued each April; norms available following testing program; no data on reliability; 4¢ per test; 4¢ per scoring key; postage extra; 40(45) minutes; Bureau of Educational Measurements. *

[829]
★Attitude Toward Politicians Scale. High school; 1954; 1 form; no data on validity; $2.20 per 35 tests, postpaid; specimen set not available; (5–10) minutes; Citizenship Education Project, Teachers College, Columbia University; distributed by C. A. Gregory Co. *

DONALD T. CAMPBELL, *Associate Professor of Psychology, Northwestern University, Evanston, Illinois.*

The supporting evidence for this test and the likelihood that the test will ever be used are both so small that reviewing it seems hardly justified. The test consists of 18 simply declarative statements, endorsed and scored in Likert fashion, of which the 10 most simply favorable and unfavorable are scored. The unscored items are the more interesting and indicate some of the multidimensionality which a full exploration of attitudes in this domain would involve. Of the scored items, five are positive and five negative, controlling response set. Test-retest reliability on 243 high school students is .76. No evidence of internal consistency or factorial structure is given. No evidence of validity or relationship to other measures is presented. Norms are provided based upon 6,342 high school students of unspecified selection or sex. The excessive size of the normative group represents a misuse of effort that might better have been placed elsewhere. The rule still holds for social attitude tests that the copyrighted tests are poorer than the uncopyrighted ones.

[830]
Civic Vocabulary Test. High school; 1951; 1 form ['51]; preliminary mimeographed manual ['51]; no norms; 5s. per 10 tests; 2s. per manual; 2s. 6d. per specimen set; postpaid within Australia; [10–30] min-

utes; S. A. Rayner; Australian Council for Educational Research. *

REFERENCE
1. RAYNER, S. A. *The Special Vocabulary of Civics.* A.C.E.R. Research Series, No. 65. Melbourne, Australia: Melbourne University Press, 1951. Pp. x, 105. *

I. G. MEDDLETON, *Deputy Head, Research Department, University of Queensland, Brisbane, Australia.*

This is a test of 36 items of the multiple choice type constructed to assess how well Australian pupils who are close to primary school leaving age understand the meaning of terms commonly used in current discussions of economic, political, and social affairs.

In establishing the validity of the test, the investigator has relied upon the careful selection (on a frequency basis) of the words used, the opinions of judges as to the value of each item for insertion in the test, and the discriminatory value of each test item when answered in a trial run using a slow learning group and an average or above group of children.

For a test compiled by an individual working with limited facilities, Rayner has done a good job. However, one feels that since the test is constructed for children "at the close of their primary schooling" and since the transfer age of primary school children in the states of Australia to secondary education varies from 12 to 14 years, the time has now arrived for the establishment of different norms in the various states based on representative samples of children and also for the calculation of more adequate estimates of reliability and validity based on the final form of the test.

[831]
*Constitution: Every Pupil Scholarship Test. High school; 1926–58; new form usually issued each January; norms available following testing program; no data on reliability; 4¢ per test; 4¢ per scoring key; postage extra; 40(45) minutes; Bureau of Educational Measurements. *

[832]
*Contemporary Problems. Grades 7–9, 10–12; 1951–54; 2 forms; 2 levels; manual ('54); separate answer sheets must be used; postpaid; specimen set not available; (20–40) minutes; Citizenship Education Project, Teachers College, Columbia University; distributed by C. A. Gregory Co. *
a) JUNIOR HIGH SCHOOL FORM. Grades 7–9; Form R ('54, identical with test copyrighted in 1951); $3.50 per 35 tests.
b) HIGH SCHOOL FORM. Grades 10–12; Forms C, D ('51); $2.65 per 35 tests.

HARRY D. BERG, *Professor, Office of Evaluation Services, Michigan State University, East Lansing, Michigan.*

The *Contemporary Problems Test* of the Citizenship Education Project is not concerned with intellectual outcomes, as such, but seeks to measure in the difficult and often controversial field of beliefs and attitudes. Specifically, an attempt is made to rate students according to their democratic or undemocratic tendencies. This is to be accomplished by presenting students with a series of realistic problems and asking them to select from alternative courses of action related to those problems, the course of action they think best in the situation. Some of these courses have been previously judged to be more "democratic" than others. Scoring is comparatively simple. It consists of adding together the weights assigned to the courses of action selected by any one student. Single scores secured in this manner can then be made meaningful by reference to a table of norms set up in terms of standard scores and percentiles.

The test was validated, to the extent that this kind of test can be validated, by submitting the problem situations and action alternatives to a distinguished panel of judges. The judges were asked to assign weights of one to five to the choices according to the democratic or undemocratic content of each course of action suggested. To assist them in the process, the judges were furnished with a set of points outlining the authors' concept of the democratic method. One such point was "acceptance of a spirit of fair play, open discussion, and respect for ideas." Another was "acceptance of public service and public duty as a primary obligation of life." The amount of agreement among judges was determined by computing Spearman coefficients for pairs of judges. It is significant that the agreement was considerably less than perfect. For the three forms, agreement ranged from a mean of .75 to a mean of .79, with some coefficients dropping as low as .43. By achievement test standards, the reliabilities were not high, either. The split halves method yielded coefficients of .76 for Form C, .81 for Form D, and .71 for Form R.

Leaving aside subjective judgments about the validity of the test, the statistical data available would indicate that the test results should be used with caution. Certainly not too much confidence should be placed in the score of a single pupil. To this reviewer, one of the most valuable uses of this test would not be for rating at all, but rather to provide the basis for a stimulating class discussion.

[833]

★Dimond-Pflieger Problems of Democracy Test: Evaluation and Adjustment Series. High school; 1952–54; IBM; Forms AM, BM ('52); manual ('53); expectancy chart ['54]; separate answer sheets must be used; $3.60 per 35 tests; $1.40 per 35 IBM answer sheets; postage extra; 35¢ per specimen set, postpaid; 40(50) minutes; Stanley E. Dimond and Elmer F. Pflieger; World Book Co. *

REFERENCE

1. LUNTZ, LESTER. "Some Reliability and Validity Data on the Dimond-Pflieger Problems of Democracy Test, Form Am." *Ed Rec B* 66:69–72 Jl '55. * (*PA* 30:5166)

JOHN H. HAEFNER, *Professor of Social Studies Education, State University of Iowa, Iowa City, Iowa.*

There are two forms of this test, each containing 80 items. The items, arranged in three parts, include 34 multiple choice items, 15 matching items, and 31 statements requiring the weighing of two or three possible answers. According to the classification of the authors, approximately 30 per cent of the items deal with government, 24 per cent with economics, 34 per cent with sociology, and 12 per cent with international affairs.

The technical construction of the items is, in general, acceptable, though the matching items in particular could be much improved. Directions to the students for some of the items in Part C, which are not typical multiple choice or "best answer" items, are not as clear as they might be. The parts of the test are so arranged that a single perforated stencil can be used for hand scoring and machine scoring both forms of the test. This is a convenient feature.

The standardization group consisted of 1,372 students attending 20 high schools in 15 states. This reviewer is not an expert on test standardization procedures; however, an analysis of the location of the 20 schools leads him to raise a question about the adequacy of the standardization population. In terms of the geographic areas and divisions employed by the U.S. Bureau of the Census, it appears that 8 of the 20 schools were in the Northeast Region and 11 in the North Central Region. Only one of the 20 schools was located in the Western Region, and none were from the Mountain Western, South Atlantic, East South Central, or West South Central states.

The manual states that "some knowledge of the more basic measurement concepts by the test user is presupposed, particularly those concepts pertaining to the general nature and purpose of standardized achievement tests, measures of central tendency and variability, the nature of interpretative scores, and measurement error." The nature of the subsequent paragraphs dealing with the interpretation of test results leads the reviewer to the conclusion that the test publishers are unduly optimistic in their presuppositions. Some portions of the suggestions for interpretation of the test are difficult to decipher and certainly presuppose specialized training in testing theory. Many teachers using the test have not had such training.

The manual also states that the test is not a diagnostic instrument nor does it furnish analytical measures of the individual student's mastery of various aspects of the subject. Instead, it is designed to measure the degree to which students have achieved "the important objectives of a high school course in problems of democracy." Unfortunately, no indication is given what these important objectives may be. An examination of the test items forces this reviewer to infer that the major objective of such a course is the memorization of factual material, much of it of questionable significance. The acquisition of certain mental abilities or skills, which are nowhere clearly defined, seems to be a second objective. There is little indication that the authors began their test building with a clearly formulated set of specific objectives. The content included in the 89 topics selected seems to have been the major point of departure, rather than the objectives of the problems course. The result is that the test as a whole seems to put a premium upon, and encourages, verbalistic learning.

The 34 multiple choice items in Part A of each form of the test illustrate this. With one or two exceptions, the content of these items is such that they should be cast in the true-false rather than the multiple choice form. They require no mental operation beyond that of recognizing the one correct fact and eliminating the four incorrect facts. Likewise, the matching items in Part B call for recognition (with no evidence that there is also understanding) of terms like gerrymandering, parity, and the like.

The 31 items in Part C of both forms are of a somewhat different nature. Some of these items represent an attempt to measure the ability to interpret materials in paragraph or chart form or to relate concepts with each other. Others measure the ability to arrange events in chronological order or to recognize when certain population trends emerged. In general, the items in this section do not reflect a high degree of expertness or ingenuity in constructing items of this kind. Some items in Form AM seem to be measuring skills and abilities quite different from those measured in Form BM. Thus, while the two forms may be comparable as regards validity and difficulty of items, they may not be measuring the same skills and abilities.

Measuring achievement over content as fluid as that contained in a problems of democracy course presents special difficulties. Many of these difficulties are represented in the Dimond-Pflieger test. Some of the items are obsolete or "dated." Some reflect a point of view commonly held at the time the test was constructed, but significantly modified since that time. Particularly in Part C, "correct" responses are often based quite largely on value judgments, for example, Items 14 and 61, Form BM. In other items, "correct" answers are based on unstated premises, for example, Items 66–70, Form AM.

The attempt to provide a standardized instrument to measure achievement in problems of democracy courses is a worthy one. It presents difficulties not encountered in other areas such as American or world history. The Dimond-Pflieger test impresses the reviewer as only a little better than the end of course examination which most teachers would build for themselves. Its chief limitation seems to be the failure to formulate clearly the objectives it is intended to measure (of which the knowledge of important factual details is certainly one). Techniques for measuring the subtler and more sophisticated mental abilities, such as the ability to draw inferences or the ability to compare and contrast points of view, are known and should be employed in a test of this kind. Properly revised, the Dimond-Pflieger test could be developed into a useful and much needed measuring instrument.

DOUGLAS E. SCATES, *Professor of Education, University of Florida, Gainesville, Florida.*

The manual states that this test "has been constructed to measure the extent to which students have achieved the important objectives of a high school course in problems of democracy." Under the names of the Director and the Evaluation Director of the 5-year Citizenship Education Study conducted in the Detroit Public Schools, this statement is nothing short of shocking. It may be that the authors of the test did not see copy for the manual; if not, whoever wrote the statement is, in the reviewer's mind, guilty of inexcusable carelessness or unethical procedure.

One quickly searches the manual in the hope of finding evidence that the opening statement, as quoted, is a misprint. He finds rather confirmation of the point of view: he reads that material was selected to "represent a balanced coverage of objectives." In a time when any employee of a major test publishing house would insist that he understood the meaning of the word "objectives," this statement becomes as misleading and indefensible as the first. On page 7 of the manual is the third unblushing statement that "the primary purpose of this test is to provide a valid, objective measure of achievement in problems of democracy for the individual student." The final paragraph of the manual attempts to atone: it is written in the spirit of someone who knew the truth and wanted to say what he knew but felt censored, either overtly or through his understanding that the publisher would not be made happy through allusions to possible limitations of the test.

Turning to the test itself, the reviewer's feeling is one of disappointment. The predominantly factual, relatively sterile group of items, most of which might be part of any routine course in modern history or formal civics, when set over against the outcomes that one might hope for in the area of "problems of democracy," stirs the reviewer's sense of professional integrity. For the authors of this test are the ones who wrote: "The quality of citizenship is directly related to the emotional development of the child." (This finding is apparently too basic to be considered among "the important objectives of a high school course.") "Civic lethargy is a disease that can destroy our way of life." (If it is a disease, it is obviously not an objective. But what about the alleviation of the disease?) "There is need....for participation in democratic activities." [1] (Ap-

1 DIMOND, STANLEY E. *Schools and the Development of Good Citizens,* pp. 2, 40, 209. Final Report of the Citizenship Education Study. Detroit, Mich.: Wayne University Press, 1953. Pp. 215.

parently this is of no concern for a course in problems of democratic living.) Our concern should be "not to give answers....but to supply students with technics for analyzing critically." [2] (Analysis in the sense of detecting problems or diagnosing them was not found in the test.) "Emotional adjustment leads to good citizenship." [3] (Not even knowledge of the importance of emotions is deemed worthy of a place in a test of problems of living.) "Keys to good citizenship" [4] include better emotional adjustment, clear thinking, engagement in civic action. (Yet these factors are negligible in a test of "the important objectives.")

Of course, the reviewer is confusing citizenship and the problems of democracy, something on the order of confusing members of the human race and people. Are we to assume that problems of democracy, when packed into the mold of a high school course, become mere intellectual statements—verbal pawns to be pushed at each other by teacher and pupil, with no more meaning for real life than a leaf blown across the lawn? No doubt the authors were told (or understood) that current practice and lofty (realistic?) conceptions are different things; that one cannot expect high school pupils to be enthusiastic over the large social problems of our day; that a test, to be successful (to sell), must be geared to the common practices of the average high school. Accordingly, with almost complete disregard for what the authors have contributed to our understanding of the essential ingredients in citizenship, a relatively commonplace group of facts from recent American history are described as representing "the important objectives of a high school course." The reviewer has an understanding of, and a genuine respect for, our American economic system; yet he must raise the question of how far it is necessary for publishers (and authors) to go, under the influence of competitive sales, in their distortions in a professional field of endeavor.

One need not take his departure from the published views of the authors; he may turn to his own expectations as an American citizen seriously interested in the public schools. A

2 COLLINGS, MILLER R., AND DIMOND, STANLEY E. "Citizenship Education." *Nation's Sch* 46:42–4 N '50.
3 PFLIEGER, ELMER F., AND WESTON, GRACE L. "Emotional Adjustment Leads to Good Citzenship." *Nation's Sch* 46:61–2 D '50.
4 DIMOND, STANLEY E. "Keys to Good Citizenship." *Nat Parent-Teach* 49:19–21 F '55.

course in problems of democracy might, apart from any survey of widespread practice, be presumed (or hoped) to give our young people insights into the character of societal problems; to cultivate the ability to sense, analyze, and define problems and issues in the contemporary news of current publications; to heighten discernment in identifying the forces at work in the day-to-day and decade-by-decade problems of his own society in his own lifetime; to develop judgment concerning the direction of social trends and their possible consequences; to stimulate interest to the point of desire for some lifelong participation in the affairs of our larger social groups; to contribute an appreciation of the role of social skills, and the need for learning them, in any social enterprise. As American citizens, we desire a degree of critical mindedness, but not without appreciation based on the awareness that "many sincere, capable, and conscientious" persons have struggled to produce what we now have (Dimond, 1953, p. 10); we recognize the need for continued evaluation by every citizen, but not without understanding of the costs met by those who have built the present; we believe in the need for persons who are forward looking, who are to some extent dissatisfied, who feel and express the urge for better things—but not without historical grounding and philosophic perspective. And if we might have some tendency to hope that our schools would attempt substantial contributions in these directions, might we not also desire that the tests by which learning and teaching success are gaged—both in the public and in the professional eye— might lend their support to a major emphasis on such goals?

Those who know high school well may say that we should not expect so much from the limited opportunities of courses in school. The point is well taken. One cannot read the careful, scientifically oriented, refreshingly candid final report of Dimond (1953; cf. p. 202) without awareness of this fact. It is not, however, so much the degree as the character of the learning that represents the tremendous hiatus between carefully formulated goals and actual practice. It is the tendency to believe and proceed on the notion that learning must begin with facts and that, after some years, one may build on these facts. In virtually all areas of human behavior such a notion is highly fallacious, and in some areas it is about the worst possible. It can be entertained only by those whose interest in the knowledge of facts is over and above their interest in practical competence. For facts are of value only to the person who is deciding and doing, and the barriers to human thought and action are greater and more serious than is the difficulty of becoming acquainted with relevant available facts. Let us therefore, as teachers, give major attention where the needs are major—such as the overcoming of complacency inertia; the breaking of the thought-action barrier; the identification of the self with the larger concern; easing through the fear of the unfamiliar—the transition from action in primary groups to action in secondary and tertiary groups; the steps necessary to avoid "going off half-cocked"— the need for punctilious care in *getting adequate relevant facts;* the importance of relating one's thoughts, attitudes, values, and plan of action to a larger context—lest one find oneself pulling in a direction embarrassing to one's other commitments; and the expectation that one will learn more as he works, and will make modifications in his ideas as he sees things partly in terms of the interests of others. (How different is such learning from that of the self-sufficient prig who knows everything in the textbook, blows the top off objective tests, gets the highest approbation of his school in terms of marks—and often knows nothing of life as it flows around and by him without making contact.) Objectives *are* important; they can be different.

It can be argued that a preponderant concern with the teaching (and learning) of facts is a serious detriment to priceless initiative, to the creative impulse, to the hope of desirable change. For one thing, the person (teacher or pupil) who starts with facts as his chief goal is likely never to separate himself from this goal. In any field, the accumulated mass is overwhelming, and new facts are produced daily at too rapid a rate for even the specialist to keep up with them. One therefore becomes ever more frantic in his lifelong squirrel-cage pursuit of what he conceives to be the mere foundation of an education. Teachers must somehow *from the start* give him an awareness that there are other things, other qualities, other learnings, other pursuits that make up the educated citizen.

Even more serious, however, than the misdirected life is the one that is stopped, bound, confined. We criticize civics texts and courses of the early part of this century because they offered young people a kind of learning about civic structure, civic processes, and civic attitudes that was akin to, let us say, learning in arithmetic. And the kind of attitude, the mental pattern, engendered in such factual teaching is what we might expect from saying day in and day out over the years, "Now young people, this is it; and if you don't do precisely as you are told you will be in trouble." For a still young and hopeful America there could be no greater trouble or danger than the stamping in of just such a mental pattern. So often in education we advertise goals of participation in constructive change, yet we teach "facts" ("This is the way it is.") in a matrix of inhibiting, fear-engendering reprisal for any hint of individuality in thought or behavior. It is difficult to say whether the social or the physical sciences are the greatest offenders. In any area such a position is a serious misconstruction. In the social sphere, we call attention to the danger of being a deviate; yet the facts are that there have been more changes in our culture in the past 50 years than in any other culture in any similar period. Do we dare teach (in problems in democracy) that our country was founded, largely peopled, and established by "deviates" of one kind or another—those who couldn't, or wouldn't knuckle down and conform to what the majority of Europeans would? In the physical sciences and mathematics, many persons regard the "facts" as inexorable, representing an ultra-human rightness that makes wrong anything one may wish to think that has not come down to him from the past. This despite the fact that mathematics during the past half century has had more *new* developments than in all its preceding history; or that physics in the past 50 years has added more to the power of mankind than it had in all its previous history. Those who think of "facts" as permanent verities must not have lived during the present century.

So the person who, in any field, is taught in such a way that he is permitted to get the impression that the world is "all set" and fixed, and that his business is to exist within the inherited confines of knowledge and propriety and to fight off any threat of change, has built into him habits of mind that ill fit him for participation in the swift currents of American cultural change, and that a long after-school

Dimond-Pflieger Problems of Democracy Test

life may never successfully alter. In an avowed democracy, should we not teach most of our courses (including problems of democracy) in such a way as to make the young person feel that he *has a place* in working out the changes that *are going to occur,* one way or the other, in his culture during his life? There are subtle but critical differences between the person who is taught primarily for the learning of facts and the person who is taught primarily to *function* as a member of his society, habitually taking the precaution to obtain the latest facts relating to his activity. The *ability to do* is not completely independent of hard facts; but creative ability so often places the "hard facts" in new perspectives, new relationships (such as 20th century mathematics has done) so that new ways of dealing with the facts are found and the old "facts to be faced" become merely relics of an obsolescent way of thinking. "Facts" can be so learned that they fit into schemes of use which are more important, more constructive, and more socially valuable than answering recall and discrimination questions at the end of a school course.

It may be felt that the reviewer is not writing from the background of current realities of the schoolroom, where problems of democracy is but one course among a number that the teacher must teach while the students, with nature on their side, exert every known form of resistance. Perhaps he is; perhaps he is making an appeal to textbook writers, testmakers, and those who prepare supplementary instructional materials not to handicap the stimulating teacher by concentrating on an inferior set of outcomes. It is difficult enough to accomplish results above the ordinary; it is cruel to have such efforts evaluated by an assessment scheme that omits them.

There are realities of many kinds—those in the classroom situation, those in our very dynamic contemporary culture, and those in curriculum and testmaking procedures. Perhaps we should be impressed when we read in the manual the serious (?) statement that the test was constructed by "(1) determining in the soundest manner possible the objectives to be measured; (2) determining the proper emphasis and weights to be assigned to the various objectives." But we are reminded of certain realities pointed out by Ralph Tyler 20 years ago: for test making purposes "each objective must be defined in terms which clarify the kind

of behavior that the course should help to develop among students." (Behavior includes all forms of reaction and doing.) "A definition of objectives in terms of expected student behavior differs from the analysis-of-content method * It does more than indicate the content to be covered. It defines the reactions which a student is expected to make to this content * With the same content it makes a great deal of difference." [5] (Tyler's statements were not meant to be coercive or restrictive; he was emphasizing that, for testing purposes, an objective needs to be stated in terms of *doing*—of which knowing is one form. But most course objectives fall outside this latter category.)

According to further statements in the manual, the "soundest manner possible" turns out to be that of analyzing textbooks and articles to find out what topics were dealt with. Topics! As though *topics* constituted the moving forces in the restless life of active youngsters sensing the dynamism of their elders in coping with a culture that surges with change. Ascertaining objectives merely by noting topics is a "sound" procedure only if one's thinking about methods of work consists essentially of a list of steps to be checked off after one has mechanically gone through certain motions. It is a far cry from topics to objectives; almost any topic lends itself to a very wide range of different objectives.

It is an interesting commentary on the technological age in which we live that professional judgment is virtually banned. In its place we have the respectability of "rigid standards" representing the imposition of relatively fixed (and often inappropriate) formalities, the spell cast by any sort of mumbo-jumbo reference to "the scientific method," the mesmerizing allure of a display of esoteric statistical terms, and, above all, the unquestioning belief in the miraculous revealing power of the modern pencil point wiggle.

The reviewer must, in fairness, note that the Dimond-Pflieger test has a number of qualities in which all persons concerned can take some satisfaction. Of the 80 items, nearly one third call for something other than recall and association: they require deduction, critical discrimination, inference, and general understand-

5 HAWKES, HERBERT E.; LINDQUIST, E. F.; AND MANN, C. R., EDITORS. *The Construction and Use of Achievement Examinations,* pp. 10–11. Boston, Mass.: Houghton Mifflin Co., 1936. Pp. x, 497.

ing (presumably untaught association). This is undoubtedly "better" than most teacher-made tests would do. The test has many earmarks of successful application of currently approved test-making procedures. The work has been done with technical sophistication. The test manual is commendably written, primarily to teachers. It is written simply, though at points carelessly or studiedly misleading, with no attempt to overawe the reader with technical flamboyancy. The test can be widely used with no more harm than centering the attention of students and teachers on the minor, relatively inconsequential outcomes of a subject area fundamentally important and potentially potent in the outlook and large social abilities of those who will soon inherit the real problems of our American democracy where we lay them down.

[834]

★General Knowledge Test of Local, State, and National Government. Grades 11–16; 1952; 8 scores: general, local, state, national executive, national legislative, national judiciary, national total, total; 1 form; norms ['52]; $3.95 per 25 tests; 40¢ per manual ['52]; 65¢ per specimen set; postpaid; 50(60) minutes; Mae Pullins Claytor; C. A. Gregory Co. *

WAYNE A. FREDERICK, *Social Studies Department, Isidore Newman School, New Orleans, Louisiana.*

This test is a comprehensive examination in local, state, and national government. Several sound features place the scope of the test beyond that of simple measurement of knowledge in terms of memorized factual data.

For one thing, although many items are designed to explore only the factual knowledge of the student, many more measure his ability to perceive relationships among basic concepts, and some call for an evaluation of perceived relationships. In this respect, Section 1, Government in General, is most carefully drawn.

For another, the items have been carefully selected to emphasize basic concepts in the several areas. Relatively few items concern themselves with trivia. The attention paid to pertinent historical concepts is to be commended.

Finally, the items have, in general, been well constructed. They are precise and cogent, with most of the options being parallel in construction and pertinent to the concept which the item is attempting to measure. Because of their weak construction a few items appear to be very easy. However, in no case does poor workmanship result in a confused or ambigu-

ous item. There are five true-false type items in Section 1 which cover concepts which could have been better tested by well made items of the multiple choice type. Also, in each of Sections 1 and 2 there is a set of sequential items carrying the same options. Most of these items test only factual knowledge, consequently weakening the test. Significant relationships concerning these same concepts could have been tested by some other device.

Basically this test appears to be what its author intended it to be—a sound comprehensive measure of the kind of knowledge that should be achieved by students in secondary schools and colleges. Since the items have been carefully drawn to measure concepts which are general in nature, the test can be used anywhere in the United States.

[835]

*The Graduate Record Examinations Advanced Tests: Government. College seniors and graduate students; 1939–56; for more complete information, see 601; IBM; 180(200) minutes; Educational Testing Service. *

CHRISTINE McGUIRE, *Assistant Professorial Lecturer in the Social Sciences, and Examiner, The University of Chicago, Chicago, Illinois.* [Review of Form EGR.]

This examination, for college seniors majoring in political science, is designed primarily to test their competence in their field of concentration. Test results are used to evaluate the student's mastery of the materials as a part of a comprehensive departmental examination or to select among applicants for graduate study or special graduate appointments.

Descriptive material furnished with the examination does not specify the major objectives nor the particular areas of subject matter sampled in the test. However, copies of the examination are available to prospective users for inspection. Approximately half of the test consists of objective items sampling a miscellaneous array of discrete information. This reviewer could detect no skill required in answering items in this section of the test other than the rather simple recall of facts at various levels of detail. The balance of the test consists of objective questions based on quite interesting and often ingenious charts, diagrams, verbal descriptions of hypothetical situations, and passages representing a variety of points of view. In the questions related to these contextual statements the student is required to demonstrate the ability to read and understand the material in the form presented, to recall relevant information, and to apply general principles in interpreting the material and drawing conclusions or making predictions based on it. The questions in this section of the examination vary greatly with respect to clarity, freedom from ambiguity in the correct answer, and level of skill and understanding required of the student. The length of the test in itself (more than one item per minute, including time required for reading and studying the numerous charts and statements) precludes the inclusion of questions requiring any very complex form of analysis. Despite these deficiencies, this section of the test provides a very useful framework which it is hoped can be more successfully exploited to require the kinds of skills and understanding that might reasonably be expected of college graduates majoring in government.

In the absence of explicit criteria for determining the choice of subject matter and skills to be sampled, it is difficult to evaluate the coverage of the examination. However, in this reviewer's opinion some areas (for example, public administration) are given undue weight at the cost of neglecting or seriously undervaluing other equally important areas (for example, political theory, comparative government, international law and diplomacy, and analysis of the dynamics of public opinion formation and political behavior). Secondly, in the areas that are extensively represented, the particular questions asked suggest a more or less random (rather than a systematic) sampling of basic concepts and principles. Third, the test places too heavy a premium on the more simple skills of recall and comprehension and inadequate weight on the more analytical and integrative skills.

In addition to an individual score report for each student taking the test, the user is supplied with the usual data on reliability and correlations with aptitude tests, and with statistical tables relevant to the interpretation of the scaled scores in terms of which test results are reported. Two cautions should be observed in utilizing these data. First, the scale values were initially determined by a series of steps which require estimating, on the basis of the actual performance of a subgroup, the probable performance of a total group from "eleven colleges selected to be representative of colleges using the Graduate Record Examinations." The *estimated* means and standard deviations may therefore be subject to certain errors, and the appropriateness of the scaling group for use as a reference group is exceedingly difficult to judge. The Score Interpretation Handbook for Deans and Advisers, November 1957, makes clear that for these and other reasons "a given college will probably find that norms collected at their own college or at a group of similar schools, will be more useful for their own purposes." Secondly, in the summary statistics provided for any given year, the only information about the group on which percentile rankings are based is a listing of the number of examinees from each participating institution. Under certain conditions the Educational Testing Service is willing to provide data on special groups that may be more appropriate for use as reference groups by a particular institution. However, in this reviewer's opinion, reports in the form of per cent of correct responses would generally be more useful to graduate schools to which a candidate is applying, and an analysis of responses to particular items would be more useful to departments from which groups of examinees are graduated.

In summary, this examination covers in considerable detail, but not necessarily in a manner that is systematically appropriate to any given department, several areas in the very broad field of government. It omits certain important areas and perhaps minimizes certain important skills in which majors in government should be able to demonstrate respectable achievement. The data supplied with test results are comprehensive but of limited usefulness in the absence of local norms.

For a review by Harold Seashore of the entire series, see 601.

[836]
★The Kansas Constitution Test. High school and college; 1957; Form A ['57]; mimeographed manual; no college norms; $1.20 per 25 tests, postage extra; 25¢ per specimen set, postpaid; 40(45) minutes; Louise Gardner and M. W. Sanders; Bureau of Educational Measurements. *

DAVID K. HEENAN, *Assistant Professor, Department of Humanities, and Office of Evaluation Services, Michigan State University, East Lansing, Michigan.*

This test consists of 125 items based on the formal structure and functions of the United

States Constitution. It covers vocabulary, history, and application of the Constitution. The items are drawn from the document itself or from textbooks which deal with the Constitution and related American history.

On the whole, the test is made up of incidental details which could be recalled only after an exhaustive study of the subject or memorization of the document. While the test adequately samples the factual information the student might have, it makes little effort to measure the student's *understanding* of these facts. Though a student might score well by being able to recall bits and parcels of information on the Constitution, rarely is he forced to compare or evaluate his accumulation of details.

Some of the items seem unnecessarily petty: "Closure is observed in the Senate to (stop a filibuster)." This is something that happens so rarely that it is hardly worth mentioning; certainly little time would be spent on this subject in class. Too many items call for "the number of this" or "the name of that," as in "The usual number of years given to a state to ratify an amendment is (seven)"; "The number of ways to become a citizen is (three)"; "The Elastic Clause of the Constitution is found in (Article I, Section 8)."

The test should be carefully checked by an authority on the subject of Constitutional history (this reviewer is not such an authority) to eliminate stem statements which lead to misunderstanding and confusion. For example, "If neither of the candidates for President receive a majority of all the electoral votes then the President is chosen by (the House of Representatives)." The word "none" should be substituted for "neither." "Neither" implies that there were only two candidates—in which case a majority of the electoral votes would be a mathematical certainty. Another item reads: "The framers of the Constitution were principally (lawyers)." Here perhaps there would be less chance of confusion if "delegates to the Constitutional Convention" were substituted for "framers" since some of the more active "framers" (Washington, Franklin, Jefferson, etc.) were not lawyers.

The test should be further checked for errors. In the item, "Congress created the Immigration and Nationalization Service which is regulated by the Department of (Justice)," "Naturalization" should be substituted for

"Nationalization." Again, in the item, "One of the first examples of the use of implied powers was the establishment of (the Federal bank)," "United States" should be substituted for "Federal."

It is unfortunate that in the few questions which require some exercise of judgment the testmaker has chosen subject matter on which there is strong disagreement. For example, "The method of choosing the President and Vice President provided for by the Constitution (has become obsolete and should be changed)." While this reviewer would also choose the expected answer, perhaps it is unfair to ask all students to concur in this judgment.

The test probably exemplifies the teaching approach used in most American secondary schools in dealing with the Constitution. The *details* of the Constitution become the object of emphasis at the expense of the philosophy of the document. Perhaps the best way to cut down on the trivial elements in the test is to shorten it. The whole test could stand editing and should be rewritten if it is to be a reliable instrument to measure students' knowledge and understanding.

[837]

★Newspaper Reading Survey: What Do You Read? High school; 1954; 4 interest scores: local, national, international politics, total; 1 form; $2.50 per 35 tests, postpaid; specimen set not available; (20–35) minutes; Citizenship Education Project, Teachers College, Columbia University; distributed by C. A. Gregory Co. *

FREDERICK H. STUTZ, *Professor of Education, Cornell University, Ithaca, New York.*

This test is designed to gauge the level of interest in political events relative to interest in other types of events. Students are expected to select from each of 10 groups of nine simulated newspaper headlines those three headlines which represent stories they would like most to read and the three which represent stories they would like least to read. Each group of nine headlines includes one each on local, national, and international political events.

Teachers of the social studies or citizenship education, especially those in junior high schools, will find this interest test to be worth using in an experimental fashion. By pretesting, they may discover something of the kinds of reading interests students have and be able to guide the development of interest in reading about political affairs. Post testing may help the teacher to determine shifts in reading interests as a result of instruction. The test is brief, well constructed technically, fairly easy to score, and accompanied by a useful set of instructions of admirable brevity.

The user should be fully aware of the limitations of a test of this sort. The scoring norms are derived from a limited administration of the test. Though validity has been sought by including headlines selected by groups with known special interests, it is by no means certain that the test will fully appraise relative levels of interest in political events. The headlines themselves, though they have been generalized by having names and dates removed, become rather quickly dated. Pupil choices of the nonpolitical headlines may be influenced by the fact that some of the political items are no longer of current interest.

The test represents a worthwhile effort to get at one of the neglected aspects of citizenship education, interest in politics. It should be used experimentally by teachers who are specially concerned with the teaching of citizenship ideas and practices. The test has limitations which should be fully recognized by users.

M. J. Wantman, *Visiting Director of Educational Measurement and Research, University of Malaya, Singapore.*

This test is designed "to enable teachers to evaluate the level of student interest in local, national, and international political events as compared with other interests." The student is presented with 10 groups of headlines which are similar to those found in newspapers. In each group there is a headline dealing with each of the following areas: music or art, religion, human interest, sports, science, economics, and local, national, and international political affairs. Thus, each group consists of nine headlines, three of which are political ones. The student is instructed to mark a plus sign next to three headlines for stories that he would MOST like to read, to mark a minus sign next to three headlines for stories that he would LEAST like to read, and to leave three headlines blank.

In the scoring of the test, a student is given 2 points for each political headline that he marked as "MOST liked to read," 1 point for each political headline left blank, and no points for each political headline that he marked as "LEAST liked to read." Thus, a student marking all 30 political headlines, 10 local, 10 national, and 10 international, as "MOST like to read" would receive the maximum possible score of 60.

The norms for the test are based on 692 students in the 10th, 11th, and 12th grades in 20 high schools. The authors express the hope that "more complete norms may be included in future editions of this test." Four years after its initial publication, more complete norms are still not available.

Norms are presented in the form of percentiles, with separate values for the local, national, international, and total scores. The values recorded indicate that girls have a greater interest in political affairs than do boys. The authors make no comment on this result.

Test-retest (after three weeks) reliabilities are reported for 75 high school seniors as .89, .72, .81, and .78 for total, local, national, and international scores, respectively. Neither standard deviations nor standard errors of measurement are reported. Estimating the standard deviations from the table of norms, and using the reliability coefficients reported above, one can estimate the standard errors of measurement for the part scores to be in the neighborhood of 2 points, and for the total score to be in the neighborhood of 3 points. The low reliabilities with the accompanying relatively large standard errors of measurement are not surprising when one recalls that the test is in reality a 30-item test.

This instrument designed to measure interest in political affairs has the usual weaknesses of interest inventories. Fudging is possible in spite of the confident statement of the authors that the probability of the purpose of the instrument being detected by students is not great provided it is presented as a survey of reading interests. No evidence is presented for the validity of the instrument for its stated purpose. The method of choosing the items to be included in the inventory is described briefly. This description supposedly supports the contention of face validity for the classification of the headlines.

The *Newspaper Reading Survey* is not recommended by this writer to teachers who might wish "to evaluate the level of student interest in local, national, and international political events as compared with other interests."

[838]

★Patterson Test or Study Exercises on the Constitution of the United States. Grades 9–16 and adults; 1931–53; 1 form ('53, same as test copyrighted in 1937 except for minor changes); directions sheet ['53]; no data on reliability and validity; $2.25 per 25 tests; 35¢ per specimen set; postpaid; (40–50) minutes; Raymond G. Patterson; Public School Publishing Co. *

[839]

★Patterson Test or Study Exercises on the Declaration of Independence. Grades 9–16 and adults; 1931–52; 1 form ('52, combination of Forms A and B copyrighted in 1931 with minor changes); manual ('52); no data on reliability and validity; no norms; $2.25 per 10 tests; 35¢ per specimen set; postpaid; (40–50) minutes; Raymond G. Patterson; Public School Publishing Co. *

[840]

★Peltier-Durost Civics and Citizenship Test: Evaluation and Adjustment Series. High school; 1958; 2 scores: achievement, attitude; IBM; Forms AM, BM; $3.80 per 35 tests; separate answer sheets may be used; $1.40 per 35 IBM answers sheets; postage extra; 35¢ per specimen set, postpaid; 55(65) minutes; Charles L. Peltier and Walter N. Durost; World Book Co. *

[841]

★Principles of American Citizenship Test. Grades 11–12; 1952–53; formerly called *Premises of American Government Test*; Forms A, B ('52); manual ('53); $3.50 per 35 tests, postpaid; specimen set not available; 40(50) minutes; Citizenship Education Project, Teachers College, Columbia University; distributed by C. A. Gregory Co. *

REFERENCE

1. CITIZENSHIP EDUCATION PROJECT. *Premises of American Liberty, With Citation of Basic Documentation.* New York: Teachers College, Columbia University, 1952. Pp. 15.

HOWARD R. ANDERSON, *Professor of Education, and Dean, University School of Liberal and Applied Studies, The University of Rochester, Rochester, New York*

The manual for this test states that it was developed to measure the attainment of three objectives: "1. Knowledge of the documented accomplishments of liberty as these are revealed in history. 2. Knowledge of the principles and ideals upon which our democratic society is based and how these ideals apply to everyday life. 3. Knowledge of the problems and issues which beset our society to-day." Actually the test concerns itself chiefly with the second. No items specifically test knowledge of the historical evolution of liberty or its attainment in lands other than the United States. Nor does the test contain any item on unemployment, inflation, high taxes, the cold war, communism, or anti-Western feeling in former colonial areas, which surely are among "the problems and issues which beset our society."

The explanation that this test "measures the student's understanding of the United States citizen's rights and responsibilities and his ability to apply to specific situations the 'Premises of American Liberty' (formulated by the staff of the Citizenship Education Project)" is more accurate. But even this statement seems to exaggerate the function of such test items as "An individual nominated for public office is called (a candidate)," "A tax on money earned during the year is called (an income tax)," and "A unique power of the Senate....is....to (approve treaties)."

Undoubtedly this test includes items which measure knowledge commonly acquired in courses in civics, American history, and problems of American democracy. Some of the items go beyond direct recall to measure the pupil's understanding of how a democratic principle applies in a given situation. The 54 four-response multiple choice items included in each form of the test are almost always clearly phrased and free of technical imperfections. Two items in Form A may be dated, however. Item 37 gives as the "essential difference between a scientist in a democracy and a scientist in a totalitarian country" this statement: "[The latter] is under pressure to produce results in line with political beliefs." That may have been true in certain fields at one time but will hardly hold as a generalization. Item 40 calls for "made the public aware of its neglected responsibilities" as the correct response to "The greatest immediate value of the Senate investigation of organized crime (1951)." No high school youngster would remember this investigation nor would he be likely to have read about it. Doubtless he could, however, figure out the answer since the foils are: "eliminated most big-time gambling," "brought criminals to justice," and "taught the public how the Senate operates."

Percentile norms are provided for junior and senior high schools. These would not be too useful in evaluating achievement in a given grade. Social studies teachers naturally could not depend on this test alone to measure achievement in civics, American history, and problems of American democracy classes; but the test might well be used to supplement more traditional tests.

Principles of American Citizenship Test

M. J. WANTMAN, *Visiting Director of Educational Measurement and Research, University of Malaya, Singapore.*

This test was originally designed to measure a student's mastery of the "Premises of American Liberty" compiled by the Citizenship Education Project of Teachers College, Columbia University. The subsequent change of the name of the test to its present title is misleading since the test content is still restricted to the project's list of 90 premises.

The stated purposes of the test are so broad that one would hesitate to attempt to achieve them in a 54-item multiple choice test. There is no evidence presented that the authors even approached their goal.

The suggested uses of the results of the test include appraisal of class position as compared with that of other classes in the United States, appraisal of an individual's standing in a class, and teaching. Since separate norms are not presented for the various grades, comparison with other classes is impossible; the advice to teachers on the use of results to appraise an individual's standing in a class is couched in such words of caution that a teacher could not be expected to use the test for this purpose; there are no doubt better ways to teach the premises of American liberty than by means of this test.

The typography and format of the test are excellent. A single typographical error was noted—a misspelling in the correct option for Item 48 in Form A. The answer sheet is easily managed. The system for assigning letters to options is designed to minimize the student's mismarking his answer sheet.

The norms provided are based on 2,742 and 2,899 cases for Forms A and B, respectively. Since the cases for each form include both junior and senior high school students, the numbers on which the norms for each of these groups are based must be considered inadequate. In view of the limited number of cases, it is difficult to understand the authors statement that the norms are "representative of the national high school population." They even indicate that "regional norms are available on request."

Separate norms are provided for Form A and Form B. The norms include only the nine deciles. Form A appears to be the easier of the two forms for junior high school students, while Form B is the easier one for senior high school students. No explanation is provided for this result.

The reliability of the two forms, computed by the split-half method, yielded values of .90 and .91 for Forms A and B, respectively. The number of cases on which these coefficients are based is not given.

There is no evidence presented that this test is valid for measuring the "student's understanding of the United States citizen's rights and responsibilities and his ability to apply to specific situations the 'Premises of American Liberty.' " The acceptance by a test user of the claims made for the test depends on the user's confidence in the judgment of the authors.

The *Principles of American Citizenship Test* should be used only in those situations where the "Premises of American Liberty" have been taught. Even then, as the authors warn, the results of individual students should be interpreted with caution. In view of the limitations of the test, the weaknesses of its norms, and its specificity for the "Premises of American Liberty," a classroom teacher would probably do well to devise his own test if he felt compelled to test for an understanding of the principles of American citizenship.

SOCIOLOGY

[842]
*The Graduate Record Examinations Advanced Tests: Sociology. College seniors and graduate students; 1939–56; for more complete information, see 601; IBM; 180(200) minutes; Educational Testing Service. *

For a review by Harold Seashore of the entire series, see 601.

[843]
★Sare-Sanders Sociology Test. High school and college; 1958; Form A; mimeographed manual; $1.20 per 25 tests, postage extra; 25¢ per specimen set, postpaid; 40(45) minutes; Harold Sare and Merritt W. Sanders; Bureau of Educational Measurements. *

[844]
★Sociology: Every Pupil Scholarship Test. High school; 1943–58; new form issued each January; norms available following testing program; no data on reliability; 4¢ per test; 4¢ per scoring key; postage extra; 40(45) minutes; Bureau of Educational Measurements. *

REPRINTED FROM *The Sixth Mental Measurements Yearbook*

SOCIAL STUDIES — SIXTH MMY

REVIEWS BY *Howard R. Anderson, Harry D. Berg, William C. Bingham, Henry Chauncey, Richard E. Gross, John H. Haefner, David K. Heenan, Christine McGuire, Jonathon C. McLendon, Donald W. Oliver, Robert J. Solomon, Morey J. Wantman, and J. Richard Wilmeth.*

[963]

*American School Achievement Tests: Part 4, Social Studies and Science.** Grades 4-6, 7-9; 1941-63; 2 scores: social studies, science; Forms D ('57), E ('57), F ('57), G ('58), (2 sheets); 2 levels; $3 per 35 self-marking tests; 50¢ per specimen set of either level; postage extra; 50(60) minutes; Willis E. Pratt, Robert V. Young (manuals), and Clara E. Cockerille; Bobbs-Merrill Co., Inc. *

a) INTERMEDIATE BATTERY. Grades 4-6; battery manual ('61, 17 pages).

b) ADVANCED BATTERY. Grades 7-9; battery manual ('63, 17 pages).

For reviews of the complete battery, see 2, 5:1, 4:1, and 3:1.

[964]

★Christian Democracy Test (Civics, Sociology, Economics): Affiliation Testing Program for Catholic Secondary Schools. Grades 9–12 and students who are candidates for the high school diploma issued by the Catholic University of America; 1949–63; administered annually in May at individual schools; IBM; Form Z ('63, 16 pages) used in 1963 program; tests loaned only; separate answer sheets must be used; 50¢ per test and IBM answer sheet; postpaid; fee includes scoring and other services; specimen set of the complete battery free; for more complete information, see 758; 90(100) minutes; Program of Affiliation, Catholic University of America. *

HENRY CHAUNCEY, *President, Educational Testing Service, Princeton, New Jersey.* [Review of Forms Y and Z.]

In the booklet describing the Program of Affiliation, it is stated that each ATP examination in social studies "seeks to measure the achievement of the student not only in the actual course content....but in the application of such content to special assignments in current events classes." If this purpose were achieved in the Christian Democracy Test, it might well represent a significant step forward in social studies tests. However, a review of these two test forms indicates that, although current situations provide the context or vehicle for the posing of many questions, the questions typically do not require the application of social science knowledge to understand, explain, or interpret current phenomena. Questions dealing with a current situation usually require the student to recall some fact about the situation. The following question is illustrative (Form Y, item 2): "If you are considering buying a home, you need to know about how the . . . operates. 1. PHA 2. FHA 3. HOLC 4. FDIC 5. FRS."

The major criticism that can be made of the Christian Democracy Test pertains to the superficiality of the knowledge required to deal with most of the questions; that is, it appears to the writer that most of the questions can be answered on the basis of a rote association between name and name, or name and object, or name and idea. However, it should be mentioned that some promising item types dealing with relationships among ideas, and between ideas and situations, are present in each of the two forms. These more significant item types comprise approximately one fourth of the test in each case.

A second criticism of the Christian Democracy Test refers to the mechanics of test construction; that is, it is generally considered desirable in writing the question to state the task required of the student in the item stem. If the student is required to formulate the item task on the basis of some relationship between the item stem and the options, then the probability of ambiguity or obscurity is increased. It is readily apparent that most of the item stems in this test are incomplete. Furthermore, it is also considered good practice in test construction to provide item options with parallel construction. In this fashion irrelevant syntactical and structural cues are more easily avoided. Forms X and Y of this test include far too many irrelevant cues of this kind.

In summary, due to the particular turn of many of its questions, the Christian Democracy Test is inappropriate for general school programs emphasizing democratic principles. This review raises the question whether, in the light of observed substantive and measurement gaps, the test adequately measures many objectives postulated for the Affiliation Testing Program.

For a review of the complete program, see 758.

[965]

★Citizenship: Every Pupil Scholarship Test. Grades 8–9; 1951–57; 2 forms: April '56, January '57, (2 pages); general directions sheet ['63, 2 pages]; no data on reliability; 4¢ per test; 4¢ per key; postage extra; 30(35) minutes; Bureau of Educational Measurements. *

[966]

*College Entrance Examination Board Achievement Test: American History and Social Studies. Candidates for college entrance; 1901–64; this test and the test in European history and world cultures (see 967) replace the single test in social studies which was offered from 1937 to 1962; for more complete information, see 760; 60(80) minutes; program administered for the College Entrance Examination Board by Educational Testing Service. *

HOWARD R. ANDERSON, *Senior Consulting Editor, High School Department, Houghton Mifflin Company, Boston, Massachusetts.* [Review of Forms KAC and LAC1.]

The test is one of 15 in the regular series of subject matter achievement tests offered by the College Entrance Examination Board. Another test in this series concerns itself with European history and world cultures. From 1937 until these two tests were developed, the series included only a single test in the field of social studies—the test called Social Studies. For a review by Ralph W. Tyler of Form FAC of that examination, see 5:786. The major emphasis in the earlier test was on United States history.

The important change made in the CEEB program is of major interest to school administrators and social studies teachers. The new test on European history and world cultures gives recognition to the fact that a growing number of high school students are taking substantial courses in this broad field. Because many students tend to take CEEB tests earlier in their high school program than was the case formerly, many of them may prefer to take the new examination on non-American history. The fact that two examinations are being provided in the field of social studies has made it possible to test more adequately a broader sample of important concepts and skills in the current test on American history and social studies.

The scope of the new test is suggested by the relative emphasis given the six content areas identified by the CEEB American History and Social Studies Committee: (a) political institutions, principles, history (35 per cent), (b) economic principles and developments (20 per cent), (c) foreign affairs (20 per cent), (d) social movements (15 per cent), (e) cultural-intellectual developments (5 per cent), and (f) geography (5 per cent). About one fifth of the 100 items are based on knowledge derived from government, economics, sociology, and geography. However, a student who has had no formal courses in these subjects but has completed a good course in American history should be able to cope with these non-history items.

The current test places major emphasis on the ability to understand and use what has been learned, rather than on the recall of odds and ends of information.

The goal the Examination Committee set itself was to prepare an examination in which about one third of the items test perception of relationships (causal, chronological, means-ends, trends, historical continuity and change, attitudes-action situations); judgments of most or least appropriate options; and applications. About another third of the test items call for the interpretation of written materials.

The test is well edited. The Test Analysis

for December 1962 Achievement Examinations reports for Form KAC a mean of 49.82 and a reliability of .91. This publication also makes the point that "The configuration of entries in the two-way table has the characteristics of a power test, as distinguished from a speeded one." In other words, this test is well suited to the group which takes it.

A reviewer who has taught history to both high school students and college freshmen may question that even the present CEEB test adequately samples important concepts and skills taught at the lower level and expected to be part of the preparation of college students. But it is hard to see how test builders can do more in a one-hour objective type examination. If the present test accurately identifies students who have received good high school preparation in American history and related social studies and who are likely to do well in college social science courses, the test is indeed performing a very useful service.

For a review by Ralph W. Tyler of an earlier form of the social studies test, see 5:786; for a review by Robert L. Thorndike, see 4:662. For reviews of the testing program, see 760.

[967]

*College Entrance Examination Board Achievement Test: European History and World Cultures. Candidates for college entrance; 1901–64; available only in January and May testing programs; this test and the test in American history and social studies (see 966) replace the single test in social studies which was offered from 1937 to 1962; for more complete information, see 760; 60(80) minutes; program administered for the College Entrance Examination Board by Educational Testing Service. *

DAVID K. HEENAN, *Associate Professor, Office of Evaluation Services, Michigan State University, East Lansing, Michigan.* [Review of Forms LAC1 and LAC2.]

This test in European history and world cultures is a new addition to the College Board series of achievement tests. This is one of two new instruments—the other is American History and Social Studies—which were developed to replace the single test in social studies and which became available in January 1963.

The test consists of 100 items and has a time limitation of one hour. The test covers the material well; its items are searching and should discriminate well. Since there are no statistics available at the moment, one can only judge by appearances.

This examination is an improvement over its predecessor and most of the weaknesses of the old social studies test (see 5:786) have been eliminated. Although the student's knowledge is still tested by sampling from a large body of information, it appears that greater attention has been given to covering the most important objectives in the teaching of world history and related fields. While the content of the examination is history-oriented, it is not enough for a student merely to have a good background in historical details, for the test incorporates material outside the scope of traditional history courses, i.e., the content and objectives found in humanities or world culture courses now being offered in many secondary schools. The items which would be classified as belonging to "related fields"—e.g., religious beliefs, philosophical concepts, aesthetics, etc.—do not dominate the test but are sufficient in number to give a student who has read widely a better opportunity to score well on the examination. It is unlikely that most high school students would have read all the works which provide the substance of the "culture items," and one could reasonably expect a wide range of scores. This is not a criticism of the test—it is to be expected that few, if any, students will be able to answer all the questions correctly. The questions on art styles and techniques require only superficial knowledge, but the items dealing with religious beliefs and philosophical systems appear to be more penetrating.

Some attention is given to non-European history and non-European cultures. This is an important addition to the test and is in line with the recent change of opinion as to what constitutes world history. In the past the content of most world history courses centered on the development of the Western world; now textbooks and teachers attempt to cover, at least in general terms, Russia, Africa, India, China, Japan, and the Islamic civilization.

The primary emphasis is on the time period from 1500 to the present, but there are enough questions on ancient and medieval history to make it difficult for a student to score well unless he has some information about man and his world prior to the modern period.

The test is well edited and there is an unusually small number of items which need to be altered for clarity or accuracy. While most multiple choice items are founded on recall of knowledge, other skills are demanded of the student. There is a good balance of items which involve judgment, interpretation and identification of ideas, recognition of cause and effect relationships, analysis of trends, and the like.

In summary, this is a good test. The committee responsible for determining its content and form has done a fine job. This test provides an excellent guidepost for the kinds of objectives that should be stressed in the teaching of world history in the secondary schools.

For a review by Ralph W. Tyler of an earlier form of the social studies test, see 5:786; for a review by Robert L. Thorndike, see 4:662. For reviews of the testing program, see 760.

[968]
Cooperative General Achievement Tests: Test 1, Social Studies. Grades 9–12 and college entrants; 1937–56; formerly called *A Test of General Proficiency in the Field of Social Studies;* IBM; Forms XX ('53, c1947–53, 8 pages, revision of Form X), YZ ('55, c1948–51, 8 pages, revision of Forms Y and Z, identical with test copyrighted in 1951); battery manual ('56, 16 pages); high school norms same as those published in 1938; separate answer sheets must be used; $4 per 25 tests; $1 per 25 IBM answer sheets; 25¢ per scoring stencil; postage extra; $1 per specimen set, cash orders postpaid; 40(50) minutes; Jeanne M. Bradford (XX) and [Elaine Forsyth Cook]; Cooperative Test Division. *

For a review by Harry D. Berg of earlier forms, see 3:596. For reviews of the complete battery, see 7, 5:6, 4:5, and 3:3.

[969]
*The Iowa Tests of Educational Development: Test 1, Understanding of Basic Social Concepts. Grades 9–12; 1942–61; IBM; Forms X-3S, Y-3S, ('52, 8 pages); battery examiner's manual ('58, c1949–57, 23 pages); battery general manual ('59, 37 pages); student profile leaflet, sixth edition ('61, c1958, 2 pages); see the complete battery entry (14b) for other accessories; no data on reliability; separate answer sheets must be used; $2.40 per 20 tests; $5 per 100 IBM answer sheets; 50¢ per scoring stencil; $3 per specimen set of the complete battery; postage extra; 55(65) minutes for full length version, 40(50) minutes for class period version; prepared under the direction of E. F. Lindquist; Science Research Associates, Inc. *

MOREY J. WANTMAN, *Director of Advisory and Instructional Programs, Educational Testing Service, Princeton, New Jersey.*

As noted in the test entry above, the copyright dates for this test, the Examiner's Manual, and the General Manual for this separate booklet edition are different from each other. The reader must note these differences lest he misjudge the currency of Test 1, Understanding of Basic Social Concepts. The General Manual for the separate booklet edition of the *Iowa Tests of Educational Development,* copyrighted in 1959, has the following paragraph on page 4: "To this end, Forms X-3S and Y-3S have been prepared to offer the user a *choice* of either a *Full Length Version* or a *Class Period Version.*" The reader might easily interpret this statement to mean that Forms X-3S and Y-3S were prepared just before this manual was issued. The fact is that these forms were seven years old when the above statement was made. Similiarly, in the Examiner's Manual for the separate booklet edition the following statement appears in the general introduction of the tests: "The tests are designed to be given to college freshmen as well as high school students." This may have once been the case, but there are no norms for grade 13 in the 1959 General Manual. Finally, the fact that the test was actually copyrighted in 1952 makes a number of questions out of date. For example, in Form X-3S: (*a*) Question 15, option 3 was written when there were only 48 states in the Union. (*b*) Question 48 relates to the control of countries in tropical areas of the world, most of which have earned their independence, thus making the key incorrect. (*c*) Options 2 and 3 of question 49 fail to take into account that the AFL and the CIO have merged into one organization. (*d*) With the recent strengthening of the Republican Party in the South, question 90 becomes dubious. In Form Y-3S: (*a*) Question 49 contains a reference to Albert Einstein as if he were still alive. (*b*) In question 85, Alaska and Hawaii are referred to as territories.

The above test entry indicates that the test can be administered either as a "full length version" requiring 55 minutes or as a "class period version" requiring 40 minutes. The claim is made on page 4 of the General Manual that "the two versions of each test are similar with respect to the average difficulty of test questions, the rate of work required to complete all questions in the version, and the standard and percentile scores obtained." The class period version uses the first 65 items of the 90 items in the full length version. These 65 items are actually 72.2 per cent of the 90 items. It is not clear from the conversion tables of raw scores to standard scores appearing on the scoring stencils how the raw score equivalents were obtained. For Form Y-3S a raw score for the class period version having a given standard score is 72.2 per cent of the raw score in the full length version having the same standard score. If the equivalents on the stencil for Form Y-3S were indeed obtained by use of the 72.2 per cent as a multiplying factor, the procedure is completely indefensible. In the case of Form X-3S, the 72.2 per cent multiplying factor seems to be operative from about the standard score of 11 and higher but it does not seem to be operative for lower standard scores. Incidentally, it should be pointed out in connection with the conversion of raw scores to standard scores that the directions for obtaining the standard score from the table given on the keys (pages 21 and 22 of the Examiner's Manual for the separate booklet edition) are confusing with respect to "columns."

The quality of the questions in the test is good. Aside from the out-dated options, the only error detected by this reviewer appears in the keyed option of question 69 of Form X-3S where "native-born" appears in place of "natural born," the term used in the United States Constitution.

On the last page of the Examiner's Manual a list of materials for "profiling and interpreting" is presented. Among these is the General Manual with Catalog Number 7-1024. The descriptive paragraph about the General Manual states that it contains, among other things, all of the statistics for the "reliabilities of the tests, the inter-correlations of the tests, the equivalence of versions." When one looks in the General Manual, Catalog Number 7-1024, he finds no data on reliabilities, intercorrelations, or equivalence of versions.

On page 15 the General Manual presents a profile of percentile ranks of grade averages of "Midtown High School, Grade 10." Average standard scores for this school are given. The reader learns from the next row of the profile and from the discussion on page 24 that an average standard score of 14.1 on Test 1 yields a 76th percentile on school averages. (The test, incidentally, changes its name here to "Social Studies Background.") The conversion table for this situation appearing on page 32 does not show any entry for 14.1 nor does it show a percentile rank of 76. A straight linear interpolation does yield the result. The reader should not have to infer the method for obtaining the result nor should he in fact be asked to do such computations if the authors intend him to use percentiles rather than the nearest decile. The 99 percentile values should be presented in the table.

In a leaflet which is made available to students, the last sentence is as follows: "Remember that a well-educated person is one who has equally high scores on all the *Iowa Tests.*" A student with "equally high scores" (for example, all at the 5th percentile) might be reassured by this statement but he hardly would be judged to be well educated.

CONCLUSION. This reviewer cannot recommend the use of this test. A test in this field which is more than 12 years old is of limited usefulness. Furthermore, the unavailability of statistical data in the auxiliary materials for this edition of the test limits the use of the test for most school purposes.

For reviews of the complete battery, see 14 and 5:17; for reviews of earlier forms, see 4:17 and 3:12.

[970]
*****Metropolitan Achievement Tests: [Social Studies].** Grades 5–6, 7–9, 9–12; 1932–64; subtest of *Metropolitan Achievement Tests;* IBM and MRC; 3 levels; $2 per 100 Harbor answer cards (machine scoring service, by Measurement Research Center, Inc., may be arranged through the publisher); 40¢ per specimen set of any one level; postage extra; Walter N. Durost, (for *a* and *b*) Harold H. Bixler, Gertrude H. Hildreth, Kenneth W. Lund, and J. Wayne Wrightstone, and (*c* only) William H. Evans, James D. Leake, Howard A. Bowman, Clarke Cosgrove, and John G. Read; Harcourt, Brace & World, Inc. *
a) INTERMEDIATE SOCIAL STUDIES TEST. Grades 5–6; 1932–62; 2 scores: information, study skills; Forms AM ('60, c1958), BM ('59), CM ('61), (7–8 pages); combined directions for administering ('59, 11 pages) for this and the advanced level; battery manual for interpreting ('62, 121 pages); $4.60 per 35 tests; separate answer sheets or cards may be used; $1.75 per 35 IBM answer sheets; 20¢ per scoring stencil; $1.20 per manual for interpreting; 46(52) minutes.
b) ADVANCED SOCIAL STUDIES TEST. Grades 7–9; 1932–62; details same as for intermediate level except: 56(62) minutes.
c) HIGH SCHOOL SOCIAL STUDIES TESTS. Grades 9–12; 1962–64; 3 scores: study skills, vocabulary, information; Forms AM ('62), BM ('63), (9 pages); manual ('64, c1962–64, 22 pages); content outline ['64, 4 pages]; revised interpretive manual for the battery ('64, c1962–64, 16 pages); separate answer sheets or cards must be used; $6 per 35 tests; $1.80 per 35 IBM answer sheets; 40¢ per set of scoring stencils; 74(88) minutes.

RICHARD E. GROSS, *Associate Professor of Education, Stanford University, Stanford,*

California. [Review of the intermediate and advanced levels.]

These tests are the separate social studies subtests of the *Metropolitan Achievement Tests* and appear for the first time as independent entities in these 1959–61 copyrighted forms. The tests are each separated into two parts: the first on factual knowledge of history, geography, and civics; the second on basic social studies skills. The information test at both the intermediate and advanced levels includes 60 items approximately evenly divided between the three above-mentioned subjects and requiring 20 minutes in either case. The skills tests at both levels are subdivided into two parts, the first being devoted to map reading and interpretation, the second to the reading and interpretation of tables, graphs, and charts.

The majority of items in the social studies information sections are four-foil completion type multiple choice questions. The duplication of items between intermediate and advanced levels varies but in some subsections goes well beyond the one third claimed to be common to both levels. For example, 11 of the 21 history items in Form AM of the advanced test are duplications of items found in Form AM of the intermediate test. While there is a clear progression of more difficult items in the advanced forms, one wonders if there is really sufficient differentiation between the capabilities at these age levels and particularly if the so-called advanced tests reveal what a true achievement test should. It is this reviewer's opinion that achievement tests must measure attainments and competencies far beyond subject matter recall and recollection and the limited skills called for in these tests. If teachers desire a broad assessment of pupil grasp of the many fundamental aims typically held for the social studies, they must go far beyond such tests in attempting to ascertain the attainment of purposes. The skill portions of these tests are quite good as far as they go; yet, coupled with the informational sections, in total these instruments are highly limited as comprehensive measures of achievement.

How well do our students read and comprehend in the social studies area? How well can they differentiate cause and effect? How well can they demonstrate the understanding of basic concepts and generalizations? Can they recognize propaganda? Can they decide if con-

Iowa Tests of Educational Development: Understanding of Basic Social Concepts

clusions are warranted by the evidence? Can they state the relationships between former events and current issues? Do they hold the essential capabilities of analysis and attitudes of openmindedness fundamental for the resolution of social problems? These are the queries I would want to put when examining pupils for true achievement of my social studies goals and these are elements upon which these tests throw very little light. As long as standardized tests are so lacking in scope of measurement they promise not to provide the needed leadership towards improvement in curriculum and instruction, but rather to further inculcate the distressing fact-depository school of social studies "education."

As suggested above, the skills portions of these tests do a satisfactory job of screening abilities of map, chart, and tabular interpretation and in some ways go on towards the more adequate measurement this reviewer seeks. When the geography section of the informational part of the tests is coupled with the map queries in the skills portion, one does get a fairly good view of geographical attainment. In fact, geography is the only one of the social studies subjects that comes near adequate treatment in these tests. In view of the need to extend measurement to other areas and for questions of other types, it might well be wise to even cut some of the map reading in future editions unless the tests are materially extended. The road map reading exercises in the intermediate forms seem to be the most expendable to this reviewer. The last page of the advanced forms are now overly cluttered and may confuse testees; the content should be spread out over another page in revised editions. Even though the geography sections are the superior portions of the tests, individual items call for correction and up-dating. For example, item 4, intermediate Form BM, asks where a magnetic compass points: south, north, east, or west? It does not allow for the pupil who knows of the south polar attraction; item 17, intermediate Form CM, lists silk, seemingly in error, as Japan's biggest "money product." The "correct" answer for item 18, advanced Form CM, is in error, as the population of China now approaches one quarter of the total world population. There are some shades of out-of-style geographic determinism in certain queries. In general, as is typical of most objective type

tests, the pupils who really know the most and who grasp the interrelationships and complexities overlooked by the test constructors may be frustrated by a number of the answers elicited in each of the subject matter portions of these tests.

If these tests are to be billed as a "social studies" test, this reviewer feels that further development of items in the areas of sociology, anthropology, and economics is called for and that these areas should be included in future editions. As it is, however, the history items are sadly short of what should be included for a comprehensive assessment of knowledge in just this discipline. Twenty items are included in each form to survey knowledge of world, as well as U.S., history from the Stone Age to the United Nations! Most of the items are on American history, but then one quarter of these precious few are used to identify battles and wars and the inventor of the telephone. In addition, in the "history" items there are questions about which South American country raises the most cattle (item 33, intermediate Form AM); on the other hand, in the civics sections there are items dealing with the New Deal (item 53, advanced Form AM, which, by the way, does not include as the correct answer the major reason behind the creation of the A.A.A.).

It is easy to carp about numerous items in these tests, but this should not be so if the items were really carefully scrutinized by experts, as is claimed. Pupils have to choose, for example, between the British Isles and the British Commonwealth in an answer to a query on the United Kingdom (item 39, intermediate Form CM) in which either answer is correct for the pupil who remembers that Ireland is a separate entity in the British Isles. What is the correct answer to item 60, intermediate Form BM, "Which of the following groups most recently obtained the right to vote in the United States?" The "correct" choice is "Women" from among the other foils of "Negroes," "Indians," and "aliens." The child who knows Indians only gained full voting rights as late as 1924 or who sees the daily papers or the TV screen full of civil rights and integration stories knows that it must be the Negroes or possibly the Indians, but how could it possibly be his Mommy? Certain questions are confusing because of factors stretching from vocabulary

Metropolitan Achievement Tests: Social Studies

(item 10, advanced Form AM) to point of view (item 41, intermediate Form CM) and from bad concepts (item 40, intermediate Form BM) to oversights (item 25, advanced Form AM).

A number of roads towards the improvement of tests of this nature are open. The reviewer has indicated a number of these. They range from improved scope and more careful construction to better discrimination and a wider variety of items. It would also seem essential to review just what are the basic contributions and processes of each of the social sciences and then to be sure to include such in the items. When, for example, of all the history items in a form (20) only 3 or 4 seem to deal with cause and effect relationships, we have missed one of the major contributions that should come from exposure to history. Perhaps some form of subtotals in the scores on each of the extended sections would also be an aid. Very probably the best way to meet many of the criticisms of this reviewer would come through providing a large reservoir of tried items that could be selected and used in varying ways depending upon purposes of the teacher, emphases and type of course, kinds of pupils, and the use to which the test results are to be put. Equally important will be unending efforts to develop tests like STEP, which move toward the application of knowledge rather than its mere reproduction.

ROBERT J. SOLOMON, *Vice President, Educational Testing Service, Princeton, New Jersey.* [Review of the intermediate and advanced levels.]

The intermediate and advanced levels of the Metropolitan social studies tests are intended to measure the knowledge and skills that are the important outcomes of social studies instruction in grades 5 through 9. The Intermediate Social Studies Test is intended for grades 5 and 6; the Advanced Social Studies Test, for grades 7, 8, and 9.

The intermediate level test consists of the social studies information and study skills subtests from the Intermediate Battery of the *Metropolitan Achievement Tests.* The advanced level test is similarly taken from the Advanced Battery of the *Metropolitan Achievement Tests.* In actuality, each form of the intermediate and advanced tests consists of two

tests, separately timed and separately scored tests of information and study skills, with separate norms for each. Each form of the information test contains 60 questions to be answered in 20 minutes. Each form of the study skills test for the intermediate level contains 29–30 questions to be answered in 26 minutes. Each form of the study skills test at the advanced level contains 39–40 questions to be answered in 36 minutes. (One wonders why Form AM for each level contains one more question than Forms BM or CM.)

Although no data on speededness are presented in the manual, the tests appear to satisfy the authors' objective that the tests are "not intended to measure the speed with which children can answer test questions." A rate of three questions per minute for the information tests may ordinarily seem high for the typical student in grades 5–9, but these questions are for the most part quite short and require relatively little reading time. In the skills tests, the pace of approximately one question per minute seems adequate. Also, in the skills tests provision is made for internal timing so that the student will not spend too much time on the first parts. Thirteen minutes before the end of each skills test, students are directed to turn to the last group of 14–15 questions.

No classroom teacher, guidance counselor, or school administrator should select an achievement test without a careful analysis of its content. In the opinion of this reviewer, the test authors are entirely accurate in their description of the test. Nevertheless, it remains for the test user to judge, by his examination of the test questions, the extent to which the content of the test is an appropriate and sufficient measure of social studies achievement. In the words of the authors, the test "seeks to measure attainment of certain important objectives of social studies instruction in the elementary and junior high school grades." These objectives "are largely in the realm of knowledge and study skills. The Social Studies Information Test is primarily a measure of the pupil's acquisition of certain factual information generally covered in social studies textbooks." The study skills test consists of two parts. "The first part....is a measure of the ability to read and interpret maps. * The second part provides a measure of ability to read and interpret information presented in the form of tables, charts, and graphs." The questions in the several forms of the skills test at each level are well constructed and appear to measure exactly what the authors intended them to measure. A major reservation one may have about this test concerns whether the two parts constitute a comprehensive measure of the important social studies study skills for the grades intended. To be fair, it must be noted that the authors do not claim that they do.

In deciding on the content of the information test, "the authors analyzed the content of all series of social studies textbooks in common use at the time the tests were developed." This analysis, "together with the opinions of social studies educators as to probable trends in social studies instruction and as to desirable distributions of emphasis among various content areas, made it possible to develop an outline of the content of both levels of the social studies test." Despite this effort, the result is disappointing. The authors' description of the test as a measure of the acquisition of certain factual information is all too accurate. Although it may appear unfair to expect that which was never promised, the information test at each level seems too little concerned with the measurement of understanding. Too many questions require the naming of a person, place, or event, and too few the knowledge, comprehension, or application of a principle, generalization, or concept.

Except for the study skills test at the intermediate level, the reliabilities reported for the tests are satisfactory. Although it is not so specified, these reliabilities are for Form AM of each test, but one would expect the reliabilities of the other forms to be very similar. The reliabilities reported for the intermediate study skills test range from .64 to .77. To quote the manual, "one must consider with skepticism the score on any test that has a reliability coefficient below .80." However, in comparing these reliabilities with those for other tests, one should keep in mind that the reliabilities reported for the Metropolitan series are, quite appropriately, based on single-school-system, single-grade groups. Such reliabilities tend to be lower than those based on more than one grade or more than one school system.

In the view of the authors, the validity of the Metropolitan social studies tests rests on their careful efforts to reflect in the content of the tests the important outcomes of social studies instruction. This emphasis on the content validity of tests is not unusual for achievement tests. Indeed, there is a school of thought that holds that the only criterion of validity for an achievement test is the test itself. For these tests, no evidence of other kinds of validity is offered, although it is likely that data could be obtained to show, for example, the extent to which performance on the tests will predict future social studies achievement. As for the content validity of these tests, as was indicated earlier, the user of the test will ultimately have to judge this for himself by his own careful analysis of test content.

An analysis of the content and statistics of the three forms for each level indicates that the forms may be considered parallel. In using the tests, one should be aware that there is significant item overlap between the forms of the intermediate and advanced tests having the same letter designation, but there is none between forms with different letter designations. The overlap between forms is mainly among the history questions and for one complete set of skills questions. However, should one have need to administer both an intermediate and advanced test to the same student within a span of time when the student may still remember the items on the first testing, the possibility of spuriously high scores on the second testing can be avoided by making certain that the second test administered does not have the same letter designation as the first.

In general, the format of the tests is good and the directions are simple and clear. Teachers should have no difficulty in administering the tests; students should have little difficulty in taking them. Perhaps it would have been better if the layout of the study skills tests had been less crowded, particularly in the intermediate tests where it would have been possible to use the back page of the test booklet, as was done in the advanced tests.

The manual for the tests deserves a special word of praise. Written by Walter H. Durost, it is not only a model of what a test manual should be, but it is an excellent short course in tests and measurements. It presents a wealth of sophisticated thinking concerning the meaning and use of test scores in a lucid, uncomplicated style that any intelligent reader should be able to comprehend. One hopes that teachers using the tests will take the time to study the manual.

Despite criticisms expressed or implied in this review, the Metropolitan social studies tests are the workmanlike products of professional testmakers. No *caveat emptor* applies here. The teacher who carefully examines the tests and the materials accompanying them will have no difficulty in making intelligent and effective use of them. And, if he will study the excellent manual, he will be able to use all tests more wisely.

For reviews of the complete battery, see 15; for reviews of earlier editions, see 4:18, 40: 1189, and 38:874.

[971]
*Sequential Tests of Educational Progress: Social Studies.** Grades 4–6, 7–9, 10–12, 13–14; 1956–63; IBM, NCS, and Grade-O-Mat; Forms A, B, ('57, c1956–57, 15–19 pages); 4 levels; battery directions ('57, 12 pages); interpretive manual ('57, 31 pages); battery technical report ('57, 58 pages); 1958 SCAT-STEP supplement ('58, 32 pages); 1962 SCAT-STEP supplement ('62, 49 pages); 1963 SCAT-STEP supplement of urban norms ('63, 16 pages); battery teacher's guide ('59, 85 pages); battery profile ('57, 1 page); battery student report ('58, 4 pages); no data on reliability of Form B; separate answer sheets or cards must be used; $4 per 20 tests; $1 per 20 IBM scorable answer sheets; 25¢ per scoring stencil; see 671 for prices of NCS answer sheets and scoring services; see 666 for prices of Grade-O-Mat cards; $1 per 20 profiles; $1 per 20 student reports; $1 per interpretive manual; $1 per technical report; $1 per supplement; $1 per teacher's guide; postage extra; $2 per specimen set, cash orders postpaid; 70(90–100) minutes; Cooperative Test Division. *
a) LEVEL 4. Grades 4–6; Forms 4A, 4B.
b) LEVEL 3. Grades 7–9; Forms 3A, 3B.
c) LEVEL 2. Grades 10–12; Forms 2A, 2B.
d) LEVEL 1. Grades 13–14; Forms 1A, 1B.

REFERENCES
1. LIGGITT, WILLIAM A. "An Evaluation of General Education in Elementary Teacher Preparation." *J Ed Res* 57: 156–9 N '63. *

JONATHON C. McLENDON, *Professor of Social Science Education, Florida Atlantic University, Boca Raton, Florida.*

The STEP tests in social studies continue without peer, indeed almost without available counterparts, as the leading standardized series of skill tests in social studies. As previous reviewers have indicated, the STEP tests fulfill a distinctive need in social studies, a field in which tests have generally dealt mostly or only with knowledge and understanding of facts and concepts.

Content validity of the STEP tests is dependent on the soundness of judgment of those three dozen persons who participated in the test construction. While this group included several outstanding teachers and other leaders in social studies education, additional evidences of content validity would be welcome. In light of the heavy emphasis that teachers place on interpretation of reading materials in social studies, content validity is weakened by the extent (37 to 51 per cent) of items that involve interpretation of visual materials. Data on item validity are not reported. Construct, concurrent, and predictive validity are evident only by implication. Correlations with SCAT scores are interesting, and useful in some ways; but more closely related criteria would serve better to guide teachers and students in interpreting and applying test results. Ideally, the reporting of scores would facilitate recognition of levels of achievement by individuals and groups in the use of particular skills involving specified types of instructional materials or sources.

Although the STEP tests aim chiefly to measure indicated abilities, previous knowledge concerning the subject matter presented on the test doubtless aids many test takers. The seven types of skills and eight areas of understanding listed in the Manual for Interpreting Scores on the social studies tests provide no more than general and somewhat vague identifications of related behaviors; the statements of understandings appear to restate several proposed in 1957 by the Committee on Concepts and Values, National Council for the Social Studies. Hopefully the publishers of the STEP tests will be able to furnish in the foreseeable future, as promised seven years ago in their 1957 Technical Report, "empirical checks....relating test scores to suitable criterion measures," which data have not yet appeared in the SCAT-STEP Supplements.

Reliability correlations (Kuder-Richardson formula 20) of .84 to .93 on the A forms attest to high internal consistency. Equivalence of Forms A and B is presumed on the basis of a common score scale. Test users look forward to the appearance of correlational analyses indicating equivalence of the forms. While it involves more than one might reasonably expect a test publisher to produce, a longitudinal study would be highly beneficial, following students from the middle grades through college and reporting learning as indicated by

Metropolitan Achievement Tests: Social Studies

the STEP tests in relation to the curricular content and instructional emphases of varying school programs.

This reviewer joins those who would like to see wider use and further refinement and expansion of the STEP tests. The apparent popularity of these tests suggests the practicability, as well as desirability, of applying the approach to other areas of skill development and to additional types of instructional material in social studies.

DONALD W. OLIVER, *Associate Professor of Education, Harvard University, Cambridge, Massachusetts.*

This social studies series is one of seven tests in the series *Sequential Tests of Educational Progress.* All were developed on the basis of certain common assumptions and presumably have similar properties. All assume that the focus of education is upon the development of critical skills and understandings rather than upon teaching only the facts of lesson material and that success in education is to be measured in terms of the student's ability to apply school-learned skills to the solution of "new problems." The tests are not to be tied to specific "courses," or to specific bodies of content.

This approach is, of course, not particularly radical. The explicitness of problem areas covered in the material, however, is novel and refreshing. The items for each level (there are four levels at median grade difficulties for grades 5, 8, 11, and 13) are categorized in terms of skills, understandings, type of material, and subject matter. The skills presumably measured are the ability to: identify generalizations, identify values, distinguish facts from opinions, assess data, compare data, and draw conclusions. The understandings are described as those involving social change, the geographic environment, forces of nature, democratic society, economic wants, interdependence, and those related to understanding one's environment. The items are further classified under the "type of material" on which items are based and "subject matter." Types of material include maps, graphs, cartoons, photographs and drawings, and text material. The subject matter is classified as American history, geography, social anthropology, government, economics, and world history. Items described by "under-

standing" and "subject matter" are often double classified; e.g., an item may be classified as both American history and government.

While the "skills" and "understandings" are those most commonly stated in lists of objectives compiled by "experts," one might question the actual utility of such a breakdown. For example, one skill is described as the ability to "identify, compare, and contrast underlying values, attitudes, assumptions, biases, and motives." Item 8 (Form 1A), which is classified as testing this objective, asks the question, "What is the likelihood that the problem depicted in the cartoon will exist and be significant ten years from now?" Item 2 (Form 2B), also classified under the same objective, asks "Which of the following is the main idea of Cartoon I?" More commonly, however, items classified under "identify values" require the student to infer the opinion or policy of the author of a statement. The point is that we have little assurance (and no information) regarding the validity of the process by which the questions were categorized. This situation is, of course, as much an indictment of the utility of objectives as stated by experts in the profession as it is a criticism of the tests; it raises the question of whether the testmaker is to lead or follow. In this case the testmakers probably chose to follow the leaders in the profession in the hope of encouraging teachers to state objectives in broader terms than subject matter content. Considering the present emphasis on analyzing the "structure" of the social science disciplines and on identifying the major procedures and concepts underlying these disciplines, one would expect that the use of the tests as a point of influence on the existing fact-oriented curriculum (which is implied on page 14 of the teacher's guide) is already an obsolete goal. Probably 70-item tests of all the social sciences, including both information and problem analysis, are much too gross to get at the structure of anything.

It should be pointed out that perhaps the strongest feature of the test series is the attempt to measure dimensions of social problem analysis, rather than recall or comprehension of facts or generalizations in standard social studies courses. (Obviously this is not true of all the items, or the tests would simply be general reasoning tests.) The fact that the series does emphasize general skills and understandings rather than specific fragments of knowledge, however, leads one to ask: Are these simply reading or intelligence tests rather than "social studies" tests? This question is answered in part in the Technical Report issued with the tests. Correlations ranging between .73 and .89 are reported for the relationship between STEP Social Studies and total SCAT, the latter of which is designed to measure general academic attitude. It is interesting to note that somewhat lower correlations are reported between STEP Reading and SCAT. In the 1958 SCAT-STEP Supplement a correlation of .77 is reported for one study between SCAT and WISC, WISC being a reputable standard measure of general intelligence. Moreover, in the same study, the correlation between a STEP social studies test and social studies grades is reported as .55, while the correlation between SCAT and average grades is reported as .70. Looking at these data, one gets the impression that the STEP social studies tests measure very little that is *unique* to the understanding of problem analysis in the social studies, and very much that is common to general measures of reading and academic aptitude. The irony is that what is unique to the social studies in this series is probably the technical knowledge and factual information which the tests are attempting to subordinate to the more general problem solving goals.

In summary, this is the most comprehensive and probably the most carefully constructed series of sequential social studies tests available in the field. It has the bonus of an excellent teacher's guide, including assistance on how to use the instrument for instructional diagnosis and as a teaching aid. Presently there is a Technical Report and three supplements, which include norms for urban schools. Within the field of existing commercial tests to measure general social studies skills and understandings, this series stands alone. It is important to note, however, that it is constructed on the same assumptions and format as many tests of general reasoning and critical thinking and probably reflects very little that is unique to social studies as a field of teaching or knowledge. The field of achievement testing in the social studies still awaits an analysis of objectives related to those concepts, intellectual processes, and skills that are uniquely

the contribution made through the study of history and the social sciences. Until the time that such objectives can be defined and measured, we might ask whether or not it makes sense to call available instruments "social studies tests."

For reviews by Richard E. Gross, S. A. Rayner, and Ralph W. Tyler, see 5:792. For reviews of the complete battery, see 25 and 5:24.

[972]
*Social Studies: Every Pupil Scholarship Test. Grades 7–8; 1935–64; new form (2 pages) usually issued each January and April; forms from previous testing programs also available; general directions sheet ['63, 2 pages]; no data on reliability; norms for new forms available following testing program; 4¢ per test; 4¢ per key; postage extra; 30(35) minutes; Bureau of Educational Measurements. *

[973]
★Social Studies: Minnesota High School Achievement Examinations. Grades 7, 8, 9; 1961–63; series formerly called *Midwest High School Achievement Examinations;* new form issued each May; norms available in June following release of new form; Form F ('63, 6–7 pages) used in 1963 testing; 3 levels; no specific manual; series manual ('63, 4 pages); series norms ['63, 4 pages]; series cumulative profile ('62, 2 pages); no data on reliability; no description of normative population; 12¢ per test; $2.50 per 100 profiles; postage extra; 20¢ per specimen set, postpaid; 60(65) minutes; American Guidance Service, Inc.

[974]
*Social Studies: National Teacher Examinations. College seniors and teachers; 1940–63; for more complete information, see 700; 80(90) minutes; Educational Testing Service. *

HARRY D. BERG, *Professor, Office of Evaluation Services, Michigan State University, East Lansing, Michigan.* [Review of Form LNT.]

This is one of the optional tests of the National Teacher Examinations. It is intended to be given to college seniors who are applicants for teaching positions so that they may show their competency in a field of greatest strength. The test should be judged within the limited purposes set forth for it by the program directors. The Handbook for School and College Officials states that "the purpose of the NTE program is....to provide objective examinations of measurable intellectual competencies which are commonly considered basic to effective classroom teaching." The phrases "objective examinations" and "measurable intellectual competencies" should be noted. It is admitted without apology that the examinations in the series cannot measure all of the qualities which contribute to effective teaching. Many of these qualities are at present poorly defined and many will probably never become amenable to objective testing. One implication of the limited purpose of the test is that no attempt has been made to establish its validity on a basis of on-the-job success.

Whatever the nature of the other qualities of the good teacher, understanding of subject content and methodology is an essential quality and one that can be defined and measured. It is the opinion of this reviewer that the present test has great potentialities for providing needed data on teaching applicants within this area. The various fields of the social studies are covered in a well balanced fashion and the items are so constructed as to emphasize reasoned understanding rather than the mere recall of facts. Many of the items pose hypothetical classroom situations in which the applicant must choose from a number of courses of action. Other items require a knowledge of teaching materials and their most appropriate uses. The various ways in which social studies data may be presented to pupils have been explored; some items are based on reading passages and others on cartoons, maps, and graphs.

The available statistics are all good. The test requires 80 minutes and has 105 items. The mean raw score is 48.03 (correction is made for guessing). The K-R 20 reliability is .92 and the mean item discrimination index (biserial r) is .43. The format, directions, and provisions for scoring are of the usual high quality associated with the Educational Testing Service. National norms based on scaled scores are made available to the concerned colleges and secondary schools. Provision is made for making the scores comparable from form to form.

All things considered, this test should provide prospective employers with one piece of useful information on teacher candidates. It is instructive to note, in this connection, that mean scores show considerable variance from one teacher training institution to another.

For reviews of the testing program, see 700, 5:538, and 4:802.

[975]

Social Studies: Teacher Education Examination Program. College seniors preparing to teach secondary school; 1957; an inactive form of *Social Stud-*

ies: National Teacher Examinations; for more complete information, see 709; IBM; 80(95) minutes; Educational Testing Service. *

For a review of the testing program, see 5:543. For reviews of the National Teacher Examinations, *see 700, 5:538, and 4:802.*

[976]

*Social Studies 12 (American Problems): Minnesota High School Achievement Examinations. Grade 12; 1955–63; series formerly called *Midwest High School Achievement Examinations;* new form issued each May; norms available in June following release of new form; Form F ('63, 7 pages) used in 1963 testing; no specific manual; series manual ('63, 4 pages); series norms ['63, 4 pages]; series cumulative profile ('62, 2 pages); no data on reliability; no description of normative population; 12¢ per test; $2.50 per 100 profiles; postage extra; 20¢ per specimen set, postpaid; 60(65) minutes; American Guidance Service, Inc. *

[977]

*Stanford Achievement Test: Social Studies Test. Grades 5.5–6.9, 7–9; 1940–64; subtest of *Stanford Achievement Test* [1964 *Revision*]; previous edition (see 5:799) still available; IBM and MRC; 2 levels; manual ['64, 8 pages] for each level; supplementary directions ['64, 1 page each] for use with IBM answer sheets, Harbor answer cards; separate answer sheets or cards may be used; $1.50 per 35 IBM answer sheets; 20¢ per scoring stencil; $2 per 100 Harbor answer cards (machine scoring service, by Measurement Research Center, Inc., may be arranged through the publisher); 40¢ per specimen set of either level; postage extra; Truman L. Kelley, Richard Madden, Eric F. Gardner, and Herbert C. Rudman; Harcourt, Brace & World, Inc. *
a) INTERMEDIATE 2. Grades 5.5–6.9; Form W ('64, 6 pages); $4 per 35 tests; 50(56) minutes.
b) ADVANCED. Grades 7–9; Form W ('64, 9 pages); $6 per 35 tests; 52(58) minutes.

For a review by Harry D. Berg of the 1953 revision, see 5:799; for a review by Ray G. Wood of the previous edition, see 3:595. For a review of the complete battery, see 26; for a review of the 1953 revision, see 5:25; for reviews of earlier editions, see 4:25 and 3:18.

[978]

★T.C. Social Studies Test. Teachers college entrants; 1955–58; 5 scores: geography, civics, history, critical thinking, total; 1 form ['56, 6 pages]; mimeographed manual ['58, 7 pages]; no data on reliability; no norms for subscores; distribution restricted to teacher training institutions; separate answer sheets must be used; 6s. per 10 tests; 2s. per 10 answer sheets; 4s. per key; 2s. 6d. per manual; 7s. 6d. per specimen set; postpaid within Australia; 35(40) minutes; Australian Council for Educational Research. *

[Other Tests]

For tests not listed above, see the following entries in *Tests in Print:* 1706, 1711–3, 1717–8, and 1724–5; out of print: 1714 and 1720.

CONTEMPORARY
AFFAIRS

[979]

*Contemporary Affairs: Every Pupil Test.
Grades 10–12; 1939–64; new test (4 pages) usually
issued each December and April; general directions
sheet ('63, 2 pages); no data on reliability; Ohio
norms for new forms available following testing program; 5¢ per test; 3¢ per key; postpaid; 40(45) minutes; Ohio Scholarship Tests. *

[980]

★Cooperative Test on Foreign Affairs. Grade 16;
1962, c1960–62; IBM; Form IBI ('62, c1960, 14
pages); manual ('62, 23 pages); separate answer
sheets must be used; $4 per 20 tests; $1 per 20 IBM
scorable answer sheets; 25¢ per scoring stencil; $1
per manual; postage extra; $2 per specimen set, cash
orders postpaid; (60–65) minutes; Cooperative Test
Division. *

REFERENCES

1. BIDWELL, PERCY W. Appendix A, "A Test on Foreign
Affairs," pp. 146–80. In his *Undergraduate Education in Foreign Affairs.* New York: King's Crown Press, 1962. Pp. viii,
215. *

CHRISTINE MCGUIRE, *Assistant Director, Research in Medical Education, University of
Illinois College of Medicine, Chicago, Illinois.*

According to the excellent accompanying
manual, this test was developed "to determine
to what extent seniors enrolled in the colleges
[included in a recent study of undergraduate
education in international relations] had acquired a background of information necessary
for an understanding of international relations
—and could apply it, even in an elementary
way." The test was constructed by asking over
a hundred "distinguished" scholars in the field
to submit topics that warranted inclusion in an
instrument designed to "cover a variety of information of *more than passing significance*
for an understanding of American foreign policy [italics added]." The manual further ad-
vises that the materials included are "as varied
as the sources of information about the international scene: cartoons, maps, charts, excerpts
from important documents." The items "require students not only to recall facts but also
to draw inferences and to apply their knowledge and understanding."

In several important respects the test
achieves the promise implied in the statement
of purpose and description of materials: many
of the questions are challenging; many are
based on data presented in a fresh and interesting form; many involve an unfamiliar juxta-
position of facts that requires the student to

reorganize his information into a structure not
frequently encountered in conventional instruction. Practically all of the items are technically
satisfactory; the common pitfalls of test construction have generally been avoided in this
highly professional product.

Unfortunately, the test also has certain deficiencies which appear to be a direct consequence of carrying to an extreme some of the
same qualities that account for its excellence.
In the attempt to provide an unusual context
for essentially factual questions, some of the
items have become unduly strained and con-
trived. In a number of cases, orientation to the
graph or chart presented is often more complex than the question itself. For example, one
rather simple question about the direction and
volume of trade in specified resources is based
on an intricate chart depicting flows of goods
by means of arrows of varying widths superimposed on a map. Again, a quite complex
graph showing variation over time with respect to political party affiliation is used as the
basis of an elementary question about the political composition of four national legislatures.
To this reviewer, only esthetic values would be
compromised if such questions were asked
more directly without the interposition of essentially irrelevant complications in the contextual materials. Secondly, an unduly large
proportion of the questions based on cartoons
or excerpts from documents are uncomfort-
ably reminiscent of the game of "guess what I
am thinking about." Third, the combination
of facts required to answer some questions de-
rives not from necessary relations in the content being sampled, but is imposed by artificial-
ities in the item itself. For example, one question asks the student to select the pair of nations in which one is characterized by X and
the other by Y; no comparison or relation is
implied, merely simultaneous matching of discrete qualities with specified political units. Finally, there are some questions in which the
complexity of the instructions presents the only
real obstacle to a correct answer.

Quite aside from these somewhat carping
criticisms of what is most certainly a stimulating and provocative test, this reviewer has
certain reservations about the balance of items
in a test purporting to measure *knowledge* and
understanding of *international relations.* Approximately one quarter is devoted to "map

questions": What countries have common borders? What is the likely date of a given map? Where are certain physical features located on a Mercator projection? The distribution of what resource is depicted by a given pattern of shading? Despite the ingenuity of some of these materials, they appear to be overemphasized, in view of the importance of political, cultural, ethnic, and other basic economic factors in the world situation. The relatively few questions on chronology suggest that the authors are striving to test the students' understanding of a sequence of events; one nevertheless suspects that students are often forced to answer in terms of isolated knowledge of specific dates, rather than in terms of the inexorable logic of events. Finally, despite this reviewer's special love for economics and economic geography, it must be said that the test seems to include an overly large proportion of questions that can be answered only in terms of some fairly detailed knowledge of resources, industrial production, and direction of trade.

The manual accompanying the test is superb. It contains very clear and detailed instructions for administration, scoring, and interpretation of results. The norms are based on a 1960 administration to 1,854 randomly selected seniors in 175 colleges. The data are appropriately organized to provide norms for various populations arranged according to curriculum (business, education, engineering, and liberal arts), major subject (social sciences, natural sciences, and humanities), type of institution (private universities, state universities, liberal arts colleges, etc.), and geographic location of institution. Both the item statistics and the total scores are separately reported for the several groups in each category. Differences among groups confirm our stereotypes: students in liberal arts colleges perform better than those in business or teachers colleges; students with a social science major achieve more than students in the natural sciences and humanities; students in the coastal regions score higher than students elsewhere; men are more fully informed in this area than women. That the differences among groups are in the expected direction and that the test yields a high reliability coefficient (.89, Kuder-Richardson formula 20) are both strong support for a favorable judgment about the technical and statistical adequacy of the test.

From the point of view of its technical ex-

cellence, the superior manual which accompanies it, and the aid the manual provides to useful interpretation of results, this test can be highly recommended to all who are interested in an assay of rather sophisticated information about international affairs. However, since most questions require new combinations of factual material rather than its interpretation and analysis, this reviewer cannot recommend the test as a valid measure of *understanding* of international relations and *ability to apply* that understanding to an interpretation of contemporary events. Finally, in the words of the manual, "this test was constructed for administration in 1960. The relevance and accuracy of some of the items will, of necessity, suffer with the passage of time." Consequently, specific items should be reviewed before use since, in the opinion of this reviewer, time is already beginning to impose its stamp.

J Counsel Psychol 9:283–4 f '62. Laurence Siegel. * The Handbook is an interesting document containing the kinds of information usually found in "administrators' manuals" and "technical manuals." In addition, five brief "Technical Notes" are boxed within its text. These notes, written for the relatively naïve test user, concern (a) computation of *t*-ratio; (b) the meaning of standard deviation, median and quartile; (c) the concept of reliability; (d) the meaning of significance levels; (e) the use of item-test biserials for item analysis. The inclusion of these Technical Notes is an interesting device, and they are extremely well-written. Whether or not they will enhance the ability of relatively unsophisticated users to interpret data presented in the Handbook remains to be seen. * Researchers wishing to measure knowledge of foreign affairs will find the test well-suited to their needs. The fact that validity (other than content validity) is not established and that norms are not available for groups other than college seniors should not prove too disturbing to them. However, counselors wishing to assess achievement in this area may be exasperated by a test with tremendous potential but lacking certain fundamental corollary information prerequisite to its intelligent use by them. The normative data for college seniors are good, but the major thrust of counseling is experienced prior to the senior year. The counselor usually needs to know something about the test performance of standardization groups representative of high school seniors, college freshmen, and perhaps the general adult population. Many interesting validity studies are self-evident for the Test on Foreign Affairs. The Handbook stops short with evidence that, of liberal arts seniors, those majoring in the social sciences have a higher mean score than either natural science or humanities majors. However, this begs the question of the test's predictive usefulness for vocational attainment. Also concurrent validities, perhaps, involving well-known interest inventories as well as other cognitive measures, are not cited. It is at least conceivable that the Test on Foreign Affairs may share considerable variance with tests of general ability and verbal fluency. It is very difficult to judge the feasibility of including this test in either a counseling battery or a school-wide achievement battery without evidence on this point.

[981]

*Current Affairs: Every Pupil Scholarship Test. High school; 1935–64; new form (2 pages) usually issued each January and April; general directions sheet ['63, 2 pages]; no data on reliability; norms available following testing program; 4¢ per test; 4¢ per key; postage extra 40(45) minutes; Bureau of Educational Measurements. *

[982]

★Nationwide Current Events Examination. Grades 4–12; 1960–63; new form issued each April; norms available following the testing program; 1 form ('63, 2 pages); no manual; mimeographed norms ('63, 1 page); no data on reliability; 10¢ per test, postage extra; (40–45) minutes; [Donald R. Honz]; Educational Stimuli. *

[983]

★New York Times Current Affairs Test. High school; 1947–64; new test (4 pages) issued monthly during school year; no data on reliability; no norms; distribution restricted to schools subscribing to the publisher's School Service Program; program includes daily copy of The New York Times for each student, monthly copy of the test for each student, and other teaching aids; subscription price: 25¢ per student per week, postpaid; (35–40) minutes; New York Times. *

[984]

★New York Times Current Affairs Test for Colleges. College; 1947–64; new test (4 pages) issued monthly during school year; no data on reliability; no norms; distribution restricted to schools subscribing to the publisher's School Service Program; program includes daily copy of The New York Times for each student, monthly copy of the test for each student, and other teaching aids; subscription price: 40¢ per student per week, postpaid; (35–55) minutes; New York Times. *

Cooperative Test on Foreign Affairs

[985]

★Newsweek Current News Test. Grades 9–12; 1951–64; 2 new tests (8 pages) issued annually: spring term review (covering mid December–mid April) issued each May, fall term review (covering September–mid December) issued each January; no data on reliability; no norms; distribution restricted to schools subscribing to one of the publisher's quantity subscription plans; plans include subscriptions to Newsweek magazine for student use, semester copy of this test and monthly copy of test 986 for each subscription, and other teaching aids; subscriptions may be entered in bulk (mailed to the school) at 15¢ each per issue or by individual student (placed by the teacher but mailed to the student, cash orders only) at $1.75 for 17 weeks, $2.75 for 34 weeks, or $3.50 per year; 2-week trial subscription, 30¢ per student; postpaid; administration time not reported; Newsweek Educational Division. *

[986]

★Newsweek NewsQuiz. Grades 9–12; 1951–64; formerly called Newsweek Monthly Objective Test; new test (4 pages) issued monthly during school year; no data on reliability; no norms; distribution restricted to schools subscribing to one of the publisher's quantity subscription plans; plans include subscriptions to Newsweek magazine for student use, monthly copy of this test and semester copy of test 985 for each subscription, and other teaching aids; subscriptions may be entered in bulk (mailed to the school) at 15¢ each per issue or by individual student (placed by the teacher but mailed to the student, cash orders only) at $1.75 for 17 weeks, $2.75 for 34 weeks, or $3.50 per year; 2-week trial subscription, 30¢ per student; postpaid; administration time not reported; Newsweek Educational Division. *

[Other Tests]

For tests not listed above, see the following entry in Tests in Print: 1731.

ECONOMICS

[987]

*The Graduate Record Examinations Advanced Tests: Economics. Grades 16–17; 1939–62; for more complete information, see 762; 180(200) minutes; Educational Testing Service. *

REFERENCES

1. RILEY, ROBERT C., AND LOVE, JEAN O. "The Predictive Value of College Test Scores." J Higher Ed 29:393–5+ O '58. *

For a review of the testing program, see 5:601.

[988]

★A Standard Achievement Test in Economic Understanding for Secondary Schools, Sixth Revision. High school; 1954–57; 1 form ('57, 9 pages, mimeographed); no manual; no data on reliability; no norms; separate answer sheets must be used; 25¢ per test, postpaid; [50] minutes; E. C. Alft and the Illinois Council on Economic Education; [Joint Council on Economic Education]. *

[989]

★Test of Economic Understanding, Preliminary Edition No. 2. High school and college and industry; 1963; IBM; Forms A, B, (13 pages); manual (7 pages); tentative norms based upon the first preliminary edition; no college or industrial norms; separate answer sheets must be used; $3 per 20 tests; $4 per 100 IBM scorable answer sheets; 25¢ per scoring stencil; 35¢ per manual; 75¢ per specimen set; postage extra; 60(70) minutes; Committee for Measurement of Economic Understanding, Joint Council on Economic Education (test); Science Research Associates, Inc. *

[Other Tests]

For tests not listed above, see the following entries in *Tests in Print:* 1736 and 1738–9.

GEOGRAPHY

[990]

★Brandywine Achievement Test in Geography for Secondary Schools. Grades 7–12; 1962; Forms A, B, (6 pages); no manual; no data on reliability; no norms; separate answer sheets must be used; $7 per 35 tests; 20¢ per specimen set; postpaid; [50–55] minutes; John A. Bonham and Harry R. Martini; [Brandywine Achievement Test]. *

[991]

*Geography: Every Pupil Scholarship Test. Grades 5–7; 1933–64; new form (2 pages) usually issued each January and April; forms from previous testing programs also available; general directions sheet ['63, 2 pages]; no data on reliability; norms for new forms available following testing program; 4¢ per test; 4¢ per key; postage extra; 30(35) minutes; Bureau of Educational Measurements. *

[992]

*[Geography]: Every Pupil Test. Grades 4–6, 7; 1935–64; new form (4 pages) usually issued each December and April; forms from previous testing programs (which included separate tests for grades 4, 5, 6, and 7) also available; 2 levels; general directions sheet ('63, 2 pages); no data on reliability; Ohio norms for new forms available following testing program; 5¢ per test; 3¢ per key; postpaid; 40(45) minutes; Ohio Scholarship Tests. *
a) GRADES 4–6. 2 tests.
  1) *Geography of the Americas.*
  2) *Geography of the Eastern Hemisphere.*
b) GEOGRAPHY OF THE WORLD. Grade 7.

[993]

★Physical Geography: Every Pupil Scholarship Test. High school; 1943; 1 form (2 pages); general directions sheet ['63, 2 pages]; no data on reliability; 4¢ per test; 4¢ per key; postage extra; 40(45) minutes; Bureau of Educational Measurements. *

[994]

*Survey Test in Geography: California Survey Series. Grades 7–9; 1946–59; subtest 3 of the elementary level (for grades 4–8) of *California Tests in Social and Related Sciences,* Form AA; IBM; Form 1 ('59, 11 pages, identical with test copyrighted in 1953 and identical with test copyrighted in 1946 except for format, changes in option order, and revision of 13 items); combined manual ('59, 15 pages) for this test and test 1010; $2.80 per 35 tests; separate answer sheets may be used; 5¢ per IBM answer sheet; 20¢ per scoring stencil; 10¢ per series class record sheet; 2¢ per series individual record sheet;

postage extra; 50¢ per specimen set, postpaid; 38(45) minutes; Georgia Sachs Adams and John A. Sexson; California Test Bureau. *

JONATHON C. MCLENDON, *Professor of Social Science Education, Florida Atlantic University, Boca Raton, Florida.*

Previously published tests in this series were reviewed in *The Fourth* and *The Fifth Mental Measurements Yearbooks,* with much of the comment there still applicable to the nature and construction of each test. Retention of content which is the same as that in the 1953 edition and essentially the same as that in the 1946 edition of the geography test is unfortunate in two respects particularly: (*a*) inaccuracy of such items as item 12 which is keyed to identify Chicago as important for its meat packing industry, and (*b*) general outdatedness of some of the content, with much attention to transportation by water and rail but little to air and motor vehicle transport, for example. Indeed, it is difficult to find, in this test, item content that was not equally usable a quarter of a century ago. While major natural features are relatively permanent, there have been significant shifts in man's relationships to them. The test content includes some relationships, but it consists preponderantly of factual items and geographical terms, largely achievable through memoriter learning.

The publishers report a commendable procedure for establishing validity, involving survey of courses of study and textbooks and reports of research, trials to determine item discrimination and difficulty, and the judgments of a sizable number of teachers and supervisors. Desirably, the test consultants would include geographers. The reviewer is tempted to speculate on the commonsensical character of several items; they appear as appropriate to a test of general intelligence as to an achievement test in geography. Current trends in teaching of geography, reported for example in the National Council for Geographic Education's *Curriculum Guide for Geographic Education,* indicate further the need for revising the contents of the test. Coverage of the test is full in relation to conventional emphases in geography. One may question the suitability of a test as long as 105 items, especially for the lower grades of the grades 7–9 range. The test format is generally satisfactory, though less so in readability of maps, especially that on page 5. While answer sheets are available, the provisions for recording of responses in the test booklet encourage a maximum but uneconomical rate of test booklet use and inefficient scoring.

The eight school systems listed as providing 1957 and 1958 data beyond the 1953 data obtained for the earlier test battery scarcely seem adequate to provide a desirably broad base for norms. No large city school systems are included in the later group. Ideally, there would be made available norms for different kinds of school systems in varying cultural environments.

Use of standard scores in reporting norms represents a step in the right direction. Many users, however, may find the tables giving raw and standard scores and percentile rank equivalents inconvenient, if not incomprehensible. More importantly, the sizable standard error of measurement makes difficult a meaningful interpretation of individual test scores. The grade placement and age norms reported are attributed vaguely to an "independent nationwide survey"; the arithmetical precision with which raw score advances almost exactly one point for each month of grade ranking from 4.7 to 10.2 suggests the possibility of as much speculation as careful establishment of norms. Statistically sophisticated users will not be satisfied with the normative data; other users may unhappily be misled.

In sum, the test appears appropriate for schools that have or desire in geographic instruction a considerable emphasis on memorization of facts and definitions. Those who wish a test with more up-to-date content and with greater stress on geographic understanding and a variety of skills will look elsewhere.

For a review by David R. Krathwohl of the California Tests in Social and Related Sciences, see 5:4; for reviews by Harry D. Berg and J. Raymond Gerberich of an earlier edition of the elementary level, see 4:23.

[995]
★World Geography: Every Pupil Scholarship Test. High school; 1952–59; 1 form ('59, 4 pages); general directions sheet ['63, 2 pages]; no data on reliability; 4¢ per test; 4¢ per key; postage extra; 50(55) minutes; Bureau of Educational Measurements. *

[Other Tests]
For tests not listed above, see the following entries in *Tests in Print*: 1742, 1747-8, and 1751; out of print: 1741 and 1743-4.

Survey Test in Geography

HISTORY

[996]
*American History: Every Pupil Scholarship Test. High school; 1926–64; forms from previous testing programs also available; 2 tests; general directions sheet ['63, 2 pages]; no data on reliability; norms for new forms available following testing program; 4¢ per test; 4¢ per key; postage extra; 40(45) minutes; Bureau of Educational Measurements. *
a) AMERICAN HISTORY TO 1865. New form (4 pages) usually issued each January.
b) AMERICAN HISTORY SINCE 1865. New form (4 pages) usually issued each April.

[997]
*American History: Every Pupil Test. Grades 7–9, 10–12; 1931–64; new form usually issued each December and April; 2 levels; general directions sheet ('63, 2 pages; no data on reliability; Ohio norms for new forms available following testing program; 5¢ per test; 3¢ per key; postpaid 40(45) minutes; Ohio Scholarship Tests. *
a) GRADES 7–9. 1935–64; test booklet titles vary.
b) GRADES 10–12. 1931–64.

[998]
★American History Test: Affiliation Testing Program for Catholic Secondary Schools. Grades 9–12 and students who are candidates for the high school diploma issued by the Catholic University of America; 1949–63; administered annually in May at individual schools; IBM; new form issued annually; Form Z ('63, 16 pages) used in 1963 program; separate answer sheets must be used; 50¢ per test and IBM answer sheet; postpaid; fee includes purchase of test booklets, scoring, and other services; specimen set of the complete battery free; for more complete information, see 758; 90(100) minutes; Program of Affiliation, Catholic University of America. *

HENRY CHAUNCEY, *President, Educational Testing Service, Princeton, New Jersey.* [Review of Forms Y and Z.]

In the introductory statement to the description of the American history course which this test is designed to cover, it is implied that the primary objectives of the course are to teach a student the facts of American history and an understanding of some of the causal connections between events in American history. The most serious criticism of these two forms of the test, which purport to measure a student's achievement in these areas, must be that none of the questions meet the laudable second objective. The tests are composed entirely of items requiring rote recall of factual-type information, such as "The Atlantic Charter dealt with" (Form Y, item 36) or "Washington's Cabinet included all of these men except" (Form Y, item 41). Completion questions which do ask about the effects of a particular policy or event merely require recall of memorized results, and not reasoned understanding of why one thing caused another; for example, "Jackson's policy toward the United States Bank resulted in 1. A shortage of farm credit 2. improved national banks　3. a sound monetary system　4. state control of banking activities" (Form Z, item 15).

Both forms also include sections made up of a less common item type which tries to deal with causal relations directly, but the novel format only overcomplicates the questioning and oversimplifies the events. For example, in Form Y, item 124 lists "one crop system" in one column and "industrial development of the South" in a second column; the connecting link (the key) is supposed to be "prevents.... [the second-column item] from occurring or coming into existence." The absence of any date makes the item ambiguous, since the situation differed in the nineteenth and twentieth centuries; moreover, the implication that a single factor caused a complicated, pervasive development is misleading, if not in error. (The instructions for this section are improved in Form Z, but the technique is still doubtful.)

Three further objectives described in the introductory statement to the course description suggest that students of American history should learn "the truth," as opposed to "opinion, or pious belief," should apply their learning to current events, and should become better informed citizens. These goals are nowhere more specifically defined, but neither form includes any questions which ask for application to novel situations of principles learned from history; such questions might reflect a student's achievement of these objectives.

With relation to the content which the test purports to cover, the balance seems faulty in terms of chronology and emphasis, both within and between the two forms. The introductory statement indicates that the courses taught in Catholic schools should divide American history at 1850 into two equal terms of work. Yet in Form Y, only a little more than one third of the items concern post-1850 history. More specifically, one seventh of the test covers the colonial period, which seems to be a larger proportion than is justified by the attention given to that period in typical high school courses. In comparison to this emphasis, the Revolution, the Constitution, and the 1920's are neglected. Form Z weights the distribution in the opposite direction, with nearly two thirds of the

questions on post-1850 happenings. Thus, the forms are hardly parallel in content. Furthermore, neither form gives enough attention to two themes that are increasingly emphasized in newer textbooks, namely, the reasons for the ways in which the economy and the power of the Federal Government have developed.

The introduction to the American history course description also suggests that the course should encourage the student's appreciation of the contributions of Catholics to American life, and help "to correct the distortion and peculiar emphasis now found in so many high school textbooks." The test acknowledges this intention by including three items in Form Y and eight in Form Z on the history of the Church, but on the whole the items reflect no markedly different interpretation of United States history than that found in tests prepared for public as well as parochial schools.

Tables 1, 2, and 3 (giving data on the norms population and student and class norms) in the ATP American History Test and Item Analysis Report for Form Y are helpful for teachers who know how to use them, but Table 4 (providing item content classifications and difficulty indices) has a fundamental organizational problem which makes the findings therein often useless. The problem is that the content areas are vaguely defined and are used part of the time as straight chronological divisions and other times as strand divisions of American history. While there may be some logic to the system, the titles of the eight content categories (there are nine for Form Z) do not themselves provide a thorough enough explanation of what each category includes and why. For example, an item on the mugwumps (Form Y, item 29) and one on imperialism (Form Y, item 27) are both lumped together in a category labeled "Expansion"; a question on legislation of the Progressive period (Form Y, item 49) and one on the Korean War (Form Y, item 143) both fall into a group called "World Power." One fourth of the items are classified in categories which lead to this type of confusion. Consequently, the interpretation of subscores based on such categories is bound to be a misleading indication of the strengths and weaknesses of a class.

Overall, the test includes items which are weak in the following aspects of verbal construction: Some stems are not directive enough

American History Test: Affiliation Testing Program

to tell the student clearly what he is to do (for example, Form Y, items 135 and 150); ambiguities in other stems make the keys debatable (for example, Form Y, items 3, 31, 32, and 94); answer options are not always written in parallel construction (for example, Form Y, items 10, 15, and 42); awkward construction unnecessarily complicates many issues (for example, Form Y, items 11, 17, 22, 27, 34, 44, 45, and 149).

Two difficulties occur in terms of factual content: (*a*) in a few instances, historical facts and interpretations appear to be faulty (for example, Form Y, items 16 and 139; the sample questions for 133–150), and (*b*) a few obscure titles make several items unjustifiably difficult (Form Y, items 109, Transcontinental Treaty, and 113, the abbreviation ODT; Form Z, item 65, Transcontinental Treaty, and 93, Glass-Owens Bill for the Federal Reserve Act).

The Affiliation Testing Program makes ambitious claims to measure students' historical and social attitudes, skills, and knowledge; but in fact, the tests demand only rote recall of tired maxims about the American past. The method of inquiry is equally conventional, and occasionally faulty, in terms of language, facts, interpretation, organization, and questioning technique.

For a review of the complete program, see 758.

[999]

★**Ancient History: Every Pupil Scholarship Test.** High school; 1933–58; 1 form ('58, 2 pages); general directions sheet ['63, 2 pages]; no data on reliability; 4¢ per test; 4¢ per key; postage extra; 40(45) minutes; Bureau of Educational Measurements. *

[1000]

*****College Entrance Examination Board Advanced Placement Examination: American History.** High school students desiring credit for college level courses or admission to advanced courses; 1956–63; for more complete information, see 761; 180(200) minutes; program administered for the College Entrance Examination Board by Educational Testing Service. *

REFERENCES

1. "CEEB Advanced Placement Examination: American History." Reproduction of an earlier examination and commentary by Henry F. Graff. *Social Ed* 26:251–62 My '62. *

HARRY D. BERG, *Professor, Office of Evaluation Services, Michigan State University, East Lansing, Michigan.* [Review of Form KBP.]

The *College Entrance Examination Board*

Advanced Placement Examination: American History is a three-hour test with objective and essay sections. The objective portion has 75 items with a 45-minute time allotment; during the remainder of the time the candidate is to write on three essay questions drawn from a limited number of options. After a rather complex scoring procedure, composite scores are reported to the colleges on a 5-point scale. The amount of time devoted to the test should be adequate for securing a reliable sample, and the items, both objective and essay, seem appropriate in difficulty and coverage for an introductory college course in American history.

The objective portion of the test is up to the high standards of the College Entrance Examination Board. It has a reliability of .85, a mean raw score of 33.7 (corrected for guessing), and an unusually high mean index of discrimination of .38 (biserial correlations of item scores with total raw scores). Except for a few key-list items, undoubtedly included to increase the number of scoring units, the items are of the multiple choice variety. The items do a good job of sampling the various forms in which American history data are presented. Some are grouped items based on cartoons, graphs, and reading selections, while others are discrete items which require the student to analyze quotations, make comparisons, draw inferences, and exhibit other like abilities. Nearly all measure for concepts of broad significance and emphasize reasoned understanding rather than memorized content detail. This reviewer's only criticism would be that the objective test should be given more of the time and have greater influence in arriving at the composite score.

The essay portion of the examination is more open to criticism, not on the grounds of question selection, which is excellent, but on the grounds of reader and reading reliability. Low reliability has always been the great shortcoming of essay tests, and particularly so when national programs are involved. Despite complex efforts to make scoring more objective and despite the accumulated experience of the Board and ETS, the problem seems not much closer to solution than ever. Two pieces of statistical evidence to support this conclusion are presented. First, the intercorrelations among the subscores of the three essay questions (each question answered by a student is graded by a different reader) is very low, ranging in the neighborhood of .30. Secondly, the means of the options which students may select differ widely. One would expect that each option would attract about the same range of ability. Unless some unexplained selective factor is at work, the conclusion can hardly be escaped that reader standards change from one option to another. In brief, students with the same writing ability and knowledge may be receiving different scores depending upon the options selected. The fact that students who did poorly on a particular option did well on the objective portion, and the reverse, helps to confirm the observation. Perhaps the use of options should be reexamined. What is gained in reliability in offering the student more opportunities for showing his writing ability may be more than lost in the increased difficulty of establishing reader standards.

The comments which have just been made are in no way intended to reflect on the value of the Advanced Placement Program. The program is needed in American education and it is well that it is growing. It should be added that the test scores are only one part of the information given to colleges. Secondary school grades and recommendations, as well as the test papers themselves, are provided. It is, therefore, on a wide array of evidence that decisions to give advanced placement or credit can be made. It speaks well for the program that the selected freshmen do as well or better in their advanced courses than do sophomores in the same courses.

For reviews by James A. Field, Jr. and Christine McGuire of an earlier form, see 5:812.

[1001]

College Entrance Examination Board Advanced Placement Examination: European History. High school students desiring credit for college level courses or admission to advanced courses; 1956–63; for more complete information, see 761; 180(200) minutes; program administered for the College Entrance Examination Board by Educational Testing Service. *

REFERENCES

1. "CEEB Advanced Placement Examination: European History." Reproduction of a 1958 Examination. *Social Ed* 25:335–43 N '61. *
2. WINKLER, HENRY R. "The Advanced Placement Program and Examination in European History." *Social Ed* 25: 332–4 N '61. *

[1002]

★*Cooperative Topical Tests in American History.* High school; 1963; title on manual is *Topical Tests in American History;* 1 form; 8 tests (6–8

pages); manual (4 pages); no data on reliability; "the norm on any one of these tests is a perfect score for all items" the examiner considers relevant to his teaching objectives; 50¢ per set of all 8 tests; 50¢ per set of keys; $1 per specimen set of all 8 tests; postage extra; 40(45) minutes; Cooperative Test Division. *

a) TEST 1, EXPLORATION, COLONIZATION, AND INDEPENDENCE: 1450–1783.
b) TEST 2, FOUNDATIONS OF AMERICAN GOVERNMENT: 1781–1801.
c) TEST 3, GROWTH OF NATIONALISM AND DEMOCRACY: 1801–1840.
d) TEST 4, EXPANSION, CIVIL WAR, AND RECONSTRUCTION: 1840–1877.
e) TEST 5, DEVELOPMENT OF INDUSTRIAL AMERICA: 1865–1898.
f) TEST 6, IMPERIALISM, DOMESTIC REFORM, AND THE FIRST WORLD WAR: 1898–1920.
g) TEST 7, PROSPERITY, DEPRESSION, AND THE NEW DEAL: 1920–1940.
h) TEST 8, THE SECOND WORLD WAR AND AFTER.

[1003]

The Graduate Record Examinations Advanced Tests: History. Grades 16–17; 1939–60; for more complete information, see 762; 180(200) minutes; Educational Testing Service. *

For a review by Robert H. Ferrell of an earlier form, see 5:818. For a review of the testing program, see 5:601.

[1004]

History: Every Pupil Scholarship Test. Grades 5–6, 7–8; 1933–64; new form (2–4 pages) usually issued each January and April; forms from previous testing programs also available; 2 levels; general directions sheet ['63, 2 pages]; no data on reliability; norms for new forms available following testing program; 4¢ per test; 4¢ per key; postage extra; 30(35) or 40(45) minutes; Bureau of Educational Measurements. *

[1005]

Kansas United States History Test. 1, 2 semesters in grades 7–8; 1957–58; IBM; Forms A ('57), B ('58), (2 pages); 2 levels labeled Tests 1, 2; manual ('57, 5 pages); no data on reliability of Form B; no norms for Form B; $1.20 per 25 tests; separate answer sheets may be used; 85¢ per 25 IBM answer sheets; 30¢ per scoring stencil; postage extra; 25¢ per specimen set, postpaid; 30(35) minutes; Shirley Meares and M. W. Sanders; Bureau of Educational Measurements. *

For reviews by Wayne A. Frederick and John Manning, see 5:820.

[1006]

★*Objective Tests in American History.* 1, 2 semesters high school; 1960; 1 form; 13 tests: 10 unit tests (3–4 pages), 2 semester tests (4–6 pages), and a final examination (4 pages); no manual; no data on reliability; no norms; separate answer sheets must be used; 5 or more tests with answer sheet, 10¢ each; 75¢ per 25 answer sheets; 15¢ per key (free with 24 or more copies of any one test); $3.25 per specimen set; cash orders postpaid; [50] minutes per test for unit tests, [60] minutes per test for other tests; Earl Bridgewater; Perfection Form Co. *

[1007]

★**Objective Tests in World History.** 1, 2 semesters high school; 1961; 1 form; 16 tests: 13 unit tests (3–4 pages), 2 semester tests (4 pages), and a final examination (4 pages); no manual; no data on reliability; no norms; separate answer sheets must be used; 5 or more tests with answer sheet, 10¢ each; 75¢ per 25 answer sheets; 15¢ per key (free with 24 or more copies of any one test); $4.15 per specimen set; cash orders postpaid; [50] minutes per test for unit tests, [60] minutes per test for other tests; Earl Bridgewater; Perfection Form Co. *

[1008]

*Social Studies 10 (American History): Minnesota High School Achievement Examinations.** Grade 10; 1955–63; earlier forms called *American History: Midwest High School Achievement Examinations;* new form issued each May; norms available in June following release of new form; Form F ('63, 8 pages) used in 1963 testing; no specific manual; series manual ('63, 4 pages); series norms ['63, 4 pages]; series cumulative profile ('62, 2 pages); no data on reliability; no description of normative population; 12¢ per test; $2.50 per 100 profiles; postage extra; 20¢ per specimen set, postpaid; 60(65) minutes; American Guidance Service, Inc. *

For a review by Howard R. Anderson of earlier forms, see 5:810.

[1009]

*Social Studies 11 (World History): Minnesota High School Achievement Examinations.** Grade 11; 1955–63; earlier forms called *Modern World History: Midwest High School Achievement Examinations;* new form issued each May; norms available in June following release of new form; Form F ('63, 6 pages) used in 1963 testing; no specific manual; series manual ('63, 4 pages); series norms ['63, 4 pages]; series cumulative profile ('62, 2 pages); no data on reliability; no description of normative population; 12¢ per test; $2.50 per 100 profiles; postage extra; 20¢ per specimen set, postpaid; 60(65) minutes; American Guidance Service, Inc. *

[1010]

*Survey Test in Introductory American History: California Survey Series.** Grades 7–9; 1946–59; subtest 1 of the elementary level (for grades 4–8) of *California Tests in Social and Related Sciences,* Form AA; IBM; Form 1 ('59, 10 pages, identical with test copyrighted in 1953 and identical with test copyrighted in 1946 except for format, 2 new items, option order in 16 items, order of 2 items, wording changes in 15 items, and other revisions in 3 items); combined manual ('59, 15 pages) for this test and test 994; $2.80 per 35 tests; separate answer sheets may be used; 5¢ per IBM answer sheet; 20¢ per scoring stencil; 10¢ per series class record sheet; 2¢ per series individual record sheet; postage extra; 50¢ per specimen set, postpaid; 40(45) minutes; Georgia Sachs Adams and John A. Sexson; California Test Bureau. *

RICHARD E. GROSS, *Associate Professor of Education, Stanford University, Stanford, California.*

This test and the accompanying survey test in geography have been taken from the battery

of the *California Tests in Social and Related Sciences* without any change of content from the material copyrighted in 1953 and with only modest changes from the original edition of that battery copyrighted in 1946. The tests are claimed to sample the pupil's ability to understand and apply principles as well as his knowledge of facts.

The 95 items would seem to parallel an outdated emphasis too typically found in elementary school United States history offerings and the test probably fails to satisfactorily differentiate between more recently recommended areas of concentration for the usual fifth grade and eighth grade American history offerings. Twenty-two items are devoted to the Colonial Period, 28 to the Westward Movement, and 20 to other aspects of our history stretching from before the Civil War to World War II. The test concludes with 25 items supposed to be related to the understanding of democracy and citizenship education, although several of these are historical also. It would seem that teachers who wish to include some history of the past quarter century, who do not want to just reemphasize much of the same content taught in the fifth grade course, and who want to teach in important areas going beyond a few key personalities and the problems of exploration, settlement, pioneers and Indians, and life on the plains would find this test quite unsatisfactory.

Most of the items are quite clear and vocabulary is certainly within the ken of junior high pupils. About two thirds of the items are multiple choice with four foils; the remaining are true-false. If one is satisfied with the content being tested, the majority of the items seem quite satisfactory. No dates are included as such, but pupils have to know sequence or the periods in which certain events happened. A number of questions require the testee to indicate if a development occurred before, after, or during the "War Between the States" or some other war; one would wish that other events besides wars, or perhaps even dates themselves, were used to so classify periods. It also seems imperative that teachers continue to use the outmoded term, the "War Between the States," placed in most such tests to get Southern sales, instead of the commonly accepted "Civil War." In items 32 and 84, "negroes" should be capitalized. Several other items call for alteration

—or should be rejected in future editions of the test. Items 64 and 65, for example, could confuse the bright pupil. In the former, among the results of the "War Between the States" the student is expected to pick the right answer from four choices, two of which are "The Union was preserved" and "Manufacturing was developed"; any good student knows that both were important results of the war. In the next item, pupils are expected to select the statement that is true "concerning the first World War"; the "correct" answer describes an event which occurred *after* the war.

On the other hand, some items are so clear as to the correct foil that one is led to question just what really important understandings they are expected to differentiate; examples are items 3, 34, and 86. Item 19 is one of the poorer examples of the objective item that penalizes the pupil who knows his history. It asks, "Which one of the following factors helped to bring about the discovery of America?" Among the choices are "the desire to obtain the wealth of the Orient" and "the adventurous spirit of the seamen of the day." Is the reference to the Vikings or to Columbus? In the latter case, were not both motivations? When will competent historians become more involved in such test construction?

Some will not like certain of the emphases and queries in the civics aspect of the test; but, in conclusion, the greatest fault of this test is its failure to include items and emphases that might help lead teachers to improved instruction that incorporates updated concepts and developments and social studies aims beyond primarily the reproduction of content.

For a review by David R. Krathwohl of the California Tests in Social and Related Sciences, see 5:4; for reviews by Harry D. Berg and J. Raymond Gerberich of an earlier edition of the elementary level, see 4:23.

[1011]

*World History: Every Pupil Scholarship Test. High school; 1926–64; new form (4 pages) usually issued each January and April; forms from previous testing programs also available; general directions sheet ['63, 2 pages]; no data on reliability; norms for new forms available following testing program; 4¢ per test; 4¢ per key; postage extra; 40(45) minutes; Bureau of Educational Measurements. *

[1012]

*World History: Every Pupil Test. High school; 1933–64; new form (4 pages) usually issued each De-

cember and April; forms from previous testing programs also available; general directions sheet ('63, 2 pages); no data on reliability; Ohio norms for new forms available following testing program; 5¢ per test; 3¢ per key; postpaid; 40(45) minutes; Ohio Scholarship Tests. *

[1013]

★World History Test: Affiliation Testing Program for Catholic Secondary Schools. Grades 9–12 and students who are candidates for the high school diploma issued by the Catholic University of America; 1949–63; administered annually in May at individual schools; IBM; new form issued annually; Form Z ('63, 12 pages) used in 1963 program; separate answer sheets must be used; 50¢ per test and IBM answer sheet; postpaid; fee includes purchase of test booklets, scoring, and other services; specimen set of the complete battery free; for more complete information, see 758; 90(100) minutes; Program of Affiliation, Catholic University of America. *

HENRY CHAUNCEY, *President, Educational Testing Service, Princeton, New Jersey.* [Review of Forms Y and Z.]

The test is probably not too difficult or too speeded for the educational level at which it is directed. If, however, a candidate's course has followed the general aims outlined in the publisher's statement about the world history course the test is designed to cover, he would presumably find much in the test which he has not covered in the required detail, and much which he has studied that is not covered by either form. Though called World History Test, both forms are really tests of western civilization, with very few questions on other areas, and a large number on ancient and medieval history. Similarly, according to the course description the second term covers history after the end of the French Revolution. Actually, only approximately one fifth of the questions in the test relate to the nineteenth and twentieth centuries. Also, the questions are of such a nature that they measure detail rather than broad historical developments—another contradiction of stated aims. Similarly, little attention is paid to economic and social history. Moreover, the two forms do not contain similar item types. The stated objectives of the course in world history could be more adequately tested by the broader subject matter coverage indicated above and by the use of item types which would require the candidate to use his historical knowledge in new situations. Form Y would be improved by questions, not purely factual in nature, based on maps, passages, and quotations. Form Z would be improved by questions such as those in Part 1 of Form Y, and by more searching questions on stimulus materials.

Thè instructions for taking the test are clear, with the following exceptions: The sample question given on the front cover of both forms, which purports to be a sample for all questions in the test, is actually a sample for Part 1, the other parts each having a different sample question. Also, samples indicate five answer positions, whereas some item types have but four options.

In Form Y the questions in Part 4 (which involve first picking out the option which does not belong with the others in the group and then ordering the remaining options chronologically) are time consuming and, within the sets, dependent on one another in such a way that one error can cause the loss of more than one point. Certain types of questions, notably those in Parts 2 and 4, which involve association or relation of individuals or ideas, require the candidate to think as the examiner has thought. In questions of this type the advantage is with the candidate whose information is more stereotyped, not with the candidate whose knowledge is more sophisticated. The questions in Part 5 frequently test only a knowledge of dates, not cause and effect, as is the stated purpose. Some options contain specific determiners (items 14, options 2 and 3, and 24, options 1 and 2), some answers seem very obvious (items 8 and 100), and some answers seem of questionable accuracy (item 50). A minor point: the name Bismarck is twice misspelled.

In Form Z, there are no questions like those in Part 1 of Form Y, which may be described as discrete informational questions. All questions are based on types of stimulus material or require the candidate to make an association of some sort. Also in Form Z, Part 4 purports to test chronological knowledge, but the periods are so large that for many questions there can be only one alternative. On the other hand, a few questions require an exact date close to the beginning or end of a period. The questions in Part 3, which are based on a world map, are poor. The five regions numbered as possible answers are so far apart that only occasionally would the candidate have to make any real choice among the options. Also, a single number may be used with more than one meaning (for example, 1 refers to the continent of Africa, which is also called a country,

to Carthage, and to Morocco). Part 2 consists of spot quotations which must be identified. Quotations representing points of view or schools of thought, or describing places, people, or events would provide a better test of the candidate's historical understanding.

In view of the subject matter and the time span covered by this test and the types of questions employed, a potential user would be advised to review the test carefully to be sure it will meet his needs.

For a review of the complete program, see 758.

[Other Tests]
For tests not listed above, see the following entries in *Tests in Print:* 1755, 1757–9, 1763–6, 1768–9, 1775, 1777, 1779–81, 1787, and 1790–4; out of print: 1756, 1767, 1770, 1773–4, and 1785–6.

POLITICAL SCIENCE

[1013a]
American Civics and Government Tests for High Schools and Colleges, Revised Edition. High school and college; 1930–54; Forms A, B, ['54, 8 pages, same as forms copyrighted in 1949 except for minor changes]; directions sheet ['49, 2 pages]; reliability, validity, and normative data based on 1949 forms; $3.15 per 35 tests; 50¢ per specimen set; postage extra; high school: 40(50) minutes; college: 35(45) minutes; F. A. Magruder, R. J. Clinton, and M. M. Chambers; [Bobbs-Merrill Co., Inc.]. *

JOHN H. HAEFNER, *Professor of Social Studies Education, State University of Iowa, Iowa City, Iowa.*

Form A consists of 63 multiple response items, each with four responses, and 57 matching items grouped into five sections. The answer key, consisting of a single sheet with the correct responses printed in six columns, is exceedingly awkward to use and very inefficient in terms of teacher time. A single sheet of directions provides information concerning the purposes of the test, its construction, the norms employed; directions for administering and scoring the test; and a minimum of data on reliability and validity. A class record sheet also accompanies the test.

The 63 multiple response items test exclusively for memoriter recall of isolated, and for the most part relatively insignificant, factual material. None of the items in this part could properly be classified as testing any reflective abilities, or any understanding of the processes of government. Furthermore, the items do not adequately sample the subject matter of American government, leaving large areas such as federal-state relationships, the civil service, and government finances—to mention only a few—completely untested. The items throughout the test are completely unimaginative in format, and at least five (items 57, Part 1; 30, 32, 20, and 27, Part 2) are obsolescent and the keyed responses no longer correct. The format of the matching items in Part 2 does not conform with accepted practice today.

The information provided on the directions sheet is entirely inadequate. In two separate places the sheet claims diagnostic values for the test—an unsupported claim which is warranted only in the vaguest and most general sense. The reliability is reported as ".85 (240 cases)," without any additional information as to specific techniques used to arrive at this figure. Validity "was determined by correlating a known criterion (teachers' marks) with scores on the test." On this basis, validity is reported as .65, based on 109 cases.

Both high school and college and "normal school" norms are provided. High school norms were based on 2,016 high school students, but nothing further about the nature of this sample is reported. College and normal school norms are based on a sample of 616 students, and no other information about the sample is provided.

The directions sheet states, "Each item included is found in the majority of the commonly used textbooks now in use, and each was carefully analyzed before it was put in the preliminary form." This appears to be the only criterion employed in the construction and selection of the items included. By inference, therefore, the authors were concerned only with measuring students' ability to recall material appearing in textbooks. The claims that the test will measure "the effectiveness of classroom instruction," that it will "test a pupil's understanding in the field," that it "makes it easy for a teacher to diagnose the pupil's difficulties," and that it can be used to "measure pupil progress" are certainly inadequately supported, if not downright misleading.

Except as an indication of students' ability for memoriter recall, this test has little to recommend it for high school use, and even less

for college use. In the judgment of this reviewer, the test should be removed from sale as a public service.

[1014]
*American Government and Citizenship: Every Pupil Test. Grades 11–12; 1935–64; new form (4 pages) usually issued each April; forms from previous testing programs also available; general directions sheet ('63, 2 pages); no data on reliability; Ohio norms for new forms available following testing program; 5¢ per test; 3¢ per key; postpaid; 40(45) minutes; Ohio Scholarship Tests. *

For a review by Elizabeth C. Adams of the 1951 form, see 4:699.

[1015]
*American Government: Every Pupil Scholarship Test. High school; 1930–63; new form (4 pages) usually issued each April; forms from previous testing programs also available; general directions sheet ['63, 2 pages]; no data on reliability; norms for new forms available following testing program; 4¢ per test; 4¢ per key; postage extra; 40(45) minutes; Bureau of Educational Measurements. *

[1016]
*Constitution: Every Pupil Scholarship Test. High school; 1926–64; new form (4 pages) usually issued each January; forms from previous testing programs also available; general directions sheet ['63, 2 pages]; no data on reliability; norms for new forms available following testing program; 4¢ per test; 4¢ per key; postage extra; 40(45) minutes; Bureau of Educational Measurements. *

[1017]
★Duke University Political Science Information Test (American Government). Grade 13; 1958; 5 scores: federal government, constitutional system, politics, programs and policies, total; Forms A, B, (7 pages, must be reproduced locally from sample copy); mimeographed manual (8 pages); no data on reliability and no norms presented in manual; $1 per test and manual, postpaid; 40(50) minutes; Robert H. Connery, Richard H. Leach, and Henry Weitz; distributed by Richard H. Leach. *

[1018]
*The Graduate Record Examinations Advanced Tests: Government. Grades 16–17; 1939–61; for more complete information, see 762; 180(200) minutes; Educational Testing Service. *

For a review by Christine McGuire of an earlier form, see 5:835. For a review of the testing program, see 5:601.

[1019]
Peltier-Durost Civics and Citizenship Test: Evaluation and Adjustment Series. High school; 1958; 2 scores: achievement, attitude; IBM; Forms AM, BM, (6 pages); manual (9 pages); expectancy chart (2 pages); separate answer sheets must be used; $4.10 per 35 tests; $1.45 per 35 IBM answer sheets; 40¢ per specimen set; postage extra; 55(65) minutes; Charles L. Peltier and Walter N. Durost; [Harcourt, Brace & World, Inc.]. *

HOWARD R. ANDERSON, *Senior Consulting Editor, High School Department, Houghton Mifflin Company, Boston, Massachusetts.*

The manual states that the *Peltier-Durost Civics and Citizenship Test* is designed to to measure three broad objectives: "the acquisition of information concerning the structure and functions of government at federal, state, and local levels; development of understanding of certain concepts and processes central to a democratic type of government; and development of certain attitudes considered to be characteristic of the good citizen in a democracy." This test is primarily intended for use in grade 9.

Each form of the test includes four parts. Part 1 is made up of 50 four-response multiple choice items. Part 2 contains 15 statements about the functions of officials. In each case the appropriate title is to be selected from an alphabetical list of 49 officials. Part 3 consists of 4 matching exercises, each made up of three statements and five responses. Part 4 includes 32 statements which briefly describe ways of behaving. The pupil is expected to mark each statement A (agree), D, ? (in some circumstances, agree; in others, disagree), DK (don't know), DU (don't understand).

The majority of the items in Part 1 test recall of information. For example, "Responsibility for protecting the President....rests with...." The answer is "Secret Service" (item 4, Form AM). The items have been carefully edited; e.g., the stems are well phrased and the wrong responses are plausible but not unfair.

To do well on Part 2 the pupil would need to be able to recall the titles of the officials identified, for it would be difficult and time consuming to "match" the right name in an alphabetized list of 49 items. The example provided for this exercise seems farfetched: "This official might help to determine the rate you would have to pay for shipping a crate of oranges from Florida to Illinois." The answer is "Interstate Commerce Commissioner." Somehow one does not associate one of the Commissioners with the setting in which a tourist normally sends a crate of oranges to a friend.

One of the matching exercises in Part 3 (Form AM) seems difficult, or dated, or both. The three questions asked concern (*a*) the number of countries in the UN in 1953, (*b*) the number of amendments to the U.S. Constitution in 1953, and (*c*) the number of states required to ratify a constitutional amendment. The answers are to be chosen from these numbers: 18, 22, 36, 48, 60. Perhaps a student should be able to figure out that 22 is the right answer for *b*. Ten years later few pupils would know, though some might guess, that 60 is the answer for *a*. But surely 36 is not the correct answer for *c*.

The statements of attitude in Part 4 include some directly related to the experiences of children but more that are related to the experiences of grownups. They are focused on significant issues. The directions state: "Be sure you answer just as you really feel. This section is not like the rest of the test, where there are definitely right or wrong answers. These statements are matters of opinion on which people may have different ideas." Although students are asked to indicate their attitudes by checking agree, disagree, don't know, or don't understand, all correct answers are either agree or disagree. Might it not be better to include statements that actually are so controversial that varying degrees of agreement could be indicated? It seems unfair, somehow, to suggest to the student that the "right answer" may be in doubt when actually it is not. Requiring a yes or no answer doubtless would affect the mind set of the pupils tested.

The manual describes how the test was validated. Content specifications were derived from an analysis of seven widely used civics textbooks. This analysis suggested the following distribution of content: 25 per cent economics, 40 per cent government, 20 per cent sociology, 10 per cent personal development, 5 per cent consumer education. One wonders if the percentage of content derived from government is not higher in present-day civics courses.

Preliminary forms of the test were administered to more than 2,500 New England pupils, and the items revised in the light of criticisms made by teachers as well as of statistical analysis. For standardization purposes the test was then administered to 2,500 students in 13 high schools in 10 states in May 1954. The manual includes a table for translating raw scores into standard scores and percentile ranks. It also provides difficulty values for all items in both tests. The medians of the several estimates of reliability are .88 for the achievement section and .76 for the attitude section.

Teachers who wish an estimate of how well their pupils have mastered traditional information can use the two forms of the Peltier-Durost test for beginning (or end) of the year testing. Because the junior high school civics course has long been fluid, it might be desirable to construct a test that places major emphasis on skills and includes selections providing the content on which test items are based.

CHRISTINE McGUIRE, *Assistant Director, Research in Medical Education, University of Illinois College of Medicine, Chicago, Illinois.*

In the opening paragraph of the manual, this test is described as one "designed to measure attainment of certain of the generally accepted outcomes of instruction in a civics and citizenship course such as is commonly offered in the 9th grade....[including] the acquisition of information concerning the structure and functions of government at federal, state, and local levels; development of understanding of certain concepts and processes central to a democratic type of government; and development of certain attitudes considered to be characteristic of the good citizen in a democracy." The test was developed through a review of seven textbooks in widest use at the time of its construction (now somewhat remote). Five major areas (economics, 25 per cent; government, 40 per cent; sociology, 20 per cent; personal development, 10 per cent; and consumer education, 5 per cent) were subdivided into several hundred specific subtopics. "Tabulation was then made of the frequency of occurrence of the subtopics in the seven selected textbooks."

The achievement section of the test gives evidence of a slavish conformity to this frequency count. The items are randomly arranged, uncoordinated, and extremely dull. For example, such questions as the following abound: "Responsibility for protecting the President of the United States and his family rests with the" (followed by the names of four agencies); "How many members were there in the United Nations in 1953?" (followed by five numbers); "The sheriff is the principal law enforcement agent for a" (followed by names of four territorial jurisdictions). Interspersed among the factual questions are a few questions which can

only be regarded as articles of faith. For example, such a question as: "Which of the following is the best reason for staying in school until you graduate from high school?" must be viewed as a matter of opinion even though the "right" answer conforms to our most cherished stereotypes about the relationship between quantity of education and preparation for earning a living. Finally, in the achievement portion of the test there are a few questions requiring identification of an example or the definition of a basic concept; these are, by far, the least objectionable.

The last section of the test is designed to measure the "development of certain attitudes considered to be characteristic of the good citizen in a democracy." Throughout the manual there are many subtle and some explicit references to "right attitudes." In the opinion of this reviewer, uncritical acceptance of such a dangerous concept denies the philosophic position it purports to identify and vitiates valid efforts toward constructive citizenship education. The manual reports that:

As a basis for defining the attitudinal outcomes to be measured by the test, the authors relied upon the report, "Characteristics of a Good Democratic Citizen," prepared by the Working Committee on Citizenship of the National Council for the Social Studies, National Education Association (February 1950). This statement lists understandings, beliefs, and actions of a good citizen in a democracy. On the basis of the committee report 78 declarative statements were composed to which the student [responds] by marking one of the five options * The answers considered "right" are those which agree with the point of view embodied in the National Council report.

In the words of the manual: "To the extent to which this report is an adequate description of the good citizen and to the extent to which the test items are representative of what is in the report, *the student's responses reflect the degree to which he espouses desirable citizenship attitudes.*" (Italics are those of the reviewer.) If so, either the authors of the report or the authors of the test, or both, have failed. These "declarative statements" have two serious deficiencies: most are such obvious platitudes (for example, "One who keeps well informed on current events is a better citizen than one who doesn't") as to lead this reviewer to have doubts about the brain rather than the heart of any ninth grade student who fails to respond in the "expected" manner. Other items (for example, those concerning the right to strike or the particular definition of property rights applicable to natural resources) deal superficially, in some cases almost flippantly, with serious issues. Such cavalier treatment of basic constitutional questions that still occupy the highest courts of the land can only be a disservice to legitimate goals of citizenship education. The implication that there is an easy "right answer" must be misleading to the thoughtful student.

In addition to these basic deficiencies, the test entails unnecessary complexities of administration including internal time limitations of undue precision (e.g., 23 minutes for Part 1, 7 minutes for Part 2). While the test is reported to have been standardized on the basis of an administration to several thousand students in a number of states, other than number of schools and states represented and grade level (ninth grade), mean IQ, and approximate size of the group, there is no specific description of the sample population.

The accompanying manual is formally complete in that it gives directions for administration, scoring, and interpretation of results, and reports data about reliability, standard scores, and correlation with other measures of aptitude and achievement, although on the whole, it is so poorly written as to be confusing to the uninitiated. More seriously, however, it recommends what this reviewer regards as a positive misuse of the test. It not only suggests, but encourages the use of this single examination in conjunction with an intelligence test to perpetuate the identification, at best dubious, of "under-achievers" and "over-achievers" in civics and citizenship classes.

In short, the test is not recommended for use with any group, since it offers neither intellectual challenge nor serious concern about the basic democratic values which it purports to sample. The parallel forms are strictly equivalent in this respect. The very misuses for which testing programs are responsibly criticized, are advocated. The concept of scoring attitudes as right or wrong rather than as multidirectional, patterned, and almost infinitely contingent, the implicit approval given to comparing individuals and groups to poorly identified norms, the advice given to use the test as an aid in the labeling of individuals as underachievers and overachievers, and, finally, the tacit encouragement to teachers to emphasize

trivia and platitudes in their civics courses, can only be viewed as shocking.

[1020]

★**Principles of Democracy Test.** Grades 9–12; 1961, c1960–61; IBM; Form A ('61, c1960, 8 pages); manual ('61, 24 pages); separate answer sheets must be used; $3 per 20 tests; $4 per 100 IBM answer sheets; 25¢ per scoring stencil; 75¢ per specimen set; postage extra; 40(45) minutes; Nathaniel L. Gage, Neil F. Garvey, Charles B. Hagan, and Roland Payette; Science Research Associates, Inc. *

WILLIAM C. BINGHAM, *Lecturer in Education, Rutgers, The State University, New Brunswick, New Jersey.*

The *Principles of Democracy Test,* according to the authors, is "designed to measure student knowledge and understanding of democratic principles as they are interpreted in the United States." To a great extent, this purpose is achieved very adequately in that many of the items deal effectively with understandings and application of facts. This quality is highly desirable and should be incorporated in more achievement tests.

In general, the manual is very good. Directions for both administration and scoring are simple, clear, easy to follow, and adequate in all respects. Time limits are appropriate for high school classroom use and are liberal enough to permit most students an opportunity to attempt all items.

Standardization procedures are reported in more detail than is often found, but one or two improvements in this connection would be helpful to the test user. While the standardization group is appropriately representative as a national sample, more specific description of the groups composing that sample could assist the test user in determining how well his own group is represented. This is particularly so because the standardization group apparently includes some students who were, and others who were not, studying related subject matter when the data were collected. Thus, the teacher who uses this test in association with an appropriate instructional unit (probably the most frequent use that can be anticipated) is likely to overestimate the relative performance of his own students because of the extent to which "uninstructed" students are represented in the standardization population.

Percentile norms are reported for grades 9 through 12 with suggestions for interpretation. Although separate norms are not reported for boys and girls, it is demonstrated that differences in means and variances for the sexes are not significant. The authors offer helpful suggestions for the development of local norms, the need for which should be reaffirmed in view of the observation made in the preceding paragraph.

The manual includes a Discussion Guide which is designed to serve as a study aid to the teacher. The guide includes suggestions for reporting scores to students, rationale for discussion of correct answers, and an indication of the percentage of the national sample which responded correctly to each item. The basic idea of the Discussion Guide is a good one, but in the case of the reviewer's copy, the print-through on some pages made it difficult to read. If use of the Discussion Guide is to be maximized, it would be helpful to have local norms established for some point in time other than the end of the second semester, as is the case with the reported national norms. An appropriate time may be at the end of a related teaching unit in social studies classes.

While the data reported on reliability and validity are not based on the total standardization group, they are based on representative research samples selected from that group.

In terms of reliability, appropriate information is reported on both internal consistency and stability. In this connection, the test performs satisfactorily (e.g., r's from .85 to .89).

Very appropriately, the authors caution the test user to make his own judgment about content validity, and that point bears repeating here. The test user, by examination of the test, should determine for himself whether the test samples the kind of content he is concerned with measuring. It would be helpful to the test user, however, if the title of the test more adequately represented the content. For example, this reviewer classified 49 of the 65 items as dealing with either content or interpretation of the United States Constitution. Most social studies teachers would probably regard a concept such as "principles of democracy" as having a somewhat broader base than the Constitution. A more specific title might reduce the danger of misleading relatively unsophisticated test users.

Part of the concurrent validity data includes correlation coefficients between this test and grades in a variety of social studies courses (r's from .33 to .83). The usefulness of these data is limited to the extent that the proportion of each course devoted to relevant subject matter is unknown, and whether the people assigning the grades had access to the test scores is not reported. It is of interest that many of the courses bearing titles similar to that of the test appear to be highly related to it. However, it is of particular interest, in terms of face validity, that the lowest reported coefficient (.33) was observed between the test and a course bearing the identical title.

The authors should be commended for the inclusion of data relating the test to other standardized measures, but it should be noted that the relatively high correlation with ability tests (e.g., .71 with the *Terman-McNemar Test of Mental Ability*) may, to some extent, be related to the increase in scores through the school years.

In summary, the test has a number of important assets and also a number of notable limitations. The *Principles of Democracy Test,* in general, does what the authors claim for it. The manual is clear and can be used by the typical consumer of achievement tests. For the most part, the limitations are in the form of missing data, especially in the description of the standardization group. The test should be useful to classroom teachers, especially to those with the interest and sophistication to develop relevant local norms.

JOHN H. HAEFNER, *Professor of Social Studies Education, State University of Iowa, Iowa City, Iowa.*

Form A of this test consists of 65 multiple response items, divided into nine sections, as follows: Constitution and Fundamental Law of the United States (10), Elections, Voting, and Ballots (9), Congress (7), President and Executive Branch (5), Judiciary and Law-Enforcement (5), National Government Powers (7), State and Local Government (6), Declaration of Independence and Articles of Confederation (3), Civil Liberties and the Bill of Rights (13). Answer sheets, which can be used for either machine or hand scoring, are required. The punched stencil provided for hand scoring is conveniently arranged for easy use. A well prepared manual accompanies the test and gives information about the authors, the purposes and uses of the test, directions for administering, scoring, and interpreting the test, suggestions for using the test in the classroom, and excellent technical information.

The section Using the Test in the Classroom is particularly helpful. Each item in the test is reprinted with the correct response, often with the source indicated, and the authors' rationale for the item. In addition, the percentages of students in grades 9, 10, 11, and 12 responding correctly to the item are provided, alongside a space in which the teacher may record the performance of his own class on the item. The rationale for each item does provide, as the manual suggests, a useful takeoff for class discussion.

The section dealing with Technical Information is above average in the data it provides on the construction of the test and the provisions made for standardization and norming. The norms are based on the scores of 7,386 students in grades 9–12 from 20 schools in 13 states, "drawn from the population of all schools that had administered the *Iowa Tests of Educational Development* in the spring of 1960." Unfortunately, the 13 states are not identified and it is somewhat difficult to judge how well the various geographic regions of the United States were, in fact, represented in the sample. The research samples on which computations of reliability, validity, and other test characteristics are based consisted of four samples of 400 students, one sample for each grade 9 through 12.

The reliability coefficients were computed by using both the split-half technique and Kuder-Richardson formula 20. These reliability coefficients are satisfactorily high, ranging from .85 to .89 for both techniques.

Pearson product-moment correlations are provided to show the relationship of scores achieved by students on the *Principles of Democracy Test* and on other instruments. Tests used for comparative purposes include portions of the *Iowa Tests of Educational Development,* the *California Test of Mental Maturity,* the *Terman-McNemar Test of Mental Ability,* the *Differential Aptitude Tests,* and portions of the *SRA Tests of Educational Ability.* It is interesting to note, particularly in the light of subsequent comments, that the lowest correlations (.30 and .31 for grades 9 and 10, respectively) are to be found when comparison is made with results on the rea-

Principles of Democracy Test

soning test of the *SRA Tests of Educational Ability.* The samples, however, are quite small (145 for grade 9 and 129 for grade 10).

The technical construction of the items is generally good. There appears to be no sound reason, however, why 9 of the 65 items should have five responses instead of four as the other items do. There are 7 "negative" items; the negative in the stem of each of the items is italicized, but no special directions or warnings to students are provided, and the items are not grouped together at the end of a section or of the test as a whole. Correction of these minor technicalities would prove helpful to students and could affect the test's validity.

Individual items do reveal weaknesses in construction. In taking the test, this reviewer found the stems of items 15, 23, 38, and 40 to be somewhat confusing and not as clearly formulated as they might be. On several items, notably 5, 22, 42, and 50, there is some reason to believe that experts would not all agree on the correct response, and these items would consequently penalize students with a more thorough knowledge of government and political science.

Perhaps the most disturbing items are those included under the heading "Civil Liberties and the Bill of Rights," particularly items 55–65. The purpose of these appears to be to test students on the meaning and significance of the provisions in the Bill of Rights. As written, however, the items do not clearly test knowledge of the constitutional amendments as they apply to hypothetical situations, but are cast in the form of items of opinion or judgment. This is particularly disturbing in an area as complex and controversial as that of civil rights, where even among knowledgeable adults there is considerable disagreement over what *is,* what *should be,* and what *can be.* These 10 items would be a good deal more effective in what purports to be an *achievement* examination if they tested for knowledge of the Bill of Rights rather than for the judgment of the student as to what ought to be done in a hypothetical situation.

In the manual accompanying the test, under the heading Validity, the authors state: "In the final analysis....each teacher who uses the instrument should attempt to judge its content validity for himself by evaluating how well each item individually, and all items collectively, relate to his own teaching objectives." This reviewer took this injunction seriously and classified the items into five broad categories, as follows: (*a*) Items which are almost wholly devoted to the recall of specific factual material; (*b*) items which require recognition of terms, or the definition of terms, but which go beyond mere recall of a textbook sentence or definition; (*c*) items which require some degree of thought or the application of simple reflective abilities beyond recall; (*d*) items which are sophisticated in that they demand considerable knowledge as well as the application of some of the more difficult reflective abilities; and (*e*) items which call for the expression of a judgment or opinion rather than a knowledge of the facts or issues involved. To be sure, these are somewhat fuzzy criteria and they must be subjectively applied. Using them as carefully as possible, however, this reviewer found that 23 of the items should be classified in category *a*, 8 in category *b*, and 21 in category *c*. At best, only 2 items should be classified in category *d*, and it would be doubtful if even these 2 would really qualify. The 10 items in category *e* do not properly belong in an achievement examination since they really test value judgments.

This analysis, inadequate as it is, suggests that the description of the test, a test of *"knowledge* and *understanding"* (italics supplied), is not entirely accurate. Overall, it is more nearly a test of information. With some exceptions, the facts tested are important to a knowledge of American governmental institutions. The arrangement of the test into sections keeps the items, in part, from testing unrelated or isolated facts. But the test could, and in this reviewer's opinion should, go further and test for students' ability to reason with the facts.

The authors do not seem to have formulated the educational objectives for teaching the principles of democracy before devising the items. If this were to be done in terms of understandings and skills or abilities, and if the objectives were to be phrased so concretely as to be amenable to measurement, then the number of items requiring more than mere recall would almost certainly be increased. In addition, if less emphasis in writing the items were placed on the way in which the information appears in typical textbooks, memoriter recall would be reduced.

In summary, this test is acceptable for purposes of meeting state legislative requirements that students must demonstrate familiarity with "the principles of representative government" before graduating. With adequate revision, it could become a very fine instrument for measuring the outcomes of topnotch instruction in American government and governmental institutions.

[Other Tests]

For tests not listed above, see the following entries in *Tests in Print:* 1801, 1805, 1808, 1810, and 1812–5; out of print: 1798–9, 1802, 1806–7, and 1809.

SOCIOLOGY

[1021]

*The Graduate Record Examinations Advanced Tests: Sociology. Grades 16–17; 1939–61; for more complete information, see 762; 180(200) minutes; Educational Testing Service. *

J. Richard Wilmeth, *Associate Professor of Sociology, State University of Iowa, Iowa City, Iowa.* [Review of Form JGR.]

This test provides a rigorous examination of the kinds of knowledge and skill which are typically developed during graduate study in sociology. Items cover a wide range of concepts, theory, and principles. The test faithfully reflects the importance of quantitative methods in contemporary sociological research. A few of the questions require a knowledge of elementary statistical techniques, but what is called for in a much broader sense is some evidence of the habit of quantitative thinking in the interpretation of data. The student who has never carefully examined a table or a graph will find himself seriously handicapped on many of the items.

The substantive areas covered are legitimately within the realm of sociology today, with a minimum of intrusion into the neighboring fields of economics, political science, and psychology. Some acquaintance with anthropological literature is expected, and this is thoroughly in accord with the merging interests of the two disciplines. While many sociologists might object to the particular "mix" represented by this test, few would argue that any particular item should be excluded.

Form JGR was first used in 1961 and a preliminary analysis indicates that it is much more difficult than earlier forms. This is not at all surprising and it is doubtful that the difficulty is the result of technical flaws in item building. On the contrary, the test shows every evidence of thorough competence in test construction. Very few items can be answered on the basis of a low level recognition of vocabulary, or names, or books. Basic concepts and principles are more often tested as they apply to illustrative examples and as they relate to other concepts and principles. If the difficulty of the test is a basis for criticism, it would be on the ground that the test is a measure of achievement in graduate study rather than of aptitude for graduate study. Thus it might be argued that a student who has an easy familiarity with the knowledge on which Form JGR is based is ready at least for his master's degree.

It should be noted that a considerable gap continues to exist between undergraduate and graduate work in sociology. A student may accumulate a respectable looking record in his undergraduate years and be exposed very little to quantitative methods or to the great theoretical issues. Such a background provides little basis on which to predict success in graduate school. On the other hand, an increasing number of students are being advised to begin serious preparation for graduate study before they complete the bachelor's degree, and for students in this category Form JGR is an appropriate test. Making the test less difficult would seriously interfere with the purpose for which it is designed. It should be added, however, that even the most intensive preparation at the undergraduate level is not likely to give a student both the breadth and depth which are are required for high performance in all parts of the test. Therefore, the reporting of subscores might be very useful both to the student and to a graduate faculty.

In the present state of the discipline, one cannot conclusively say that a low score on Form JGR indicates that a student will not do well in graduate school. It may only indicate the inappropriateness of his undergraduate experience. A high score, on the other hand, would be a very strong indicator of probable success. This positive value should not be jeopardized by making the test easier. Sociology is in a stage of very rapid development and it is entirely justifiable that the GRE test in sociology be designed with an eye on the future rather than on the past.

Graduate Record Examinations Advanced Tests: Sociology

For a review of the testing program, see 5:601.

[1022]

Sare-Sanders Sociology Test. High school and college; 1958; IBM; Form A (4 pages); mimeographed manual (3 pages); $1.20 per 25 tests; separate answer sheets may be used; 85¢ per 25 IBM answer sheets; 30¢ per scoring stencil; postage extra; 25¢ per specimen set, postpaid; 40(45) minutes; Harold Sare and Merritt W. Sanders; Bureau of Educational Measurements. *

J. RICHARD WILMETH, *Associate Professor of Sociology, State University of Iowa, Iowa City, Iowa.*

According to the manual, this is an achievement test for high school and college classes pursuing introductory courses in sociology. Preparing such a double-purpose test is a rather perplexing task in view of the sharp discontinuities which exist between high school and college sociology. For contrast, we may consider American history, a field in which it would certainly be less difficult to compare the achievement of high school and college students. Sociologists are generally agreed that students in high school have little exposure to their field of study, and at least a few of them argue that this is no great cause for professional concern. Nevertheless, there now exists a committee of the American Sociological Association which is attempting to develop improved resource materials for the high school social studies program. Much more intensive efforts have been made in the same direction by economists in recent years.

Constructing a test for both high school and college students of sociology calls into play a kind of pedagogical Gresham's Law. The process is quite apparent in the instrument under consideration here. It consists of 142 items which are to be completed in 40 minutes. The first 115 items are in multiple choice form with three or four responses (usually single words or brief phrases) and the remainder are truefalse. Under this format, little can be accomplished beyond low-level testing for vocabulary and simple descriptive facts. But even if this limited purpose is accepted, the test still has a number of shortcomings.

The test as a whole seems to have a rather secondhand quality which may be explained by a statement in the manual that "the items were selected from the basic content of several leading textbooks." Reliance on textbooks rather than on a general familiarity with the field can lead to simple errors of fact (males do *not* outnumber females in the United States, as one item asserts) and to such embarrassing lapses as the use of "more" as the singular of "mores." Casual reference to both high school and college texts may account for the appearance of items on government, labor relations, and consumer economics. These might be included under the rubric of social studies, but the test is neither broad enough to justify this label nor is it restricted to the typical interests of practicing sociologists. Other items are based on implicit value judgments which most sociologists would prefer either to make explicit or to avoid altogether.

One may criticize the form as well as the content. It requires no special competence in test construction to point out that an instrument which is offered for sale should be free of grammatical errors or that items which require nothing more than the ability to read should be discarded. An item which is based on an association between two variables should specify the direction of association as well as asserting that the relationship exists. Using the completion form of multiple choice question offers a temptation toward greater and greater brevity of statement until in the extreme case a stem may consist of a single word. The extreme is reached in this examination.

Both sociology and objective testing have been the targets of severe criticism, the former on the ground that it merely elaborates what everybody knows already, and the latter because it does not discriminate between those who understand and those who do not. This test will not improve the reputation of either.

[Other Tests]

For tests not listed above, see the following entry in *Tests in Print:* 1818 (out of print).

SOCIAL STUDIES — SEVENTH MMY

REVIEWS BY *Howard R. Anderson, Harry D. Berg, Vincent N. Campbell, Edward J. Furst, Hulda Grobman, Richard E. Gross, Dana G. Kurfman, Christine H. McGuire, John Manning, Howard D. Mehlinger, Virginia M. Rogers, and William J. Webster.*

[884]

*College Board Achievement Test in American History and Social Studies.** Candidates for college entrance; 1901–71; test administered each January, March, May, July, and December at centers established by the publisher; for more complete information, see 663; 60(80) minutes; program administered for the College Entrance Examination Board by Educational Testing Service. *

REFERENCE

1. PUGH, RICHARD C.; MORGAN, JAMES M.; AND LUDLOW, H. GLENN. *Predicting Success for Indiana University Freshmen Using the CEEB Achievement Tests, the CEEB Scholastic Aptitude Test, and High School Rank.* Indiana Studies in Prediction, No. 13. Bloomington, Ind.: Bureau of Educational Studies and Testing, Indiana University, April 1970. Pp. xi, 39. *

For a review by Howard R. Anderson of earlier forms, see 6:966; for a review by Ralph W. Tyler, see 5:786; for a review by Robert L. Thorndike, see 4:662. For reviews of the testing program, see 6:760 (2 reviews).

[885]

*College Board Achievement Test in European History and World Cultures.** Candidates for college entrance; 1901–71; test administered each January and May at centers established by the publisher; for more complete information, see 663; 60(80) minutes; program administered for the College Entrance Examination Board by Educational Testing Service. *

For a review by David K. Heenan of earlier forms, see 6:967. For reviews of the testing program, see 6:760 (2 reviews).

[886]

★College Placement Test in American History and Social Studies.** Entering college freshmen; 1962–

70; irregularly scheduled reprintings of inactive forms of *College Board Achievement Test in American History and Social Studies;* Forms NPL ('65, reprint of 1962 test), PPL ('67, reprint of 1964 test) in a single booklet (25 pages); for more complete information, see 665; 60(70) minutes; program administered for the College Entrance Examination Board by Educational Testing Service. *

For a review by Howard R. Anderson of Form NPL (formerly KAC), see 6:966; for a review by Ralph W. Tyler of an earlier form, see 5:786; for a review by Robert L. Thorndike, see 4:662. For a review of the testing program, see 665.

[887]

★College Placement Test in European History and World Cultures.** Entering college freshmen; 1963–70; irregularly scheduled reprintings of inactive forms of *College Board Achievement Test in European History and World Cultures;* Form OPL ('66, 16 pages, reprint of 1963 test); for more complete information, see 665; 60(70) minutes; program administered for the College Entrance Examination Board by Educational Testing Service. *

For a review by David K. Heenan of Form OPL (formerly LAC1), see 6:967. For a review of the testing program, see 665.

[888]

*Metropolitan Achievement Tests: High School Social Studies Test.** Grades 9–13; 1962–64; catalog uses the title *Metropolitan High School Social Studies Test;* subtest of *Metropolitan Achievement Tests: High School Battery;* 3 scores: study skills, vocabulary, information; Forms Am ('62, 9 pages), Bm ('63, 9 pages); manual ('64, 24 pages); for battery accessories, see 15; separate answer sheets (Digitek, Harbor, IBM 805, IBM 1230) must be used; $7 per 35 tests; $2.30 per 35 IBM 805 answer sheets; $2.80 per 35 Digitek or IBM 1230 answer sheets; $3 per 100 Harbor answer cards; $1.40 per set of Digitek or IBM scoring stencils; $1.25 per specimen set; postage extra; Harbor scoring service, 19¢ and over per test; IBM scoring service, 33¢ and over per test; 70(84) minutes; Walter N. Durost, William H. Evans, James D. Leake, Howard A. Bowman, Clarke Cosgrove, and John G. Read; Harcourt Brace Jovanovich, Inc. *

HARRY D. BERG, *Professor, Office of Evaluation Services, Michigan State University, East Lansing, Michigan.*

This test is divided into three subtests: study skills (38 items), vocabulary (45 items), and information (56 items). Except for the vocabulary section, all items are of the four-response multiple choice type. As is so often the case with subtests, the number of items in any one is probably too small for the subtest to be reliable for individual diagnosis.

The study skills test is limited to measuring the ability to read and interpret maps, tables, charts, and graphs. Part A, the map skills section, is very well done. Students are required to use different projections, and the questions are directed toward using a scale of miles, identifying symbols, recognizing land forms and the like. Occasionally an item based solely on outside information creeps in, but not very often. The maps were drawn specifically for these tests to preclude answering merely from remembering previously seen maps.

Part B of the skills section does not contain the same variety of items as the map section. In Form BM, one set of items is based on a line graph, with nearly all of the items measuring the same skill—the ability to determine percentages. The corresponding set in Form AM involves circle graphs. In both forms, a second set requires the reading of a stock market report. This set, it would appear, chiefly rewards persistence in determining when one number is larger than another. One might also question the use of stock market reports, since students who have been exposed to this rather specialized information should have an advantage.

One useful kind of skills exercise is conspicuously missing. I refer to the reading selection with related items. Most social studies information is presented in verbal form, and the reading selection to be interpreted provides an excellent opportunity to determine whether students can generalize, draw conclusions, detect assumptions, and show a variety of other abilities.

The vocabulary test consists of terms each of which is to be placed in one of four categories. For example, the term "siege" would be placed under "military action" rather than under "American elections" or "type of government organization." Such items can measure for vocabulary in only generalized terms. It might have been well to measure for some terms in a more specific sense. This reviewer also wonders about the value of having separate vocabulary and information tests. The two seem to measure quite similar forms of knowledge.

The information test is admittedly of a highly factual nature. Few of the items require the student to demonstrate an understanding of the properties of his knowledge. A rote memory question such as "the discoverer of the Pacific Ocean was" is not atypical of the test. This reviewer would have preferred items requiring a higher level of command of information such as those found in the *Tests of Academic Progress: Social Studies.*

Some of the items in the information test might have been more precisely worded. The "blockade and impressment policies carried on by the British" were not the "primary cause of the War of 1812," but the ostensible or apparent cause. It is also questionable whether Churchill was "one of the world's greatest leaders in time of war and peace." This reviewer would also recommend that tests containing what amounts to current affairs items be revised more often. Today's headlines may be only a footnote to history ten years hence. The test being discussed has not been revised since 1963, and one of the items asks for the nations attending the Summit Conference of 1955.

To conclude this appraisal of the information subtest, it should be pointed out that most of the items are drawn from the field of American history, with the next largest number from world history. There are almost no sociology or economics items. The prospective user of the test should make a comparison with the TAP Social Studies to determine the kind of content balance he wants. The weighting on the side of American history can perhaps be explained on the grounds that nearly all students have been exposed to this area.

From a technical point of view, the items are

carefully constructed. The questions, for the most part, are direct and there are few clues and little nonfunctioning content. The items in the two forms of the test are carefully balanced as to difficulty, content coverage, and discriminating quality. The statistical data with regard to indices of discrimination are particularly impressive. Mean item validities for subtests range from .38 to .54. But as is the case with all tests, good item data, while necessary, are not a sufficient criterion of a curricularly valid test. Items should always be subjectively scrutinized to determine whether they measure for what we wish the students to learn.

Meticulously prepared and useful norms are provided in easy-to-use form. Raw scores are to be converted into standard scores and these, in turn, into percentiles and stanines. While the same test is to be used for all four grades, age-controlled norms are provided for each grade. There are also separate norms for college preparatory students.

VINCENT N. CAMPBELL, *Associate Program Director, Social and Educational Research Program, American Institutes for Research, Palo Alto, California.*

According to the manual, the battery which includes the Social Studies Test "can be used in appraising student progress, in guiding students educationally and vocationally, in evaluating instructional programs as a basis for curriculum revision, in evaluating instructional material, and for other administrative purposes." To achieve these purposes in an area of achievement as broad as social studies requires a great deal more information than can be provided by this brief test, no matter how high the quality of the test.

Test sellers naturally want to sell their tests to as many consumers for as many purposes as is reasonably possible. But there is something misleading about the subtle implication that a brief testing program of this sort will provide the bulk of the information needed for individual student guidance and curriculum revision in the area of social studies. The authors do point out that the tests merely provide "data about students" and do not provide cookbook solutions to all educational problems. They even suggest that test results should be taken "in conjunction with other reliable information" in inferring needed modifications in instruction. Perhaps it is the fault of educators' limited per-

spective rather than of test makers that standardized tests are relied upon as the principal source of information for purposes of guidance and curriculum change. Certainly the Metropolitan test makers are no more to blame in this regard than the makers of other standardized social studies tests.

Given the above limitations, educators may find this test helpful as a rough guide to placement in high school and early college social studies courses emphasizing map and graph skills, civics, and history. For curriculum revision, I would recommend it only for those course segments involving map and graph skills.

The main weakness of the test is that it samples only a limited portion of the domain of important social studies objectives. The test could, of course, be used to check achievement in only those areas measured—namely, maps, graphs, tables, vocabulary, and factual information. But I fear that the main purpose for which an achievement measure of this sort is sought is to conduct a comprehensive survey of achievement in broad curriculum areas such as "social studies." There are differences of opinion as to what is important in social studies, but I think most leading social studies educators would agree that a list of top priority objectives for social studies should include the following: skills of inquiry, problem solving, and question asking; critical analysis of communications; knowledge of useful sources of social studies information, including social roles as well as stored information (the latter may be partially covered in the language arts test); effective personal interaction; planning and social organization; and the application of generally useful social studies concepts to a variety of specific settings. Most social studies educators would, I believe, include development of a well examined set of personal values about important social issues. Admittedly, many of these objectives are difficult to measure, especially with objective tests, but measures do exist for all of these objectives, some of them in current achievement test batteries. For example, the STEP battery includes measures of critical analysis skills, and the ACT battery measures knowledge of sources of social studies information. Limited coverage of objectives, however, is a general failing of existing standardized tests in social studies and is not a unique deficiency of the Metropolitan test.

It appears the authors relied mainly on widely

used textbooks and courses of study as their sources of objectives. It is generally acknowledged among social studies educators that most textbooks are sadly out of keeping with current thinking on what objectives are important in social studies, and test makers commit a strategic error in relying on current texts and courses of study.

In the study skills test, over half the items concern map skills. This is the best part of the entire test. The items are strong and straightforward and cover a wide range of commonly needed and important map skills. The items measuring graph skills are adequate, although each form of the test refers to only one type of graph. In both forms, use of tables is measured by reference to a portion of the daily quotations from the New York Stock Exchange. The authors made the grave error of assuming the student would be familiar with the meaning of the cryptic headings and abbreviations in the stock listings. In the one form I checked, four of the six items suffer from this failing.

The vocabulary test measures a low order of word knowledge in that students are asked to assign each word to one of four broad classes of social studies vocabulary. Ability to do this probably indicates general familiarity with the context in which a word is used, but it does not indicate sufficient understanding for accurate use of the word.

The social studies information test is the weakest. It is approximately 90 percent history, mostly of the last four centuries. At least one quarter of the items in both forms call for trivial knowledge (e.g., "In 1898, American influence in the Far East was established after a naval battle at—(a) Manila, (b) Guam, (c) Honolulu, (d) Tutuila"). On the other hand, some of the items concerning civics and political science are quite good. For a few items the choice of a correct answer is a matter of opinion (e.g., "Which of the following was *not* favorable to the United States? (*e*) India became an independent nation, (*f*) Chiang Kai-shek was driven to Formosa, (*g*) The Philippines gained independence, (*h*) The South East Asia Treaty Organization was formed"). The test as a whole leans toward the traditional and sides noticeably with the Establishment. This is probably a minor failing, but modern activists and reformers might be disappointed to find no reference to current social problems and issues. Also, there is no coverage of anthropology, so-

cial psychology, non-Western cultures, or environmental geography.

The two forms of the social studies test appear quite comparable in content. The manual indicates high correlations in student performance for the two forms, but, oddly, no evidence is given as to whether the mean level of difficulty of the two is comparable. ("Standard score distributions for the two forms were combined at each grade level, test-by-test, and percentile ranks and stanines were derived from the resulting distributions.")

The makers of the test followed quite adequately the traditional routine for item analysis and standardization. Unfortunately, the traditional routine is itself of little value if the test is not measuring the most important objectives. The norm sample for standardization included over 31,000 students from 29 school systems throughout the country. Two questions concerning the selection of the sample are worth noting. First, how many school districts were invited to participate? If we knew what percentage of the schools refused, we would be in a better position to judge how biased the norm sample may be. Second, the sample was drawn only "from communities with populations between 10,000 and 99,999." Why? Does this range include virtually the total market for standardized tests? Or is it just more expensive and difficult to obtain valid data from very small and very large communities? Since rural and inner-city students often perform more poorly on school tests, this limitation in the nature of the norms should be noted by test users.

The test is to be commended for its administrative instructions and adjunct scoring materials. The wording of the instructions and the test items is clear and straightforward. Procedures for administration are spelled out thoroughly. The test user is offered tables for interpreting raw scores on three different scales: standard scores, percentile ranks, and stanines. The advantages of each scale are explained quite clearly in the manual and the guide for interpreting, and the authors wisely recommend the use of stanines for most purposes. Generally, the authors are appropriately modest in advising how to interpret test scores. The one bad suggestion which they repeatedly make is that a student's achievement scores should be compared with his "capacity (as measured by the intelligence test)." The basis for using an intelligence test for this purpose is

Metropolitan Achievement Tests: High School Social Studies Test

very weak, and the use of an intelligence test for guidance and counseling in a particular area of achievement, such as social studies, is probably not worth the dangers of miscalculation and misinterpretation.

SUMMARY. The tests are of limited usefulness, all in all. They serve well as a measure of map skills, but coverage of important objectives is inadequate for a comprehensive measure of achievement in the social studies.

For reviews of the complete battery, see 15 (2 reviews) and 6:15 (3 reviews).

[889]

*National Teacher Examinations: Social Studies. College seniors and teachers; 1940–70; Forms RNT1 ('69, 21 pages), RNT2 ('69, 23 pages), SNT ('70, 22 pages); descriptive booklet ('70, 8 pages); for more complete information, see 582; 120(165) minutes; Educational Testing Service. *

For a review by Harry D. Berg of an earlier form, see 6:974. For reviews of the testing program, see 582 (2 reviews), 6:700 (1 review), 5:538 (3 reviews), and 4:802 (1 review).

[890]

★Primary Social Studies Test. Grades 1–3; 1967; PSST; no reading by examinees; 1 form; 2 editions: hand scorable booklets (14 pages), MRC scorable booklets (19 pages); manual (26 pages); $6 per 35 hand scorable tests; $15 per 35 MRC scorable tests; $1.20 per specimen set; postage extra; MRC scoring service, 54¢ and over per test; (35–40) minutes; Ralph C. Preston and Robert V. Duffey; Houghton Mifflin Co. *

VIRGINIA M. ROGERS, *Assistant Professor of Education, University of Kentucky, Lexington, Kentucky.*[1]

The *Primary Social Studies Test* purports to evaluate the social studies understandings of students in grades 1–3. It was constructed to test "relevant knowledge" which children have acquired rather than to analyze the extent to which they have mastered the social science generalizations. It is questionable whether some items could be considered "relevant," e.g., that Abraham Lincoln read books by firelight, or that a baby is the symbol for New Year's Day. But more to the point, it seems to this reviewer that an evaluation of the extent to which a child has mastered certain generalizations and skills is exactly what a teacher needs. A test which focuses on the accumulation of facts reinforces teaching for the accumulation of factual infor-

mation. It appears that this test was designed to evaluate social studies programs of the last decade. A review of current programs at both the local level and the national level indicates a multidisciplinary and conceptual approach which de-emphasizes facts and focuses on broader understandings which have wide applicability. Standardized evaluative instruments should play a role in encouraging this approach.

Items which relate to the areas of sociology and anthropology are noticeably omitted from the test, even though they are included in the majority of the series and programs published by major companies and are the primary focus of at least two national social studies projects.

The sampling validity of items must also be questioned if items are to reflect generalizations from the social science disciplines. That is, if the test items are to be representative of the generalizations which usually are included in primary social studies, do they sample extensively enough from the population of items which might represent those generalizations? In some cases, there seems to be only one item in this test pertaining to a given generalization.

The intended answers to several items are ambiguous. For example, one question asks the student to identify the picture of a swamp. One of the incorrect responses is a picture, showing dense trees and undergrowth of vines and bushes, which looks very much like the swamps in certain areas of this country. The correct response is a picture of water with cattails and ducks or geese flying over, which would be defined by many as a lake rather than a swamp.

Relative to the marking of the booklets by children, a positive feature of the test is that items are identified by objects, e.g., stars, bells, or balls, rather than by numerals. However, facing pages use the same objects, thereby increasing the likelihood of a child's being on the wrong page. It would seem more efficient to alternate item identification objects or to use different colors.

The first four or five pages of the booklets have two columns of items. Since primary children are seldom accustomed to reading by columns, this could be a distracting variable.

One good feature of this test is the reliability and standardization program which is reported in the test manual. The norming sample of schools used for the program was a subsample of the norming sample used for the *Iowa Tests of Basic Skills* and the *Lorge-Thorndike In-*

---

1 In reviewing technical considerations, the writer gratefully acknowledges the assistance of Professor Daniel S. Arnold, University of Kentucky.

telligence Tests. The use of a sample on which considerable additional data were available allowed a much tighter description on the characteristics of students upon whom norms are based. As a consequence, the reported norms are adjusted so as to reflect the makeup of the total population of primary children in the U.S. with respect to geographic region, urban-rural ratio, and reading level. Unfortunately, separate norms for regions or size of city of residence are not reported. Methods of determining reliability and the data regarding reliability are completely reported. The reliability estimates obtained are remarkably stable between test times and among grade levels. The reported estimates of reliability are sufficiently high that the test can be used validly to interpret group performance and growth.

A shortcoming of the manual section on interpretation is that it fails to suggest to the teacher what reservations he should exercise in using the test. While the manual cautions that a given student should be expected to grow more or less than one grade equivalent in a year's time depending upon his ability, nowhere does it caution against abusing the test by applying it to the case of the individual student and his expected and observed growth. Inasmuch as the reported standard error of measurement represents from three-tenths to five-tenths of a grade equivalent, the error component of the score attained by a single child in a single testing might easily equal or exceed the grade equivalent growth expected in one year of study. This consideration alone should not dissuade the teacher from using the test for group evaluation purposes, since the standard error operates randomly and in either a positive or negative direction and will presumably be cancelled out when the total group is considered. The teacher should, however, be cautioned that overly strict application to the individual student exceeds the power of the test.

Another flaw in the description of how the test can be used is that the manual does not address itself to the problem of diagnosis of specific content strengths and weaknesses of a given class. The section of the teacher's manual on how to use the test results is really a synopsis of teaching strategies applied to social studies. That material seems more appropriate to a full semester's study of that problem than to this test manual. More appropriate to the test manual would be a description of the method that a classroom teacher might use in doing an item analysis of the test for his class in order to determine which particular concepts or processes require further development in that school's social studies curriculum.

This reviewer cannot recommend the use of this test. A broader view of the concepts and processes of the social studies is needed to evaluate current programs in the primary grades.

[891]

*****SRA Achievement Series: Social Studies.** Grades 4-9; 1963-69; Forms C, D, ('63, 11 pages); 3 levels: blue (grades 4.5-6.5), green (grades 6.5-8.5), and red (grades 8.5-9) in a single booklet; no specific manual; for series manuals and accessories, see 18; separate series answer sheets (Digitek, DocuTran, IBM 805, IBM 1230) must be used; $8.70 per 25 tests; $9.30 per 100 DocuTran answer sheets; postage extra; 30(40) minutes; Louis P. Thorpe, D. Welty Lefever, and Robert A. Naslund; Science Research Associates, Inc. *

For reviews of the complete battery, see 18 (2 reviews), 6:21 (1 review), and 5:21 (1 review).

[892]

*****Social Studies: Minnesota High School Achievement Examinations.** Grades 7, 8, 9; 1961-71; new or revised form issued each May; Form EH Rev. ['71, c1968, 6-8 pages]; 3 levels; no specific manual; series manual ('71, 16 pages); no data on reliability; 15¢ per test; separate answer sheets (IBM 1230) may be used; 10¢ per answer sheet including scoring service; $1 per series manual; postage extra; $1.10 per specimen set, postpaid; 60(65) minutes; edited by V. L. Lohmann; American Guidance Service, Inc. *

[893]

*****Social Studies 12 (American Problems): Minnesota High School Achievement Examinations.** Grade 12; 1955-71; new or revised form issued each May; Form EH Rev. ['71, c1968, 6 pages]; no specific manual; series manual ('71, 16 pages); no data on reliability; 15¢ per test; separate answer sheets (IBM 1230) may be used; 10¢ per answer sheet including scoring service; $1 per series manual; postage extra; $1.10 per specimen set, postpaid; 60(65) minutes; edited by V. L. Lohmann; American Guidance Service, Inc. *

[894]

*★Stanford Achievement Test: High School Social Studies Test.** Grades 9-12; 1965-66; catalog uses the title *Stanford High School Social Studies Test;* subtest of *Stanford Achievement Test: High School Basic Battery;* Forms W, X, ('65, 7 pages); no specific manual; battery manual ('65, 48 pages); supplementary directions ('66, 4 pages) for each type of answer sheet; separate answer sheets (IBM 805, IBM 1230) must be used; $8.20 per 35 tests; $2.30 per 35 IBM 805 answer sheets; $2.80 per 35 IBM 1230 answer sheets; 70¢ per scoring stencil; $1.20 per battery manual; $2 per specimen set; postage extra; scoring service, 19¢ and over per test; 40(45) minutes; Eric F. Gardner, Jack C. Merwin, Robert Callis, and Richard Madden; Harcourt Brace Jovanovich, Inc. *

[895]
***Stanford Achievement Test: Social Studies
Tests.** Grades 5.5–6.9, 7.0–9.9; 1940–68; catalog uses
the title *Stanford Social Studies Test;* 2 forms; 2
levels; battery technical supplement ('66, 55 pages);
expected grade score tables ('68, 10 pages) based on
Otis-Lennon Mental Ability Test available on request;
supplementary directions ['64–66, 1–2 pages] for each
type of answer sheet; $5.20 per 35 tests; 70¢ per key;
separate answer sheets (Digitek, Harbor, IBM 805,
IBM 1230) may be used; $2.30 per 35 IBM 805 an-
swer sheets; $2.80 per 35 Digitek or IBM 1230 answer
sheets; $3 per 100 Harbor answer cards; 70¢ per
Digitek or IBM scoring stencil; $2 per technical sup-
plement; $1.75 per specimen set of either level; post-
age extra; Harbor or IBM scoring service, 19¢ and
over per test; Braille and large type editions available
from American Printing House for the Blind; Truman
L. Kelley, Richard Madden, Eric F. Gardner, and
Herbert C. Rudman; Harcourt Brace Jovanovich,
Inc. *
a) INTERMEDIATE 2. Grades 5.5–6.9; Forms W, X,
('64, 6 pages); combined manual ('64, 10 pages) for
this and test 802; 50(56) minutes.
b) ADVANCED. Grades 7.0–9.9; Forms W, X, ('64, 9
pages); combined manual ('64, 11 pages) for this and
test 802; 52(58) minutes.

VIRGINIA M. ROGERS, *Assistant Professor of
Education, University of Kentucky, Lexington,
Kentucky.*[1]

This test was designed to measure the significant "knowledges, skills, and understandings
commonly accepted as desirable outcomes" of
the social studies programs in grades 5–9. The
authors have to a commendable degree succeeded in accomplishing their purpose. The test
rises above the treatment of achievement as a
reservoir of factual information which requires
the student to function almost entirely at the
memory level. It succeeds in testing some of the
higher processes, such as interpretation, application, translation, and analysis, recently incorporated in more progressive textbooks and
curricula.

The test is divided into two parts—Content
and Study Skills. The Study Skills section is
designed to require students to use data and
interpretive tools to respond to the questions.
This section of the test is an excellent example
of testing for problem-solving or critical thinking achievement.

The test represents a broad sampling from
many social studies disciplines, rather than being restricted almost completely to geography,
history, and civics, as tests with similar titles
have traditionally been. One example from the
test reads:

[1] In reviewing technical considerations, the writer gratefully
acknowledges the assistance of Professor Daniel S. Arnold,
University of Kentucky.

Bob is a new boy in town. When he chooses his
new friends, he should know—
5 the kind of house they live in
6 if they have many good clothes
7 how much allowance they get
8 if they have interests like his

This item seems to draw from sociological or
psychological considerations. Other items test
for anthropological, economic, and political
science concepts, as well as for history, geography, and government.

One caution seems to be in order. Teachers
or others who use this test should be advised as
to exactly what is meant by "social studies
achievement" as interpreted by the authors of
this test. If the program of instruction which
students have received is of a traditional nature,
the use of this test might not be an adequate
measure of achievement, both because of the
breadth of disciplines drawn upon and because
of its testing for higher cognitive processes.

From the viewpoint of technical considerations, the test is an excellent one. The norms
for the test are complete and well reported. The
reliability reported for all forms is adequate for
group interpretation. The directions for the
administration and scoring of the test are clear
and complete.

Considering the directions for interpretation
of the test, one criticism should be made. The
Directions for Administering report, along with
the statistics on test reliability, the standard
error of measurement for the test, with no explanation of how that statistic affects the interpretation of test results. In view of the number of school systems that have discontinued
standardized testing because of teachers' alleged misuses of the results, it would appear
that test publishers might help correct one abuse
by treating in the manual the concept of standard error and the limitations which it places
upon interpretation. The reviewer strongly
recommends that the publishers of this test
make such an addition.

*For a review by Harry D. Berg of an earlier
edition, see 5:799; for a review by Ray G.
Wood, see 3:595. For reviews of the complete
battery, see 25 (1 excerpt), 6:26 (1 review, 1
excerpt), 5:25 (1 review), 4:25 (2 reviews),
and 3:18 (2 reviews).*

[896]
★Tests of Academic Progress: Social Studies.
Grades 9–12; 1964–66; Form 1 ('64, 14 pages); 4
levels (grades 9, 10, 11, 12) in a single booklet; no
specific manual; battery teacher's manual ('64, 62

pages) ; battery manual for administrators, supervisors, and counselors ('65, 45 pages) ; battery norms booklet for IQ levels ('66, 26 pages) ; separate answer cards (MRC) must be used ; 30¢ per test ; $3 per 100 MRC answer cards ; MRC keys not available ; scoring service, 27¢ per test ; $1.20 per battery teacher's manual ; 96¢ per battery administrator's manual ; 60¢ per battery norms booklet ; $3 per specimen set of the complete battery ; postage extra ; 60(70) minutes ; Dale P. Scannell and Alvin H. Schild ; Houghton Mifflin Co. *

REFERENCE
1. GOOLSBY, THOMAS M., JR. "The Appropriateness of the Tests of Academic Progress for an Experimental School." *Ed & Psychol Meas* 30(4):967-70 w '70. *

HARRY D. BERG, *Professor, Office of Evaluation Services, Michigan State University, East Lansing, Michigan.*

The developers of the battery of which this test is a part state that "the *Tests of Academic Progress* are designed to provide an efficient and comprehensive appraisal of student progress toward the most widely accepted academic goals of secondary-school education." In the social studies, for purposes of this test, these goals are taken to be the acquisition of (*a*) "a meaningful, functional knowledge which leads to understandings and valid generalizations....," and (*b*) "the skills necessary to acquire additional knowledge and understandings, and the ability to apply these skills to the intelligent solution of problems." It is admitted that there are other desirable goals, but not ones adapted to measurement by paper-and-pencil tests. Several distinguishing features of the test have convinced this reviewer that the instrument is a valid measure of progress toward the two limited goals stated above.

A test can be no better than its component items. The authors state their concern for good item writing. Such statements are made as "the most important and perhaps the most difficult aspect of test development is the translation of test plans into specific items," and "most of the items require students to apply their knowledge and to make judgments." More than lip service has been paid to these assertions; they have been translated into practice. The items are of consistently high quality. All of the technical procedures of good item writing have been followed. But of even greater importance, the items deal with broad, significant concepts which should be included in any social studies program, regardless of specific organization. Instead of asking for rote-learned and highly factual information, the questions require students to apply knowledge in new situations. This is done by asking students to generalize, select

examples and illustrations, make comparisons, understand broad trends, relate cause and effect, and the like. The responses have been carefully selected and phrased to make these significant questions effective for their purposes.

The content outline upon which item selection was based has seven major categories : American history, geography, world history, American government, economics, sociology, and skills. The items included in the test for each grade reflect a good balance among these areas, and all areas are covered at each level with items of appropriate difficulty. Also, the items are clearly drawn from each of the disciplines. For example, economics items are from economics and not economic history. Too often tests only pretend to be general social studies tests while actually having items concentrated in only one area, usually American history.

Skills, as well as content concepts, are well covered at each grade level, even though there is no skills subtest as such. In fact, there is broader coverage with regard to kinds of skills than in the well-known Metropolitan test, which in this field deals primarily with map and graph interpretation. The TAP includes items which require the student to recognize valid generalizations, to distinguish between primary and secondary sources, to recognize consistency, to distinguish between descriptive statements and value judgments, as well as to interpret maps, graphs, and tables. With regard to the latter, an important point should be noted. While a variety of maps and graphs are used throughout the test, only one or two items are based on each. It is not uncommon in other tests to have six or eight items for a single piece of stimulus material. It is my feeling that having so many items results in overemphasizing particular skills and, consequently, in item duplication.

As previously indicated, this social studies test is not divided into subtests, although it could easily have been if the authors had so desired. There are advantages in using only total scores : subtests are commonly too short to provide reliable measures, items are often arbitrarily classified, and differences in what is measured in the subtests may be superficial. For those who do desire subscores, a content outline is given. The specific parts of this can be related to particular items by using an item classification table. No norms are given for such possible divisions of the test.

All of the tests for grades 9-12 are included

Tests of Academic Progress: Social Studies

in a single booklet of 130 items, with overlapping items for each grade. The use of overlapping tests has an advantage over identical items for all grades in that optimum difficulty levels can be secured for each grade. The overlapping feature also makes possible the addition of content and skills coverage when most appropriate for a given grade level.

All in all, this is the best social studies test for multi-grade use that I have seen in many years. I wish to compliment its authors. I hope that another form will be forthcoming so that the norms can be used for measuring within-grade progress.

For a review of the complete battery, see 31.

[897]
★**Tests of Basic Experiences: Social Studies.**
Prekgn–kgn, kgn–grade 1; 1970–71; 1 form; Levels K ('70, 34 pages), L ('70, 18 pages); for battery manual and accessories, see 33; $9 per 30 tests, postage extra; scoring service, $1.20 per test; (25) minutes; Margaret H. Moss; CTB/McGraw-Hill. *

For a review of the complete battery, see 33.

[898]
*Zimmerman-Sanders Social Studies Test. 1, 2 semesters in grades 7–8; 1962–64; first published 1962–63 in the Every Pupil Scholarship Test series; Forms A, B, ('64, 2 pages); 2 levels labeled Tests 1, 2; manual ('64, 3 pages); $1.75 per 25 tests, postage extra; 75¢ per specimen set, postpaid; 30(35) minutes; John J. Zimmerman and M. W. Sanders; Data Processing and Educational Measurement Center. *

ECONOMICS

[899]
★**CLEP Subject Examination in Introductory Economics.** 1 year or equivalent; 1964–70; for college accreditation of nontraditional study, advanced placement, or assessment of educational achievement; tests administered monthly at regional centers throughout the United States; tests also available for institutional testing at any time; Form MCT ('64, 16 pages); optional essay supplement: Form MCT-A ('64, 2 pages); for program accessories, see 664; rental and scoring fee, $5 per student; postpaid; essay supplement scored by the college; 90(95) minutes, same for essay supplement; program administered for the College Entrance Examination Board by Educational Testing Service. *

For reviews of the testing program, see 664 (3 reviews).

[900]
*The Graduate Record Examinations Advanced Economics Test. Graduate school candidates; 1939–70; 6 current forms ('65–70, 28–36 pages); descriptive booklet ('70, 9 pages); descriptive booklet for

faculty ('70, 13 pages); for more complete information, see 667; 180(200) minutes; Educational Testing Service. *

REFERENCE

1. See 6:987.

For reviews of the testing program, see 667 (1 review) and 5:601 (1 review).

[901]
*Test of Economic Understanding. High school and college; 1963–64; Forms A, B, ('63, 13 pages, same as preliminary edition no. 2, also published in 1963, except for booklet cover and shorter time limit); manual ('64, 36 pages); norms based on grade 12 only; separate answer sheets (IBM 805) must be used; $5.95 per 25 tests; $8.40 per 100 answer sheets and 3 manuals; 45¢ per scoring stencil; $1.35 per specimen set; postage extra; 40(50) minutes; test by Committee for Measurement of Economic Understanding, Joint Council on Economic Education; manual by George Leland Bach, Walter R. Jones, and Suzanne R. Meyer; Science Research Associates, Inc. *

REFERENCES

1. PAUL, JOEL HARRIS. *An Analysis of Economic Understanding in Selected Georgia High Schools.* Doctor's thesis, University of Georgia (Athens, Ga.), 1964. (*DA* 25:5643)
2. DAUGHTREY, ANNE SCOTT. *An Analysis of the Economic Understanding of the June 1966 Graduates of Norfolk, Virginia Public Schools.* Doctor's thesis, University of South Dakota (Vermillion, S.D.), 1967. (*DA* 28:8-4A)
3. KASTNER, HAROLD H., JR., AND JACKSON, HARRY D., JR. "Economics and United States History." *J Sec Ed* 42:34-7 Ja '67. *
4. SMITH, ALFRED J., JR. *The Relationship Between the Economic Understanding of Graduating High School Seniors and Certain Personal and Curricular Factors.* Doctor's thesis, Indiana University (Bloomington, Ind.), 1967. (*DA* 28:2461A)
5. HOPKINS, CHARLES RUSSEL. *A Measure of Economic Understanding and General Business Knowledges of Tenth Grade Students.* Doctor's thesis, University of Minnesota (Minneapolis, Minn.), 1968. (*DAI* 30:60A)
6. HUNT, EUGENE HAROLD. *An Experimental Study to Determine the Effectiveness of Teaching Economics at the Secondary-School Level.* Doctor's thesis, University of Maryland (College Park, Md.), 1968. (*DA* 29:1474A)
7. ALEXANDER, LINDA ANN. *An Analysis of Economic Understanding of High School Seniors in Selected Schools in Alabama.* Doctor's thesis, University of Alabama (University, Ala.), 1969. (*DAI* 30:1740A)
8. GENTRY, ATHAL DENNIS. *Economic Understanding of Non-College-Bound Seniors in Public High Schools in Indiana.* Doctor's thesis, University of Denver (Denver, Colo.), 1969. (*DAI* 31:61A)
9. GABLE, MYRON. *The Value Orientations and Actual and Perceived Level of Economic Understanding of New York Businessmen.* Doctor's thesis, New York University (New York, N.Y.), 1970. (*DAI* 31:3411A)
10. GANSER, CARL J. "Understanding of Economic Concepts by Business Education and Social Studies Undergraduate Teaching Majors." *Delta Pi Epsilon J* 12(4):10-21 Ag '70. *

EDWARD J. FURST, *Professor of Education, University of Arkansas, Fayetteville, Arkansas.*

The primary purpose of this test is to help meet the "needs of the schools for standards by which to measure the effectiveness of their instruction." A secondary purpose is to aid learning through follow-up discussion.

In keeping with the first purpose, the authors developed two parallel forms, each having 50 four-choice items, to assess "understanding of the basic economic concepts essential for good citizenship." In keeping with the second, they developed an Item Discussion Guide that gives an explanation of the choice of best answer for each item.

The authors have made a commendable effort to carry out the emphasis upon basic understandings rather than upon "an elaborate set of technical terms, abstract theory, or detailed masses of factual information." In this respect the test reflects a modern educational view.

Such an emphasis has its difficulties, however. One difficulty stems from the vagueness of the word "understanding," which was to be the guiding concept here. The inevitable result of this lack of definition of outcomes, as distinct from subject matter, is that the test consists of some unspecified miscellany. It includes knowledge of specific terms, of specific but nonetheless important facts, of principles and generalizations; interpretation of data; and application of principles. Unless the prospective user undertakes his own classification of items, he will not know the relative emphasis given to different kinds of outcomes.

A second difficulty is that the understandings may represent outcomes so general that they fail to reflect the unique contribution of a formal course in economics, let alone of an entire curriculum. A student may acquire many of these "understandings" incidentally through media such as newspapers, magazines, radio, television, and conversation. If the purpose of this test is to register such informal gains, well and good. But if the primary purpose of educational evaluation is to be honored, the test will not do. (For that matter, *any* 50-item test will fall far short of a comprehensive evaluation of a course or curriculum.)

Related to the previous difficulty is a third, one that follows from the highly verbal nature of the test content. General verbal ability, apart from specific understanding of economics, may be expected to influence scores appreciably. The test presupposes a good general vocabulary; a knowledge of such words as "accelerates" (trend on graph), "deficit," "dilemma," "dispense with," "divert," "inflation," and "reconcile" will aid the person in his comprehension of certain questions and alternatives. This reviewer [1] obtained correlations of .69 and .64 before and after a trial course in economics, respectively, between scores on Form A of this

test and scores on standardized tests of vocabulary. To overcome somewhat these first three difficulties, the reviewer would prefer that general vocabulary be kept simple where it is not intended to be discriminatory (e.g., in item 33, Form A, answer B, use "keep prices from rising" instead of "fight inflation") and that a separate section or test be devoted entirely to knowledge of basic vocabulary of economics.

General verbal ability also shows itself through reading and general reasoning. Again, apart from what a person knows about economics, his skill in these operations will affect his score on the TEU. Many examples could be given of such items on both forms. Take item 17 on Form A, which asks for "the best use of economic reasoning, using the alternative (or opportunity cost) principle." A person may not be able to define this principle yet be able to piece together clues as to its meaning from alternatives A, B, C, which mention things given up as a result of increased public expenditures on education. The use of the word "compare" in A, the best answer, gives a strong suggestion of weighing alternatives. This reviewer found that only 2 of a sample of 36 graduate students in Education, who were not generally well-informed on economics, could give a rough definition of this principle, but 25 of them could get the multiple choice item right! The difference in proportions was well beyond what one would expect by chance. To substantiate the part that reading and general reasoning most likely play, the reviewer will again draw on the curricular project cited above. Several samples of representative ninth grade classes yielded correlations of about .65 to .70 between TEU scores, either pre- or post-test, and scores on well-known tests of general verbal ability and of .75 or better between either pre- or post-test and scores on well-known tests of reading comprehension.

Test-wiseness, as distinct from such verbal abilities, is also likely to influence scores slightly, but by and large the items are of high technical quality and the effects of test-wiseness are likely to be small.

A combination of the influences described in the preceding paragraphs should go far in explaining some of the results reported in the manual and elsewhere.[2] The results indicate that students without a formal course in economics

1 LOVENSTEIN, MENO L.; FURST, EDWARD J.; JEWETT, R.; AND MACCIA, E. S. *Development of Economics Curricular Materials for Secondary Schools.* An unpublished report to the U.S. Office of Education, Cooperative Research Project No. HS-082, Ohio State University, 1966. Pp. 915. (ERIC ED 014 430)

2 *Op. cit.*

Test of Economic Understanding

score considerably higher than a chance score and on the average only 5 to 6 raw score points below students who have had a course.

The test manual is quite comprehensive. A competent teacher should have little need, however, for the Item Discussion Guide, the 21 pages of which might well have been given over to a classification of each item by subtopic and by educational objective and to data on the frequency of choice of item alternatives before and after instruction.

Overall, the TEU seems to fall short of meeting the stated primary purpose of providing standards for evaluating instruction. It lacks the scope and depth to be sensitive enough for that purpose. Yet it is technically sound, physically attractive, and adequately reliable to provide a good general measure of those essentials of economics that the citizen should know.

CHRISTINE H. McGUIRE, *Professor of Medical Education; Assistant Director and Chief of the Evaluation Studies Section, Center for Educational Development; College of Medicine, University of Illinois, Chicago, Illinois.*

This test consists of two parallel forms, each containing 50 multiple choice questions, designed for use with high school and college classes in introductory economics; in this reviewer's opinion, it is too elementary for use with college classes unless supplemental exercises requiring more sophistication are added. The questions sample fundamental concepts and principles regarding the common functions of any economic system, comparisons of the ways in which these functions are performed in different types of economic organizations, economic growth and stability (including monetary and fiscal policy), and distribution of income.

The test was designed by a committee of eminent economists and the guide they prepared for classroom discussion (which is included in the manual) will be of special assistance to many teachers.

The test items are technically satisfactory, generally clear, unambiguous, and addressed to basic concepts. There are a few questions that involve easy interpretation of limited amounts of data, and a few requiring simple application of principles; for the most part, however, the test appears to sample the student's comprehension rather than his ability to apply and analyze economic concepts and principles. From this reviewer's point of view, that is the greatest weakness of this test. Given the kinds of issues on which citizens are now required to have an opinion and the rhetoric characteristic of so much of our current political and economic debate, this test would be significantly more valuable if additional exercises requiring a somewhat more analytical and interpretative approach were added.

As implied above, the manual contains unusually explicit instructions for administering and scoring, interpreting the results, and using these as a basis for classroom discussion. The discussion guide includes not only a brief rationale explaining the correct answer to each question but also, more importantly, a summary report which helps to structure the classroom discussion of individual items around a few basic kinds of issues. This structured summary includes specific identification of the individual items in each form which sample the several major topics around which the summary is organized, thus enabling the teacher to make a more informed judgment about the relevance of the test to his curriculum and to use the test as a basis for a more integrated and insightful discussion.

The technical data supplied in the manual explain the use of Forms A and B as pre- and post-tests and the method of converting raw scores on each to equivalent scaled scores. The sample population on which the test was normed is adequately described and the standard statistics are provided for that sample. In addition, the percentage in each of two subsamples (those with and those without prior instruction in economics) is reported. The data regarding reliability and validity indicate that the test can be used with reasonable confidence in individual evaluation (reliability coefficients are all greater than .80) and that the differences in mean scores before and after instruction are statistically significant at the .01 level of significance for six of the seven groups tested. However, as the manual itself indicates, content validity must ultimately be judged by the teacher in relation to his own objectives. In considering the validity of the test, one also notes that a correlation of .61 is reported "between intelligence and test performance" and that, given the data used in computing this correlation, that can be considered as "a conservative estimate of the true relation between intelligence test scores and scores on the *Test of Economic Understanding* for students without economic instruction."

Test of Economic Understanding

This reviewer would observe that, under the circumstances, there appears to be an extraordinarily close relation between intelligence test scores and scores on this test; this relation raises some question as to precisely what this test measures.

Given the limitations noted above, the test can be highly recommended to the typical classroom teacher who is interested in obtaining some comparative measure of the level of student achievement in economics or in evaluating the impact of a brief elementary high school course in economics. The data obtained from the test should also prove useful to the classroom teacher in highlighting those areas of instruction in which a specific course has been relatively effective or ineffective.

J Ed Meas 2:252–3 D '65. Robert L. Ebel. This is an excellent test, well deserving of imitation by scholars in other subject fields. * It shows careful regard for modern criteria of excellence in test development and standardization. A comprehensive manual that emphasizes effective use of the test, but does not neglect technical information, accompanies it. Finally it is printed in a readable, attractive style. All of those involved in its production merit high praise. * Scores....were found to yield reliability coefficients in the low .80s. This is about as high as one can expect for a 50-item test of this type. If the test were longer, it could not be administered effectively in a single 50 minute class period. * Form B tended to yield very slightly (0 to 2 units) lower raw scores than Form A. To make the scores from the two forms interchangeable, a system of scaled scores having a mean of 20 and a standard deviation of 5 was devised. One who is not committed to scaled scores as an essential part of the apparatus of mental measurement may wonder whether the slight addition they make to precision of score interpretation is worth the trouble they cost to establish and to interpret, and the meaning they cost by divorcing the reported scores from any direct relation to the test content. An alternative that would avoid the complicaion of scaled scores and preserve some of the content-related meaning of the raw scores, would be to exchange (during test development) some more difficult items from Form B for easier items in the same content classification from Form A. An uncommon but highly useful feature of the manual is a long section (21 pages of the 36 in the manual) intended to guide discussion of the items in each form of the test. This section displays, in parallel columns (1) each test item (2) a paragraph explaining the choice of the best answer, and (3) figures reporting how many students in the national sample answered the item correctly. In addition to encouraging the use of the tests as foci of discussion, and helping to make that discussion productive of sound learning, this section provides direct evidence of the thoughtful care that went into the writing of each test item. If tests of this kind are used widely and intensively as supplementary teaching tools they may tend to lose their effectiveness as measures of achievement. Teachers may begin to teach too specifically the answers to these particular questions, and students may learn to know the answers without understanding them. This raises the question of whether or not it will be possible to produce, every few years, new, equally good forms that do not duplicate the content of the present forms. These tests emphasize general principles and relationships. Most test specialists will approve this emphasis. A few may be inclined to ask whether achievement in economics consists mainly in grasping these generalizations; or whether it may consist also, and perhaps even more extensively, in knowledge of specific facts that justify or illuminate the general principles? Do we, when we emphasize principles and generalizations exclusively in our tests, encourage a kind of abstract, theoretical, verbalistic learning quite divorced from the detailed specific facts needed to establish, and to really understand, the principles and generalizations? If so, and if it is legitimate to test understanding of specific facts as well as understanding of general principles, the field of available questions would be greatly enlarged. Perhaps the validity of the measures of achievement the test yields might even increase. For it may be that tests that emphasize applications and problem solving play into the hands of the bright, test-wise student whose special knowledge of economics is limited. That the tests may lack a very high degree of specificity to special study of economics is suggested by the relatively small mean difference (5 to 6 raw score units out of 50) between students having and students lacking training in economics. This difference might be much greater if the tests placed more emphasis on technical terminology and factual knowledge. Of course, the questions then might also seem

Test of Economic Understanding

less significant, so that the apparent validity of the tests might suffer. The present tests are excellent, but their very excellence raises some hard questions about replacing them or extending their scope. In view of the importance of sound measures of educational achievement in economics (as in all other areas of special study) one may hope that the Committee for Measurement of Economic Understanding will continue to function, and that its example will be emulated in other fields.

[902]

★Test of Understanding in College Economics. 1, 2 semesters college; 1967–68; TUCE; Forms A, B; 2 tests: part 1 ('67, 6 pages) for first semester (macroeconomics), part 2 ('68, 6 pages) for second semester (microeconomics); manual ('68, 19 pages); separate answer sheets (NCS) must be used; $7.50 per 25 tests; $3 per 50 answer sheets; $3 per set of keys and manual; $4 per specimen set; postage extra; scoring service, 35¢ per test; 45(50) minutes; Committee for a College-Level Test of Economic Understanding, Joint Council on Economic Education; Psychological Corporation. *

CHRISTINE H. McGUIRE, *Professor of Medical Education; Assistant Director and Chief of the Evaluation Studies Section, Center for Educational Development; College of Medicine, University of Illinois, Chicago, Illinois.*

A stellar cast of both economists and psychometricians was assembled to prepare this test; its approach, as described in the manual, represents a model which should be more widely emulated. The test specifications with respect to both content categories and objectives are fully detailed; a convincing rationale for those selected is cogently presented; and the specific questions assigned each content and behavioral category are clearly identified.

The test consists of two forms, originally designed as a pre- and post-test for students in an introductory, basic college course in economics. Each form is composed of two parts, each part containing 33 questions designed to sample a semester's work in a typical introductory course. Part 1 is concentrated mainly on macroeconomics and samples basic concepts and principles relating to the functioning of economic systems, income and expenditure theory, monetary and fiscal policies, and economic stabilization and growth; Part 2 is concentrated mainly on microeconomics and samples basic concepts and principles relevant to an understanding of the theory of the firm, factor markets, allocation of resources, international

trade and comparative cost, and comparative economic systems.

Given this splendid introduction, this reviewer was anticipating a much more challenging set of exercises than has actually been provided. While the questions are for the most part technically adequate, clear, well formulated, free of ambiguity, and focused on important concepts and principles, even those designed to test understanding and application are limited to rather simple, obvious situations of the conventional, textbook type. Indeed, the manual includes an explicit caveat warning that the committee "agreed that, in the interests of time, complicated diagrams and extensive tabular material should be avoided." Consequently, the tests contain only a very few questions involving the kind of interpretation and analysis required in reading ordinary newspaper accounts of economic phenomena.

One further limitation of the test must be noted, namely, the relatively low reliability reported. The K-R 20 reliability is especially low (.55 and .57) when Part 1 is used independently as a pre-test; it ranges from .67 to .76 when either part is used as a post-test. While this restricted reliability is undoubtedly attributable to the brevity of the tests, it means that the instruments have serious limitations for use in estimating individual student growth. However, in all fairness, it should be noted that the manual is quite explicit in making these limitations clear to the user and in providing information which is exceedingly helpful in interpreting results under these circumstances.

Further, the manual meets high professional standards in reporting all relevant test statistics, including essential information regarding the groups from which those statistics were derived. Finally, it is extremely helpful in suggesting concrete ways in which the tests can be used and in which the derived data can be legitimately interpreted.

So long as the user is aware of the narrow range of objectives sampled, and of the test's limited usefulness as a measure of individual achievement, it can be highly recommended as a convenient instrument for evaluating the most simple and basic outcomes of an introductory course. This reviewer can only hope that the committee appointed by the Joint Council on Economic Education to design this instrument will continue its work in the direction of developing more sophisticated exercises that will be

Test of Economic Understanding

useful in assessing the kinds of economic understandings that it is so urgent for our citizenry
to develop.

[903]

★The Undergraduate Record Examinations: Economics Test. College; 1969–70; Forms RUR ('69,
21 pages), SUR ('70, 19 pages); descriptive booklet
('70, 8 pages); for more complete information, see
671; 120(140) minutes; Educational Testing Service. *

*For reviews of the testing program, see 671
(2 reviews).*

GEOGRAPHY

[904]

★Geography Achievement Test for Beginning
High School Students. Grade 10; 1965–68; 1 form
('68, 15 pages); manual ['65, 5 pages]; no data on
reliability; separate answer sheets must be used; $5
per 20 tests; 50¢ per specimen set; cash orders postpaid; answer sheets must be provided locally; 75(85)
minutes; Geography Tests Committee (original edition), George Tompkins (revision), and John J.
Doerr (manual); National Council for Geographic
Education. *

REFERENCE
1. GREEN, JOE L. *An Analysis of Factors Related to Academic Achievement in Introductory Geography at the University of Arkansas.* Doctor's thesis, University of Arkansas
(Fayetteville, Ark.), 1970. (*DAI* 31:1510A)

DANA G. KURFMAN, *Supervisor of Social Studies, Prince George's County Public Schools,
Upper Marlboro, Maryland.*

This test for beginning high school students
includes the kinds of questions geography
educators would like to encourage. Most of the
questions fit the comprehension and application
categories of Bloom's Taxonomy. They require
students to interpret information found in a
variety of geographical sources and to apply
their geographic understandings in somewhat
new contexts.

If the test included only such questions, it
would be an effective instrument for determining how well students can read and interpret
geographic materials. However, the meaning of
scores on this test is blurred by the inclusion
of 24 items—about a quarter of the test—
dealing with general geographic knowledge. A
separate test devoted to general knowledge
might be desirable, but the inclusion of general
knowledge items in a test of geographic *skills*
is unfortunate.

The first quarter of the test requires students
to interpret photographs and a large-scale map.
Some of the questions require only a direct
reading of what is present. Others require both

an interpretation of a photograph or map and
the recall of knowledge about similar areas. For
example, an aerial photograph of midwestern
farm terrain is an occasion for students to
identify the kind of relief indicated in the
photograph. Students are also asked to indicate
which of four states is probably represented in
the photograph and the relative size of the
farms shown in comparison to farms in other
parts of the world.

The largest single section of the test consists
of 30 items based upon two small-scale maps.
Most of these items require students to recall
knowledge about various parts of the world and,
particularly, about North America. A student
must know, for example, that a certain letter
on the map indicates Manchuria, rather than
Laos, western Siberia, or Tibet. On another
question, he must know where Alaska is and
in which of four regions on the map most of
Alaska's people and farmlands are found.

A third section of the test includes several
sets of questions based on a table, a series of
graphs, and a series of descriptions. The table
indicates Japanese imports at two different
points in time. Six questions are asked, each
of which requires the ability to interpret and
compare information found in the table. No
external knowledge is necessary to answer the
questions. The set of questions based on pre-
cipitation and temperature graphs of four locations requires external knowledge on the part
of the student, as well as the ability to read
graphs. Finally, the questions based on descriptions are all of the type requiring only external
knowledge on the part of students.

The point is that even questions based on
maps, graphs, and photographs commonly require students to bring external knowledge to
bear. Since this is the case, it is important to
note the kinds of knowledge students are required to have in order to do well on the test.
Unfortunately, the knowledge necessary to do
well on the test is not emphasized in American
schools. Both seventh grade and ninth grade
geography, which students taking this test might
have studied, tend to be cultural-regional geography with relatively little attention given to
Anglo-America. Yet fully one-third of the items
in this test require knowledge of economic and
commercial geography. The second most common type of item requires knowledge of physical geography. Very few items deal with the
cultural geography emphasized in most world

geography courses. Moreover, as many items are based on Anglo-American content as on all the other world regions combined. This means, then, that the test has questionable content validity for United States students.

Although tenth grade norms are provided, additional data are needed. Norms for other grades, particularly seventh and ninth grade, would be useful to teachers and administrators. Item difficulty data would make it possible for teachers to compare their students with the performance of a national sample on particular types of abilities, such as graph reading. However, the most obvious lack is any estimate of test reliability.

A number of minor changes could be made to improve the quality of the test as a measurement instrument. In the first place, it is important that the instructions to students make clear the consequences of guessing. Second, the suggestion that the test be divided into one 30-minute and one 45-minute part is questionable. Students who finish the early part of the test could certainly look at the questions that follow and perhaps answer successfully some that would otherwise have been incorrect. Moreover, the timing of the two sections will make administration of the 45-minute section difficult for schools which have only 40- or 45-minute class periods. Finally, some of the terminology used in discussing the norms, such as the British term "marks," will be difficult for American teachers to understand.

Clearly, this test by the National Council for Geographic Education includes a large number of exemplary items. Unfortunately, this does not assure an exemplary test. To make it so, the authors must decide what will be measured—presumably the ability to read and interpret geographic material—and then base far more of the items on content derived from culture regions other than Anglo-America. In spite of these drawbacks, this is probably the best geography test presently available for high school students.

[905]

★The Graduate Record Examinations Advanced Geography Test. Graduate school candidates; 1966–70; 4 current forms ('66–70, 32–44 pages) ; descriptive booklet ('70, 8 pages) ; for more complete information, see 667; 180(200) minutes; Educational Testing Service. *

For reviews of the testing program, see 667 (1 review) and 5:601 (1 review).

[906]

*Hollingsworth-Sanders Geography Test. 1, 2 semesters in grades 5–7; 1962–64; first published 1962–63 in the Every Pupil Scholarship Test series; Forms A, B, ('64, 2 pages) ; 2 levels labeled Tests 1, 2; manual ('64, 4 pages) ; $1.75 per 25 tests, postage extra; 75¢ per specimen set, postpaid; 30(35) minutes; Leon Hollingsworth and M. W. Sanders; Data Processing and Educational Measurement Center. *

DANA G. KURFMAN, *Supervisor of Social Studies, Prince George's County Public Schools, Upper Marlboro, Maryland.*

If a teacher wishes to determine how well his fifth, sixth, or seventh grade students perform on a test of geographic information, this test has considerable face validity. Multiple choice completions are provided for a large number of descriptive, definitional, and locational facts. Acceptable reliabilities of from .88 to .93 are reported for each of the forms. However, it is difficult to imagine a geography test for the intermediate grades that places no emphasis on geographic skills or relationships. No maps or graphs are used. Question after question asks students to recall locational and definitional information. Moreover, there are problems with the several forms of the test as adequate measures of geographic information.

There are two forms, A and B, of Test 1 and two forms, A and B, of Test 2. Test 1 is intended for use at the end of the first semester and Test 2 at the end of the second semester. There do not appear to be any content differences between Tests 1 and 2, so the basis for assigning one to the first semester and one to the second semester is not very clear. Since about half of the questions deal with the United States and about half with the rest of the world, any given form of the test would be relevant for any group of students whose preparation was roughly of this proportion. This certainly is not the case for most fifth grade students, whose geographic background is based primarily on information about the United States.

More important, perhaps, is the claim that the forms of the test are equivalent. Form A of Test 2 has 17 items based on Africa. This is almost 30 percent of the test. On the other hand, Form B of Test 2 has no African items. Instead, there is an emphasis on Latin America and Asia not found in the other form of the test. If the test makers mean that the forms are equivalent in terms of difficulty, there are problems here, too. A raw score of 36 on Form B places a seventh grade student at the 40th percentile; an identical raw score on Form A places him at the 55th percentile.

It is questionable whether geography tests placing exclusive reliance on informational recall should be used in our schools. Teachers desiring tests of this sort are advised to choose the test form that fits most closely the information conveyed in their geography program. The forms of the *Hollingsworth-Sanders Geography Test* simply are not derived from the same informational domains.

[907]

★The Undergraduate Record Examinations: Geography Test. College; 1969–70; Form K-RUR ('69, 33 pages); descriptive booklet ('70, 8 pages); for more complete information, see 671; 120(140) minutes; Educational Testing Service. *

For reviews of the testing program, see 671 (2 reviews).

HISTORY

[908]

*Advanced Placement Examination in American History. High school students desiring credit for college level courses or admission to advanced courses; 1956–70; Forms RBP ('69, 16 pages), SBP ('70, 18 pages) in 2 booklets (objective, essay); for more complete information, see 662; 180(200) minutes; program administered for the College Entrance Examination Board by Educational Testing Service. *

REFERENCE

1. See 6:1000.

For a review by Harry D. Berg of an earlier form, see 6:1000; for reviews by James A. Field, Jr. and Christine McGuire, see 5:812. For a review of the testing program, see 662.

[909]

*Advanced Placement Examination in European History. High school students desiring credit for college level courses or admission to advanced courses; 1956–70; Forms RBP ('69, 16 pages), SBP ('70, 15 pages) in 2 booklets (objective, essay); for more complete information, see 662; 180(200) minutes; program administered for the College Entrance Examination Board by Educational Testing Service. *

REFERENCES

1–2. See 6:1001.

For a review of the testing program, see 662.

[910]

★CLEP Subject Examination in American History. 1 semester or equivalent, 1 year or equivalent; 1970; for college accreditation of nontraditional study, advanced placement, or assessment of educational achievement; 2 editions: 90 and 45 minute tests; for program accessories, see 664; program administered for the College Entrance Examination Board by Educational Testing Service. *

a) 90 MINUTE EDITION. 1 year or equivalent; tests administered monthly at regional centers throughout the United States; tests also available for institutional testing at any time; Form SCT1 (17 pages); optional essay supplement: Form SCT1A (2 pages); separate answer sheets (SCRIBE) must be used; rental and scoring fee, $5 per student; 90(95) minutes.
b) 45 MINUTE EDITION. 1 semester or equivalent; available only for institutional testing; 2 tests (items in the two tests together parallel those in 90 minute test); separate answer sheets (Digitek-IBM 805, IBM 1230) must be used; rental fee, 75¢ per student; scoring service not available; 45(50) minutes.
  1) *CLEP Subject Examination in American History—Before 1865.* Form SSL2 (9 pages).
  2) *CLEP Subject Examination in American History—After 1865.* Form SSL4 (8 pages).

For reviews of the testing program, see 664 (3 reviews).

[911]

★CLEP Subject Examination in Western Civilization. 1 year or equivalent; 1964–70; for college accreditation of nontraditional study, advanced placement, or assessment of educational achievement; tests administered monthly at regional centers throughout the United States; tests also available for institutional testing at any time; Form MCT ('64, 16 pages); optional essay supplement: Form MCT-B ('64, 2 pages); for program accessories, see 664; rental and scoring fee, $5 per student; postpaid; essay supplement scored by the college; 90(95) minutes, same for essay supplement; program administered for the College Entrance Examination Board by Educational Testing Service. *

For reviews of the testing program, see 664 (3 reviews).

[912]

★Cooperative Social Studies Tests: American History. Grades 7–8, 10–12; 1964–65; Forms A ('64, 9 pages), B ('64, 10 pages); 2 levels: junior high school, senior high school; no specific manual; series manual ('65, 44 pages); student bulletin ('65, 2 pages) for each test; separate answer sheets (Digitek, IBM 805, IBM 1230, SCRIBE) must be used; $6 per 20 tests; $4 per 100 answer sheets; $1.25 per 10 IBM scoring stencils (answer pattern must be punched out locally); Digitek scoring stencils not available; $2 per series manual; $3 per 100 student bulletins; $3 per specimen set of this and 5 other social studies tests; cash orders postpaid; SCRIBE scoring and statistical analysis service, 35¢ per test; 40(50) minutes; Cooperative Tests and Services. *

WILLIAM J. WEBSTER, *Director, System-Wide Evaluation, Dallas Independent School District, Dallas, Texas.*

The junior high school level of the American History test was normed on seventh and eighth graders and places major content emphasis on that period of American History between exploration and the end of the Civil War. The senior high school level was normed on tenth, eleventh, and twelfth graders and places major content emphasis on the period from 1865 to the present. Both levels profess to assess achievement in American History in terms of knowledge and understanding of historical events, issues, and ideas; application of basic knowledge to the generalization of principles and concepts; analysis of relationships; and interpretation of graphs, maps, charts, cartoons, and other communication tools of the social sciences.

The handbook which accompanies the tests supplies information on the technical aspects of the six tests in the series. One of the interesting features of the handbook is a group of tables which classify each item on both forms of each test in the series according to the subject matter content of the item and the level of cognitive skill that is presumed to be required in responding to the item. Since there is a high positive relationship between the nature of a given student's previous experience and the level of cognitive skill used to respond to a given item, some guesswork was required in classifying items on the skill dimension. In cases where doubt existed as to the level of cognitive skill that a particular item was measuring, as was the case in most instances of higher order classification, the item was classified according to the highest skill level that could conceivably be required. This naturally tends to bias the classifications—which generally depict about 31 percent of the items as measuring recall and recognition, 43 percent as measuring understanding, and 26 percent as measuring analysis—toward the higher order cognitive skills. This is particularly true when items are classified as measuring understanding when, for many students, they may be measuring only recall or recognition. The measurement of developed abilities in the skills of synthesis and evaluation is not attempted in either of these tests; however, the measurement of student attainment of these skills is a complex problem which, to this reviewer's knowledge, has never been successfully accomplished in a standardized achievement test of the type reviewed here.

The handbook also provides details on the norming procedures which were used. National norms for each of the tests are based on a combined group of the adjacent grade levels for which each of the tests was designed. A stratified random sample of 44 junior high schools and 73 senior high schools, drawn in May of 1963 and selected in such a manner as to reflect the proportions of public, Roman Catholic, and independent school students in

the national population, formed the norming samples for the junior high and senior high levels.

Internal consistency reliabilities, computed by using the K-R 20, are reported for each form of the test. For Form A of the junior high school level, the reported reliability is .88, while it is .90 for Form B. For the senior high level, both forms yielded a reliability coefficient of .90. Reported reliabilities for each form are based on a sample of 450 students. Since these reliabilities were computed on the basis of groups selected from several schools, they represent overestimates of the coefficients which would be obtained for a more homogeneous group of students within a single school.

The equivalency of alternate forms is assured statistically by providing a common score scale by which raw scores on each form of each test can be equated. The alternate-form reliability for the junior high test is .87, just slightly lower than the previously reported coefficient of internal consistency for that test. The alternate-form reliability for the senior high test is .79, considerably lower than the previously reported coefficient of internal consistency for that test. This would suggest that the two forms of the senior high test are not equivalent. However, further study reveals that the mean biserial correlations for the two forms, a measure of a test's ability to discriminate between low and high ability students, are the same, as well as the percentage of students finishing each form of the test and the previously reported coefficients of internal consistency. Form A is apparently easier, as evidenced by the higher mean raw score attained by the sample given that form. This could be because Form B contains four more items that purport to measure the cognitive skill of analysis than does Form A, and, generally speaking, the higher the cognitive skill required, the more difficult the item.

In summary, both levels of the American History test are relatively superior standardized achievement tests. They represent a sophisticated, scholarly attempt to measure some of the more important outcomes of instruction in American history. Clear and concise suggestions for administering the tests and utilizing the results are included. These tests would provide a fine component part of an overall testing program which should include an assessment of the degree of development of those affective behaviors which are also important objectives of social studies instruction. Despite this reviewer's endorsement of these instruments as valuable standardized achievement tests, it must be emphasized that each test user must make an individual judgment of the validity of each test relative to his own course content and educational objectives.

[913]

★Cooperative Social Studies Tests: Modern European History. Grades 10-12; 1964-65; Forms A, B, ('64, 10 pages); no specific manual; series manual ('65, 44 pages); student bulletin ('65, 2 pages); separate answer sheets (Digitek, IBM 805, IBM 1230, SCRIBE) must be used; $6 per 20 tests; $4 per 100 answer sheets; $1.25 per 10 IBM scoring stencils (answer pattern must be punched out locally); Digitek scoring stencils not available; $2 per series manual; $3 per 100 student bulletins; $3 per specimen set of this and 5 other social studies tests; cash orders postpaid; SCRIBE scoring and statistical analysis service, 35¢ per test; 40(50) minutes; Cooperative Tests and Services. *

JOHN MANNING, *Professor, Department of Humanities and the Office of Evaluation Services, Michigan State University, East Lansing, Michigan.*

There are 70 items in each form of this test, including some items based on maps, charts, cartoons, and one item based on an illustration of a work of art. The items involving recall of factual knowledge outnumber those involving judgment or interpretation. The items based on the cartoons (2 each on 2 cartoons in Form A, 3 each on 2 cartoons in Form B) give some welcome variety. In the latter case, however, the 2 additional items (3 instead of 2 on each cartoon) are purely chronological. Form A, moreover, has 4 strictly chronological items based exclusively on a time chart. In Form A there are 13 items based on 3 maps; in Form B there are 8 based on 2 maps. The map items are mainly factual, and the practice (followed in both forms in connection with an identical map depicting voyages of exploration and discovery) of not identifying the explorer concerned is unnecessarily confusing.

Because of the above and other facts, such as Form B having four items based on three stanzas of verse, it is apparent that the two forms are somewhat disparate in content. *On the whole,* the items per se show good technical construction. There are caveats, nonetheless. Precise dates, for inventions or the application thereof, for example, are open to challenge. How *long* is "long" in the answer option, "a long period of relative stability which fol-

lowed"? Items with stems using such words as "chief goal" or "most important" do not leave enough room for honest differences of opinion or judgment when the optional foils are too close for scholarly comfort.

On the whole, the test format—printing, spacing of items and foils, clarity, and ease of reading—is excellent. The map, identical on both forms, depicting voyages of discovery, however, is fuzzy and confusing to the eye, and should be improved in clarity and enlarged in size. The alternating item notation of options ("A, B, C, D" alternating with "F, G, H, I") forces administrators of this test to purchase answer sheets specifically tailored to this alternating notation, at greater expense to the taxpayer.

The traditional subject matter is well covered; it could be improved by giving the test a more modern emphasis and increasing the number of items based on the 20th Century (at present about one-fourth of the items).

The series manual reports an alternate-forms reliability of .75 and K-R 20 reliabilities of .87 and .89. On the whole, the test seems a bit difficult—the mean scores for Forms A and B being approximately 46 percent of the possible score.

Notwithstanding the above criticisms, if I were teaching the designated high school grades, I would not hesitate to use this test.

[914]

★Cooperative Social Studies Tests: World History. Grades 10-12; 1964-65; Forms A, B, ('64, 11 pages); no specific manual; series manual ('65, 44 pages); student bulletin ('65, 2 pages); separate answer sheets (Digitek, IBM 805, IBM 1230, SCRIBE) must be used; $6 per 20 tests; $4 per 100 answer sheets; $1.25 per 10 IBM scoring stencils (answer pattern must be punched out locally); Digitek scoring stencils not available; $2 per series manual; $3 per 100 student bulletins; $3 per specimen set of this and 5 other social studies tests; cash orders postpaid; SCRIBE scoring and statistical analysis service, 35¢ per test; 40(50) minutes; Cooperative Tests and Services. *

[915]

*Cooperative Topical Tests in American History. High school; 1963-65; CTTAH; 1 form; 8 tests ('63, 6-8 pages); handbook ['65, 30 pages]; "the norm on any one of these tests is a perfect score for all items" the examiner considers relevant to his teaching objectives; $7.25 per 10 sets of all 8 tests; $1 per set of keys; $2 per handbook; $3 per specimen set of all 8 tests; cash orders postpaid; 40(45) minutes; Cooperative Tests and Services. *
a) TEST I, EXPLORATION, COLONIZATION, AND INDEPENDENCE: 1450-1783.
b) TEST 2, FOUNDATIONS OF AMERICAN GOVERNMENT: 1781-1801.

c) TEST 3, GROWTH OF NATIONALISM AND DEMOCRACY:
1801–1840.
d) TEST 4, EXPANSION, CIVIL WAR, AND RECONSTRUC-
TION: 1840–1877.
e) TEST 5, DEVELOPMENT OF INDUSTRIAL AMERICA:
1865–1898.
f) TEST 6, IMPERIALISM, DOMESTIC REFORM, AND THE
FIRST WORLD WAR: 1898–1920.
g) TEST 7, PROSPERITY, DEPRESSION, AND THE NEW
DEAL: 1920–1940.
h) TEST 8, THE SECOND WORLD WAR AND AFTER.

RICHARD E. GROSS, *Professor of Education,
Stanford University, Stanford, California.*

These eight tests are somewhat misleading in
their overall title, since they cover a given
chronological period in American history and
are not topical in the sense that most teachers
use the term; that is, that one be devoted to
foreign affairs, one to labor and economics, etc.
The coverage of the total set of tests, each with
60 items, is comprehensive and there is an
attempt to gain a balance with attention to
chronology, maps, personalities, documents, and
quotations, as well as events. For teachers ap-
proaching American history primarily in terms
of a chronological organization, these tests will
assist in evaluating the progress of their students at the end of a unit. Teachers who are
concerned primarily with the measurement of
achievement but who do not have the time or
skills to produce valid and reliable instruments
will be aided by the use of these tests. The total
battery is too long to serve as a final examination for a course, at least within the amount
of time normally given for such assessment at
the end of the high school year.

Each of the eight tests is divided into several
subsections—a total of 28 major subheadings—
and some of these, but not most, are topical.
These particular headings could be used to
assess weaknesses in specific areas and could
provide guidance for remedial or review work.
The information resulting from this use could
also be helpful in planning for future content
emphasis, as well as in suggesting ways in which
to individualize instruction. Items dealing with
topics not part of the content of the unit taught
by the teacher could also be eliminated in the
taking or scoring of the test.

Unfortunately, most items are knowledge
reproduction questions. Very few attempt to get
the pupil to think analytically, in depth, on his
own. (This is possibly an inherent weakness of
all tests of this sort as they are normally constructed and for the purposes for which they
are typically used.) Few items are skill oriented

in terms of the expectations of the "new" social
studies. There is little attention to generalizing
abilities. Indeed, in terms of the process and
structural orientation now recommended for
the field, in toto these tests can be questioned
as to whether they really meet emerging prime
objectives. At least some questions, however,
call for the use of higher mental processes.
Items 35–37 of Test 1 do, for example, ask for
evidence in support of particular conclusions.
Certain questions vary from the typical objective query and may prove interesting to the
testee, as well as intriguing to the mentor
seeking a greater variety in test items; examples
here are items 24–28 in Test 4, 22–25 in Test 6,
and 27–31 in Test 7. Nevertheless, the test
would be strengthened by the inclusion of more
cartoons, graphs, tables, pictures, and other
elements measuring analytical abilities. A number of individual tests have no such visual items,
and Test 8, item 42, for example, provides a
lone picture which really serves no purpose.
Pupils could just as well have been asked which
reason has led workers to strike in recent years
rather than presenting a picture of striking
laborers. Something in a picture should be an
integral part of the test item; otherwise, it
seems useless. While one does not wish to be
overly querulous about individual items, the
above item is an example of several on each
test for which teachers might question the
appropriateness of the foils. Two of the most
important reasons for strikes in recent years,
mounting inflation and the struggle for increased fringe benefits, are not even mentioned
in the item and may be more important than the
correct answer given.

There is an overemphasis on questions pertaining to political and economic history. Items
devoted to black history, social and cultural
history, and economic geography are either
absent or, at best, minimal. There is no question
that items pertaining to some of the most recent
serious developments in the United States are
in inadequate balance.

This reviewer found only one outright printing error in the tests. The word "people" in
item 45, Test 6, should be changed to read
"peoples." The test booklets are not reusable.
The handbook accompanying the tests is quite
complete, including data on reliability, validity,
item discrimination characteristics, and test
difficulty. Some might differ on the high reliability reported because of contrary opinions on

Cooperative Topical Tests in American History

the appropriateness of the number of students used to establish reliability or because of a question as to the representativeness of the schools employed and their student populations.

As stated initially, this is a good test of a comprehensive chronological nature when the teacher is satisfied with a heavy emphasis on simple recall or recognition questions. If, in addition to measuring knowledge, testing abilities to interpret, assay evidence, and build social studies skills is of concern to the teacher, these tests would not by themselves allow him to evaluate the fulfillment of his objectives adequately.

[916]

*Crary American History Test, Revised Edition. Grades 10–13; 1950–65; Forms E, F, ('65, 8 pages); manual ('65, 18 pages); $8.70 per 35 tests; $1 per key; separate answer sheets (Digitek, IBM 805, IBM 1230) may be used; $2.30 per 35 IBM 805 answer sheets; $2.80 per 35 Digitek or IBM 1230 answer sheets; 70¢ per key; $1.50 per specimen set; postage extra; scoring service, 19¢ and over per test; 40(50) minutes; Ryland W. Crary; Harcourt Brace Jovanovich, Inc. *

REFERENCES

1–2. See 5:816.

RICHARD E. GROSS, *Professor of Education, Stanford University, Stanford, California.*

Each form of this 76-item test represents a comprehensive survey of American history from the colonial period to recent years. Because items from different periods are mixed together, the test is useful only at the end of a course, unless the teacher wishes to use it as a pretest. Thus, unfortunately, the test is of little practical benefit in identifying strengths or weaknesses during the school year and cannot be used to aid in instructional planning for classes or individual students undergoing the course. The survey nature of the test also makes it less desirable for measuring achievement in courses which have emphasized a depth approach on certain topics or which have focused on certain eras at the expense of general coverage. As is usual with these kinds of objective tests, many of the aims frequently stated for the high school United States history course do not seem to be evaluated by this instrument.

Perhaps 76 items are sufficient to assay the spread of knowledge over the general field of American history, but this reviewer would wish to couple the spotty coverage with other kinds of evaluation. The test does include some items which measure the understanding of historical facts by attempting to have the pupil make

applications; examples include item 1, Form F, and item 43, Form E. There is some attempt to include study skill questions which should help measure these increasingly important objectives—for example, items 45–47, Form E, and item 44, Form F. Each form also includes one map question, which focuses on the territorial growth of the United States, but aside from this, there is no use of pictures or cartoons and the analysis of charts, graphs, and tables is entirely disregarded. Too many of the questions emphasize primarily simple recognition or recall. Too many items seek merely the identification of specific dates or events, of particular men and women, of specialized terminology, and of quotations from documents. There are very few "why" questions or items calling for any analysis in depth using the higher mental processes. Even though some skill-type queries are included, more of these are in order.

As is true of most tests which focus on the attainment of facts, this examination fails to meet the emerging purposes of the new social studies, such as process and inquiry competencies, the assessment of many key concepts, and the ability to generalize as a result of a grasp of the structure of the discipline. Another weakness is the failure to include items of great social import in the 1960's; this includes, particularly, domestic difficulties such as the racial conflict and urban unrest that have characterized America during this period. A new edition of this test should certainly update questions of this nature to reflect changing concerns. Contemporary problems should serve to a greater extent as guides to the selection of earlier historical content to be examined.

The test manual provides helpful information for the teacher for interpreting results in terms of percentiles and stanines based on various population groups. The availability of alternate forms of the test for separate classes of students or to provide different makeup tests contributes to confidence in the security of the evaluation. The availability of separate answer sheets permits the reuse of test booklets and helps reduce costs. In addition, the tests can be machine scored, which is of advantage when dealing with large numbers of students.

For teachers emphasizing a factual evaluation of a survey-type which focuses on a number of key persons, events, and institutions in American society, this test will suffice. For teachers wishing to emphasize many of the analytical and skill-oriented objectives now commonly listed for the field, this test will be insufficient.

For a review by Frederick H. Stutz of the original edition, see 5:816; for a review by Edgar B. Wesley, see 4:688.

[917]

Cummings World History Test, Revised Edition. Grades 9–13; 1950–66; Forms E, F, ('66, 8 pages); manual ('66, 18 pages); no norms for grade 13; $8.70 per 35 tests; $1 per key; separate answer sheets (Digitek-IBM 805, IBM 1230) may be used; $2.30 per 35 Digitek-IBM 805 answer sheets; $2.80 per 35 IBM 1230 answer sheets; 70¢ per scoring stencil; $1.50 per specimen set; postage extra; scoring service, 19¢ and over per test; 40(50) minutes; Howard H. Cummings; Harcourt Brace Jovanovich, Inc. *

REFERENCE

1. See 5:817.

JOHN MANNING, *Professor, Department of Humanities and the Office of Evaluation Services, Michigan State University, East Lansing, Michigan.*

This test was constructed in conformity with generally accepted standards and procedures. It is a 1966 revision of a 1950 edition. Standardized in 1965, it suffers, as do most such tests, from being partially outdated almost from the onset of publication. The test has been cut from 80 to 70 items chosen from 130 preliminary items (an improvement over the 80 selected from 100 preliminary items in 1949). The 1966 manual, increased from 7 to 19 pages, is impressive in its presentation of information concerning the nature and content of the test, the procedures followed in its development, its analysis, and standardization; directions for administration and scoring; explanation of stanines, standard scores, percentiles, norms, and method of scoring; and suggested interpretation and possible uses of the results.

The item selection process was based on the scores of 4,685 students in 32 high schools in 23 states (which is an improvement in comparison to a base of 1,900 students in 17 high schools in 7 states used in 1949). Yet, all three schools selected as representative samples of the Midwest were in Wisconsin!

National percentile and stanine norms are given, and the results for each test may be expressed in normalized standard scores. The test manual gives clear procedures for comparing a student's score on the history test with his intelligence score by means of tables presenting concurrent scores on the history test and on the *Otis Quick-Scoring Mental Ability Test* so that a measure of the student's learning ability may be compared with his achievement in history. The problem remains, however, that high or low learning ability may, or may not, be the sole reason for low or high achievement.

The format of the tests and manual, the spacing of both items and options, the type, the clarity of the directions are all commendable. Answer sheets may be scored by hand or by IBM machine or scanner, which gives good adaptability.

A great deal is made in the manual of the inclusion of a fifth foil to each item, marked DK, for "don't know," as a "distractor" for guessing. "Students at all levels tended to make increasing use of this fifth option as the difficulty of the items increased," boasts the manual. What may not be obvious to the 10th grade teacher, however, is that student use of this option per se automatically gives a higher coefficient of difficulty for those items in which it is selected *in lieu of* the correct option, no matter how arrived at. What may be gained, therefore, in eliminating contamination of students' scores through guessing, by use of the DK, is offset by contamination of the statistics. Since the test purports to be a measure of *achievement,* it would appear that objectivity of statistics should not be sacrificed in attempts to gain student psychological or personality data. Another factor that may not be obvious to the 10th grade teacher is that not only is the coefficient of difficulty pushed up slightly by the use of the DK but also that the coefficient of discrimination follows suit and, when added to the Flanagan formula, gives rather optimistic figures for item discrimination. An astute student (or any student if so instructed), moreover, could conceivably raise his score simply by ignoring the DK option altogether.

The gimmick of using "a, b, c, d, DK" to number the options in one item with the alternating use of "e, f, g, h, DK" in the next item is repeated in the revised test forms. This forces test users to purchase the publisher's answer sheets specifically designed to match this peculiar notation—at greater expense to purchasers of the test (namely, the taxpayer) than would be the case if more standardized numbering of all options were followed.

The manual claims that the test measures not only "factual knowledge" but also "conceptual understanding," yet tabulations indicate that, in

Form E, of the 46 items measuring political content, 72 percent measure factual knowledge over against only 28 percent measuring understanding.

Moreover, while the manual claims that the test measures appropriate topics included "in current educational material," nevertheless, problems remain for a test purporting to be of national use. For example, some world history courses put a major stress on the history of ancient Greece and Rome, yet Form E contains only 5 items, and Form F only 6 items relevant to history before 500 A.D., while Form E contains only 17 items, and Form F only 18 items concerning history before 1700. Under such circumstances, teachers obviously would have to make additional items of their own. This necessity would make the standardized test, with all its complicated statistical information, of very limited value.

The same difficulty could arise with the small number of items on the Orient and in regard to only 3 items on Russia, compared to 6 on Great Britain, or 4 on the Balkans in Form E, or 4 on Russia compared to 6 on Great Britain and 5 on France in Form F. A noteworthy improvement in the revised test, however, is the inclusion of many more items involving history since World War II and also of items which attempt to reflect changes of content and emphasis in the instruction of world history during the past 10 to 12 years.

The technical quality of the items themselves *on the whole* is better than average. But the revised tests still show some of the technical weaknesses of the old. For example, item 23 in Form F: "His book, *The Origin of Species*, attempted to account for the beginnings of life forms—[a] Charles Darwin [b] Adam Smith [c] John Locke [d] Isaac Newton [DK]." In the first place, the "stem" is not strictly accurate, and probably should read something like "the diversity (rather than *beginnings*) of life forms"; in the second place, only one of the options has reference to a biologist; Mendel or Lamarck, for example, would have been more plausible distractors than Adam Smith or John Locke! A set of 10 items in both Forms E and F based on options consisting entirely of lists of names seems a bit too factual; for example, surely something less purely factual than Darwin's being the author of *The Origin of Species* could be substituted. In both forms, however, items 61 through 66, keyed to a set

of options involving understanding, are much superior. One could not say the same for the set in Form E, items 67–70, based on a genealogy of a royal family of Europe in comparison with a slightly better analogous set, in Form F, based on a diagram of the United Nations organization. Other items objectionable because of the disparity of the options given include 22, 29, 40, and 42 in Form E; and 20, 25, 35, and 56 in Form F.

WILLIAM J. WEBSTER, *Director, System-Wide Evaluation, Dallas Independent School District, Dallas, Texas.*

The *Cummings World History Test*, designed to measure the "extent to which high school students have attained important educational objectives of world history courses as typically taught in grade 10," consists of two forms, each of which includes 70 multiple choice items. The fifth choice in the 5-response items is a guessing distracter which allows the student to respond "don't know." The rationale for the guessing distracter is that its use in the experimental tryout of the test revealed that students tended to make increasing use of it as the difficulty of items increased, while the number of questions omitted tended to remain constant throughout the progressive ranges of difficulty. In an actual testing situation, however, students would tend to guess rather than use the distracter, since no provision is made for providing penalties for guessing in the scoring of the test. If such penalties were provided for, the guessing distracter would serve a more useful function.

The manual asserts that the objectives and content of the test were drawn from "widely-used textbooks....representative courses of study, publications of educational and social studies societies, recommendations by experts in the field of social studies education, and pronouncements of national and state committees." According to the manual, test items were designed to measure "factual knowledge and conceptual understanding." The majority of items (the manual claims approximately 70 percent) measure the student's ability to recognize historical facts. Many of the items in this category are uninspiring, particularly the ones requiring rote recall of the names of various people throughout history (items 20–29 on both forms of the test). The remaining 30 percent of the items on each form purport to measure "conceptual understanding." Success in this endeavor is difficult to ascertain from studying the items, since the nature of previous instruction is often the deciding factor as to whether or not a given item is measuring "understanding" or rote recall for a particular student.

The test has two major failings in the realm of content. First, it fails to provide the student with any opportunity to exercise developed abilities in such skills as application, analysis, synthesis, and evaluation, all legitimate objectives of social studies. This is admittedly a difficult task; however, it is time that those concerned with the construction of standardized tests in the social studies address themselves to the reality of the testing problem. Second, it fails to measure important affective objectives of world history instruction. The manual states that "a primary obligation and objective of world history instruction is the development of social awareness and intelligent citizenship," a statement with which this reviewer wholeheartedly concurs. However, unlike the author of the test, the reviewer feels that such behaviors can and must be measured in an objective manner if a test is to do an adequate job of measuring the outcomes of a year's instruction in world history.

The 70 items that comprise each form of the test were selected, on the basis of item analysis data and teacher comments, from preliminary forms of 130 items each. The item tryout and standardization were carried out simultaneously in a dual research program conducted in the spring of 1965. It would have been more appropriate to carry out the item tryout, make adjustments on the basis of the data, and then carry out the standardization procedures on a new sample. Split-half reliabilities for various groups range from .87 to .94, with median .92.

The manual reports that the forms are equivalent in both content and level of cognitive performance measured and provides equivalency charts to illustrate this point. These charts, however, can only provide approximations with regard to the level of cognitive performance measured because of the aforementioned relationship between the nature of previous instruction and the cognitive level at which a given student is actually performing in response to a particular stimulus. In addition to the similar reliability coefficients, the two forms have the same mean difficulty index (.49). Furthermore, it was found that the two

raw score distributions were equivalent at all points along the distribution curves. Unfortunately, the conclusive evidence for equivalence, the correlation between the two forms, is not available.

The manual contains clear and explicit instructions for the administration and scoring of the test. Norms are reported for college-preparatory, non-college-preparatory, and all students, based on 4,685 world history students from 32 public schools in 23 states. A lucid explanation of the interpretation of results includes suggestions for interpreting the percentile ranks, stanines, and normalized standard scores.

In summary, the technical aspects of the test appear to be better than average for tests in the social studies area. It could be used by those whose objectives of world history instruction include a considerable emphasis on the memorization of historical facts. Close scrutiny of the test is recommended for any potential user to insure that the facts required by the test are the same facts that are considered important in the user's world history program.

For reviews by Dorothy C. Adkins and Howard R. Anderson of the original edition, see 4:689.

[918]

*Emporia American History Test. 1, 2 semesters high school; 1962–64; first published 1962–63 in the Every Pupil Scholarship Test series; Forms A, B, ('64, 4 pages); 2 levels labeled Tests 1, 2; manual ('64, 3 pages); $1.75 per 25 tests, postage extra; 75¢ per specimen set, postpaid; 40(45) minutes; Shirley Meares and M. W. Sanders; Data Processing and Educational Measurement Center. *

HOWARD R. ANDERSON, *Senior Consulting Editor, Social Studies, Houghton Mifflin Company, Boston, Massachusetts.*

The two-page manual for the *Emporia American History Test* states that it "was constructed for use as an achievement test in high school classes which cover the field in a one-year course. * Test I is designed to cover the work of the first semester; Test II covers the second semester." The allocation of items suggests that a class will "cover" the period from the discovery of America through the Civil War in the first semester, from Reconstruction to the present in the second semester. This assumption is much less valid today than it was a decade or more ago. Today courses in American history tend to include concepts and materials

Cummings World History Test

from other social sciences and even from the humanities. The course may not be taught in consecutive semesters, and quite often the division is made not at 1865 but following Reconstruction. Or the course may be organized topically. The publisher's catalog provides this one-sentence description of the test: "Covers historical events, concepts, vocabulary and personages." There is no suggestion that the test is concerned with values or the skills of analysis.

The four forms include no items based on maps, charts, graphs, cartoons, pictures, or reading selections. Most of the items stress simple recall of information.

Some of the test items have stems that are burdened with too much information: "White servants who bonded themselves to a colonial master for a fixed number of years in exchange for transportation to the colonies from Europe were called: 1. serfs 2. dissenters 3. indentured servants 4. loyalists." The fact that the word "servants" is found both in the stem and in one of the responses provides a "give-away" clue to the answer. It should be remembered that the first blacks brought to Virginia were indentured servants and not slaves. The white indentured servant obtained his passage to America from a ship captain, who in turn received money covering the cost of transportation from the planter taking over the indenture. For various reasons, therefore, this is not a good test item; it is merely representative of many weak items.

At times the foils provided for an item are so carelessly selected that a correct answer by no means proves that the pupil knows the information that seemingly is called for.

A pupil who recalls item 8, Test 2B will certainly find it easier to answer item 10, and vice versa. The former item states, "From the end of the Civil War until 1900 the pace of industrial change in the United States: 1. grew faster and faster 2. was unchecked by panics or depressions 3. remained relatively slow 4. was halted by the growth of labor unions." The latter states, "The spectacular growth of industry following the Civil War was: 1. limited almost entirely to the Northeast 2. not evident in the Midwest 3. not confined to any one section of the country 4. based on a very unstable foundation." Actually, the stem of item 10 suggests the answer to item 8. How many of the four possible responses to item 10 make sense?

The two forms of each semester test seem less "equivalent" than might be desirable. Form

1A includes four items on Spain's role in the New World prior to 1588; Form 1B has none. Form 2A includes 12 items dealing with wars and international affairs in the period since World War I, compared to four such items in Form 2B.

The manual reports 50th percentile scores of 68 for Form 1A and 69 for Form 1B. Yet Form 1A includes 135 items; Form 1B only 120. The 50th percentile scores are 59 for Form 2A and 72 for Form 2B. The former has 130 items; the latter, 135. The reliabilities of the four forms of the test by the split-half method are .94, .94, .92, and .91, respectively.

The manual promises, "The test results may be profitably used....(1) for determining pupil achievement; (2) for checking the efficiency of instruction; (3) for assigning school marks; (4) for analyzing pupil and class weaknesses; and (5) for motivation of pupil effort." These claims have no merit unless one accepts the *Emporia American History Test* as a valid instrument for evaluating the outcomes of instruction in American history. This reviewer doubts that the test in question squares with present goals of instruction. Indeed, it seems not to be a good test even by the standards of a generation ago.

[919]
*The Graduate Record Examinations Advanced History Test.** Graduate school candidates; 1939–70; 5 current forms ('64–70, 36–40 pages); descriptive booklet ('70, 11 pages); for more complete information, see 667; 180(200) minutes; Educational Testing Service. *

REFERENCE
1. LANNHOLM, GERALD V.; MARCO, GARY L.; AND SCHRADER, WILLIAM B. *Cooperative Studies of Predicting Graduate School Success*, pp. 46-53. Graduate Record Examinations Special Report No. 68-3. Princeton, N.J.: Educational Testing Service, August 1968. Pp. 92. *

For a review by Robert H. Ferrell of an earlier form, see 5:818. For reviews of the testing program, see 667 (1 review) and 5:601 (1 review).

[920]
*Hollingsworth-Sanders Intermediate History Test.** 1, 2 semesters in grades 5–6; 1962–64; first published 1962–63 in the Every Pupil Scholarship Test series; Forms A, B, ('64, 4 pages); 2 levels labeled Tests 1, 2; manual ('64, 3 pages); $1.75 per 25 tests, postage extra; 75¢ per specimen set, postpaid; 30(35) minutes; Leon Hollingsworth and M. W. Sanders; Data Processing and Educational Measurement Center. *

[921]
*Meares-Sanders Junior High School History Test.** 1, 2 semesters in grades 7–8; 1962–64; first published 1962–63 in the Every Pupil Scholarship Test

series; Forms A, B, ('64, 4 pages); 2 levels labeled Tests 1, 2; manual ('64, 3 pages); $1.75 per 25 tests, postage extra; 75¢ per specimen set, postpaid; 30(40) minutes; Shirley Meares and M. W. Sanders; Data Processing and Educational Measurement Center. *

[922]
*Sanders-Buller World History Test. 1, 2 semesters high school; 1962–64; first published 1962–63 in the Every Pupil Scholarship Test series; Forms A, B, ('64, 4 pages); 2 levels labeled Tests 1, 2; manual ('64, 3 pages); $1.75 per 25 tests, postage extra; 75¢ per specimen set, postpaid; 40(45) minutes; M. W. Sanders and Robert Buller; Data Processing and Educational Measurement Center. *

JOHN MANNING, *Professor, Department of Humanities and Office of Evaluation Services, Michigan State University, East Lansing, Michigan.*

This test is intended to cover a one-year high school course in world history—ancient, medieval, and modern. According to the manual, the items were selected from the "content of several leading textbooks." Forty minutes is allotted for each form, although the number of items per form varies from 85 to 120. The score is the number of correct responses per test. Percentile norms are based on 9,661 students from 452 schools participating in four nationwide testing programs.

The median difficulties of the four forms in the standardization population range from 40 to 45 percent of a possible score. All forms seem to be excessively factual and too difficult, and a number of individual items and/or options seem confusing. On the other hand, some items appear too easy. There is the confusing practice of matching a book and a man, or a man and a historical period, incorrectly in three out of the four options. A number of items have an excessive amount of reading per item, involving only four (but long) choices. Consider a single option which reads: "American victories at Guadalcanal, Coral Sea, the Battle of Midway, Tarawa, Saipan, Guam, Tinian, Iowa Jima, Leyte Gulf, and Okinawa." Presumably, testing time could be used to better advantage than reading such a long option. It is difficult to see, moreover, how an average student could be expected to do 85 to 120 items besprinkled with such lengthy options and items in the allotted 40 minutes. The time limit allows one-third to one-half minute per item; an average of three-fourths minute per item is more customary.

In some items containing *not* in the stem, the "correct" option is tainted with half truth and half falsehood: "The increase in the supply

of gold and silver which caused general deflation as prices increased." Students should be provided with options that are clear-cut, not those which may be construed as neither fish nor fowl!

High school students who can score in the upper percentiles on this test would most likely be "up" in their knowledge of facts in world history, be rapid readers, and have high IQ's. For the less scholastically inclined student, the test would be unnecessarily discouraging.

[923]
*Social Studies 10 (American History): Minnesota High School Achievement Examinations. Grade 10; 1955–71; new or revised form issued each May; Form EH Rev. ['71, c1968, 8 pages]; no specific manual; series manual ('71, 16 pages); no data on reliability; 15¢ per test; separate answer sheets (IBM 1230) may be used; 10¢ per answer sheet including scoring service; $1 per series manual; postage extra; $1.10 per specimen set, postpaid; 60(65) minutes; edited by V. L. Lohmann; American Guidance Service, Inc. *

For a review by Howard R. Anderson of earlier forms, see 5:810.

[924]
*Social Studies 11 (World History): Minnesota High School Achievement Examinations. Grade 11; 1955–71; new or revised form issued each May; Form EH Rev. ['71, c1968, 7 pages]; no specific manual; series manual ('71, 16 pages); no data on reliability; 15¢ per test; separate answer sheets (IBM 1230) may be used; 10¢ per answer sheet including scoring service; $1 per series manual; postage extra; $1.10 per specimen set, postpaid; 60(65) minutes; edited by V. L. Lohmann; American Guidance Service, Inc. *

[925]
★The Undergraduate Record Examinations: History Test. College; 1969–70; Forms K-RUR ('69, 24 pages), SUR ('70, 22 pages); descriptive booklet ('70, 8 pages); for more complete information, see 671; 120(140) minutes; Educational Testing Service. *

For reviews of the testing program, see 671 (2 reviews).

POLITICAL SCIENCE

[926]
★CLEP Subject Examination in American Government. 1 semester or equivalent; 1965–70; for accreditation of nontraditional study, advanced placement, or assessment of educational achievement; tests administered monthly at regional centers throughout the United States; tests also available for institutional testing at any time; Form NCT ('65, 16 pages); optional essay supplement: Form NCT-A ('65, 2 pages); for program accessories, see 664; rental and scoring fee, $5 per student; postpaid; essay supplement scored by the college; 90(95) minutes, same

for essay supplement; program administered for the College Entrance Examination Board by Educational Testing Service. *

For reviews of the testing program, see 664 (3 reviews).

[927]

★Cooperative Social Studies Tests: American Government. Grades 10–12; 1964–65; Forms A ('64, 10 pages), B ('64, 11 pages); no specific manual; series manual ('65, 44 pages); student bulletin ('65, 2 pages); separate answer sheets (Digitek, IBM 805, IBM 1230, SCRIBE) must be used; $6 per 20 tests; $4 per 100 answer sheets; $1.25 per 10 IBM scoring stencils (answer pattern must be punched out locally); Digitek scoring stencils not available; $2 per series manual; $3 per 100 student bulletins; $3 per specimen set of this and 5 other social studies tests; cash orders postpaid; SCRIBE scoring and statistical analysis service, 35¢ per test; 40(50) minutes; Cooperative Tests and Services. *

HOWARD D. MEHLINGER, *Associate Professor and Director, Social Studies Development Center, Indiana University, Bloomington, Indiana.*

The subject matter for this American government test was selected from five major topics: the Constitution and the national government; state and local government; citizenship and political participation; government services, controls, and finances; national defense and international relations. These topics and the related test items constitute a fair and equitable representation of excellent American government instruction. Somewhat more attention is given to "national defense and international relations" than may be true of many high school courses, and one might wish for a few items that measure explicitly students' comprehension of the social-psychological bases of politics. Nevertheless, the test transcends the narrow legalistic approach toward American government that has too frequently marred other achievement tests and it samples students' understanding of political processes in the United States.

The test items have been designed to test three levels of cognition: remembering, understanding, and analyzing. Approximately equal proportions of items are directed toward remembering and analyzing; a slightly higher percentage measure students' understanding of American government. Taken as a group, the items exemplify imaginative test construction; and they are fair measures of student knowledge of American government without regard to specific textbooks. In addition, the writers suc-

ceeded in preparing a test remarkably free of items that were important four or five years earlier but are now out of date.

The quality of the test reflects the attention given to its preparation. The publishers used many leading professionals—social studies education professors, political scientists, and social studies teachers and supervisors—as advisors, item writers, and test reviewers. The result is a test that will reward excellent teaching of American government.

The manual not only provides answers to the test, item content classification, and norms tables; it also provides the means by which the user can equate scores on this test with those of earlier Cooperative tests of social studies. The manual has been designed for use by those without special training in statistics and test construction. Even teachers who lack special training in the use of achievement tests will readily learn from the manual how to administer the test, interpret the results, and utilize test results to evaluate and improve instruction.

While this test is probably the best of its kind and accurately reflects better-than-average classroom instruction about American government, this reviewer believes that it also demands too little of formal instruction. Studies by Langton and Jennings and by others [1] reveal that courses in American government are largely redundant for many students. Students acquire their political knowledge from many sources, including parents, mass media, and peer groups. Much of the information presented in typical American government courses is already known to many high school seniors prior to instruction. On the basis of the Jennings study, one is led to speculate that bright students who have high political interest are likely to perform as well on this test as high achievers in American government classes. If this proved to be true, it would be less the fault of the test makers and more the fault of course designers. Nevertheless, such an outcome would question the efficacy of an achievement test that aspires to measure instruction.

If achievement tests influence instruction, as is frequently asserted, test designers can move

1 LANGTON, KENNETH P., AND JENNINGS, M. KENT. *Political Socialization and the High School Civics Curriculum in the United States.* Ann Arbor, Mich.: Department of Political Science, University of Michigan, 1967. For a useful, nontechnical review of research on political socialization and its relationship to high school civics and government courses, see *Political Socialization of American Youth: Implications for Secondary Social Studies* by John J. Patrick. Washington, D.C.: National Council for the Social Studies, 1967. Pp. 88.

instruction along desirable paths by the types of items they include. With regard to American government instruction, it seems useful to encourage teachers to include topics that would enhance pupils' understanding of politics, especially the kind of understanding that is not easily available outside the classroom. Currently, high school civics and American government courses lag far behind modern social scientific approaches to the study of politics. Not only do the courses fail to include recent knowledge about politics acquired through social science investigation—for example, knowledge about the political behavior of typical citizens—but also little attention is devoted to teaching students the rudimentary skills of social scientific study, e.g., operationalizing definitions, identifying and relating social variables, stating testable hypotheses. Students are not likely to acquire these skills outside the classroom. American government teachers can and should teach such skills.

In summary, this test is an excellent achievement test for existing high school courses in American government. It fairly and equitably measures good instruction in current courses. Whatever weaknesses it may have stem primarily from gaps in current instructional practices rather than from failures in the test itself.

[928]

★Cooperative Social Studies Tests: Civics. Grades 8–9; 1964–65; Forms A, B, ('64, 11 pages); no specific manual; series manual ('65, 44 pages); student bulletin ('65, 2 pages); separate answer sheets (Digitek, IBM 805, IBM 1230, SCRIBE) must be used; $6 per 20 tests; $4 per 100 answer sheets; $1.25 per 10 IBM scoring stencils (answer pattern must be punched out locally); Digitek scoring stencils not available; $2 per series manual; $3 per 100 student bulletins; $3 per specimen set of this and 5 other social studies tests; cash orders postpaid; SCRIBE scoring and statistical analysis service, 35¢ per test; 40(50) minutes; Cooperative Tests and Services. *

VINCENT N. CAMPBELL, *Associate Program Director, Social and Educational Research Program, American Institutes for Research, Palo Alto, California.*

This is a better than average achievement test in civics. Its coverage of knowledge of civics is quite comprehensive, and it emphasizes the realities of contemporary political and economic institutions, not just the traditional textbook structure of government so often found in tests in the past. As is usual with standardized tests, there is, unfortunately, no indication of the specific educational objectives being measured.

This lack is partially compensated for by provision in the manual of a two-way table showing the classification of each item in one of five content areas and one of three general skills. The content areas are the Constitution and the national government; state and local government; citizenship and political participation; government services, controls, and finances; and national defense and international relations. The three skill areas are remembering, understanding, and analyzing. Comparing the two forms by this classification suggests that they are testing generally similar domains of performance.

The manual indicates that the test may be used to evaluate and compare the achievement of groups, to guide individual students, and to evaluate and revise curriculums. For the last purpose, the publisher recommends that schools use results to evaluate achievement of specific goals in the social studies curriculum, which is commendable advice, though they leave it entirely up to the schools to decide what specific goals are measured by the test items. They recommend that each test user make an individual judgment of content validity with respect to his own course content and educational aims. Some users may notice in doing this that there is no coverage of civil rights and only slight attention to constitutional liberties. The specific area given least attention, in my opinion, concerns what individual citizens can do to influence civic decisions. This should be the main focus of a civics course if participation in the democratic process is a general goal. This opens up the whole area of measuring to what extent the student actually does participate in civic matters, an area untouched by all standardized tests which restrict themselves to questions with multiple choice answers.

Nearly all items in both forms seem well constructed and have excellent foils. The test makes good use of cartoons as a basis for questions on political conflict over current social issues. Poor readers at grades 8 and 9 may be handicapped somewhat by some of the longer words used, but it can be argued that this knowledge of vocabulary is an integral part of achievement in civics.

The instructions for administration of the test and interpretation of results are clear, adequate, and sensible. Users are provided with tables of percentile ranks and percentile bands. The manual is cautious in recommending interpretation of score differences and in relating achievement scores to verbal ability scores. As with other standardized tests, there is too much emphasis on ranking individuals relative to each other and not enough on assessing specifically what a given individual or group has achieved. There is a good description of the procedure used to equate the two forms as to mean difficulty. The description of how norms were established seems honest and thorough and at the end includes a list of the schools involved. The sample for setting norms included Roman Catholic and independent schools as well as public schools.

The manual presents a table showing the number of schools invited to participate in the norming program for the social studies tests along with the number of schools which actually provided data. This information enables the test user to estimate the possible bias in the norms due to differences between responding and non-responding schools. Unfortunately, the figures for total number of schools invited are available only for senior high school tests and not for the two junior high tests, which include civics.

SUMMARY. This is a quite good test of *knowledge* of civics. Although there are minor gaps of coverage, it is adequately comprehensive, the items are well constructed, and the manual is clear and complete. Test users who wish to measure noncognitive objectives, such as actual student involvement in civic affairs or the development of personal values on civic issues, will have to look elsewhere, however, and will probably fail to find any standardized test which serves these purposes.

[929]

★Cooperative Social Studies Tests: Problems of Democracy. Grades 10–12; 1964–65; Forms A ('64, 11 pages), B ('64, 10 pages); no specific manual; series manual ('65, 44 pages); student bulletin ('65, 2 pages); separate answer sheets (Digitek, IBM 805, IBM 1230, SCRIBE) must be used; $6 per 20 tests; $4 per 100 answer sheets; $1.25 per 10 IBM scoring stencils (answer pattern must be punched out locally); Digitek scoring stencils not available; $2 per series manual; $3 per 100 student bulletins; $3 per specimen set of this and 5 other social studies tests; cash orders postpaid; SCRIBE scoring and statistical analysis service, 35¢ per test; 40(50) minutes; Cooperative Tests and Services. *

REFERENCE
1. FARNEN, RUSSELL F., JR., AND WILLS, G. ROBERT. "Nationwide Test Scores on International and Other Social Studies Material." *Ed Horizons* 47(2):51–60 '68. *

HULDA GROBMAN, *Professor of Education, New York University, New York, New York.*

This test provides a welcome change from the "who," "when," and "how much" type of

social studies test that, unfortunately, is still with us. The subject matter covered is varied and non-stereotyped; the questioning strategy is also varied, with maps, cartoons, diagrams, and quotations included.

From a statistical standpoint, the test is satisfactory. It was normed in the spring of 1964. For the norm group (grades 10–12), the raw score means are 61 percent of the possible score, with 86 and 81 percent of the students reaching the last item in Forms A and B, respectively. K-R 20 reliabilities of .90 for each form and an alternate-form reliability of .86 are reported.

The manual is relatively complete and understandable. It is commendably cautious in describing the test and its limitations for a particular evaluation situation. Particularly noteworthy is the discussion of interpretation of item scores and clusters of item scores, a type of test analysis too often neglected.

The converted scores provide some degree of comparability between the two forms; users are advised by the publisher against comparing scores of individuals on the two forms. Comparability of converted scores is in terms of item difficulty and discrimination; the relative emphases in the forms differ somewhat. The manual provides a grid by subject area (international affairs and national defense, political problems, economic problems, and social problems) and by cognition levels (remembering, understanding, and analyzing). No criteria or definitions are provided for the cognitive skills "remembering," "understanding," and "analyzing," and an examination of the items and their classifications does not make the criteria evident.

The relative emphases among the four subject areas tested and the distribution of items among cognitive skills are open to question. "Problems of Democracy" is a relatively new course offering in the social studies and there is no standard course content. Current POD texts reflect a diversity of subjects treated and of emphases. Further, the social studies have been a center of the ferment in curriculum in the last half dozen years, with emphasis centering on inquiry, problem solving, and relevance. Thus, it is difficult to prepare a test that will reflect the emphases appropriate to a wide variety of POD courses over a period of time.

In both forms, the greatest emphasis is on economic problems and the least emphasis is on social problems. The manual classifies 54 percent of the items on international affairs and national defense in the combined forms as measuring "remembering." This should be contrasted with the corresponding percentages of 10 and 19 for economics and social problems, respectively. These may not be the emphases a potential user wishes to communicate to the student.

Given the care taken in preparation of the test, the layout of Form B is surprisingly poor. For items 14–18, the diagram appears on the left-hand page of the test booklet and four of the questions pertaining to it, on the right-hand page. For both forms, the use of cartoons and diagrams is occasionally farfetched and unnecessarily complicates what would otherwise be rather straightforward questions.

In the years since the test was written, the implications of some questions and foils have changed. For example, in Form B, item 41 asks which region of the world has been characterized by political instability since 1950, with the correct response being South America. The foil referring to the region including Greece, Hungary, and Czechoslovakia is certainly more attractive than it was in 1964. To tie a test question down to a given year or a limited time span may give an undue emphasis to the year or time period; yet, given the rapid pace of change in public affairs, the risk of test questions becoming obsolete or the keyed answer becoming incorrect makes it imperative for users to review such tests as this prior to each use, to check on validity of items in the context, not just of the course taught or the educational goals espoused, but also of the context of the time for which use is considered and of possible changes in the implications of the items because of such time factors.

[930]

*The Graduate Record Examinations Advanced Political Science Test. Graduate school candidates; 1939–70; formerly called *The Graduate Record Examinations Advanced Tests: Government;* 4 current forms ('67, 36 pages); descriptive booklet ('70, 8 pages); for more complete information, see 667; 180(200) minutes; Educational Testing Service. *

For a review by Christine McGuire of an earlier form, see 5:835. For reviews of the testing program, see 667 (1 review) and 5:610 (1 review).

[931]

*Sare-Sanders American Government Test. High school and college; 1962–64; first published 1962–63 in the Every Pupil Scholarship Test series; Forms A, B, ('64, 4 pages); manual ('64, 3 pages); $1.75 per 25 tests, postage extra; 75¢ per specimen set, postpaid; 40(45) minutes; Harold V. Sare and M. W. Sanders; Data Processing and Educational Measurement Center. *

HOWARD D. MEHLINGER, *Associate Professor and Director, Social Studies Development Center, Indiana University, Bloomington, Indiana.*

This test is a poor and insufficient effort to measure student understanding of American government. It has many inadequacies; only four weaknesses will be discussed here: (*a*) a number of items are out of date; (*b*) the test represents a narrow conception of American government and the political process; (*c*) contrary to stated claims, it measures primarily the student's ability to recall specific data rather than his capacity "to make applications of his knowledge"; (*d*) the test makes claims about its utility that are not demonstrated and are highly unlikely.

A number of items from Forms A and B were designed to measure a student's ability to recall specific facts that might have been salient in 1962–63 but are now out of date, for example, from Form A: "President Kennedy's policy toward labor has called for: 1. an increase in the minimum wage 2. a decrease in the minimum wage 3. less unemployment benefits 4. none of these" and from Form B: "The United States government budget for 1962 is about: (1) $50 billion (2) $60 billion (3) $80 billion (4) $90 billion." Of 225 items on the two tests, at least 15 are items that might have been fair in 1962–63 but are no longer appropriate in a test of general understanding of American government.

If it is true that school instruction is influenced by achievement tests, this test will contribute to bad instruction about American government and the political process. The test reflects a narrow, legalistic conception of American government and fails to represent the impact of new knowledge in political science. For example, students are asked about the "reserved" powers in the Constitution but are not asked any questions regarding the influence of social class on political behavior of citizens. Not only do many of the items seem too narrow in focus, but it is difficult to imagine any rationale for such items as "The Constitution of the United States is about how long? 1. one hundred pages 2. fifty pages 3. thirty pages 4. ten pages" or "The seating arrangement of the House of Representatives may be described as: 1. semicircular 2. square 3. rectangular 4. none of these."

The test manual asserts that the test "covers theory and factual data concerning government and problems which test the student's ability to make applications of his knowledge." In fact, nearly every item is a recall item in which the student is expected to know such things as the number of terms the President can serve, the number of representatives Alaska sends to Congress, the percentage of income a typical American citizen pays in income tax, the primary topic of the 19th Amendment, the term of office of a federal judge, and which state was not represented at the Constitutional Convention.

Moreover, students have no opportunity to reveal their skill at deriving generalizations from statistical data, at offering testable hypotheses about political behavior, of selecting among useful operational definitions, etc. In short, good American government teachers try to accomplish much more than imposing discrete bits of information on their students' minds. Good teaching is not rewarded by this test.

The publishers assert that the "test results may be profitably used....(1) for determining student achievement; (2) for checking the efficiency of instruction; (3) for assigning school marks; (4) for analyzing student and class weaknesses; and (5) for motivation of student effort." If these utilities were ever valid, they no longer are, for reasons specified in the paragraphs above. A particularly questionable use of this test would be for assigning school marks according to the suggestions in the test manual. The manual presents a formula for translating scores on the test to letter grades for a class, in which 75 percent is considered to be the lowest passing mark. Not only does this represent a questionable grading policy, but in view of the earlier comments about the test items, the manual's suggestion in this regard should be totally ignored.

In summary, this is a poor test of American government. The description of the process to establish test validity and reliability, contained in the test manual, is brief and inadequate. Whatever the validity and reliability of this test might have been in 1963, the weaknesses indicated in the preceding paragraphs should cause one to be very skeptical of the test's performance with regard to these factors today. Indeed

a teacher need not feel proud if his students do well on this test nor feel guilty if they fail.

[932]

*Sare-Sanders Constitution Test. High school and college; 1962–64; first published 1962–63 in the Every Pupil Scholarship Test series; Forms A, B, ('64, 4 pages); manual ('64, 3 pages); no college norms; $1.75 per 25 tests, postage extra; 75¢ per specimen set, postpaid; 40(45) minutes; Harold V. Sare and M. W. Sanders; Data Processing and Educational Measurement Center. *

[933]

★The Undergraduate Record Examinations: Political Science Test. College; 1969–70; Forms K-RUR ('69, 23 pages), SUR ('70, 22 pages); descriptive booklet ('70, 8 pages); for more complete information, see 671; 120(140) minutes; Educational Testing Service. *

For reviews of the testing program, see 671 (2 reviews).

SOCIOLOGY

[934]

★CLEP Subject Examination in Introductory Sociology. 1 year or equivalent; 1965–70; for college accreditation of nontraditional study, advanced placement, or assessment of educational achievement; tests administered monthly at regional centers throughout the United States; tests also available for institutional testing at any time; Form NCT ('65, 15 pages); optional essay supplement: Form NCT-A (no date, 1 page); for program accessories, see 664; rental and scoring fee, $5 per student; postpaid; essay supplement scored by the college; 90(95) minutes, same for essay supplement; program administered for the College Entrance Examination Board by Educational Testing Service. *

For reviews of the testing program, see 664 (3 reviews).

[935]

*The Graduate Record Examinations Advanced Sociology Test. Graduate school candidates; 1939–70; 3 current forms ('66–70, 32–40 pages); descriptive booklet ('70, 7 pages); for more complete information, see 667; 180(200) minutes; Educational Testing Service. *

For a review by J. Richard Wilmeth of an earlier form, see 6:1021. For reviews of the testing program, see 667 (1 review) and 5:601 (1 review).

[936]

★The Undergraduate Record Examinations: Sociology Test. College; 1969–70; Forms RUR ('69, 17 pages), SUR ('70, 20 pages); descriptive booklet ('70, 8 pages); for more complete information, see 671; 120(140) minutes; Educational Testing Service. *

For reviews of the testing program, see 671 (2 reviews).

TIP II SCANNING INDEX

This classified index of all tests in *Tests in Print II* can be used to determine what tests are available in areas besides social studies. Citations are to test entry numbers in TIP II. The population for which a test is intended is included. Stars indicate tests not previously listed in an MMY; asterisks indicate tests revised or supplemented since last listed. The social studies portion of this index, the only part relevant to this monograph, is repeated at the end of this volume.

ACHIEVEMENT BATTERIES

Academic Proficiency Battery [South Africa], college entrants, see 1

Adult Basic Education Student Survey, poorly educated adults in basic education classes, see 2

Adult Basic Learning Examination, adults with achievement levels grades 1–12, see 3

American School Achievement Tests, grades 1–9, see 4

Bristol Achievement Tests [England], ages 8–13, see 5

*CLEP General Examinations: Humanities, 1–2 years of college or equivalent, see 6

*California Achievement Tests, grades 1–14, see 7

Canadian Tests of Basic Skills [Canada], grades 3–8, see 8

Classification and Placement Examination, grade 8 and high school entrants, see 9

*College-Level Examination Program General Examinations, 1–2 years of college or equivalent, see 10

*Comprehensive Tests of Basic Skills, grades kgn–12, see 11

Cooperative Primary Tests, grades 1.5–3, see 12

★Educational Skills Tests: College Edition, open-door college entrants, see 13

General Tests of Language and Arithmetic [South Africa], standards 5–7, see 14

Gray-Votaw-Rogers General Achievement Tests, grades 1–9, see 15

★Guidance Test for Junior Secondary Bantu Pupils in Form 3 [South Africa], see 16

High School Fundamentals Evaluation Test, grades 9–12, see 17

Iowa High School Content Examination, grades 11–13, see 18

*Iowa Tests of Basic Skills, grades 1.7–9, see 19

*Iowa Tests of Educational Development, grades 9–12, see 20

Ligondé Equivalence Test [Canada], adults who left elementary or secondary school 15–20 years ago, see 21

*Metropolitan Achievement Tests, grades kgn–9, see 22

National Achievement Tests, grades 4–9, see 23

*National Educational Development Tests, grades 7–10, see 24

*National Teacher Examinations: Common Examinations, college seniors and teachers, see 25

Peabody Individual Achievement Test, grades kgn–12, see 26

★Primary Survey Tests, grades 2–3, see 27

Public School Achievement Tests, grades 3–8, see 28

*SRA Achievement Series, grades 1–9, see 29

*SRA Assessment Survey, grades 1–12, see 30

*SRA High School Placement Test, grade 9 entrants, see 31

*STS Closed High School Placement Test, grade 9 entrants, see 32

*STS Educational Development Series, grades 2–12, see 33

*Scholastic Proficiency Battery [South Africa], standards 8–10, see 34

*Sequential Tests of Educational Progress, grades 4–14, see 35

*Stanford Achievement Test, grades 1.5–9, see 36

Stanford Achievement Test: High School Basic Battery, grades 9–12, see 37

*Stanford Early School Achievement Test, grades kgn–1.5, see 38

★Stanford Test of Academic Skills, grades 8–12 and first year junior/community college, see 39

Survey of College Achievement, grades 13–14, see 40

*Teacher Education Examination Program: General Professional Examinations, college seniors preparing to teach, see 41

*Test for High School Entrants, high school entrants, see 42

Test of Reading and Number: Inter-American Series, grade 4 entrants, see 43

*Tests of Academic Progress, grades 9–12, see 44

Tests of Adult Basic Education, adults at reading levels of children in grades 2–9, see 45
★*Tests of Arithmetic and Language for Indian South Africans* [South Africa], standards 6–8, see 46
Tests of Basic Experiences, prekgn–grade 1, see 47

Tests of General Educational Development, candidates for high school equivalency certificates, see 48
Undergraduate Program Area Tests, college, see 49
Wide Range Achievement Test, ages 5 and over, see 50

ENGLISH

Advanced Placement Examination in English, high school students desiring credit for college level courses or admission to advanced courses, see 51
American School Achievement Tests: Language and Spelling, grades 4–9, see 52
Analytical Survey Test in English Fundamentals, grades 9–13, see 53
Barrett-Ryan English Test, grades 7–13, see 54
★*Berry-Talbott Language Test: Comprehension of Grammar,* ages 5–8, see 55
Bristol Achievement Tests: English Language [England], ages 8–13, see 56
Business English Test: Dailey Vocational Tests, grades 8–12 and adults, see 57
CLEP General Examinations: English Composition, 1–2 years of college or equivalent, see 58
CLEP Subject Examination in English Composition, 1 year or equivalent, see 59
★*CLEP Subject Examination in Freshman English,* 1 year or equivalent, see 60
California Achievement Tests: Language, grades 1–14, see 61
Canadian Achievement Test in English [Canada], grade 10, see 62
Canadian English Achievement Test [Canada], grades 8.5–9, see 63
★*Canadian English Language Achievement Test* [Canada], candidates for college entrance, see 63A
College Board Achievement Test in English Composition, candidates for college entrance, see 64
College English Placement Test, college entrants, see 65
College English Test: National Achievement Tests, grades 12–13, see 66
College Placement Tests in English Composition, entering college freshmen, see 67
Comprehensive Tests of Basic Skills: Language, grades 2.5–12, see 68
Cooperative English Tests, grades 9–14, see 69
Cooperative Primary Tests: Writing Skills, grades 2.5–3, see 70
Cotswold Junior English Ability Test [Scotland], ages 8.5–10.5, see 71
Cotswold Measurement of Ability: English [Scotland], ages 10–12, see 72
English Expression: Cooperative English Tests, grades 9–14, see 73
English IX–XII: Achievement Examinations for Secondary Schools, grades 9–12, see 74
English Progress Tests [England], ages 7-3 to 15-6, see 75
English Test FG [England], ages 12–13, see 76
English Test: Municipal Tests, grades 3–8, see 77
English Test: National Achievement Tests, grades 3–12, see 78
English Tests (Adv.) [England], ages 12–13, see 79
English Tests 14–20 and 22 [England], ages 10–11, see 80
Essentials of English Tests, grades 7–13, see 81
★*Functional Grammar Test,* high school and college, see 82
Grammar and Usage Test Series, grades 7–12, see 83

Grammar, Usage, and Structure Test and Vocabulary Test, college entrants, see 84
Hoyum-Sanders English Tests, 1–2 semesters in grades 2–8, see 85
Iowa Placement Examinations: English Aptitude, grades 12–13, see 86
Iowa Placement Examinations: English Training, grades 12–13, see 87
Iowa Tests of Educational Development: Correctness and Appropriateness of Expression, grades 9–12, see 88
★*Language Arts Diagnostic Probes,* grades 3–9, see 89
Language Arts: Minnesota High School Achievement Examinations, grades 7-12, see 90
Language Arts Tests: Content Evaluation Series, grades 7–9, see 91
Language Perception Test, business and industry, see 92
Language Usage: Differential Aptitude Tests, grades 8–12 and adults, see 93–4
Moray House English Tests [England], ages 8.5–14, see 95
National Teacher Examinations: English Language and Literature, college seniors and teachers, see 96
Nationwide English Composition Examination, grades 4–12, see 97
Nationwide English Grammar Examination, grades 4–12, see 98
New Purdue Placement Test in English, grades 11–16, see 99
Objective Tests in Constructive English, grades 7–12, see 100
Objective Tests in Punctuation, grades 7–12, see 101
Pacific Tests of English Attainment and Skills: Pacific Test Series [Australia], job applicants in Papua New Guinea, see 102
Picture Story Language Test, ages 7–17, see 103
Pressey Diagnostic Tests in English Composition, grades 7–12, see 104
Purdue High School English Test, grades 9–12, see 105
RBH Spelling Test and Word Meaning Test, business and industry, see 106
RBH Test of Language Skills, business and industry, see 107
SRA Achievement Series: Language Arts, grades 2–9, see 108–9
Schonell Diagnostic English Tests [Scotland], ages 9.5–16, see 110
Senior English Test [England], technical college entrants, see 111
★*Sequential Tests of Educational Progress, Series 2: English Expression,* grades 4–14, see 112
Sequential Tests of Educational Progress: Writing, grades 4–14, see 113
Stanford Achievement Test: High School English and Spelling Tests, grades 9–12, see 114
Stanford Achievement Test: Spelling and Language Tests, grades 4–9, see 115
Survey Tests of English Usage, grades 9–13, see 116
Teacher Education Examination Program: English Language and Literature, college seniors preparing to teach secondary school, see 117

FINE ARTS

ART

FOREIGN LANGUAGES

GERMAN

GREEK

HEBREW

ITALIAN

LATIN

RUSSIAN

INTELLIGENCE

GROUP

INDIVIDUAL

SPECIFIC

MATHEMATICS

ARITHMETIC

CALCULUS

GEOMETRY

Cooperative Mathematics Tests: Geometry, grades 10–12, see 746
Diagnostic Test in Basic Geometry [Australia], 1–2 years high school, see 747
Geometry (Including Plane and Solid Geometry): Minnesota High School Achievement Examinations, high school, see 748–9
Howell Geometry Test, grades 9–12, see 750
Iowa Geometry Aptitude Test, high school, see 751
Mid-Year Geometry Test, high school, see 752
★*Modern Geometry Test: Content Evaluation Series,* grades 10–12, see 753
★*Objective Tests in Mathematics: Geometry* [England], ages 15 and over, see 754
Orleans-Hanna Geometry Prognosis Test, grades 8–11, see 755
Plane Geometry: Achievement Examinations for Secondary Schools, high school, see 756
Plane Geometry: National Achievement Tests, high school, see 757
Solid Geometry: Achievement Examinations for Secondary Schools, high school, see 758

Solid Geometry: National Achievement Tests, high school, see 759

SPECIAL FIELDS

★*Decimal Currency Test* [England], primary and secondary school, see 760
★*NM Consumer Mathematics Test,* grades 9–12, see 761

TRIGONOMETRY

CLEP Subject Examination in Trigonometry, 1 semester or equivalent, see 762
Cooperative Mathematics Tests: Trigonometry, high school and college, see 763
Plane Trigonometry: National Achievement Tests, grades 10–16, see 764
Trigonometry: Minnesota High School Achievement Examinations, high school, see 765

MISCELLANEOUS

Modern Photography Comprehension Test, photography students, see 766
★*NM Consumer Rights and Responsibilities Test,* grades 9–12, see 767

AGRICULTURE

★*Agribusiness Achievement Test,* grades 9–12, see 768

BLIND

Colorado Braille Battery: Literary Code Tests, grades 1 and over, see 769
Colorado Braille Battery: Nemeth Code Tests, grades 4 and over, see 770
Lorimer Braille Recognition Test [England], students (ages 7–13) in grade 2 Braille, see 771
Roughness Discrimination Test, blind children in grades kgn–1, see 772
★*Stanford Multi-Modality Imagery Test,* blind and partially sighted ages 16 and over, see 773
Tooze Braille Speed Test [England], students (ages 7–13) in grades 1 or 2 Braille, see 774

BUSINESS EDUCATION

Bookkeeping: Achievement Examinations for Secondary Schools, high school, see 775
Bookkeeping: Minnesota High School Achievement Examinations, high school, see 776
Bookkeeping Test: National Business Entrance Tests, grades 11–16 and adults, see 777
Business Fundamentals and General Information Test: National Business Entrance Tests, grades 11–16 and adults, see 778
Business Relations and Occupations: Achievement Examinations for Secondary Schools, high school, see 779
Clerical Aptitude Test: Acorn National Aptitude Tests, grades 7–16 and adults, see 780

Clerical Speed and Accuracy: Differential Aptitude Tests, grades 8–12 and adults, see 781
Clerical Tests FG and 2 [England], ages 12–13, see 781A
Detroit Clerical Aptitudes Examination, grades 9–12, see 782
General Office Clerical Test: National Business Entrance Tests, grades 11–16 and adults, see 783
Hiett Simplified Shorthand Test (Gregg), 1–2 semesters high school, see 784
Machine Calculation Test: National Business Entrance Tests, grades 11–16 and adults, see 785
National Business Entrance Tests, grades 11–16 and adults, see 786
National Teacher Examinations: Business Education, college seniors and teachers, see 787
★*Office Information and Skills Test: Content Evaluation Series,* high school, see 788
Reicherter-Sanders Typewriting I and II, 1–2 semesters high school, see 789
Russell-Sanders Bookkeeping Test, 1–2 semesters high school, see 790
SRA Clerical Aptitudes, grades 9–12 and adults, see 791
SRA Typing Skills, grades 9–12 and adults, see 792
Shorthand Aptitude Test [Australia], high school, see 793
Stenographic Aptitude Test, grades 9–16, see 794
Stenographic Test: National Business Entrance Tests, grades 11–16 and adults, see 795
Tapping Test: A Predictor of Typing and Other Tapping Operations, high school, see 796
Teacher Education Examination Program: Business Education, college seniors preparing to teach secondary school, see 797
Turse Shorthand Aptitude Test, grades 8 and over, see 798
Typewriting Test: National Business Entrance Tests, grades 11–16 and adults, see 799
Undergraduate Program Field Tests: Business Test, college, see 800
United Students Typewriting Tests, 1–4 semesters, see 801

COMPUTATIONAL & TESTING DEVICES

COURTSHIP & MARRIAGE

DRIVING & SAFETY EDUCATION

EDUCATION

National Teacher Examinations: Media Specialist—Library and Audio-Visual Services, college seniors and teachers, see 876

Ohio Teaching Record: Anecdotal Observation Form, teachers, see 877

★*Oral School Attitude Test,* grades kgn–3, see 878

Pictographic Self Rating Scale, high school and college, see 879

Purdue Instructor Performance Indicator, college teachers, see 880

Purdue Rating Scale for Instruction, college teachers, see 881

Purdue Student-Teacher Opinionaire, student teachers, see 882

Purdue Teacher Evaluation Scale, grades 7–12, see 883

Purdue Teacher Opinionaire, teachers, see 884

Remmlein's School Law Test, teacher education classes in school law, see 885

★*School Administration and Supervision,* prospective elementary school administrators and supervisors, see 886

★*School Atmosphere Questionnaire,* grades 7-12, see 887

★*School Attitude Test,* grades 4–6, see 888

★*School Personnel Research and Evaluation Services,* teachers and prospective administrators and supervisors, see 889

★*School Survey of Interpersonal Relationships,* teachers, see 890

★*Secondary School Administration,* prospective secondary school administrators, see 891

★*Secondary School Supervision,* prospective secondary school supervisors, see 892

Self Appraisal Scale for Teachers, teachers, see 893

★*Student Instructional Report,* college teachers, see 894

★*Student Reactions to College,* two-year college, see 895

Student's Rating Scale of an Instructor, high school and college, see 896

★*Survey of Educational Leadership Practices,* teachers and school administrators, see 897

Teacher Education Examination Program, college seniors preparing to teach, see 898

Teacher Education Examination Program: Early Childhood Education, college seniors preparing to teach kgn–grade 3, see 899

Teacher Education Examination Program: Elementary School Education, college seniors preparing to teach grades 1–8, see 900

Teacher Opinionaire on Democracy, teachers, see 901

Teacher Preference Schedule, elementary school teachers and prospective teachers, see 902

★*Teacher Self-Rating Inventory,* teachers, see 903

Teaching Aptitude Test, grades 12–16, see 904

Teaching Evaluation Record, teachers, see 905

Undergraduate Program Field Tests: Education Test, college, see 906

Wilson Teacher-Appraisal Scale, ratings by students in grades 7–16, see 907

HANDWRITING

Ayres Measuring Scale for Handwriting: Gettysburg Edition, grades 5–8, see 908

Expessional Growth Through Handwriting Evaluation Scale, grades 1–12, see 909

HEALTH & PHYSICAL EDUCATION

★*AAHPER Cooperative Health Education Test,* grades 5–9, see 910

AAHPER Cooperative Physical Education Tests, grades 4–12, see 911

AAHPER-Kennedy Foundation Special Fitness Test for the Mentally Retarded, ages 8–18, see 912

AAHPER Sport Skills Tests, ages 10–18, see 913

AAHPER Youth Fitness Test, ages 10–30 (grades 5–16), see 914

Action-Choice Tests for Competitive Sports Situations, high school and college, see 915

Attitude Inventory, college women, see 916

Basic Fitness Tests, ages 12–18, see 917

Belmont Measures of Athletic Performance, females grades 9–16, see 918

CAHPER Fitness-Performance Test [Canada], ages 7–44, see 919

CLEP Subject Examination in Human Growth and Development, 1 semester or equivalent, see 920

College Health Knowledge Test, college, see 921

★*Drug Abuse Knowledge Test,* grades 10–12, see 922

Drug Knowledge Inventory, grades 7–16 and adults, see 923

Emporia Elementary Health Test, grades 6–8, see 924

Emporia High School Health Test, high school and college, see 925

Health and Safety Education Test, grades 3–6, see 926

Health Behavior Inventory, grades 3–16, see 927

Health Education Test: Knowledge and Application, grades 7–13, see 928

Health Knowledge Test for College Freshmen, grade 13, see 929

Health Test: National Achievement Tests, grades 3–8, see 930

Illinois Ratings of Character in Physical Education, high school, see 931

Indiana Physical Fitness Test, grades 4–12, see 932

Information Test on Drugs and Drug Abuse, grades 9–16 and adults, see 933

Information Test on Human Reproduction, grades 9–16 and adults, see 934

Kilander-Leach Health Knowledge Test, grades 12–16, see 935

Modified Sjöstrand Physical Work Capacity Test [Canada], ages 7–44, see 936

National Teacher Examinations: Men's Physical Education, college seniors and teachers, see 937

National Teacher Examinations: Women's Physical Education, college seniors and teachers, see 938

Patient's Self-History Form, patients, see 939

★*Self Administered Health Questionnaire for Secondary School Students,* high school, see 940

Swimming Ability Scales for Boys in Secondary Schools: National Swimming Norms [England], boys ages 11–18, see 941

Teacher Education Examination Program: Physical Education, college seniors preparing to teach secondary school, see 942

★*Tests for Venereal Disease Education,* junior high school, high school and college, see 943

★*Thompson Smoking and Tobacco Knowledge Test,* grades 7–16, see 944

Undergraduate Program Field Tests: Physical Education Test, college, see 945

★*VD Knowledge Test,* grades 6 and over, see 946

Wetzel Grid Charts, ages birth–18, see 947

HOME ECONOMICS

Compton Fabric Preference Test, females in grades 7 and over, see 948

Emporia Clothing Test, high school, see 949

Emporia Foods Test, high school, see 950

Minnesota Check List for Food Preparation and Serving, grades 7–16 and adults, see 951

*National Teacher Examinations: Home Economics Education, college seniors and teachers, see 952

*Nutrition Information Test, grades 9–16 and adults, see 953

Scales for Appraising High School Homemaking Programs, pupils, teachers, community members, and administrators, see 954

★*Teacher Education Examination Program: Home Economics Education*, college seniors preparing to teach secondary school, see 955

★*Test of Family Life Knowledge and Attitudes*, grade 12 boys and girls seeking Betty Crocker college scholarships and awards, see 956–66

INDUSTRIAL ARTS

Drawing: Cooperative Industrial Arts Tests, 1 semester grades 7–9, see 967

Electricity/Electronics: Cooperative Industrial Arts Tests, 1 semester grades 7–9, see 968

Emporia Industrial Arts Test, high school, see 969

General Industrial Arts: Cooperative Industrial Arts Tests, 1 year grades 7–9, see 970

Metals: Cooperative Industrial Arts Tests, 1 semester grades 7–9, see 971

*National Teacher Examinations: Industrial Arts Education, college seniors and teachers, see 972

*Teacher Education Examination Program: Industrial Arts, college seniors preparing to teach secondary school, see 973

Technical and Scholastic Test: Dailey Vocational Tests, grades 8–12 and adults, see 974

Woods: Cooperative Industrial Arts Tests, 1 semester grades 7–9, see 975

LEARNING DISABILITIES

★*Automated Graphogestalt Technique*, grades 1–4, see 976

★*Basic Screening and Referral Form for Children With Suspected Learning and Behavioral Disabilities*, grades 1–12, see 977

★*Cutrona Child Study Profile of Psycho-Educational Abilities*, grades kgn–3, see 978

First Grade Screening Test, first grade entrants, see 979

★*Grassi Basic Cognitive Evaluation*, ages 3–9, see 980

Illinois Test of Psycholinguistic Abilities, ages 2–10, see 981; *Filmed Demonstration of the ITPA*, see 982

★*Individual Learning Disabilities Classroom Screening Instrument*, grades 1–3, see 983

Meeting Street School Screening Test, grades kgn–1, see 984

★*Psychoeducational Inventory of Basic Learning Abilities*, ages 5–12 with suspected learning disabilities, see 985

Psychoeducational Profile of Basic Learning Abilities, ages 2–14 with learning disabilities, see 986

★*Pupil Rating Scale: Screening for Learning Disabilities*, grades 3–4, see 987

Screening Test for the Assignment of Remedial Treatments, ages 4-6 to 6-5, see 988

Screening Tests for Identifying Children With Specific Language Disability, grades 1–4, see 989

Specific Language Disability Test, "average to high IQ" children in grades 6–8, see 990

Valett Developmental Survey of Basic Learning Abilities, ages 2–7, see 991

LISTENING COMPREHENSION

*Assessment of Children's Language Comprehension, ages 2–6, see 992

Brown-Carlsen Listening Comprehension Test, grades 9–16 and adults, see 993

Cooperative Primary Tests: Listening, grades 1.5–3, see 994

Orr-Graham Listening Test, junior high school boys, see 995

★*Progressive Achievement Tests of Listening Comprehension* [New Zealand], standards 1–4 and Forms I–IV (ages 7–14), see 996

Sequential Tests of Educational Progress: Listening, grades 4–14, see 997

★*Tests for Auditory Comprehension of Language*, ages 3–7, see 997A

PHILOSOPHY

*Graduate Record Examinations Advanced Philosophy Test, graduate school candidates, see 998

*Undergraduate Program Field Tests: Philosophy Test, college, see 999

*Undergraduate Program Field Tests: Scholastic Philosophy Test, college, see 1000

PSYCHOLOGY

Aden-Crosthwait Adolescent Psychology Achievement Test, college, see 1001

*CLEP Subject Examination in Educational Psychology, 1 semester or equivalent, see 1002

*CLEP Subject Examination in General Psychology, 1 semester or equivalent, see 1003

Cass-Sanders Psychology Test, high school and college, see 1004

*Graduate Record Examinations Advanced Psychology Test, graduate school candidates, see 1005

*Undergraduate Program Field Tests: Psychology Test, college, see 1006

RECORD & REPORT FORMS

*A/9 Cumulative Record Folder, grades kgn–12, see 1007

American Council on Education Cumulative Record Folders, grades 1–16, see 1008

California Cumulative Record and Health Insert, grades 1–12, see 1009

*Cassel Developmental Record, birth to death, see 1010

Florida Cumulative Guidance Record, grades 1–12, see 1011

G.C. Anecdotal Record Form [Canada], teachers' recordings of student actions, see 1012

*Guidance Cumulative Folder and Record Forms, grades kgn–12, see 1013

*Height Weight Interpretation Folders, ages 4–17, see 1014

Junior High School Record, grades 7–10, see 1015

*Ontario School Record System [Canada], grades kgn–13, see 1016

★*Permanent Record Folder*, exceptional children, see 1017

★*Psychodiagnostic Test Report Blank*, psychologists' test data on clients, see 1018

*Secondary-School Record, grades 9–12, see 1019

RELIGIOUS EDUCATION

Achievement Test in Jewish History, junior high school, see 1020
★*Achievement Test—Jewish Life and Observances,* grades 5–7, see 1021
★*Achievement Test—The State of Israel,* "pupils who have completed an organized course of study on the State of Israel," see 1022
★*Bible and You,* ages 13 and over, see 1023
★*Biblical Survey Test,* college, see 1024
Concordia Bible Information Inventory, grades 4–8, see 1025
Inventory of Religious Activities and Interests, high school and college students considering church-related occupations and theological school students, see 1025A
Religious Attitudes Inventory, religious counselees, see 1026
Standardized Bible Content Tests, Bible college, see 1027
Theological School Inventory, incoming seminary students, see 1028
Youth Research Survey, ages 13–19, see 1029

SCORING MACHINES & SERVICES

Automata EDT 1200 Educational Data Terminal, see 1030
Hankes Scoring Service, see 1031
IBM 1230 Optical Mark Scoring Reader, see 1032
★*IBM 3881 Optical Mark Reader,* see 1033
MRC Scoring and Reporting Services, see 1034
NCS Scoring and Reporting Services, see 1035
NCS Sentry 70, see 1036
OpScan Test Scoring and Document Scanning System, see 1037
Psychological Resources, see 1038

SOCIOECONOMIC STATUS

American Home Scale, grades 8–16, see 1039
Environmental Participation Index, culturally disadvantaged ages 12 and over, see 1040A
Home Index, grades 4–12, see 1040A
Socio-Economic Status Scales [India], urban students, adults, and rural families, see 1041

STATISTICS

CLEP Subject Examination in Statistics, 1 semester or equivalent, see 1042
★*Objective Tests in Mathematics: Statistics* [England], ages 15 and over, see 1043

TEST PROGRAMS

ACT Assessment, candidates for college entrance, see 1044
Advanced Placement Examinations, high school students desiring credit for college level courses or admission to advanced courses, see 1045
Canadian Test Battery, Grade 10 [Canada], see 1046
Canadian Test Battery, Grades 8–9 [Canada], grades 8.5–9.0, see 1047
College Board Admissions Testing Program, candidates for college entrance, see 1048
★*College Guidance Program,* grade 11, see 1049
College-Level Examination Program, 1–2 years of college or equivalent, see 1050
College Placement Tests, entering college freshmen, see 1051
Comparative Guidance and Placement Program, entrants to two-year colleges and vocational-technical institutes, see 1052
Graduate Record Examinations: National Program for Graduate School Selection, graduate school candidates, see 1053
Junior College Placement Program, junior college entrants, see 1054
National Guidance Testing Program, grades 1.5–14, see 1055
National Science Foundation Graduate Fellowship Testing Program, applicants for N.S.F. fellowships for graduate study in the sciences, see 1056
★*Ohio Survey Tests,* grades 4, 6, 8, and 10, see 1057
Project Talent Test Battery, grades 9–12, see 1058
Secondary School Admission Test, grades 5–10, see 1059
★*Service for Admission to College and University Testing Program* [Canada], candidates for college entrance, see 1060
★*Testing Academic Achievement,* high school students desiring credit for college level courses or advanced placement, entering college freshmen, and 1–2 years of college or equivalent, see 1061
Undergraduate Program for Counseling and Evaluation, college, see 1062

MULTI-APTITUDE BATTERIES

Academic Promise Tests, grades 6–9, see 1063
★*Academic-Technical Aptitude Tests* [South Africa], "coloured pupils" in standards 6–8, see 1064
★*Aptitude Test for Junior Secondary Pupils* [South Africa], Bantus in Form I, see 1065
Aptitude Tests for Occupations, grades 9–13 and adults, see 1066
★*Armed Services Vocational Aptitude Battery,* high school, see 1067
Detroit General Aptitudes Examination, grades 6–12, see 1068
Differential Aptitude Tests, grades 8–12 and adults, see 1069
Differential Test Battery [England], ages 7 to "top university level," see 1070
Employee Aptitude Survey, ages 16 and over, see 1071

Flanagan Aptitude Classification Tests, grades 9–12 and adults, see 1072
General Aptitude Test Battery, grades 9–12 and adults, see 1073
Guilford-Zimmerman Aptitude Survey, grades 9–16 and adults, see 1074
High Level Battery: Test A/75 [South Africa], adults with at least 12 years of education, see 1075
★*International Primary Factors Test Battery,* grades 5 and over, see 1076
Jastak Test of Potential Ability and Behavior Stability, ages 11.5–14.5, see 1077
Job-Tests Program, adults, see 1078
★*Junior Aptitude Tests for Indian South Africans* [South Africa], standards 6–8, see 1079
Measurement of Skill, adults, see 1080

Multi-Aptitude Test, college courses in testing, see 1081

Multiple Aptitude Tests, grades 7–13, see 1082

N.B. Aptitude Tests (Junior) [South Africa], standards 4–8, see 1083

National Institute for Personnel Research Intermediate Battery [South Africa], standards 7–10 and job applicants with 9–12 years of education, see 1084

*National Institute for Personnel Research Normal

Battery [South Africa], standards 6–10 and job applicants with 8–11 years of education, see 1085

*Nonreading Aptitude Test Battery, disadvantaged grades 9–12 and adults, see 1086

SRA Primary Mental Abilities, grades kgn–12 and adults, see 1087

*Senior Aptitude Tests [South Africa], standards 8–10 and college and adults, see 1088

PERSONALITY

NONPROJECTIVE

★*Ai3Q: A Measure of the Obsessional Personality or Anal Character* [England], sixth form and intelligent adults, see 1089

A-S Reaction Study, college and adults, see 1090

*Activity Vector Analysis, ages 16 and over, see 1091

*Adaptive Behavior Scales, mentally retarded and emotionally maladjusted ages 3 and over, see 1092

Addiction Research Center Inventory, drug addicts, see 1093

Adjective Check List, grades 9–16 and adults, see 1094

Adjustment Inventory, grades 9–16 and adults, see 1095

★*Adolescent Alienation Index,* ages 12–19, see 1096

★*Affect Scale,* college, see 1097

Alcadd Test, adults, see 1098

★*Animal Crackers: A Test of Motivation to Achieve,* grades kgn–1, see 1099

Anxiety Scale for the Blind, blind and partially sighted ages 13 and over, see 1100

Attitude-Interest Analysis Test, early adolescents and adults, see 1101

Attitudes Toward Industrialization, adults, see 1102

Attitudes Toward Parental Control of Children, adults, see 1103

Ayres Space Test, ages 3 and over, see 1104

Babcock Test of Mental Efficiency, ages 7 and over, see 1105

Baker-Schulberg Community Mental Health Ideology Scale, mental health professionals, see 1106

★*Balthazar Scales of Adaptive Behavior,* "profoundly and severely mentally retarded adults and the younger less retarded," see 1107

★*Barclay Classroom Climate Inventory,* grades 3–6, see 1108

Barron-Welsh Art Scale, ages 6 and over, see 1109

Behavior Cards, delinquents having a reading grade score 4.5 or higher, see 1110

Behavior Status Inventory, psychiatric inpatients, see 1111

Bristol Social Adjustment Guides [England], ages 5–15, see 1112

Brook Reaction Test [England], ages 13 and over, see 1113

Burks' Behavior Rating Scale for Organic Brain Dysfunction, grades kgn–6, see 1114

Burks' Behavior Rating Scales, preschool and grades kgn–8, see 1115

C-R Opinionaire, grades 11–16 and adults, see 1116

Cain-Levine Social Competency Scale, mentally retarded children ages 5–13, see 1117

California Life Goals Evaluation Schedules, ages 15 and over, see 1118

California Medical Survey, medical patients ages 10–18 and adults, see 1119

California Preschool Social Competency Scale, ages 2.5–5.5, see 1120

California Psychological Inventory, ages 13 and over, see 1121; **Behaviordyne Psychodiagnostic Lab Service,* see 1122

California Test of Personality, grades kgn–14 and adults, see 1123

Cassel Group Level of Aspiration Test, grades 5–16 and adults, see 1124

Chapin Social Insight Test, ages 13 and over, see 1125

Child Behavior Rating Scale, grades kgn–3, see 1126

*Children's Embedded Figures Test, ages 5–12, see 1127

Children's Hypnotic Susceptibility Scale, ages 5–16, see 1128

*Children's Personality Questionnaire [South Africa], ages 8–12, see 1129

Client-Centered Counseling Progress Record, adults and children undergoing psychotherapeutic counseling, see 1130

Clinical Analysis Questionnaire, ages 18 and over, see 1131

Clinical Behavior Check List and Rating Scale, clinical clients, see 1132

College and University Environment Scales, college, see 1133

College Inventory of Academic Adjustment, college, see 1134

*College Student Questionnaires, college entrants and students, see 1135

★*College Student Satisfaction Questionnaire,* college, see 1136

Community Adaptation Schedule, normals and psychiatric patients, see 1137

Community Improvement Scale, adults, see 1138

Comrey Personality Scales, ages 16 and over, see 1139

Concept Formation Test, normal and schizophrenic adults, see 1140

★*Concept-Specific Anxiety Scale,* college and adults, see 1141

★*Conceptual Systems Test,* grades 7 and over, see 1142

Conservatism Scale [England], ages 12 and over, see 1143

Cornell Index, ages 18 and over, see 1144

Cornell Medical Index, ages 14 and over, see 1145

Cornell Word Form 2, adults, see 1146

Cotswold Personality Assessment P.A.1 [Scotland], ages 11–16, see 1147

★*Crawford Psychological Adjustment Scale,* psychiatric patients, see 1148

Cree Questionnaire, industrial employees, see 1149

Current and Past Psychopathology Scales, psychiatric patients and nonpatients, see 1150

DF Opinion Survey, grades 12–16 and adults, see 1151

Defense Mechanism Inventory, ages 16 and over, see 1152

Demos D Scale: An Attitude Scale for the Identification of Dropouts, grades 7–12, see 1153

Depression Adjective Check Lists, grades 9–16 and adults, see 1154

Detroit Adjustment Inventory, grades kgn–12, see 1155

Inter-Person Perception Test, ages 6 and over, see 1239

Interpersonal Check List, adults, see 1240

★*Interpersonal Communication Inventory,* grades 9–16 and adults, see 1241

★*Interpersonal Orientation Scale,* college and adults, see 1242

Interpersonal Perception Method [England], married couples and other 2-person or 2-group situations, see 1243

Inventory of College Activities, college, see 1244

Inventory of Factors STDCR, grades 9–16 and adults, see 1245

★*"Is of Identity" Test,* grades 4–16, see 1246

It Scale for Children, ages 5–6, see 1247

★*Jesness Behavior Checklist,* ages 10 and over, see 1248

Jesness Inventory, disturbed children and adolescents ages 8–18 and adults, see 1249

Job Analysis and Interest Measurement, adults, see 1250

Jones Personality Rating Scale, grades 9–12 and adults, see 1251

Junior Eysenck Personality Inventory [England], ages 7–15, see 1252

Jr.-Sr. High School Personality Questionnaire, ages 12–18, see 1253

KD Proneness Scale and Check List, ages 7 and over, see 1254

Katz Adjustment Scales, normal and mentally disordered adults, see 1255

Kuder Preference Record—Personal, grades 9–16 and adults, see 1256

Kundu's Neurotic Personality Inventory [India], adults, see 1257

★*Kupfer-Detre System,* psychiatric patients, see 1258

Leadership Ability Evaluation, grades 9–16 and adults, see 1259

Leadership Q-Sort Test, adults, see 1260

Level of Aspiration Board, mental ages 12.5 and over, see 1261

Life Adjustment Inventory, high school, see 1262

Lüscher Color Test, adults, see 1263

MACC Behavioral Adjustment Scale, psychiatric patients, see 1264

M-B History Record, psychiatric patients and penal groups, see 1265

M-Scale: An Inventory of Attitudes Toward Black/ White Relations in the United States, college and adults, see 1266

★*Maferr Inventory of Feminine Values,* older adolescents and adults, see 1267

★*Maferr Inventory of Masculine Values,* older adolescents and adults, see 1268

Manchester Scales of Social Adaptation [England], ages 6–15, see 1269

Mandel Social Adjustment Scale, psychiatric patients and others, see 1270

Manson Evaluation, adults, see 1271

Martin S-D Inventory, clients and patients, see 1272

Maryland Parent Attitude Survey, parents, see 1273

★*Mathematics Anxiety Rating Scale,* college and adults, see 1274

Maudsley Personality Inventory [England], college and adults, see 1275

Maxfield-Buchholz Scale of Social Maturity for Use With Preschool Blind Children, infancy–6 years, see 1276

Memory-For-Designs Test, ages 8.5 and over, see 1277

Mental Status Schedule, psychiatric patients and non-patients, see 1278

Middlesex Hospital Questionnaire [England], ages 18 and over, see 1279

Minnesota Counseling Inventory, high school, see 1280

Minnesota Multiphasic Personality Inventory, ages 16 and over, see 1281 ; *Behaviordyne Psychodiagnostic Lab Service,* see 1282; *MMPI-ICA Computer Report,* see 1283; *The Psychological Corporation MMPI Reporting Service,* see 1284; *Roche MMPI Computerized Interpretation Service,* see 1285

Minnesota Rating Scale for Personal Qualities and Abilities, college and adults, see 1286

★*Missouri Children's Picture Series,* ages 5–16, see 1287

★*Mood Altering Substances,* high school and college, see 1288

Mooney Problem Check List, grades 7–16 and adults, see 1289

Mother-Child Relationship Evaluation, mothers, see 1290

Motivation Analysis Test, ages 17 and over, see 1291

Multidimensional Maturity Scale, grades kgn–12, see 1292

Multiple Affect Adjective Check List, grades 8–16 and adults, see 1293

Myers-Briggs Type Indicator, grades 9–16 and adults, see 1294

Neuroticism Scale Questionnaire, ages 13 and over, see 1295

New Junior Maudsley Inventory [England], ages 9–16, see 1296

Northampton Activity Rating Scale, mental patients, see 1297

Nurses' Observation Scale for Inpatient Evaluation, mental patients, see 1298

Object Sorting Scales [Australia], adults, see 1299

Objective-Analytic (O-A) Anxiety Battery, ages 14 and over, see 1300

Ohio College Association Rating Scale, high school, see 1301

Omnibus Personality Inventory, college, see 1302

Opinion, Attitude, and Interest Survey, high school seniors and college students, see 1303

★*Opinions Toward Adolescents,* college and adults, see 1304

Organic Integrity Test, ages 5 and over, see 1305

Orientation Inventory, college and industry, see 1306

★*Ottawa School Behavior Check List* [Canada], ages 6–12, see 1307

PHSF Relations Questionnaire [South Africa], standards 6–10 and college and adults, see 1308

PRADI Autobiographical Form, clinical clients, see 1309

Parent-Adolescent Communication Inventory, high school and adults, see 1310

Perceptual Maze Test [England], ages 6–16 and adults, see 1311

Personal Adjustment Index, job applicants, see 1312

Personal Adjustment Inventory, ages 9–13, see 1313

Personal Audit, grades 9–16 and adults, see 1314

Personal Orientation Inventory, grades 9–16 and adults, see 1315

Personal Preference Scale, ages 15 and over, see 1316

★*Personal Values Abstract,* ages 13 and over, see 1317

Personal Values Inventory, grades 12–13, see 1318

Personality Evaluation Form, ages 2 and over, see 1319

Personality Inventory, grades 9–16 and adults, see 1320

Personality Rating Scale, grades 4–12, see 1321

Personality Research Form, college, see 1322

Personnel Reaction Blank, adults, see 1323

Philo-Phobe, ages 10 and over, see 1324

Pictorial Study of Values, ages 14 and over, see 1325

Piers-Harris Children's Self Concept Scale, grades 3–12, see 1326

Polarity Scale, college and adults, see 1327

Polyfactorial Study of Personality, adults, see 1328

Power of Influence Test, grades 2–13, see 1329

PROJECTIVE

READING

DIAGNOSTIC

MISCELLANEOUS

ORAL

READINESS

SPECIAL FIELDS

SPEED

STUDY SKILLS

SCIENCE

BIOLOGY

Cooperative Biology Test: Educational Records Bureau Edition, high school, see 1807
Cooperative Science Tests: Biology, grades 10–12, see 1808
Emporia Biology Test, 1–2 semesters high school, see 1809
General Biology Test: National Achievement Tests, high school, see 1810
Graduate Record Examinations Advanced Biology Test, graduate school candidates, see 1811
Nelson Biology Test, grades 9–13, see 1812
Undergraduate Program Field Tests: Biology Test, college, see 1813

CHEMISTRY

ACS Cooperative Examination Brief Course in Organic Chemistry, 1 semester college, see 1814
ACS Cooperative Examination in Analytical Chemistry, Graduate Level, entering graduate students, see 1815
ACS Cooperative Examination in Biochemistry, college, see 1816
ACS Cooperative Examination in Brief Physical Chemistry, 1 semester college, see 1817
ACS Cooperative Examination in Brief Qualitative Analysis, college, see 1818
ACS Cooperative Examination in General Chemistry, 1 year college, see 1819
ACS Cooperative Examination in Inorganic Chemistry, grades 15–16, see 1820
ACS Cooperative Examination in Inorganic Chemistry, Graduate Level, entering graduate students, see 1821
ACS Cooperative Examination in Inorganic-Organic-Biological Chemistry (for Paramedical Programs), 1–2 semesters of chemistry for nursing, home economics, and other paramedical students, see 1822
ACS Cooperative Examination in Instrumental Analysis, grades 15–16, see 1823
ACS Cooperative Examination in Organic Chemistry, 1 year college, see 1824
ACS Cooperative Examination in Organic Chemistry, Graduate Level, entering graduate students, see 1825
ACS Cooperative Examination in Physical Chemistry, 1 year college, see 1826
ACS Cooperative Examination in Physical Chemistry, Graduate Level, entering graduate students, see 1827
ACS Cooperative Examination in Qualitative Analysis, college, see 1828
ACS Cooperative Examination in Quantitative Analysis, college, see 1829
ACS-NSTA Cooperative Examination in High School Chemistry, 1 year high school, see 1830
ACS-NSTA Cooperative Examination in High School Chemistry: Advanced Level, advanced high school classes, see 1831
Advanced Placement Examination in Chemistry, high school students desiring credit for college level courses or admission to advanced courses, see 1832
CLEP Subject Examination in General Chemistry, 1 year or equivalent, see 1833
Chemistry: Achievement Examinations for Secondary Schools, high school, see 1834
Chemistry Achievement Test for CHEM Study or Equivalent, high school, see 1835
Chemistry: Minnesota High School Achievement Examinations, high school, see 1836
College Board Achievement Test in Chemistry, candidates for college entrance, see 1837
College Placement Test in Chemistry, entering college freshmen, see 1838
Cooperative Chemistry Test: Educational Records Bureau Edition, high school, see 1839

Cooperative Science Tests: Chemistry, grades 10–12, see 1840
Emporia Chemistry Test, 1–2 semesters high school, see 1841
General Chemistry Test: National Achievement Tests, grades 10–16, see 1842
Graduate Record Examinations Advanced Chemistry Test, graduate school candidates, see 1843
Iowa Placement Examinations: Chemistry Aptitude, grades 12–13, see 1844
Iowa Placement Examinations: Chemistry Training, grades 12–13, see 1845
RBH Test of Chemical Comprehension, employee applicants and applicants for nurses' training, see 1846
Toledo Chemistry Placement Examination, college entrants, see 1847
Undergraduate Program Field Tests: Chemistry Test, college, see 1848

GEOLOGY

CLEP Subject Examination in Geology, 1 year or equivalent, see 1849
Graduate Record Examinations Advanced Geology Test, graduate school candidates, see 1850
Undergraduate Program Field Tests: Geology Test, college, see 1851

MISCELLANEOUS

Butler Life Science Concept Test, grades 1–6, see 1852
Dubins Earth Science Test, grades 8–12, see 1853
★NM Concepts of Ecology Test, grades 6–8, see 1854
★Science Attitude Questionnaire [England], secondary school, see 1855
Test on Understanding Science, grades 9–12, see 1856
Tests of Basic Experiences: Science, prekgn–grade 1, see 1857

PHYSICS

Advanced Placement Examination in Physics, high school students desiring credit for college level courses or admission to advanced courses, see 1858
College Board Achievement Test in Physics, candidates for college entrance, see 1859
College Placement Test in Physics, entering college freshmen, see 1860
Cooperative Physics Test: Educational Records Bureau Edition, high school, see 1861
Cooperative Science Tests: Physics, grades 10–12, see 1862
Dunning-Abeles Physics Test, grades 10–13, see 1863
Emporia Physics Test, 1–2 semesters high school, see 1864
General Physics Test: National Achievement Tests, grades 10–16, see 1865
Graduate Record Examinations Advanced Physics Test, graduate school candidates, see 1866
Iowa Placement Examinations: Physics Aptitude, grades 12–13, see 1867
Iowa Placement Examinations: Physics Training, grades 12–13, see 1868
★Objective Tests in Physics, high school, see 1869
Physics: Achievement Examinations for Secondary Schools, high school, see 1870
Physics: Minnesota High School Achievement Examinations, high school, see 1871
Tests of the Physical Science Study Committee, high school, see 1872
Undergraduate Program Field Tests: Physics Test, college, see 1873

SENSORY-MOTOR

D-K Scale of Lateral Dominance, grades 2–6, see 1874

Developmental Test of Visual-Motor Integration, ages 2–15, see 1875

★*Frostig Movement Skills Test Battery,* ages 6–12, see 1876

Harris Tests of Lateral Dominance, ages 7 and over, see 1877

Leavell Hand-Eye Coordinator Tests, ages 8–14, see 1878

MKM Picture Arrangement Test, grades kgn–6, see 1879

Moore Eye-Hand Coordination and Color-Matching Test, ages 2 and over, see 1880

Perceptual Forms Test, ages 5–8, see 1881

Primary Visual Motor Test, ages 4–8, see 1882

Purdue Perceptual-Motor Survey, ages 6–10, see 1883

★*Rosner Perceptual Survey,* ages 5–12, see 1884

Southern California Kinesthesia and Tactile Perception Tests, ages 4–8, see 1885

Southern California Perceptual-Motor Tests, ages 4–8, see 1886

Southern California Sensory Integration Tests, ages 4–10 with learning problems, see 1887

★*Spatial Orientation Memory Test,* ages 5–8, see 1888

★*Symbol Digit Modalities Test,* ages 8 and over, see 1889

Trankell's Laterality Tests [Sweden], left-handed children in grades 1–2, see 1890

★*Wold Digit-Symbol Test,* ages 6–16, see 1891

★*Wold Sentence Copying Test,* grades 2–8, see 1892

★*Wold Visuo-Motor Test,* ages 6–16, see 1893

MOTOR

★*Devereux Test of Extremity Coordination,* emotionally handicapped and neurologically impaired ages 4–10, see 1894

Lincoln-Oseretsky Motor Development Scale, ages 6–14, see 1895

★*Manual Accuracy and Speed Test,* ages 4 and over, see 1896

★*Motor Problems Inventory,* preschool–grade 5, see 1897

Oseretsky Tests of Motor Proficiency: A Translation From the Portuguese Adaptation, ages 4–16, see 1898

Perrin Motor Coordination Test, adults, see 1899

Rail-Walking Test, ages 5 and over, see 1900

Smedley Hand Dynamometer, ages 6–18, see 1901

Southern California Motor Accuracy Test, ages 4–7 with nervous system dysfunction, see 1902

★*Teaching Research Motor-Development Scale,* moderately and severely retarded (preschool–grade 12), see 1903

★*Test of Motor Impairment* [Canada], ages 5–14, see 1904

VISION

A-B-C Vision Test for Ocular Dominance, ages 5 and over, see 1905

AO Sight Screener, adults, see 1906

Atlantic City Eye Test, grades 1 and over, see 1907

Basic Screen Test—Vision: Measurement of Skill Test 12, job applicants, see 1908

Burnham-Clark-Munsell Color Memory Test, adults, see 1909

Dennis Visual Perception Scale, grades 1–6, see 1910

Dvorine Pseudo-Isochromatic Plates, ages 3 and over, see 1911

Farnsworth Dichotomous Test for Color Blindness: Panel D-15, ages 12 and over, see 1912

Farnsworth-Munsell 100-Hue Test for the Examination of Color Discrimination, mental ages 12 and over, see 1913

★*Guy's Colour Vision Test for Young Children* [England], ages 3–5 and handicapped, see 1914

Inter-Society Color Council Color Aptitude Test, adults, see 1915

Keystone Ready-to-Read Tests, school entrants, see 1916

Keystone Tests of Binocular Skill, grades 1 and over, see 1917

Keystone Visual Screening Tests, preschool and over, see 1918

MKM Binocular Preschool Test, preschool, see 1919

MKM Monocular and Binocular Reading Test, grades 1 and over, see 1920

Marianne Frostig Developmental Test of Visual Perception, ages 3–8, see 1921

★*Motor-Free Visual Perception Test,* ages 4–8, see 1922

Ortho-Rater, adults, see 1923

Pseudo-Isochromatic Plates for Testing Color Perception, ages 7 and over, see 1924

School Vision Tester, grades kgn and over, see 1925

★*Sheridan Gardiner Test of Visual Acuity* [England], ages 5 and over, see 1926

★*Sloan Achromatopsia Test,* individuals suspected of total color blindness, see 1927

Southern California Figure-Ground Visual Perception Test, ages 4–10, see 1928

Spache Binocular Reading Test, nonreaders and grades 1 and over, see 1929

★*Speed of Color Discrimination Test,* college, see 1930

Stycar Vision Tests [England], ages 6 months to 7 years, see 1931

Test for Colour-Blindness [Japan], ages 4 and over, see 1932

★*3-D Test of Visualization Skill,* ages 3–8, see 1933

Titmus Vision Tester, ages 3 and over, see 1934

★*Visualization Test of Three Dimensional Orthographic Shape,* high school and college, see 1935

SOCIAL STUDIES

American History—Government—Problems of Democracy: Acorn Achievement Tests, grades 9–16, see 1936

American School Achievement Tests: Social Studies and Science, grades 4–9, see 1937

CLEP General Examinations: Social Sciences and History, 1–2 years of college or equivalent, see 1938

College Board Achievement Test in American History and Social Studies, candidates for college entrance, see 1939

College Board Achievement Test in European History

POLITICAL SCIENCE

CLEP Subject Examination in American Government, 1 semester or equivalent, see 2004

Cooperative Social Studies Tests: American Government, grades 10–12, see 2005

Cooperative Social Studies Tests: Civics, grades 8–9, see 2006

Cooperative Social Studies Tests: Problems of Democracy, grades 10–12, see 2007

★*Government/Objective Tests*, 1 semester grades 11–12, see 2008

Graduate Record Examinations Advanced Political Science Test, graduate school candidates, see 2009

★*National Teacher Examinations: Texas Government*, college seniors and teachers, see 2010

Patterson Test or Study Exercises on the Constitution of the United States, grades 9–16 and adults, see 2011

Principles of Democracy Test, grades 9–12, see 2012

Sare-Sanders American Government Test, high school and college, see 2013

Sare-Sanders Constitution Test, high school and college, see 2014

Social Studies Grade 12 (American Problems): Minnesota High School Achievement Examinations, grade 12, see 2015

Undergraduate Program Field Tests: Political Science Test, college, see 2016

SOCIOLOGY

CLEP Subject Examination in Introductory Sociology, 1 year or equivalent, see 2017

Graduate Record Examinations Advanced Sociology Test, graduate school candidates, see 2018

Sare-Sanders Sociology Test, high school and college, see 2019

Undergraduate Program Field Tests: Sociology Test, college, see 2020

SPEECH AND HEARING

★*Diagnostic Test of Speechreading*, deaf children ages 4–9, see 2021

★*Multiple-Choice Intelligibility Test*, college, see 2022

★*Ohio Tests of Articulation and Perception of Sounds*, ages 5–8, see 2023

Preschool Language Scale, ages 2–6, see 2024

Reynell Developmental Language Scales [England], children ages 1–5 with delayed or deviant language development, see 2025

Undergraduate Program Field Tests: Speech Pathology and Audiology Test, college, see 2026

HEARING

Ambco Audiometers, ages 10 and over, see 2027

Ambco Speech Test Record, ages 3 and over, see 2027A

Auditory Discrimination Test, ages 5–8, see 2028

★*Auditory Memory Span Test*, ages 5–8, see 2029

★*Auditory Sequential Memory Test*, grades 5–8, see 2030

Auditory Tests, grades 2 and over, see 2031

Beltone Audiometers, grades kgn and over, see 2032

Comprehension of Oral Language: Inter-American Series, grade 1, see 2033

Eckstein Audiometers, grades kgn and over, see 2034

★*Flowers-Costello Tests of Central Auditory Abilities*, grades kgn–6, see 2035

★*Four Tone Screening for Older Children and Adults*, ages 8 and over, see 2036

Goldman-Fristoe-Woodcock Test of Auditory Discrimination, ages 4 and over, see 2037

Grason-Stadler Audiometers, ages 6 and over, see 2038

Hearing of Speech Tests, ages 3–12, see 2039

Hollien-Thompson Group Hearing Test, grades 1 and over, see 2040

★*Kindergarten Auditory Screening Test*, grades kgn–1, see 2041

★*Lindamood Auditory Conceptualization Test*, grades kgn–12, see 2042

Maico Audiometers, grades kgn and over, see 2043

Maico Hearing Impairment Calculator, see 2044

Massachusetts Hearing Test, grades 1–16 and adults, see 2045

Modified Rhyme Hearing Test, grades 4 and over, see 2046

National Teacher Examinations: Audiology, college seniors and teachers, see 2047

New Group Pure Tone Hearing Test, grades 1 and over, see 2048

★*Oliphant Auditory Discrimination Memory Test*, grades 2–6, see 2049

★*Oliphant Auditory Synthesizing Test*, grade 1, see 2050

Pritchard-Fox Phoneme Auditory Discrimination Tests: Test Four, kgn and over, see 2051

Robbins Speech Sound Discrimination and Verbal Imagery Type Tests, ages 4 and over, see 2052

Rush Hughes (PB 50): Phonetically Balanced Lists 5–12, grades 2 and over, see 2053

Screening Test for Auditory Perception, grades 2–6, see 2054

Stycar Hearing Tests [England], ages 6 months to 7 years, see 2055

Test of Listening Accuracy in Children, ages 5–9, see 2056

★*Test of Non-Verbal Auditory Discrimination*, ages 6–8, see 2057

★*Tracor Audiometers*, infants and older, see 2058

Verbal Auditory Screening for Children, ages 3–8, see 2059

★*Washington Speech Sound Discrimination Test*, ages 3–5, see 2060

★*Word Intelligibility by Picture Identification*, hearing impaired children ages 5–13, see 2061

★*ZECO Pure Tone Screening for Children*, ages 3–8, see 2062

Zenith Audiometers, preschool and over, see 2063–4

SPEECH

Arizona Articulation Proficiency Scale, mental ages 2–14 and over, see 2065

★*Boston Diagnostic Aphasia Examination*, aphasic patients, see 2066

★*Bzoch-League Receptive-Expressive Emergent Language Scale: For the Measurement of Language Skills in Infancy*, birth to age 3, see 2067

Communicative Evaluation Chart From Infancy to Five Years, see 2068

Deep Test of Articulation, all reading levels, see 2069

VOCATIONS

CLERICAL

INTERESTS

MANUAL DEXTERITY

MECHANICAL ABILITY

MISCELLANEOUS

SELECTION & RATING FORMS

APT Controlled Interview, applicants for employment, see 2294

Application Interview Screening Form, job applicants, see 2295

Career Counseling Personal Data Form, vocational counselees, see 2296

Employee Competency Scale, employees, see 2297

Employee Evaluation Form for Interviewers, adults, see 2298

Employee Performance Appraisal, business and industry, see 2299

★*Employee Progress Appraisal Form,* rating of office employees, see 2300

Employee Rating and Development Forms, executive, industrial, office, and sales personnel, see 2301

Executive, Industrial, and Sales Personnel Forms, applicants for executive, industrial, office, or sales positions, see 2302

Job Application Forms, job applicants and employees, see 2303

Lawshe-Kephart Personnel Comparison System, for rating any aspect of employee performance by the paired comparison technique, see 2304

★*McCormick Job Performance Measurement "Rate-$-Scales,"* employees, see 2305

McQuaig Manpower Selection Series, applicants for office and sales positions, see 2306

Martin Performance Appraisal, employees, see 2307

Merit Rating Series, industry, see 2308

Nagel Personnel Interviewing and Screening Forms, job applicants, see 2309

Performance Review Forms, employees and managers, see 2310

Personal Data Blank, counselees ages 15 and over, see 2311

Personnel Interviewing Forms, business and industry, see 2312

Personnel Rating Scale, employees, see 2313

RBH Individual Background Survey, business and industry, see 2314

San Francisco Vocational Competency Scale, mentally retarded adults, see 2315

Selection Interview Forms, business and industry, see 2316

Speech-Appearance Record, job applicants, see 2317

Stevens-Thurow Personnel Forms, business and industry, see 2318

★*Tickmaster,* job applicants, see 2319

Wonderlic Personnel Selection Procedure, applicants for employment, see 2320

Work Reference Check, job applicants, see 2321

SPECIFIC VOCATIONS

ACCOUNTING

Account Clerk Test, job applicants, see 2322

American Institute of Certified Public Accountants Testing Programs, grades 13–16 and accountants, see 2323

CLEP Subject Examination in Introductory Accounting, 1 year or equivalent, see 2324

BUSINESS

Admission Test for Graduate Study in Business, business graduate students, see 2325

CLEP Subject Examination in Introduction to Business Management, 1 semester or equivalent, see 2326

CLEP Subject Examination in Introductory Business Law, 1 semester or equivalent, see 2327

CLEP Subject Examination in Introductory Marketing, 1 semester or equivalent, see 2328

CLEP Subject Examination in Money and Banking, 1 semester or equivalent, see 2329

Organizational Value Dimensions Questionnaire, adults, see 2330

COMPUTER PROGRAMMING

Aptitude Assessment Battery: Programming, programmers and trainees, see 2331

CLEP Subject Examination in Computers and Data Processing, 1–2 semesters or equivalent, see 2332

★*CLEP Subject Examination in Elementary Computer Programming—Fortran IV,* 1 semester or equivalent, see 2333

Computer Programmer Aptitude Battery, applicants for computer training or employment, see 2334

Diebold Personnel Tests, programmers and systems analysts for automatic data processing and computing installations, see 2335

★*Programmer Aptitude/Competence Test System,* computer programmers and applicants for programmer training, see 2336

DENTISTRY

Dental Admission Testing Program, dental school applicants, see 2337

Dental Hygiene Aptitude Testing Program, dental hygiene school applicants, see 2338

★*Ohio Dental Assisting Achievement Test,* grades 11–12, see 2339

ENGINEERING

AC Test of Creative Ability, engineers and supervisors, see 2340

Engineering Aide Test, engineering aides, see 2341

Garnett College Test in Engineering Science [England], 1–2 years technical college, see 2342

Graduate Record Examinations Advanced Engineering Test, graduate school candidates, see 2343

Minnesota Engineering Analogies Test, candidates for graduate school and industry, see 2344

N.I.I.P. Engineering Apprentice Selection Test Battery [England], engineering apprentices, see 2345

National Engineering Aptitude Search Test: The Junior Engineering Technical Society, grades 9–12, see 2346

Purdue Creativity Test, applicants for engineering positions, see 2347

Undergraduate Program Field Tests: Engineering Test, college, see 2348

LAW

Law School Admission Test, law school applicants, see 2349

MEDICINE

★*CLEP Subject Examination in Clinical Chemistry,* medical technologists, see 2350

★*CLEP Subject Examination in Hematology,* medical technologists, see 2351

★*CLEP Subject Examination in Immunohematology and Blood Banking,* medical technologists, see 2352

★*CLEP Subject Examination in Microbiology,* medical technologists, see 2353

Colleges of Podiatry Admission Test, grades 14 and over, see 2354
Medical College Admission Test, applicants for admission to member colleges of the Association of American Medical Colleges, see 2355
Medical School Instructor Attitude Inventory, medical school faculty members, see 2356
★*Optometry College Admission Test,* optometry college applicants, see 2357
Veterinary Aptitude Test, veterinary school applicants, see 2358

MISCELLANEOUS

Architectural School Aptitude Test, architectural school applicants, see 2359
Chemical Operators Selection Test, chemical operators and applicants, see 2360
Fire Promotion Tests, prospective firemen promotees, see 2361
Firefighter Test, prospective firemen, see 2362
Fireman Examination, prospective firemen, see 2363
General Municipal Employees Performance (Efficiency) Rating System, municipal employees, see 2364
Journalism Test, high school, see 2365
★*Law Enforcement Perception Questionnaire,* law enforcement personnel, see 2366
Memory and Observation Tests for Policeman, prospective policemen, see 2367
Police Performance Rating System, policemen, see 2368
Police Promotion Tests, prospective policemen promotees, see 2369
Policeman Examination, prospective policemen, see 2370
Policeman Test, policemen and prospective policemen, see 2371
Potter-Nash Aptitude Test for Lumber Inspectors and Other General Personnel Who Handle Lumber, employees in woodworking industries, see 2372
★*Test for Firefighter B-1,* firemen and prospective firemen, see 2373
★*Test for Police Officer A-1,* policemen and prospective policemen, see 2374
Visual Comprehension Test for Detective, prospective police detectives, see 2375

NURSING

Achievement Tests in Nursing, students in schools of registered nursing, see 2376
Achievement Tests in Practical Nursing, practical nursing students, see 2377
Empathy Inventory, nursing instructors, see 2378
Entrance Examination for Schools of Nursing, nursing school applicants, see 2379
Entrance Examination for Schools of Practical Nursing, practical nursing school applicants, see 2380
George Washington University Series Nursing Tests, prospective nurses, see 2381
Luther Hospital Sentence Completions, prospective nursing students, see 2382
NLN Achievement Tests for Schools Preparing Registered Nurses, students in state-approved schools preparing registered nurses, see 2383
NLN Aide Selection Test, applicants for aide positions in hospitals and home health agencies, see 2384
NLN Practical Nursing Achievement Tests, students in state-approved schools of practical nursing, see 2385
NLN Pre-Admission and Classification Examination, practical nursing school entrants, see 2386
NLN Pre-Nursing and Guidance Examination, applicants for admission to state-approved schools preparing registered nurses, see 2387
Netherne Study Difficulties Battery for Student Nurses [England], student nurses, see 2388
Nurse Attitudes Inventory, prospective nursing students, see 2389
PSB-Aptitude for Practical Nursing Examination, applicants for admission to practical nursing schools, see 2390

RESEARCH

Research Personnel Review Form, research and engineering and scientific firms, see 2391
Supervisor's Evaluation of Research Personnel, research personnel, see 2392
Surveys of Research Administration and Environment, research and engineering and scientific firms, see 2393
Technical Personnel Recruiting Inventory, research and engineering and scientific firms, see 2394

SELLING

Aptitudes Associates Test of Sales Aptitude, applicants for sales positions, see 2395
Combination Inventory, Form 2, prospective debit life insurance salesmen, see 2396
Detroit Retail Selling Inventory, candidates for training in retail selling, see 2397
Evaluation Record, prospective life insurance agency managers, see 2398
Hall Salespower Inventory, salesmen, see 2399
Hanes Sales Selection Inventory, insurance and printing salesmen, see 2400
Information Index, life and health insurance agents, see 2401
LIAMA Inventory of Job Attitudes, life insurance field personnel, see 2402
Personnel Institute Hiring Kit, applicants for sales positions, see 2403
SRA Sales Attitudes Check List, applicants for sales positions, see 2404
Sales Aptitude Test, job applicants, see 2405
Sales Comprehension Test, applicants for sales positions, see 2406
Sales Method Index, life insurance agents, see 2407
Sales Motivation Inventory, applicants for sales positions, see 2408
Sales Sentence Completion Blank, applicants for sales positions, see 2409
Steward Life Insurance Knowledge Test, applicants for life insurance agent or supervisory positions, see 2410
Steward Occupational Objectives Inventory, applicants for supervisory positions in life insurance companies or agencies, see 2411
Steward Personal Background Inventory, applicants for sales positions, see 2412
Test for Ability to Sell: George Washington University Series, grades 7–16 and adults, see 2413
★*Test of Retail Sales Insight,* retail clerks and students, see 2414

SKILLED TRADES

Electrical Sophistication Test, job applicants, see 2415
Fiesenheiser Test of Ability to Read Drawings, trade school and adults, see 2416
Mechanical Familiarity Test, job applicants, see 2417
Mechanical Handyman Test, maintenance workers, see 2418
Mechanical Knowledge Test, job applicants, see 2419

PUBLISHERS DIRECTORY
AND INDEX

This directory and index gives the addresses and tests of all publishers represented in this volume. References are to entry numbers, not to page numbers. Stars indicate test publishers with test catalogs listing 10 or more tests.

★American Guidance Service, Inc., Publishers' Bldg., Circle Pines, Minn. 55014:
Minnesota High School Achievement Examinations
  Social Studies, 1949
  Social Studies Grade 10 (American History), 1999
  Social Studies Grade 11 (World History), 2000
  Social Studies Grade 12 (American Problems), 2015
American Printing House for the Blind, Inc., 1839 Frankfort Ave., Louisville, Ky. 40206:
Sequential Tests of Educational Progress: Social Studies, 1948
Stanford Achievement Test: Social Studies Tests, 1953
★Bobbs-Merrill Co., Inc. (The), 4300 West 62nd St., Indianapolis, Ind. 46268:
Achievement Examinations for Secondary Schools
  Economic Geography, 1974
  Modern World History, 1997
American School Achievement Tests: Social Studies and Science, 1937
Patterson Test or Study Exercises on the Constitution of the United States, 2011
Brandywine Achievement Test, Box 526, Coatesville, Pa. 19320:
Brandywine Achievement Test in Geography for Secondary Schools, 1973
★Bureau of Educational Measurements, Kansas State Teachers College, 1200 Commercial, Emporia, Kan. 66802:
Emporia American History Test, 1993
Hollingsworth-Sanders Geography Test, 1978
Hollingsworth-Sanders Intermediate History Test, 1995
Meares-Sanders Junior High School History Test, 1996
Sanders-Buller World History Test, 1998
Sare-Sanders American Government Test, 2013
Sare-Sanders Constitution Test, 2014
Sare-Sanders Sociology Test, 2019
Zimmerman-Sanders Social Studies Test, 1957
★CTB/McGraw-Hill, Del Monte Research Park, Monterey, Calif. 93940:
Tests of Basic Experiences: Social Studies, 1956
College Entrance Examination Board, 888 Seventh Ave., New York, N.Y. 10019:
Advanced Placement Examinations
  American History, 1980
  European History, 1981
CLEP General Examinations: Social Sciences and History, 1938
CLEP Subject Examinations
  Afro-American History, 1985
  American Government, 2004
  American History, 1986

  Introductory Economics, 1963
  Introductory Sociology, 2017
  Western Civilization, 1987
College Board Achievement Tests
  American History and Social Studies, 1939
  European History and World Cultures, 1940
College Placement Tests
  American History and Social Studies, 1941
  European History and World Cultures, 1942
★Cooperative Tests and Services, Educational Testing Service, Princeton, N.J. 08540:
Cooperative Social Studies Tests
  American Government, 2005
  American History, 1988
  Civics, 2006
  Modern European History, 1989
  Problems of Democracy, 2007
  World History, 1990
Cooperative Topical Tests in American History, 1991
Sequential Tests of Educational Progress: Social Studies, 1948
★Educational Testing Service, Princeton, N.J. 08540 (See also College Entrance Examination Board, and Cooperative Tests and Services):
Graduate Record Examinations
  Advanced Economics Test, 1965
  Advanced Geography Test, 1977
  Advanced History Test, 1994
  Advanced Political Science Test, 2009
  Advanced Sociology Test, 2018
National Teacher Examinations
  Social Studies, 1945
  Texas Government, 2010
Teacher Education Examination Program: Social Studies, 1954
Undergraduate Program Field Tests
  Economics Test, 1972
  Geography Test, 1979
  History Test, 2001
  Political Science Test, 2016
  Sociology Test, 2020
★Harcourt Brace Jovanovich, Inc., 757 Third Ave., New York, N.Y. 10017:
Crary American History Test, 1992
Stanford Achievement Test: High School Social Studies Test, 1952
Stanford Achievement Test: Social Studies Tests, 1953
★Houghton Mifflin Co., 110 Tremont St., Boston, Mass. 02107:
Modern Economics Test: Content Evaluation Series, 1966
Primary Social Studies Test, 1946
Tests of Academic Progress: Social Studies, 1955

Joint Council on Economic Education, 1212 Avenue of the Americas, New York, N.Y. 10036:
     Primary Test of Economic Understanding, 1967
     Test of Elementary Economics, 1969
     Test of Understanding in College Economics, 1970
     Test of Understanding in Personal Economics, 1971

Kansas State Teachers College. *See* Bureau of Educational Measurements.

New York Times, 229 West 43rd St., New York, N.Y. 10036:
     School Weekly News Quiz, 1960

Newsweek Educational Division, 444 Madison Ave., New York, N.Y. 10022:
     Current News Test, 1958
     Newsweek NewsQuiz, 1959

Perfection Form Co. (The), 214 West Eighth St., Logan, Iowa 51546:
     American History: Junior High—Objective, 1982
     American History: Senior High—Objective, 1983
     Economics/Objective Tests, 1964
     Government/Objective Tests, 2008
     World History/Objective Tests, 2002

★Psychological Corporation (The), 304 East 45th St., New York, N.Y. 10017:

Test of Understanding in College Economics, 1970

★Psychometric Affiliates, Box 3167, Munster, Ind. 46321:
     American History—Government—Problems of Democracy, 1936
     Acorn National Achievement Tests
        Social Studies Test, 1950
        World History Test, 2003
     National Achievement Tests
        American History Test, 1984
        Geography Test, 1976
        Geography Test: Municipal Tests, 1975
        History and Civics Test, 1943
        Social Studies Test, 1951

★Science Research Associates, Inc., 259 East Erie St., Chicago, Ill. 60611:
     Iowa Tests of Educational Development: Understanding of Basic Social Concepts, 1944
     Principles of Democracy Test, 2012
     SRA Achievement Series: Social Studies, 1947
     Test of Economic Understanding, 1968

Time, Inc., Time and Life Bldg., Rockefeller Center, New York, N.Y. 10020:
     Time Current Affairs Test, 1961
     Time Monthly News Quiz, 1962

INDEX OF TITLES

This index lists (*a*) social studies tests in print as of February 1, 1974, and (*b*) social studies tests out of print or status unknown since last listed in a *Mental Measurements Yearbook* (MMY). Citations are to test entries, not to pages. Numbers without colons refer to in print tests; numbers with colons refer to tests out of print or status unknown. With one exception, all tests cited are in this volume. The guide numbers next to the outside margins in the running heads of the reprint sections should be used to locate a particular test. The first reprint section, from *Tests in Print II*, has guide numbers in the range 1936 to 2020; the second reprint section, from the 1st MMY, 1:948 to 1:1154; the third reprint section, from the 2nd MMY, 2:1614 to 2:1642; etc. Superseded titles are listed with cross references to the current title. Tests which are part of a series are listed under their individual titles and also their series titles.

INDEX OF NAMES

This analytical index indicates whether a citation refers to authorship of a test, test review, excerpted review, or a reference for a specific test. Citations are to test numbers, not to page numbers. In the reprint sections, the numbers of the first and last tests on facing pages are given in the running heads next to the outside margins. Numbers without colons refer to in print tests presented in the section reprinted from TIP II. Interpret abbreviations and numbers for in print tests as follows: "*test, 1967*" indicates authorship of test 1967; "*rev, 1978*," authorship of a review of test 1978; "*exc, 1968*," authorship of an excerpted review of test 1968; and "*ref, 1970*," authorship of one or more references for test 1970. (The Cumulative Name Index for that test must be consulted to locate the references.) Numbers with colons (e.g., 6:1019, test 1019 in the 6th MMY) refer to out of print tests included in the material reprinted from the MMY's, unless otherwise indicated. In the reprint sections, the yearbook digit preceding the colon is given in the running head only.

ABRAHAM, H. J.: *ref,* 3:617(1)
Achard, F. H.: *ref,* 4:668(2)
Adams, E. C.: *rev,* 4:693, 4:699
Adams, G. S.: *test,* 6:994, 6:1010
Adkins, D. C.: *rev,* 3:609, 3:612, 4:684, 4:689
Alexander, L. A.: *ref,* 1968
Alft, E. C.: *test,* 6:988
Allen, J. E.: *ref,* 3:613(4)
Anderson, H. R.: *rev,* 1936, 1939, 1943, 1993, 1999, 1:950, 1:1146, 2:1616, 2:1621-2, 3:607, 4:689, 5: 841, 6:1019; *test,* 1:951, 1:1019-21, 1:1148, 2:1618, 2:1633, 2: 1635-6, 3:597, 4:685
Artley, A. S.: *ref,* 4:668(1, 3)
Augspurger, E. F.: *test,* 1950
Australian Council for Educational Research: *test,* 6:978
Ayer, F. L.: *rev,* 4:702

BACH, G. L.: *test,* 1968; *ref,* 1968
Baker, P. C.: *test,* 4:696
Barr, A. S.: *test,* 2:1638
Barton, K.: *ref,* 1988
Beard, M. R.: *test,* 2:1614
Bechtoldt, H.: *test,* 1:1018, 3:598
Benton Review Publishing Co.: *test,* 4:671
Berg, H. D.: *rev,* 1943, 1945, 1953, 1955, 1980, 3:593, 3:596, 5:832, 7:888; *test,* 1:1020, 4:663, 4:684
Bidwell, P. W.: *ref,* 6:980(1)

Bingham, W. C.: *rev,* 2012
Black, W. A.: *test,* 4:708
Bobbitt, J. M.: *ref,* 1939
Boertman, C. S.: *test,* 3:610
Bolton, F. B.: *ref,* 2:1622(2)
Boney, J. D.: *ref,* 1948
Bonham, J. A.: *test,* 1973
Bornstein, H.: *ref,* 1948
Bowman, H. A.: *test,* 7:888
Bowman, L. G.: *test,* 2:1632
Boyd, P. P.: *ref,* 3:613(5)
Bradford, J. M.: *test,* 6:968
Bragdon, H. W.: *ref,* 1939
Branom, M. E.: *test,* 2:1625, 5:801
Broudy, H. S.: *ref,* 3:613(6)
Brown, N.: *ref,* 4:680(1)
Buckles, S. G.: *ref,* 1970
Buller, R.: *test,* 1998
Bureau of Educational Measurements: *test,* 5:844, 6:965, 6:972, 6:981, 6:991, 6:993, 6:995-6, 6: 999, 6:1004, 6:1011, 6:1015-6
Buzzard, G. A.: *test,* 3:601

CALKINS, E. J.: *test,* 1:1018, 3:598
Callis, R.: *test,* 1952
Campbell, D. T.: *rev,* 5:829
Campbell, M. W.: *ref,* 1968
Campbell, V. N.: *rev,* 2006, 7:888
Carman, H. J.: *test,* 2:1628
Cartwright, W. H.: *rev,* 3:591, 3: 610, 3:618

Cattell, R. B.: *ref,* 1988
Chamberlain, K.: *ref,* 1948
Chambers, M. M.: *test,* 6:1013a
Chandler, J. D.: *ref,* 1948
Chauncey, H.: *rev,* 6:964, 6:998, 6:1013; *ref,* 1939
Clark, M.: *test,* 4:706-7
Clarke, F. H.: *ref,* 4:668(2)
Claytor, M. P.: *test,* 5:834
Clinton, R. J.: *test,* 6:1013a
Cockerille, C. E.: *test,* 1937
Cole, L. W.: *test,* 4:693
College Entrance Examination Board: *test,* 1938-42, 1963, 1980-1, 1985-7, 2004, 2017; *ref,* 1939
Connery, R. H.: *test,* 6:1017
Conrad, C. C.: *rev,* 2:1637, 2:1640
Cook, E. F.: *test,* 6:968
Cooperative Bureau of Educational Research: *test,* 1:1152
Cooperative Tests and Services: *test,* 1948, 1988-91, 2005-7, 6:980
Cosgrove, C.: *test,* 7:888
Cottle, E.: *test,* 1:1011
Cowne, L.: *ref,* 1992
Crary, R. W.: *test,* 1992
Croon, C. W.: *test,* 2:1618, 2:1633, 2:1635, 3:596, 4:685
Crow, L. D.: *test,* 1950, 1976, 1984
Cummings, H. H.: *test,* 7:917

DAGGETT, C. J.: *test,* 2:1638
Dahl, T.: *ref,* 1970

SOCIAL STUDIES
SCANNING INDEX

This scanning index is an expanded table of contents listing all tests in this volume. The population for which a test is intended is presented to facilitate the search for tests for use with a particular group. Stars indicate tests not previously listed in a *Mental Measurements Yearbook*; asterisks indicate tests revised or supplemented since last listed. Numbers refer to test entries, not to pages.

SOCIAL STUDIES

★*Primary Test of Economic Understanding,* grades 2–3, see 1967
Test of Economic Understanding, high school and college, see 1968
★*Test of Elementary Economics,* grades 4–6, see 1969
Test of Understanding in College Economics, 1–2 semesters college, see 1970
★*Test of Understanding in Personal Economics,* high school, see 1971
Undergraduate Program Field Tests: Economics Test, college, see 1972

GEOGRAPHY

Brandywine Achievement Test in Geography for Secondary Schools, grades 7–12, see 1973
Economic Geography: Achievement Examinations for Secondary Schools, high school, see 1974
Geography Test: Municipal Tests, grades 3–8, see 1975
Geography Test: National Achievement Tests, grades 6–8, see 1976
Graduate Record Examinations Advanced Geography Test, graduate school candidates, see 1977
Hollingsworth-Sanders Geography Test, grades 5–7, see 1978
Undergraduate Program Field Tests: Geography Test, college, see 1979

HISTORY

Advanced Placement Examination in American History, high school students desiring credit for college level courses or admission to advanced courses, see 1980
Advanced Placement Examination in European History, high school students desiring credit for college level courses or admission to advanced courses, see 1981
★*American History: Junior High—Objective,* grades 7–9, see 1982
American History: Senior High—Objective, 1–2 semesters high school, see 1983
American History Test: National Achievement Tests, grades 7–8, see 1984
★*CLEP Subject Examination in Afro-American History,* 1 semester or equivalent, see 1985
CLEP Subject Examination in American History, 1 year or equivalent, see 1986
CLEP Subject Examination in Western Civilization, 1 year or equivalent, see 1987
Cooperative Social Studies Tests: American History, grades 7–8, 10–12, see 1988
Cooperative Social Studies Tests: Modern European History, grades 10–12, see 1989
Cooperative Social Studies Tests: World History, grades 10–12, see 1990
Cooperative Topical Tests in American History, high school, see 1991
Crary American History Test, grades 10–13, see 1992
Emporia American History Test, 1–2 semesters high school, see 1993
Graduate Record Examinations Advanced History Test, graduate school candidates, see 1994

Hollingsworth-Sanders Intermediate History Test, grades 5–6, see 1995
Meares-Sanders Junior High School History Test, grades 7–8, see 1996
Modern World History: Achievement Examinations for Secondary Schools, high school, see 1997
Sanders-Buller World History Test, 1–2 semesters high school, see 1998
Social Studies Grade 10 (American History): Minnesota High School Achievement Examinations, grade 10, see 1999
Social Studies Grade 11 (World History): Minnesota High School Achievement Examinations, grade 11, see 2000
Undergraduate Program Field Tests: History Test, college, see 2001
World History/Objective Tests, 1–2 semesters high school, see 2002
World History Test: Acorn National Achievement Tests, high school and college, see 2003

POLITICAL SCIENCE

CLEP Subject Examination in American Government, 1 semester or equivalent, see 2004
Cooperative Social Studies Tests: American Government, grades 10–12, see 2005
Cooperative Social Studies Tests: Civics, grades 8–9, see 2006
Cooperative Social Studies Tests: Problems of Democracy, grades 10–12, see 2007
★*Government/Objective Tests,* 1 semester grades 11–12, see 2008
Graduate Record Examinations Advanced Political Science Test, graduate school candidates, see 2009
★*National Teacher Examinations: Texas Government,* college seniors and teachers, see 2010
Patterson Test or Study Exercises on the Constitution of the United States, grades 9–16 and adults, see 2011
Principles of Democracy Test, grades 9–12, see 2012
Sare-Sanders American Government Test, high school and college, see 2013
Sare-Sanders Constitution Test, high school and college, see 2014
Social Studies Grade 12 (American Problems): Minnesota High School Achievement Examinations, grade 12, see 2015
Undergraduate Program Field Tests: Political Science Test, college, see 2016

SOCIOLOGY

CLEP Subject Examination in Introductory Sociology, 1 year or equivalent, see 2017
Graduate Record Examinations Advanced Sociology Test, graduate school candidates, see 2018
Sare-Sanders Sociology Test, high school and college, see 2019
Undergraduate Program Field Tests: Sociology Test, college, see 2020